NEW proficiency

Gold

coursebook

PEARSON
Longman

Contents

Exam information

Overview

The Cambridge Certificate of Proficiency in English consists of five papers.

Paper 1 **Reading** (1 hour 30 minutes)
Paper 2 **Writing** (2 hours)
Paper 3 **Use of English** (1 hour 30 minutes)
Paper 4 **Listening** (approx. 40 minutes)
Paper 5 **Speaking** (19 minutes)

Each paper tests a different area of your ability in English. The overall grade is based on all five papers, which are weighted equally; there are three pass grades (ABC) and two fail grades (DE). Typically, grade C corresponds to 60% of the total marks. There is also an optional background reading text for Paper 2 only.

Paper 1 Reading

The paper has 40 questions and is divided into four parts.

Part 1 Multiple-choice questions
There are three short unthemed cloze texts with six four-option multiple-choice questions on each text. The focus of the questions is on vocabulary, including collocations, idioms, linkers, complementation and phrasal verbs. (See Exam Focus Unit 1, page 14.)

Part 2 Multiple-choice questions
There are four short themed texts from different genres with two four-option multiple-choice questions on each text. The focus may be on content or detail, opinion, attitude, purpose of text, implication and text organisation features such as referents and comparison. (See Exam Focus Unit 10, page 146.)

Part 3 Gapped text
You will be given a single long text from which paragraphs have been removed. These are given in jumbled order for you to replace in their correct place in the base text. To do this you need to think about cohesion (linking devices), underlying ideas, the structure of the text and the overall meaning. (See Exam Focus Unit 5, page 68.)

Part 4 Multiple-choice questions
You will be given a single long text from a range of genres and sources with seven four-option multiple-choice questions. The focus of these questions is the same as for Part 2. (See Exam Focus Unit 7, page 98.)

Marking: there is one mark for each correct answer in Part 1, and two marks for each correct answer in Parts 2–4.

Paper 2 Writing

The paper is divided into two parts and you are asked to complete two writing tasks. You have to write 300-350 words for each answer.

Part 1 has one question only which is compulsory. You will be given a task with one or more short texts (from the same source) to give you ideas for your writing, and you will be expected to present and develop ideas supporting your opinions with evidence. It may be:

- an article (See Writing section in Unit 13.)
- an essay (See Writing section in Units 1 and 7.)
- a letter (See Writing section in Unit 1.)
- a proposal (See Writing section in Unit 2.)

Here is an example of a Part 1 task.

> ### TASK
>
> You have seen the email below posted on the website of your local football club. You decide to write a letter to the local council responding to the points raised and making constructive suggestions for solving the problem.
>
> **300–350 words**

> Parking on match days is an absolute nightmare. I had to park a kilometre away from the ground for the match on Saturday and then I got clamped! I've got to come in by car – the bus service is so bad – so what am I supposed to do? The council has clearly got it in for football supporters – but after all, we're bringing money into the town. There's plenty of land around that could be used for car parks. It's high time someone did something about it.

Part 2 has four optional questions, from which you choose one. Question 5 will always be on the set text. The other questions may include:

- a letter (See Writing sections in Units 4 and 8.)
- a report (See Writing sections in Units 6 and 10.)
- an article (See Writing section in Unit 9.)
- a proposal (See Writing section in Unit 5.)
- a review (See Writing sections in Units 3 and 12.)

Question 5 is made up of three questions, one on each optional prescribed background reading text (see examples in the Writing section in Unit 14). The task may be to write a letter, an essay, an article, a review or a report.

Marking: each question in the paper carries equal marks and you will be penalised for writing very short answers. Spelling and punctuation will be taken into account. It is important that you use appropriate vocabulary and style, and that you organise your writing appropriately for the task set.

Paper 3 Use of English

The paper has 44 questions and is divided into five parts.

Part 1 Open cloze text

This consists of a text with 15 gaps which you must fill in with a single appropriate word. You must write your answers in capital letters on the answer sheet. There may be more than one acceptable answer, but the focus is primarily on structure and on grammatical patterns and collocations. You may be penalised for incorrect spelling. (See Exam Focus Unit 3, page 45.)

Part 2 Word formation

This consists of a text with 10 gaps, each one corresponding to a word. The stems of these missing words are given beside the text, and you have to write the word in its correct form in capital letters on the answer sheet. You will need to be aware of prefixes and suffixes as well as compound words. (See Exam Focus Unit 2, page 32.)

Part 3 Gapped sentences

You will be given six sets of three discrete sentences, with a gap in each sentence. You need to find a single word that you can use in the gap of all three sentences in each set. You will need to think about collocation, phrasal verbs, idioms and lexical patterns. You must write your answers in capital letters on the answer sheet. (See Exam Focus Unit 8, page 114.)

Part 4 Key word transformations

This part consists of eight separate sentences. You have to transform each sentence so that it is as close as possible in meaning to the original sentence, using a given word that you may not change in any way. You will be given the beginning and end of the transformed sentence. The emphasis is on whole phrases rather than individual words or grammatical structures, though you may need to think about the effect of the given word on the grammar of the sentence. You may not use more than eight words in the gap and you may be penalised for incorrect spelling. (See Exam Focus Unit 11, page 164.)

Part 5 Comprehension questions and summary writing task

You will be given two texts on a similar topic though from different genres. Each text will be followed by two comprehension questions which focus on awareness of the style and vocabulary of the texts, and on referencing. The questions may involve interpreting meaning and identifying the function of specific language items in the text. Your answers may not need to be in full sentences, and some questions may specify that you should use your own words. These questions are testing comprehension rather than writing skills, and grammatical errors will not be penalised unless they make your answer impossible to understand.

You will then be asked to complete a summary task using relevant information taken from both texts. This tests your ability to choose relevant information to answer the given question and to express this in a clear, well-organised paragraph of 50–70 words. Your summary should not be in note form and should be in a formal or neutral style. You should always try to use your own words rather than lifting the words of the text, and you should include appropriate linkers. You will be marked on relevance, organisation and accuracy of language. If you write more than the required number of words then you will lose marks. (See Exam Focus Unit 4, page 54.)

Marking: there is one mark for each correct answer in questions 1–25 and two marks for each correct answer in questions 26–43. There are 14 marks for question 44: this is four marks for content and 10 for summary writing skills.

Paper 4 Listening

This paper has 28 questions and is divided into four parts, each with a recorded text or texts. In each part you will hear the recording twice. The texts may be taken from announcements, radio broadcasts, public speeches, interviews, talks, lectures or meetings and you may hear a variety of accents.

Part 1 Three-option multiple-choice questions

You will hear four short extracts from monologues or conversations with interacting speakers, and you will have to answer two three-option questions for each extract. This task may test your understanding of purpose, attitude, opinions and feelings expressed by the speakers as well as gist, main idea and detail. (See Exam Focus Unit 12, page 178.)

Part 2 Sentence completion

You have to complete nine gaps in sentences with information from the text, which will be a monologue or near-monologue. These sentences form a summary of the text and will focus on abstract ideas, opinions or feelings as well as specific information. Most answers are short, consisting of a word or short phrase from the text, and must fit grammatically into the sentence. Spelling must be correct. (See Exam Focus Unit 9, page 128.)

Part 3 Four-option multiple-choice questions

You will hear a conversation with interacting speakers, and there will be five four-option multiple-choice questions focusing on opinion, gist, detail and inference. (See Exam Focus Unit 6, page 83.)

Part 4 Three-way matching

You will hear a conversation between two speakers. You will then have to decide which of a series of statements reflects the views or opinion of which speaker. You will also have to decide whether the speakers agree on some statements. You will need to listen for the attitude of the speakers which may not be stated but may be given through intonation or

choice of expression. (See Exam Focus Unit 14, page 199.)

Marking: there is one mark for each correct answer.

Paper 5 Speaking

This paper consists of three parts, and you will take the test with another candidate. If there is an odd number of candidates then the last ones may take the test in a group of three. There will be two examiners, an interlocutor and an assessor. The interlocutor will manage the test by asking questions and setting up the tasks, but the assessor will not speak to you. You will be assessed throughout on your range of grammar and vocabulary, your ability to develop arguments, the clarity and appropriacy of your pronunciation, the way you communicate with your partner and your overall performance during the test.

Part 1 Conversation with the interlocutor (3 minutes)

The interlocutor will ask you and your partner to talk about yourselves and to give your own opinions on various topics.

Part 2 Two-way conversation between you and your partner (4 minutes)

You will be given a picture or group of pictures and asked to complete a task together. This will involve comparing and evaluating the picture(s) and then giving opinions and making decisions on a topic related to the picture(s).

Part 3 Long turn and discussion (2 minutes for each long turn plus 8 minutes general discussion)

You will each be given a prompt card with a written question and prompts to give you ideas for answering the question on the card. You will be asked to talk for two minutes on your question, and your partner will then be given a different (but related) question to talk about for two minutes. The interlocutor will then ask general questions related to the topic of both your long turns to generate a discussion between you and your partner.

(For help with all the sections of the Speaking paper, see Exam Focus Unit 13, page 190. These are examples of Speaking prompt cards and follow-up questions on the topic of each unit on pages 226–229. These can be used to extend your ability to talk about the topic by discussing them in class, or they can be used for further Speaking practice in exam format.)

Preparing for Proficiency

Paper 1

Paper 1 has nine texts from a range of different sources, so it is vital to read as much and as widely as possible. You should look at different types of text – novels, short stories, magazine articles, reviews, advertisements – to become familiar with different styles of writing. You will not have to identify the source of a text in the exam, but in Parts 2 and 4 you may have to identify the writer's purpose, and what sort of reader the text is aimed at. In Part 3 you need to understand the underlying organisation of the text (e.g. chronological or flashback). Short stories provide narrative in condensed form, so read as many as you can and think about how each one is organised. You could also look at the set texts, even though they are not tested in this paper.

Paper 2

Wide reading will help you to become familiar with different genres and with the style appropriate for each. The compulsory question in Part 1 may provide input in one genre and ask you to write in another, so it is important that you are comfortable with different styles and registers.

Use the Internet to help you find examples of different text types. Useful addresses are:

http://www.bbc.co.uk
http://www.sunday-times.co.uk
http://www.guardianunlimited.co.uk
http://www.the-times.co.uk
http://www.independent.co.uk

You could also use search engines and key words to find other articles.

Work on organising your writing clearly, planning your ideas and using connectors where appropriate. It is a good idea to exchange your writing with a friend so that you get used to editing each other's work. Use the editing checklist and list of linking words on pages 230–233 to help you.

Paper 3

Wide reading may enable you to come up with some answers almost instinctively. Remember to note new vocabulary in phrases rather than in single words, and use the *Longman Dictionary of Contemporary English* to find examples of the most frequent contexts in which words are found.

For Part 4, practise writing sentences in as many different ways as you can. Look at the 'Say it Again' sections in this coursebook for ideas on how to do this. This will help you develop the facility to manipulate language, which will also help you with the summary task in Part 5.

Paper 4

Listen to as much English as possible in as many different situations as you can. Use satellite television or the Internet to watch films without subtitles. Listen to the news on the BBC World Service. Songs are a good source of natural idiomatic language and collocations and they will also help your pronunciation.

Paper 5

To prepare for Part 2, collect photographs or pictures from magazines and then record yourself speaking about each one. Listen to yourself for fluency and general accuracy, but make sure that you focus on general issues suggested by the picture rather than just describing what you see.

You will need to have ideas for the long turn in Part 3, so read a wide range of newspapers and magazines. You do not have to find these ideas in English magazines – for this paper you will need to have a lot to say, so you may find it easier to read magazines in your own language and discuss the issues with friends and family.

You can practise using the prompt cards given on pages 226–229 of this coursebook by making notes then recording yourself. (Do **not** write out a script).

Nearest and dearest

Speaking

1 Look at the photos. They show scenes from an extremely popular American TV programme, *Friends*.

1 Describe the situation in each picture. Which aspect of friendship do you think each picture shows?

- sharing problems
- sharing good times
- learning together
- learning to get on

2 Why do you think programmes like this are so popular? Do you think they give a realistic picture of friendship?

2 What do you think makes a good friend? Think of three qualities or characteristics that you value in a friend.

3 Discuss the following questions.

1 What are friends for?
2 Do different personalities and different beliefs make friendship impossible?
3 'The only way to have a friend is to be one.' (Ralph Waldo Emerson) How far do you agree?
4 How far do you think that developments such as e-mail and mobile phones are affecting personal relationships?
5 Do you think that the nature of friendship remains the same throughout a person's life?

Listening
▶ Paper 4, Part 3

1 You will hear a psychologist being interviewed about friendship. Before you listen, read through the incomplete statements and the options **A–D** below. Discuss which option best completes each statement and underline it.

1 From 3 to 5 years old, children
   A are happy to play alone.
   B prefer to be with their family.
   C have rather selfish relationships.
   D have little idea of ownership.

2 From age 5 to 8 or 10, children
   A change their friends more often.
   B decide who they want to be friends with.
   C admire people who don't keep to rules.
   D learn to be tolerant of their friends.

3 According to Sarah Browne, adolescents
   A may be closer to their friends than to their parents.
   B develop an interest in friends of the opposite sex.
   C choose friends with similar personalities to themselves.
   D want friends who are dependable.

4 Young married people
   A tend to focus on their children.
   B often lose touch with their friends.
   C make close friends less easily.
   D need fewer friends than single people.

5 In middle or old age people generally prefer
   A to stay in touch with old friends.
   B to see younger friends more often.
   C to have friends who live nearby.
   D to spend more time with their friends.

 2 Now listen and choose the answer (**A**, **B**, **C** or **D**) which fits best according to what you hear. How far did your ideas match those of the psychologist?

3 **Vocabulary:** phrasal verbs

1 Read the following summary of the Listening text. Replace the verbs in italics with phrasal verbs from the box. There is one you will not need to use.

build up	carry on	fall off	give up
keep to	keep up	take on	turn to

Between the ages of 3 and 5, a child is unlikely to (1) *sacrifice* anything for a friend. After the age of 5 children co-operate more but they expect their friends to (2) *follow* certain rules. This stage will usually (3) *continue* until the child is aged between 8 and 10.

In adolescence, friendships with the same sex (4) *acquire* great importance. Young adults may initially (5) *maintain* close relationships with their friends. Later on, the number of friendships begins to (6) *decline* and after middle age, people (7) *develop* new friendships less easily.

2 Are phrasal verbs more likely to be used in spoken or written English?

Study Tip

When you record new phrasal verbs in your vocabulary notebook, look up their equivalents in the dictionary and record those too. You should also record an example sentence or sentences to help you remember the phrasal verbs in context. A good dictionary will give examples of the most frequent uses. A good knowledge of phrasal verbs and their neutral or more formal one-word equivalents is important, as they may be tested in the Proficiency exam.

get together *phr v* **1** [I] if two or more people get together, they meet each other: *We must get together some time for a drink.* | [+ **with**] *It's ages since I got together with the gang from school.* **2** [I] if two people get together, they start a romantic or sexual relationship: *Those two should get together – they have a lot in common.* **3 get yourself together** to begin to be in control of your life, your emotions etc: *She needs a bit of time to get herself together.*

(Longman Dictionary of Contemporary English)

For example:

get together = meet
We must get together some time for a drink.
It's ages since I got together with the gang from school.

Reading

▶ Paper 1, Part 2

In Paper 1, Part 2 you have to read four short extracts from different sources and answer two multiple-choice questions on each. The extracts will all be linked by a common theme. The questions may test your understanding of:

- the main ideas, detail and implication
- the writer's attitude, tone and purpose
- text organisation.

1 The following four extracts are all on the topic of friendship. Read the extracts quickly to get a general idea of the style and content. Then match them to the following sources:

- a novel or an autobiography
- a specialist journal or an academic reference book
- a popular magazine

2 Now read the extracts again and choose the answer (**A**, **B**, **C** or **D**) which you think fits best according to the text.

Ourselves and our friends

Most of us have friends as close as family, who, at a pinch, we'd call at 3 am for consolation or congratulations because we know they won't resent us. They're almost part of us, and we regale them confidently with our troubles and triumphs. But while I love these *Pour Your Heart Out* friends, I also need the energy of my *Let's Party* friends. These friends care on a different level – less intense, less deep – but they still care.

And such friendships are important. 'With some friends, you want to be playful rather than deeply disclosing,' says psychotherapist Susie Orbach. 'It's not just a relief to them that you won't give chapter and verse, it's a relief to you. It's healthy to have lots of different friends at different levels of intimacy because not only is it impossible to be close to everyone, it's also undesirable. You need the full spectrum. This is the only way you can experiment with different parts of yourself.'

Of course, it's exasperating to feel stranded with friends who can't – or won't – allow you to open up when there's opening up to be done. But if we accept our 'lite' friends for what they do want to offer us – fun, laughter, full stop – then we enrich our lives immeasurably.

1 The writer feels her relationships with her 'lite' friends
   - A are valuable but not fully satisfying.
   - B can be relied on in difficult times.
   - C offer more than laughter and enjoyment.
   - D are often frustrating.

2 In this extract, the writer is
   - A opposing an argument.
   - B describing a problem.
   - C justifying an opinion.
   - D reporting on research.

Talking to Helena

'You know what you said to Neale about underestimating friendship?' I said.

'Yes?'

'I was just thinking I've never experienced it.'

'Now you're being silly again,' said Helena. 'I'm sure you have. I'm sure you're a very warm-hearted person.'

'No. I've been in love, or acquainted with people because I wanted to use them in some way.'

'I reckon you were impatient with people,' she said. 'You wanted them to give you something, always. Still, it's natural to be impatient when you're young.'

'I once told Neale I could stand anything but a status quo.'

'And now,' said Helena, 'one would give anything for a status quo. If only it would last. What were you and Neale really looking for?'

'A moment,' I said, 'that should be immortal. A moment to set up against those moments when you wake up in the night and realize – oh, that Venice will crumble into the sea one day, and that even before that you'll be dead yourself.'

Helena nodded. 'Oh, those moments in the night,' she said. 'When they come on me now, I just say to myself: Well, you know now. You're going to die. That's all there is to it.'

I looked at her, smiling. 'Oh Helena, I do like you.'

'That's a good thing.' She gathered herself robustly in her chair. 'Because I like you.'

3 What does Helena mean by saying 'If only it would last.'?
   - A She would like to have more power over her life.
   - B She would like her friendship with the narrator to survive.
   - C She would like her situation to remain unchanged.
   - D She would like to stay young forever.

4   The two main themes of their discussion are friendship and
    A   love.
    B   patience.
    C   death.
    D   fear.

STUDYING FRIENDSHIP

ALTHOUGH friendship is a common term in modern cultures, it has not been studied much by social scientists. The word is loosely applied in Anglophone society, although there seems to be general agreement that it has a deeper meaning in Europe than in North America. Arguably, in non-Western cultures it has a more explicit meaning and is used as the basis of structured social relationships. The word 'friendship' is not used in any context to describe a family relationship, but it does imply some type of reciprocity and obligation between otherwise unrelated individuals, although this varies according to situation and context. Friendships can range from the relatively casual, depending on shared activity or setting (such as a sports club), to deep and enduring relationships of mutual support.

The systematic study of friendship has two main strands. The social-psychological study of the ways in which children develop friendships usually focuses on the correlation between type of friendship and chronological age in childhood. Studies of friendship among adults, however, concentrate on patterns of sociability and tend to focus on class differences. Graham Allen claims that working-class friendship choices are dominated by kin links, although neighbours and work-mates also feature. The middle classes, on the other hand, have a wider, more conscious choice of friends.

5   Compared with English-speaking countries, friendship in other parts of the world
    A   has a deeper meaning.
    B   is less vaguely defined.
    C   has been little studied.
    D   is more closely linked to family ties.

6   What are the two main strands in the study of friendship?
    A   social patterns and psychology
    B   patterns of friendship for children and adults
    C   working-class and middle-class friendships
    D   children's friendships and chronological age

In my own world

I spent a great deal of time inside myself, as if in my own world, screened off from everything else. But there was no world there inside me, only a kind of nothing layer, a neither-nor, a state of being hollow without being empty or filled without being full. It just was, inside myself. This emptiness wasn't tormenting in itself. I was inside the emptiness and the emptiness was inside me – no more than that. It was nothing but an extension of time – I was in that state and it just went on. But the sense of unreality and of always being wrong when I was out in the world, outside myself, was harder to bear.

I often sat in the garden, looking at something, absorbed in a flower or a leaf. Then I felt neither wrong nor right, I just was and that never stopped. I never suddenly wanted to do something else. Nothing was happening there inside me. I sat looking, observing.

I had no problem dealing with failing at something that I had decided to do on my own. I simply tried again until it worked. When I had set the goal myself, my patience was infinite. But when other people demanded something of me, I found it difficult that I failed so often. And every time it happened, I became even more sensitive and felt I was one great failure.

7   When she was apart from others and 'inside herself' the writer felt
    A   nothing at all.
    B   hopeless and lonely.
    C   at one with nature.
    D   cut off from the world.

8   The writer was demoralised when she
    A   was unable to achieve her objectives.
    B   felt unjustly condemned by other people.
    C   could not express her feelings about her situation.
    D   could not live up to the expectations of others.

3   Discuss the following questions.

1   What does the writer of the first extract mean by saying that friends help you to 'experiment with different parts of yourself'? Do you agree?
2   The author of the last extract is autistic – she has a medical condition which means that she finds it difficult to relate to other people and to develop social skills. An autistic person appears to live in his or her own world and may display the following symptoms:

   • severely limited physical abilities
   • difficulty in coping with new experiences
   • lack of outward response to people and actions
   • difficulty in forming relationships with others.

Underline evidence in the extract for one of these symptoms.

Language Focus: Grammar

Diagnostic review of verb forms and uses

In order to convey your meaning effectively in writing and speech in Papers 2 and 5, and also to complete the tasks in Paper 3, you need to be able to use a good range of grammar and vocabulary appropriately and accurately, and be aware of how they affect one another. The Language Focus sections in this book highlight specific areas of grammar and vocabulary to help you to do this.

1 Talking about the past

1 The writer of the extract 'In my own world' on page 11 managed to overcome her autism and write an account of how she did so. Some autistic people display great creative powers. The following text describes an interview with the teacher of an autistic child called Stephen Wiltshire, who was an exceptionally gifted artist. Read the text below and put the numbered verbs into the correct tense. There may be more than one possible answer.

S is for St Paul's Cathedral

T is for Tower Bridge

2 Which sentence:

a) establishes the main topic and time frame of the text?

b) sets the scene and describes an event supporting the main idea?

c) describes a repeated activity that occurred over a period of time?

d) gives information about events occurring before the time of the main event?

e) describes two different activities, suggesting that they occurred at the same time?

► Grammar reference p. 210

3 Divide into two groups. Students from **Group A** should complete the text on page 234 by filling in the gaps with the correct past tense form of the verbs given. Students from **Group B** should complete the text on page 238.

Now get together with a student from the other group and tell your completed story from memory.

Stephen's London Alphabet, drawn when he was 10.

When Chris Marris, a young teacher, (1) .... (*come*) to Queensmill in 1982, he was astonished by Stephen's drawings. Marris (2) .... (*teach*) disabled children for nine years, but nothing he (3) .... (*see*) (4) .... (*prepare*) him for Stephen.

'When I first (5) .... (*see*) him, Stephen (6) .... (*sit*) on his own in the corner of the room, drawing,' Chris told me. 'He was absolutely amazing. He (7) .... (*draw*) and draw and draw – the school (8) .... (*call*) him "the drawer". And he (9) .... (*produce*) these most unchildlike drawings, like St Paul's and Tower Bridge, in tremendous detail when other children his age (10) .... (*draw*) stick figures. It was the sophistication of his drawings, their mastery of line and perspective, that (11) .... (*amaze*) me – and these (12) .... (*be*) all there when he was seven.'

Stephen King (1) *was writing* horror stories since he was seven years old, but in his early years he had little success. Throughout his twenties he (2) *has worked* as an English teacher during the day and (3) *spent* his free time writing. One day, in despair at receiving yet another publisher's rejection slip, he (4) *was throwing* away the manuscript of his latest novel. However, his wife (5) *retrieved* it from the rubbish and soon afterwards it (6) *has been accepted* for publication. The book was called 'Carrie'. It (7) *since sold* over 2.5 million copies and the film (8) *terrified* viewers ever since its release in 1970.

The undisputed king of literary and film horror, King (9) *had made* a fortune through his writing but (10) *is still living* simply today with his family in the small American town where many of his novels (11) *are being set*.

2   Relating the past to the present

1   The extract above is about the author Stephen King, a successful writer of horror stories, many of which have been made into films.

Work with a partner. Read the extract and decide if the numbered verbs are in an appropriate tense or not. If not, correct them. Discuss and justify your decisions.

2   Find an example of each of the following in the corrected text.

a)   a verb used for a completed event occurring in the past but relevant to the present
b)   a verb used for a repeated event which first happened in the past and is still happening now
c)   a verb used to talk about a novel or film
d)   a verb that could be either in the present simple or present continuous tenses, without changing the meaning

▶ Grammar reference p. 211

3   State and event verbs

1   Complete the following definitions with the correct terms, *event verbs* or *state verbs*.

1   .... refer to activities and situations that may not have a definite beginning or end, e.g. *be*, *have*, *know*, and are not commonly used in the continuous form.
2   .... refer to activities with a definite beginning and end, e.g. *ask*, *leave*, *offer*, and may be used in the simple or continuous form.

▶ Grammar reference p. 211

2   Read the following lines from the extract on page 8 and answer the questions.

> 'You know what you said to Neale about underestimating friendship?' I said.
>   'Yes?'
>   'I was just thinking I've never experienced it.'
>   'Now you're being silly again,' said Helena. 'I'm sure you have. I'm sure you're a very warm-hearted person.'

1   Are the underlined verbs usually state verbs or event verbs?
2   What is the difference between 'I was just thinking' and 'I just thought'?
3   Why does Helena say 'you're being silly' but 'you're a very warm-hearted person'?

▶ Grammar reference p. 211

3   Both sentences in the following pairs are possible. For each pair, decide whether the verb has the same or a different meaning. If the meaning of the verb is the same, what is the effect of using simple or continuous forms?

1   a)   I have a lot of friends in Australia.
    b)   I'm having some friends round for dinner at the weekend.
2   a)   I'm feeling really hungry – let's stop and eat.
    b)   I feel it's important to do your very best.
3   a)   Did you want to see me?
    b)   Were you wanting to see the manager?
4   a)   Our tickets cost an arm and a leg.
    b)   The whole holiday was costing an arm and a leg.
5   a)   That food tastes a bit salty.
    b)   I'm just tasting the pudding to see if it needs more sugar.
6   a)   I imagine you must be tired.
    b)   Thank goodness you're safe – I've been imagining all sorts of terrible things.

▶ Exam Maximiser

Exam Focus
▶ Paper 1, Part 1

In Paper 1, Part 1 you have to read three texts taken from different sources, and unconnected in theme. Each text contains six gaps, and is followed by six multiple-choice options, testing your knowledge of the following areas of vocabulary:

- collocations
- fixed expressions
- idioms
- word complementation (the grammatical patterns that words are used with)
- phrasal verbs
- semantic precision (words with similar meanings).

The exercises in this section will help you to become aware of the types of vocabulary tested, and show you the best technique for dealing with this task. For each exercise, read the information and complete the sentences below.

1 Collocations

Collocations are words which are frequently found together. They may consist of verb + noun (*take an exam*), adjective + noun (*a huge relief*), verb + adverb (*admire enormously*), adverb + adjective (*highly successful*) or other combinations.

Choose the word or phrase which best completes each sentence. Then decide which type of collocation each combination is.

1 I'm going to .... a big party for Ella's birthday this summer.
   A make **B** do **C** throw **D** run
2 I managed to pass my driving test first time, but it was a .... thing.
   A thin **B** close **C** fine **D** narrow

2 Fixed expressions

In fixed expressions, particular words always go together. Other words cannot normally be substituted. For example:

- *People were walking **to and back** across the square.* ✗
- *People were walking **to and fro** across the square.* ✓

1 Her maths improved by leaps and .... and she got 90% in her final exam.
   A jumps **B** walks **C** races **D** bounds
2 I was in the .... of despair before I heard the good news.
   A pits **B** abyss **C** depths **D** valley

3 Idioms

Idioms are a type of fixed expression in which the meaning of the whole expression cannot be worked out from the meanings of the individual words. For example:

- *The whole thing was so easy – in fact, it was **a piece of cake**.*

1 You're just .... your head against a brick wall – you might as well give up now.
   A putting **B** hitting **C** breaking **D** banging
2 She didn't give chapter and .... but I got a general idea of what she meant.
   A line **B** book **C** verse **D** page

4 Word complementation

Some words are followed by special grammatical patterns, e.g. verbs + gerund or infinitive, nouns or adjectives + specific prepositions.

Choose the word or phrase which best completes each sentence, using the hints to help you.

1 I've always been very .... of my grandmother.
   A close **B** fond **C** affectionate **D** attached
   (**HINT**: *Which preposition – of, to, towards – follows each adjective?*)
2 His comments about our project .... me thinking.
   A made **B** began **C** got **D** encouraged
   (**HINT**: *Which of the four words A–D fits which of the following patterns?* 1 .... me think 2 .... me to think 3 .... to make me think 4 .... me thinking)

5 Phrasal verbs

You may have to choose the entire phrasal verb for a particular context, or select either the verb or particle.

Choose the word or phrase which best completes each sentence below.

1 The girl managed to .... a conversation while doing her homework.
   A carry out **B** keep up **C** make out **D** go on
2 The bedspread was .... up of hundreds of small squares of material sewn together.
   A formed **B** done **C** taken **D** made

6 Semantic precision (words with similar meaning)

Many words that have the same general meaning cannot be used interchangeably, either because they don't mean exactly the same thing or they don't have the same connotation (associations). For example, *stride*, *stroll*, *trudge* and *shuffle* all mean *walk*, but they suggest different ways of walking. You may have to look beyond the sentence with the gap to the whole text and think about very precise distinctions in meaning.

1 Local residents have complained about the music constantly .... from the club.
  A blaring **B** roaring **C** booming
  D thundering

2 The film's success is amazing .... the poor reviews it has received.
  A considering **B** seeing **C** remarking
  D evaluating

7

Read the following three texts and decide which answer (**A**, **B**, **C** or **D**) best fits each gap.

Here is a procedure to follow for this task.

- Read the text carefully. Decide what it is about and what style it is written in.
- Try to fill in the gaps without looking at the choices. This will help you to decide what kind of word you need for the gap, and will prevent you from being confused by distractors.
- Read the choices carefully. You may be able to eliminate one or two immediately or you may have already guessed the right answer.
- If several words look similar, think carefully about their meaning. They may be very different.
- If several words have similar meanings, think about
  a) their grammatical use. The words before and after the gap may suggest a particular grammatical pattern.
  b) words they collocate with. Look at words before and after the gap for help. Remember that a collocation may be found two or three words away from the gap.
- If you aren't sure, read the text again, take a chance and go for the one that 'feels' right.
- Finally, read the whole text through again to check that it makes sense.

Jessica

The trouble was that Jessica had been brought up by a strong, clear-minded and independent woman, and (1) .... with the expectation that she would be the same. This had meant that at the earliest (2) .... she had been encouraged to fly the nest and (3) .... her wings. At no time had she considered marriage or ever having children; the two things didn't (4) .... into her thinking. As a child there had been no bed-time stories of young girls being rescued by handsome princes. 'Whatever you want to do,' her mother would say when kissing her goodnight, 'believe you can do it and you will.' And more important than anything else, make sure you enjoy what you do. Which might have (5) .... some children into becoming (6) .... achievers, but not Jessica. What it did was convince her from an early age that whatever she did would be because she wanted to do it, and for no other reason.

1 **A** raised **B** grown **C** produced **D** reared
  (HINT: *Semantic precision*)
2 **A** occasion **B** possibility **C** opportunity **D** moment
  (HINT: *Fixed phrase*)
3 **A** spread **B** open **C** flap **D** try
  (HINT: *Idiom*)
4 **A** come **B** go **C** move **D** get
  (HINT: *Phrasal verb*)
5 **A** caused **B** provoked **C** incited **D** incensed
  (HINT: *Word complementation*)
6 **A** great **B** big **C** huge **D** high
  (HINT: *Collocation*)

Phone home

It was 7 a.m. and Amber Scott was driving to college. She had stopped at a level crossing when a truck ploughed into the back of her car and (7) .... her into the middle of the train. The front of her car wedged under one of the carriages and she was dragged along for more than three miles, sparks (8) ....

At this point Amber dug out her mobile phone and phoned home. 'I knew I couldn't just sit there and be scared, so I called my mom.' Her mother, more accustomed to calls about the humdrum events of the (9) .... grind, was confused. For one thing, the phone's battery was on the blink. 'She could hear the noise of the train but she couldn't (10) .... out what it was – all she heard was "Mom, mom! I've been hit!" and then the line went (11) ....'

Finally, after seven minutes, Amber was knocked clear of the train, nursing cuts and bruises, but (12) .... unharmed.

7	A shunted	B crashed	C pulled	D slipped
8	A shooting	B flying	C blazing	D jumping
9	A daily	B regular	C ordinary	D common
10	A find	B make	C work	D get
11	A cold	B blank	C quiet	D dead
12	A otherwise	B elsewhere	C nevertheless	D conversely

Child's play

Child's play? Not at all, says Dr David Campbell, consultant clinical psychologist, who explains that children as young as seven are busy (13) .... their identity outside the family. 'They are developing relationships that give them (14) .... about what kind of person they are – pretty, sporty, and so on. It's a very important time for them. As they get older, relationships become more routine.

Psychological theories indicate that women are more (15) .... to find their identity through relationships than boys, who define themselves more through activities,' he adds. 'At first, rejections are (16) .... painful for girls, so they can seem much more important than they really are.' He points out that the oldest child may feel more threatened by relationships that (17) .... wrong. 'If they lose a girlfriend at school, it reverberates with all their past experiences of (18) .... to siblings.'

13	A constituting	B establishing	C basing	D grounding
14	A feedback	B reports	C advice	D references
15	A possible	B probable	C likely	D given
16	A greatly	B extremely	C highly	D utterly
17	A come	B get	C go	D do
18	A losing out	B getting out	C bowing out	D running out

Use of English
► Paper 3, Part 1

1   Read the following statements.
Which one do you think is more likely to
be true? Give reasons for your opinions.

A   Parents and adolescents argue
mainly over everyday matters, and
these arguments seem to change
very little from generation to
generation.

B   Parents and adolescents have always
argued over small things, but these
days these arguments are becoming
more serious.

2   In Paper 3, Part 1 you have to
complete a text with fifteen gaps. To
do this successfully, it's essential to
understand what the text is about.

Read through the whole of the text,
ignoring the gaps for the moment,
and decide which of the statements in
Exercise 1 best summarises the text.

Does the text mention any of the ideas
you discussed in Exercise 1?

3   In the first paragraph the words
tested have been supplied. To help you
identify the types of words that are being
tested, match each of the following
descriptions to one of the words 0–7 in
the text.

a)   part of a phrasal verb ....
b)   part of an expression used to
introduce an example ....
c)   a preposition which follows an
adjective ....
d)   a preposition meaning *about* ....
e)   a negative ....
f)   a form of the verb often used in the
expression *to ... a discovery* ......*0*....
g)   a conjunction meaning *taking the
circumstances into account* ....
h)   an auxiliary verb ....

4   Read the second paragraph and fill in the answers that are
immediately obvious. Don't spend time thinking about difficult items.
Don't fill in anything you're not sure of at this stage, because you need
to keep an open mind when you look back at the gap.

Causes of conflict between adolescents and their parents

Some interesting discoveries have been (0) *made*
by psychologists studying conflicts between
adolescents and their parents. One notable feature
is that they seldom argue about such major topics
(1) ...*as*.... sex, drugs, or politics. This is surprising,
(2) .*given*.. that great differences often exist between
the attitudes of parents and adolescents (3) ..*on*......
such issues. Researchers suggest the explanation
may be that such topics (4) ...*do*.... not usually relate
to day-to-day family interaction and are (5) .*not*....
discussed as they are not directly relevant (6) ...*to*......
family life. Instead, parents and children tend to
(7) ...*fall*.... out over everyday family matters such as
housework.

Despite the changes that have (8) .... place over
the past fifty years, adolescents appear to have the
same kinds of arguments with their parents as their
parents had (9) .... they themselves were young.
It seems to come (10) .... to the conflict between
the adolescent's desire for independence (11) ....
the parents' authority. Teenagers spoke of their right
to be free of restrictions, while parents were equally
(12) .... of their right to exert control, backing this
up (13) .... referring to the needs of the family as
(14) .... whole. Interestingly, both groups could
see the other's (15) .... of view even though they
disagreed with it.

► Exam Maximiser Gold

17

5 Read the text again and use the hints below to help you with the more difficult items.

8 part of a collocation meaning *occur*
9 a conjunction
10 part of a phrasal verb
11 part of the structure *the conflict between (something) ... (something)*
12 an adjective followed by the dependent preposition *of*
13 a preposition
14 part of an expression meaning *altogether*
15 a fixed expression: *to see someone's ... of view*

6 Discuss the following questions.

1 Do you think the text is right about what causes arguments between parents and children nowadays?
2 Do you think your parents had similar arguments when they were young?
3 What do you think can help parents and children have a close relationship?
4 In what ways is your relationship with your grandparents similar to or different from your relationship with your parents?

Speaking
▶ **Paper 5, Part 3**

In Paper 5 you have to talk about a topic on your own for two minutes. You will be given a card with a question and some ideas to help you decide what to talk about. You don't have to use these ideas, but they will help to guide your thoughts. After you have given your talk, the examiner will ask you and your partner some short questions about it. Then your partner will be given a different card with a question on a related topic.

1 Read the prompt card below.

> How easy is it for parents and children to understand each other?
> - generation gap
> - financial problems
> - education and careers

1 First discuss the following questions, which will give you some ideas to talk about.

- What problems do you think are caused by people of different ages living together? (Think about music, living styles, etc.)
- In what ways do you think attitudes change as you get older? (Think about tolerance, priorities, etc.)
- In what ways can money cause arguments between parents and children? (Think about what people like to spend their money on.)
- Do you think that young people have a sense of the importance of money? (Think about how much young people save, what they like to do with their money.)
- Do you think that parents and children have different attitudes to school and homework? (Think about how children like to spend their time.)
- How important is academic success to children? (Think about your plans for the future.)

2 Now think about organising your talk. Use the headings below to help you. Remember that although you are giving your own opinion, you should show awareness of other points of view.

Introduction
Main part
Conclusion

3 Work in pairs. Present your talks to each other and give feedback on language, content and timing.

2 Now read the prompt card below, and follow the same procedure.

> How far do you agree that friends are more important than family?
> - having problems
> - facing problems
> - finding models

Improving your writing

In Paper 2 your writing may be assessed according to the following criteria:

a) accuracy, including grammatical accuracy, spelling, punctuation
b) range of grammatical structures used
c) range and accuracy of vocabulary used
d) consistency and appropriacy of style and register
e) effect on target reader
f) organisation and discourse management.

The exercises in this section will help you with a), b) and c). You will work on the other areas in Units 3, 9 and 13.

1 Accuracy

The sentences below have mistakes in grammar, word formation, spelling and punctuation. Identify and correct the errors.

1 I think children shouldn't be aloud to wach violence cartoons
2 I live in a city in sweden. It is a lot of small shops there.
3 Some family let theirs children to do a lot of thing after the school.
4 When a six year old children, that is watching Robocop', doesn't understand the differens between TV and reality, its because his parents don't explain him the differens.
5 When I had seen him I realised that he was the same person I saw before.

2 Range of grammatical structures

The following extracts would all lose marks because of lack of variation and range in grammatical structure. Each extract has been rewritten to express the ideas more precisely through use of appropriate structures and linking words.

1 Read Extract 1 and then complete the gaps in the rewritten version using the phrases given.

Extract 1

I am majoring in film at my university. I am writing a film script, but I keep in mind not to write anything violent. I think this is not interesting. Also it can be dangerous. People can be influenced by it.

but even more importantly   one of my main concerns here
as part of   partly because I do not find

(1) .... my university major in film, I am writing a film script. (2) .... is to avoid writing anything violent, (3) .... violence particularly interesting, (4) .... because it can be such a dangerous influence on people.

2 Read Extract 2 and then complete the rewritten paragraph by adding an appropriate linking word in each gap.

Extract 2

James is a handsome boy. He puts a lot of emphasis on his hair. His hair is short and brown but always fixed with a lot of gel. I've never seen him without gel on his hair. The strange thing about his hair is that he combs it according to the way he feels. That's very unusual. You can tell his mood only by looking at his hair.

James is a handsome boy (1) .... takes a great deal of care of his hair, (2) .... is short and brown (3) .... always held in place with gel. I've never seen him with ungelled hair. The strange thing is that he combs his hair according to the way he feels, 4) .... is very unusual, (5) .... means that you can tell his mood just by looking at his hairstyle.

3 Read Extract 3 and then combine the jumbled phrases below into a paragraph consisting of three sentences, forming an improved version of the original paragraph. Add punctuation where necessary.

Extract 3

> George was a quite short man to play basketball, his height was 1 metre and 81 centimetres, that is why he was the playmaker of the team. George was the greatest and most talented player in the whole championship. He got this title because he was extremely fast, he had an incredible dribble and shot, a superb jump and he was calm and energetic too.

> (1) At only just over 1 metre 80,
> and jump superbly
> these skills
> in addition to being extremely fast
> made him the most talented player in the whole championship
> he could dribble and shoot incredibly well
> together with his combination of calmness and energy,
> and was therefore the team's playmaker
> George was quite short for a basketball player

3   Range and accuracy of vocabulary

The following three extracts do not express the writer's meaning clearly because of problems with the range and accuracy of the vocabulary used. Complete the gaps in the three rewritten versions by choosing a word or phrase from the box below.

> arising   convicted   created
> current affairs   drunkenness
> emotional   existence   ideal
> persistent   potentially   repeatedly
> sent   shocking   unstable

Extract 1

> I think we have too many bad programmes for example tv drama and movies. When there is a bad problem we can watch tv news about that many times so young people imitate it as funny problems. I think people have some problems in its heart, people who don't have a good family, they are difficult to solve.

I think that too many of the TV dramas and movies we see are (1) .... harmful, and in addition to this, (2) .... programmes (3) .... show (4) .... events that young people sometimes imitate for fun. These people may have complex (5) .... problems (6) .... from (7) .... family backgrounds.

Extract 2

> In our country there are some schools for criminal children. Most of them come there because of their unrealisable faults: drugs, overdrinking, or just imitating the violence in films.

In our country there are some special schools for children who are (8) .... criminals. Most of them are (9) .... there because of (10) .... crimes: drug-taking, (11) ...., or just imitating violence in films.

Extract 3

> He influenced my life, because he invented the motto I was looking for. I need a motto to give my life meaning.

He influenced my life, because he (12) .... the (13) .... I was looking for, and which I need to give meaning to my (14) ....

Writing
▶ Paper 2, Part 1 (letter)

For the compulsory task in Paper 2, Part 1 you may be asked to write a **letter**, an article, an essay or a proposal. This will involve putting forward an argument and supporting it with your own ideas. You will be given information to base your writing on. In this section you will work on a formal letter.

1 Read the following writing task.

TASK

You have read the text below which is an extract from a magazine article on the lack of inspiring role models in public life. You decide to write a letter responding to the points raised and describing a person who has inspired you.

(300–350 words)

We are becoming a society of cynics, money-grabbers, people whose sole purpose in life is furthering self-interest. The sad truth is that there are no longer inspirational people among us; manipulation of the media and wealth creation have become paramount for those in public life. Most people just want an easy life; few take risks for the sake of others, or push for knowledge without anticipating financial reward. Where are the role models of today?

2 Read the following letter which was written in answer to the task. Note down:

- why the writer recommends John Glenn as the role model
- how she has used the information in the extract from the magazine to help to give her ideas for her letter
- what extra details she has added to support her argument.

Dear Sir,

I am writing in response to your article about the lack of role models today. I feel that it was most unfair and that there are many admirable role models to inspire us today. I have always felt that people who attempt to push back the frontiers of knowledge or who put their lives in danger for others should be admired. I would like to describe someone who has inspired me personally and who in my opinion has fulfilled these criteria — the American astronaut John Glenn.

Throughout his life Glenn constantly looked for new challenges. He proved his courage and adventurous spirit in 1962, becoming the first American to orbit the Earth. This was a major technological breakthrough and made him world-famous. After that spectacular trip into space it could have been difficult for him to settle back into the routine of normal life, and indeed later astronauts had psychological problems. But, admirably, he then set about carving a new career for himself in politics. He became a well-respected and popular senator, making an important contribution to the American political scene.

Even then Glenn didn't rest on his laurels. Instead, after reaching the top in these two professions, he decided to go back into space to help with medical research into the process of ageing. This would have been a major undertaking at any age, but John Glenn did it at 77, an age when most people just want to sit back and relax. Not surprisingly, there was considerable opposition, as people felt it would put too much strain on him. However, he had kept himself fit throughout his political career and was therefore ready to undertake this final challenge.

Overall, I think that I most admire his spirit and optimism. Neither cynical nor money-grabbing, he took great personal risks to push for knowledge. He achieved more in his lifetime than most people ever dream of, and was truly inspirational to others, not only of his own generation but also of mine. Who could ask for a better role model for our time?

Yours faithfully,

(348 words)

3 To show you how the writer has used the information given in the magazine extract, answer the following questions.

1 How does the writer show that John Glenn had a purpose in life other than 'furthering self-interest?'
2 What information does she give to show that he was 'inspirational'?
3 What 'risks' did he take and why?
4 What evidence does she give for showing that John Glenn did not opt for an 'easy life'?

4 To help you to think about how the letter is organised, complete the following outline by adding notes.

Opening paragraph
Reason for writing:
I am writing to respond to your article about ...

Writer's point of view:
I have always felt that ...
In my opinion ...

First supporting paragraph
Main idea: constantly looking for new challenges
Supporting details:

....

new career as US senator

Second supporting paragraph
Main idea: he kept going – didn't relax
Supporting details:

....

Closing paragraph
Summary of points made in relation to magazine article:

....

....

Return to reason for writing given in opening paragraph:

....

5

1 Read the following writing task.

TASK

You have read the text below which is an extract from a magazine article on the declining role in the family of fathers today. You decide to write a letter responding to the points raised and describing a person who, in your opinion, has been an ideal father.

(300–350 words)

A father is more than a male parent. Fathering a child is easy – being a father is not. Many people say that fathers no longer have a clear role in the family. They spend most of their time outside the home and never really get to know their children. Without models to follow, how can today's boys understand the concept of 'being a father'? Are there no real fathers left?

2 Here are some questions to start you thinking about the topic. You may find it helpful to jot down some notes from the text to give you ideas for your letter.

1 What role do you think fathers should play in a family today? Is it taking financial responsibility, feeding and clothing a child, teaching a child how to behave, or something different?
2 How do you think the person you are describing has demonstrated the best aspects of 'being a father'?

6 Using the model in Exercise 4 to guide you, prepare your own outline for the task.

Opening paragraph
Give your reason for writing.
Introduce the person you are describing and give your global reason for this.

Supporting paragraphs
Give specific examples of how this person is a model father and what makes him a caring parent. What has he contributed to maintaining 'family values'?

Closing paragraph
Summarise your points in relation to the extract.
Return to your reason for writing.

7 Now write your letter, using the outline above.

8 Exchange your letter with a partner. Evaluate each other's work and suggest improvements. Use the checklist on page 231.

9 Write an improved version of your letter.

Exam Strategy

In any piece of writing, planning in advance will save you time and help you to organise your ideas clearly. Get into the habit of always writing an outline before you start.

1 Match the two halves of each sentence in the following story.

1 Last week I invited a colleague of mine round to supper
2 It was one of the worst evenings
3 I'd only just got home from work
4 Only minutes after he'd arrived,
5 He zapped through all the channels on TV
6 He didn't leave
7 I think he's easily the most inconsiderate person

a) and didn't even try to make conversation.
b) because he didn't seem to know anyone.
c) he was lying with his feet up on the sofa.
d) I've ever met.
e) until he'd finished off all the food and drink in the house.
f) when he arrived – an hour early.
g) I've ever had.

2 For questions 1–8 complete the second sentence with three to eight words so that it has a similar meaning to the first sentence, using the word given. Do not change the word given.

1 We sometimes argue, but I get on well with him most of the time. **usually**
Despite ....
.... get on well with him.
2 My friends are the most important thing in my life. **mean**
My friends .... else.
3 I only just managed to win the race. **close**
I won the race, ...
.... thing.
4 There's been a great improvement in Hannah's relationship with her sister. **leaps**
Hannah's relationship with her sister ....
.... bounds.
5 That is the most outrageous suggestion I've ever heard! **such**
I've .... life!
6 No-one could deny that he had won all the international competitions. **undisputed**
He was .... world.
7 The music was so loud that she couldn't understand what he was saying. **make**
She couldn't ....
.... the loud music.
8 The opinion of parents often has less effect on children as they grow older. **parental**
As children grow older, ...
.... to decline.

3 Read the following text and decide which answer (**A, B, C** or **D**) best fits each gap.

As a child I lived near an American air base in central England, and so had several American friends, but after I left school I lost touch with most of them. Recently I decided to try to (1) .... them, but my efforts were in (2) .... , and I resigned myself to the fact that I would not see any of them again. Then, completely out of the (3) .... , I received a postcard from one of my old friends, now living in Seattle, bringing me up to date on her news and inviting me to pay her a visit. It's extraordinary how rapidly a single event like this can turn your life (4) .... I had been having a tough time trying to (5) .... with a job I hated and an unsatisfactory social life, which had meant that my opportunities for new experiences had been (6) .... limited – until now. Without hesitation I booked a flight and set off for new horizons.

1	A discover	B trace	C place	D identify
2	A failure	B despair	C vain	D loss
3	A sky	B blue	C distance	D past
4	A up	B out	C in	D around
5	A cope	B manage	C run	D handle
6	A strongly	B closely	C tightly	D severely

4 Look at the photo below. It has been chosen as the centrepiece for a campaign promoting the values of family life.

Discuss what positive aspects of family life the picture shows, and decide if there are any other positive aspects that are not portrayed. Would this be a good picture for the campaign? What other issues do you think could be portrayed in the campaign instead?

2 Learning for life

Speaking

1 Which of the following features do you associate with a) a traditional approach to education b) a more 'progressive' approach?

- choice of subjects
- questioning ideas
- written examinations
- continuous assessment
- individual assignments
- collaborative activities
- mixed-ability classes
- fixed curriculum
- streaming
- rote learning

Which have been features of schools you have attended?

2 The following extracts from job advertisements mention qualities which are often required in the modern working environment. Which qualities do you think are developed by schools? Which are not developed? Which of the features listed in Exercise 1 are most likely to encourage these qualities?

must be self-motivated and able to work independently

should possess well-developed leadership and communication skills

understanding of and empathy with other cultures

you will be a reliable team player with sound commercial judgement

excellent time management skills and attention to detail

good analytical ability is essential for success in this role

Reading

▶ **Paper 1, Part 4**

1 The following text is taken from a book by Charles Handy, an educator with many years' experience in business and public services, who has written extensively on the role of business in modern society.

A PROPER EDUCATION

▶ I left school and university with my head packed full of knowledge; enough of it, anyway, to pass all the examinations that were put in my path. As a well-educated man I rather expected my work to be a piece of cake, something at which my intellect would allow me to excel without undue effort. It came as something of a shock, therefore, to encounter the world outside for the first time, and to realize that I was woefully ill-equipped, not only for the necessary business of earning a living, but, more importantly, for coping with all the new decisions which came my way, in both life and work. My first employers put it rather well: 'You have a well-trained but empty mind,' they told me, 'which we will now try to fill with something useful, but don't imagine that you will be of any real value to us for the first ten years.' I was fortunate to have lighted upon an employer prepared to invest so much time in what was, in effect, my real education and I shall always feel guilty that I left them when the ten years were up.

▶ A well-trained mind is not to be sneezed at, but I was soon to discover that my mind had been trained to deal with closed problems, whereas most of what I now had to deal with were open-ended problems. 'What is the cost of sales?' is a closed problem, one with a right or a wrong answer. 'What should we do about it?' is an open problem, one with any number of possible answers, and I had no experience of taking this type of decision. Knowing the right answer to a question, I came to realize, was not the same as making a difference to a situation, which was what I was supposed to be paid for. Worst of all, the real open-ended question — 'What is all this in aid of?' was beginning to nudge at my mind.

▶ I had been educated in an individualist culture. My scores were mine. No one else came into it, except as competitors in some imagined race. I was on my own in the learning game at school and university. Not so in my work, I soon realized. Being an individual star would not help me there if it was in a failing group. Our destinies were linked, which meant that my co-workers were now colleagues, not competitors. Teams

In this extract he evaluates how useful his own education was as a preparation for the world of work. Read paragraphs 1, 5 and 6 quickly. Does the writer think his own education was useful preparation for work? What does he say about the present situation?

BY THE AUTHOR OF THE AGE OF UNREASON AND THE AGE OF PARADOX

Charles Handy

Beyond Certainty

The Changing Worlds of Organizations

were something I had encountered on the sports field, not in the classroom. They were in the box marked 'fun' in my mind, not the ones marked 'work' or even 'life'. My new challenge, I discovered, was to merge these three boxes. I had discovered, rather later than most, the necessity of others. It was the start of my real education.

4 ▶ 'So you're a university graduate are you?' said my new Sales Manager. 'In classics, is it? I don't think that is going to impress our Chinese salesmen! How do you propose to win their respect since you will be in charge of some of them very shortly?' Another open-ended problem! I had never before been thrust among people very different from me, with different values and assumptions about the way the world worked, or should work. I had not even met anyone more than two years older, except for relatives and teachers. Cultural exploration was a process unknown to me, and I was not accustomed to being regarded as stupid and ignorant, which I undoubtedly was, in all the things that mattered in their world.

5 ▶ My education, I decided then, had been positively disabling. So much of the content of what I had learned was irrelevant, while the process of learning it had cultivated a set of attitudes and behaviours which were directly opposed to what seemed to be needed in real life. Although I had studied philosophy I hadn't applied it to myself. I had assumed that the point of life was obvious: to get on, get rich, get a wife and get a family. It was beginning to be clear that life wasn't as simple as that. What I believed in, what I thought was worth working for, and with whom, these things were becoming important. So was my worry about what I personally could contribute that might not only earn me money but also make a useful contribution somewhere.

6 ▶ It would be nice to think that this sort of experience could not happen now, that our schools, today, prepare people better for life and for the work which is so crucial to a satisfactory life. But I doubt it. The subjects may appear to be a little more relevant, but we are still left to learn about work at work, and about life by living it. That will always be true, but we could, I believe, do more to make sure that the process of education had more in common with the processes of living and working as they are today, so that the shock of reality is less cruel.

2 It is important to have an overall idea of the organisation of the text and its main message before looking at the details.

Match the following main topics to the numbered paragraphs of the text. Then underline the phrase or sentence in that paragraph which answers the question below.

Personal conclusions (para. ....)
What was the writer's main conclusion about his education?

Initial expectations of work (para. ....)
What were the writer's initial expectations of how he would cope at work?

Relevance to today's educational systems (para. ....)
To what extent does the writer think that things are better today?

Broadening awareness of other cultures (para. ....)
In what ways were the people the writer worked with different from the people he had been educated with?

Dealing with problems and making decisions (para. ....)
What were the differences between the types of problem he had to deal with in education and at work?

Attitudes to colleagues (para. ....)
What difference did the writer find between his relationships at school and at work?

3 Now answer the multiple-choice questions below. Choose the answer (**A**, **B**, **C** or **D**) which you think fits best according to the text.

1 When the writer left university, he expected to succeed by
   A using the qualities his education had developed.
   B gaining further qualifications.
   C developing his decision-making skills.
   D acquiring relevant skills in his place of work.

2 He feels he treated his first employers badly because he did not
   A give them a true idea of his strengths and weaknesses.
   B contribute to the company financially.
   C repay them fully for the help they gave him.
   D stay with them any longer than he was obliged to.

3 He found that he needed to re-evaluate his approach at work because he
   A was asking the wrong types of question.
   B had been trained to deal with problems in the wrong way.
   C met new kinds of problems in his working life.
   D was dealing primarily with moral problems.

4 What was one of the first things he learned at work?
   A that he could not always be first
   B that other people were willing to help him
   C the importance of having leisure interests outside his work
   D the link between team sport and work

5 He realised that he lacked understanding of other cultures when he
   A had to work with people who had different values.
   B had to work outside his own country.
   C realised that his subordinates did not respect him.
   D found that his qualifications were not relevant.

6 What was the writer's main conclusion about his education?
   A It had taught him to value money too much.
   B It had been much too theoretical to be of any use.
   C It had been not just useless, but actually harmful.
   D It had taught him that life was not simple.

7 The writer feels that nowadays
   A life is changing so fast that schools can never prepare for it.
   B the way in which students are taught to think should be re-examined.
   C the content of syllabuses should be brought fully up-to-date.
   D educational reforms have bridged the gap between school and work.

4 How do you think Charles Handy's education could have prepared him more effectively for his working life? Using information from the text, discuss whether and to what extent the following suggestions would have helped him. Give reasons for your decisions.

- more vocational or practical subjects (*give examples*)
- compulsory involvement in competitive team sports
- school trips and exchange visits to other countries
- more cross-curricular projects
- work experience placements

Can you add any more suggestions to the list?

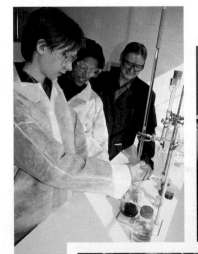
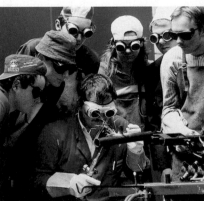

Language Focus: Vocabulary

Context and style

1   You will often find clues to the meaning of difficult words and expressions within the text itself. Find the following expressions in the text on pages 24–25 and use the context to work out what they mean. Which expressions are formal and which are informal?

1   a piece of cake (para. 1)
  (CLUE: *The following words explain the meaning of this idiom in relation to the topic.*)

2   excel (para. 1)
  (CLUE: *This is a verb related to the adjective 'excellent'.*)

3   encounter (paras. 1 and 3)
  (CLUE: *Use both contexts to work out the meaning.*)

4   closed problems/open problems (para. 2)
  (CLUE: *The text goes on to give examples and explanations.*)

5   nudge (para. 2)
  (CLUE: *This is a verb usually meaning 'to give a gentle push'. Here it is used metaphorically.*)

6   merge (para. 3)
  (CLUE: *Look back at the previous two sentences.*)

7   thrust (para. 4)
  (CLUE: *A passive verb followed by 'among people'.*)

8   undoubtedly (para. 4)
  (CLUE: *Word formation: an adverb formed from the root 'doubt' and a negative prefix.*)

9   cultivated (para. 5)
  (CLUE: *A verb usually used about farming or gardening. Here it is used metaphorically.*)

10   crucial (para. 6)
  (CLUE: *The immediate context.*)

2   Like much written English, the text on pages 24–25 contains a mixture of formal and semi-formal or even informal language. The following sentences are written in neutral language. Re-express them using a phrase from the text to replace the words in italics. Which of the expressions from the text are typical of formal language? Which are informal or idiomatic?

1   He therefore felt that starting work would be *very easy for him*.
2   He thought that he would succeed in business without *needing to work hard*.
3   The hard reality of the business world *was quite a surprise to him*.
4   He realised that he was *not adequately trained* for the demands of the business world.
5   He still felt that a well-trained mind *could be useful*, but that it was not enough for the world of work.
6   He had been trained specifically to deal with closed problems *but* now he needed to solve open-ended problems.
7   He felt unhappy and asked himself the question, 'What is *the purpose of all this effort*?'
8   He had previously only *met* the idea of being part of a team when he played sports.
9   He also knew nothing about *finding out about other cultures*.
10   He had assumed that the point of work was to *become wealthy*, but began to question this philosophy.

3   The text on pages 24–25 contains fewer phrasal verbs than would be found in a more informal written text or spoken language.

Try to think of verbs or phrases with similar meanings to the ones below. Then check your answers with the text.

non-phrasal verb	phrasal verb/expression
found (by chance)	(1) ....
(2)	went away
(3)	find out
solve	(4) ....
was involved	(5) ....
(6)	had come across
(7)	join together
(8)	go over well with
(9)	built up
succeed	(10) ....

27

Language Focus: Grammar

Conditionals (1) + wishes and preferences

1 Conditionals: review of basic patterns

1 Read through the text below, then complete it using the verbs in brackets.

My father's job took him all over the world, so I was sent to a boarding school from the age of eight to 18. Looking back on it now, I think I (1) .... (*be*) happier, and maybe better educated, if instead of sending me away, my parents (2) .... (*keep*) me with them during those years and (3) .... (*send*) me to local schools in the countries they were living in. But they did it for the best.

Now I'm trying to decide on my own career. I'd really like a job that involves travelling, and I've applied for two so far. The first one's in South America – I don't think I'll get it though. If I (4) .... (*know*) some Spanish or Portuguese, I (5) .... (*probably have*) a better chance, but we only did French at school. The second job's in Australia so there isn't a language problem, and the salary's fantastic! I'm on the short-list, so things look hopeful. If I (6) .... (*get*) it, I (7) .... (*have*) to sign a five-year contract, but that doesn't really worry me. After all, I suppose that if you (8) .... (*want*) a good job, you (9) .... (*have*) to be prepared to commit yourself.

2 Find examples in the text above of conditional structures related to:

- something regarded as a general truth
- a future situation seen as likely to occur
- a hypothetical situation in the present or future
- a hypothetical situation in the past.

▶ Grammar reference p. 211

3 Work in pairs. Complete these sentences, then compare your sentences with your partner. Have you used the right tenses?

1 If you want to get a job in my country, ...
2 ... unless I get my work finished tonight.
3 If I had the chance to go abroad to study, I ...
4 I'd never have chosen to study ... if ...
5 My parents used to let me ... as long as ...
6 We might find English easier if ...

2 wish/if only

We use *wish* to express a desire for something to be different from reality, so the tenses used after *wish* are similar to the ones used in the *if*-clause of hypothetical conditions.

1 Work with a partner. Underline the correct alternative in the following sentences.

1 I wish *I'd had/I had* the chance to do more sport when I was at school.
2 I wish our school *offered/offers* more vocational subjects. I'd like to take Information Technology.
3 I wish success *doesn't/didn't* depend so much on exam results.
4 I wish we *could/can* go on more school trips abroad.
5 I wish the authorities *will/would* do something to reduce class sizes.
6 I wish we *weren't getting/didn't get* the exam results tomorrow! I'm really nervous.

2 Now answer the following questions.

1 What verb form is used after *wish* when the statement refers to a) the past? b) the present or the future?
2 Re-express sentences 1–6 above using *if only*. Does the grammatical pattern change? Is there a difference in meaning? Which expression is more emphatic? Which is more appropriate to the context?

3 Read these sentences. Which example in each set is wrong? Cross it out. Which rule below applies in each case?

1 a) I wish you would stop smoking so much.
  b) I wish I would stop smoking so much.
  c) I wish I could stop smoking so much.
  d) I wish I didn't smoke so much.

2 a) I wish they would give us a holiday!
   b) I wish you liked me.
   c) I wish you would like me.

• We can't use *would* with verbs that describe a state.
• We can't use *would* when we ourselves are the subject. We have to use *could* or a past form.

4   Compare these examples. What is the difference in meaning between *wish* and *hope*?

1   I wish the authorities would revise the curriculum.
2   I wished the authorities would revise the curriculum.
3   I hope the authorities will revise the curriculum.
4   I hoped the authorities would revise the curriculum.

► Grammar reference p. 212

5   Which of the statements in Exercise 2.1 do you agree with? Do you have any other wishes, regrets or hopes? Make similar statements using *wish/if only* and *hope* about:

• your first school or the place where you are studying at present
• your first job or your current place of work, if you have left school.

--- **Watch Out!** *meanings of* **wish** ◄
1   I wish you were here.
2   I wish you the best of luck.
3   Do you wish to make a formal complaint?

What does *wish* mean in each of the examples?

---

3   *It's time, I'd rather/I'd prefer*

1   Read the following examples. What tenses and patterns can follow the underlined expressions? What time is referred to in each sentence? When can the infinitive be used after these expressions, and when is it not possible?

1   It's high time they changed the curriculum.
2   I didn't really want him to do that course – I'd rather he'd done something more practical.
3   I quite like my job, although I'd rather have worked somewhere where I could use my language skills.
4   I'd prefer it if you didn't invite her.
5   I'd prefer not to come on Saturday.

► Grammar reference p. 213

2   Fill in the gaps with suitable words.

1   It's high .... messing about and got down to some serious work. You've got an exam next week!
2   'Do you mind if I smoke?'   '........................ didn't, if you don't mind. I've got a horrible sore throat.'
3   I didn't really want to live in London – .... lived in the country.
4   'Are you coming to the sales conference next month?' 'Well, actually, ... not to, if you can find anyone else.'

► Grammar reference p. 213

4   **Use of English:** Paper 3, Part 4

Complete the second sentence with three to eight words so that it has a similar meaning to the first sentence, using the word given. Do not change the word given.

1   It would have been a disaster for him to be made responsible.   **put**
   If he ....
   .... would have been serious consequences.
2   I think it would be better to get on as fast as possible.   **much**
   I'd prefer us ....
   .... progress as we can.
3   I wish he would learn to make his own breakfast.
                                                                   high
   It's ....
   .... for himself.
4   If only I had travelled more widely when I had the chance.   **taken**
   I wish ....
   .... more widely.
5   I feel I must say how worried I am about the proposed changes.   **concern**
   I wish ....
   .... over the proposed changes.
6   She thinks it would be better if he discovered the answer for himself.   **found**
   She'd prefer ....
   .... for himself.
7   I'd be happier if you kept it a secret.   **rather**
   I'd ....
   .... anyone.
8   I'd prefer to be given the chance to work with other people.   **allowed**
   I think it would be better ....
   .... a team.

Listening
▶ Paper 4, Part 2

1 Look at the advertisement and discuss the following questions.

1 Have you ever done a puzzle like this? Was it easy or difficult?
2 What kind of mind do you think you need to be able to do this kind of puzzle?

It's The World's Best-Selling Puzzle

Rubik's cube is back!
Re-launched to stretch the brain cells of a new generation, this simple-looking cube puzzle can be solved in just a few moves. That is, as long as you choose the right ones from the 43 quintillion possibilities!

2 You will hear a talk about the different ways in which we think. First, read through the gapped sentences below. Can you predict any of the content of the talk?

---

1 The fastest mental process involves a reaction which is _____ and which the speaker calls our 'wits'.

2 The second mode is the function of the brain that things like _____ test.

3 We know least about the slowest level because it is _____ , and may be illogical or irrational.

4 The two girls in the science lesson wanted their teacher's help because they _____

5 The girl was using her _____ to manipulate the puzzle.

6 She was still making progress with the cube, although she appeared not to be _____

7 When the speaker questioned her, the girl initially believed he was _____ for playing with the cube.

8 When questioned, the girl was unaware of the _____ she had been using.

9 Adults who try to use their _____ are unable to do the puzzle.

---

 3 Now listen and complete the sentences with a word or short phrase. You should not need more than two or three words for any answer.

 4 Listen to the recording for the second time. Check and complete your sentences. Have you made any spelling errors?

5

1 Using ideas from the talk, decide which type of thinking is needed for each of the activities below: wits, intellect or wisdom. Discuss why.

- doing a maths problem
- writing poetry
- choosing a holiday
- driving a car
- playing the piano

2 Add three more activities to the list and discuss which type of thinking they need.

6 Discuss the following questions.

1 Does your own experience support the idea that you learn different things in different ways? Give examples.
2 Which types of skills do you think are the easiest to learn? Which are most difficult? Why?

7 Say it again

At Proficiency level you are expected to be able to produce a wide range of structures and expressions. To help you do this, you will be given regular opportunities to practise rephrasing sentences.

The following sentences are from the Listening text. Re-express them using the framework given.

1 The theory makes a lot of sense to me.
   I find .... convincing.
2 She seemed to be paying very little attention.
   She looked .... very little attention.
3 She explained it to the best of her ability.
   She explained it as .... could.
4 Adults have lost the knack of this way of learning.
   Adults .... this way any more.

▶ Exam Maximiser

Language Focus: Vocabulary
Meaning in context

1   **Use of English:** Paper 3, Part 3

In Paper 3, Part 3 you have to find one word to complete three different sentences. Read the following sentences.

Secondly there's a rather slower process, which we can .... the intellect. (*term/call*)

When I .... your name, could you please stand up? (*say/call*)

I need to .... at the dry cleaner's to collect my suit. (*stop/call*)

Although there are other correct possibilities for each gap, the word *call* can be used in all three sentences.

For questions 1–6, think of one word only which can be used appropriately in all three sentences.

1   He's a nice boy and he's very ...., but he doesn't do much work.
    A .... light shone through the open curtains.
    She likes wearing .... colours, but her sister always wears black.

2   The colourful pictures should .... the children's interest.
    My son will soon .... the majority of the shares in the company.
    Be careful! I don't think that branch will .... you.

3   She's always on the .... – I don't know how she has the energy.
    He's going to start his own company, which sounds like a smart ....
    Be careful. They'll be watching your every ....

4   She .... the tray down on a table next to his bed.
    The teacher .... the class some work to do.
    The princess was given a necklace .... with diamonds and emeralds.

5   The fog and ice meant that it was a very .... journey.
    Business is rather .... at present but we hope it will pick up soon.
    You'd better check the time – the clock might be a few minutes ....

6   She had dark .... around her eyes from too many sleepless nights.
    The thief escaped with a diamond brooch, two gold .... and some cufflinks.
    Only one of the .... on the electric cooker is working.

2   Read the following sentences and work out the meaning of the expressions in italics. What helped you to decide?

1   You need to *keep your wits about you* in Paper 3 of the Proficiency exam.

2   I've tried everything I can think of, but I still can't get him to agree – I'm *at my wits' end*.

3   I was *scared out of my wits* all alone in that huge empty house.

4   *To the best of my knowledge*, the project's going ahead as planned.

5   Didn't you realise he was married to that actress? I thought it was *common knowledge*.

6   I've got that song *on the brain* – it's driving me mad!

7   Can I come and *pick your brains*? I'm having problems with my new computer software.

8   I've been *racking my brains* trying to remember where I've met him before.

3   **Phrasal verbs with *think***

Complete the following sentences with a particle or preposition from the box. Use each word once only. There are two extra words that you won't need.

across	back	of	on
over	through	up	

1   They're still trying to think .... a name for the baby.

2   When I think .... to childhood holidays, it's the long, lazy days on the beach that I remember.

3   I wonder how anyone could ever have thought .... such a complicated story.

4   Why don't you think it .... for a while, and give me your answer in a few days?

5   Your plan isn't going to work – you haven't thought it .... carefully enough.

4   Take turns to interview a partner, using the following questions.

1   Have you ever been scared out of your wits in a film? What was the film/scene about?

2   What's the most important thing you've ever changed your mind about? What would have happened if you hadn't changed your mind?

3   Is there anything you've particularly set your mind on doing in the next few years?

4   If I ask you to name a man or woman who's in the news at present, who springs to mind? Why?

5   Think over what you've done in class today. What do you think you've learned?

Exam Focus
▶ Paper 3, Part 2

In Paper 3, Part 2 you have to read a text with ten gaps. The stems of the missing words are given in the margin of the text. You have to decide on the correct form of the word in this context. You need to think about both the grammatical use and the exact meaning of the word required.

You may need to:

- add a suffix (e.g. confirm*ation*). This usually depends on the part of speech required, e.g. noun, adjective, adverb or verb. But it may also be related to meaning (e.g. use*less*).
- add an inflection (e.g. confirmations, confirm*ing*). This gives information about singular or plural, tense, etc.
- add a prefix (e.g. **un**confirmed, **re**confirmations). Here you need to think about the meaning of the word in this context. The prefix may make the word negative or add other information such as repetition or location.
- change the stem itself (e.g. *affect* – *effect*).

Here is a procedure to follow for this task.

- Read through the whole text quickly to get a general idea of what it is about.
- Complete any gaps you feel sure of.
- For the remaining gaps, the surrounding words will help you decide what part of speech is required.
- Check whether an inflection such as a plural -s or participle ending is needed.
- Think about the meaning. Does the word need a prefix?
- Finally, read the whole text again and check that it makes sense.

1 Suffixes

1 This exercise will help you to identify and classify some common suffixes. First match the following headings to the groups of suffixes 1–7.

- making adjectives from nouns
- making adjectives from verbs
- making nouns from verbs
- making nouns from adjectives
- making nouns from other nouns
- verb suffixes
- adverb suffixes

Then complete each sentence using the word given and adding the correct suffix. You may also need to add an inflected ending such as plural -s.

1 ....
The car's cheap as it has low .... (*mile*)
I've lost the .... that came with my mobile phone. (*book*)
In his autobiography, he describes his unhappy .... (*child*)
If you would like to apply for ...., please complete this form. (*member*)

2 ....
To his .... he won the competition. (*amaze*)
We hire out glasses for big parties, but we ask for a deposit to cover any .... (*break*)
His .... to accompany them upset her more than she admitted. (*refuse*)
The press refused to divulge the names of their .... (*inform*)

3 ....
His .... with money was legendary. (*mean*)
The .... of this material makes it suitable for sportswear. (*elastic*)

4 ....
I think his behaviour's really .... – he's old enough to know better. (*child*)
Although now an old man, he was still .... in his trust and refused to see harm in anyone. (*child*)
The .... discovery of the diary led to serious problems. (*accident*)
She's got quite an .... style, but it's rather misleading. (*authority*)

5 ....
It was a very .... incident. (*regret*)
He's an .... man. (*attract*)

6 ....
You need to .... the water in the swimming pool. (*chlorine*)
You don't need to .... your language – she's very fluent. (*simple*)
The colour red in our flag .... the blood shed in the fight for independence. (*symbol*)

7 ....
In order to unscrew, turn in a .... direction. (*clock*)
We reckoned we were travelling more or less .... (*north*)

2 Can you think of any more examples of suffixes which fit these seven categories?

3 Complete the following sentences. You will need to use two or three suffixes to make the correct form of each word.

1 The .... of the facilities was more expensive than they had expected. (*modern*)
2 He unlocked the door slowly and .... (*care*)
3 ...., he wasn't hurt in the accident. (*amaze*)
4 The music blared out .... from the amplifiers. (*deaf*)
5 His .... and .... make him a very strong candidate for the job. (*adapt, resource*)
6 The village is .... located in a sheltered valley. (*picture*)

2   Prefixes

1 The sentences below do not make sense because some prefixes have been omitted. Find the words which need prefixes and choose a suitable prefix from the box for each one.

anti	sub	dis	fore
il	in	mis	multi
out	over	un	semi

1 If you do not pay your telephone bill within the next ten days the service will be connected.
2 She was not aware of any change, but consciously she must have realised something was wrong.
3 'Didn't you ask me to bring a parachute?'
  'No, you must have heard me, I asked for a pair of shoes!'
4 The essay was totally legible and so I couldn't give it any marks.
5 The river is flowing its banks and some streets are already flooded.
6 The leader sat with his back to a high wall and his followers sat in a circle around him.
7 Although most of the major transactions were shown, the accounts were complete.
8 He seems to enjoy himself at public functions, despite his social tendencies.

2 Now write sentences of your own for the four remaining prefixes.

3   Stems

As well as adding prefixes and suffixes, you will sometimes need to make changes to the stems themselves. Complete the table below with the appropriate form of the word.

noun	verb	adverb	adjective
poverty	(1)	poorly	(2) ....
safety	(3)	(4)	(5) ....
(6)	(7)	peaceably	(8) ....
(9)	honour	(10)	(11) ....
blood	(12)	(13)	(14) ....

4 Read the text below. Use the word given in **capitals** at the end of some of the lines to form a word that fits in the space in the same line. There is an example at the beginning (0).

GET THE GIRLS TO SCHOOL

The (0) *education* of girls is the surest way of   EDUCATE
reducing (1) .... So why are ninety million   POOR
primary school age girls not in school? It is
because they contribute (2) .... to the family   ECONOMY
by looking after younger children, or working
in the fields. But these girls face a life of
backbreaking work, with children who die of
(3) .... diseases, subordination to a husband   PREVENT
and his family, and an early death. And the
uneducated woman transmits to her children the
same doomed life. But it does not have to be
like this. Educational campaigns have meant
that (4) .... is almost unknown in Southern   LITERATE
India, and the infant (5) .... rate there is   MORTAL
(6) .... the lowest in the developing world.   CONSEQUENCE
And in Africa and south Asia, where women do
most of the farming, education is allowing them
to learn how to improve (7) .... farming   EFFICIENT
practices and at the same time is raising
awareness of the (8) .... needs of the land.   ECOLOGY
While to rural families it might seem an
unavoidable (9) .... to keep girls working   NEED
at home, it is in both the national and
international interest – as well as in the interest
of the girls themselves – to (10) .... the   COME
short-term difficulties and provide these girls
with the education they need.

Language Focus: Vocabulary
Education

1 Put the words in the box into the correct column below. Some words can go in more than one column.

an exam	a course	a subject	history
lessons	homework	a module	revision
a test	notes		

do	take	sit	study	pass	make	follow

2 Read the following text and fill in the gaps using verbs from Exercise 1. Try to use each verb at least once.

In secondary schools in England, students have to (1) .... 10 different subjects until they are 16, and these must include English and maths. After that they specialise, and from age 16 to 18 they usually (2) .... a maximum of four or five subjects. Sometimes timetabling problems in the school mean that not all the students are able to (3) .... the course of their choice. In their final year they (4) .... the final school exams, which are known as A-levels.

If students want to (5) .... a particular subject at university, they must normally have (6) .... the same subject, or a related one, at A-level. It's very difficult to go to university unless you have (7) .... your A-level exams with good grades. However, it is always possible to (8) .... the exam again to get a better grade. Although in the majority of courses, students (9) .... just one exam at the end of the course, many new courses involve modules where the student (10) .... smaller tests and builds up credits. These are popular with students because they are less stressful.

3 The following words are sometimes confused. Underline the best word for each sentence below.

1 The *format/formula* of examinations in the British educational system is changing.
2 He would have preferred to study more *practical/practicable* subjects at school.
3 This involves a process of *continuous/continual* assessment done by the teacher throughout the course.

4 It has the advantage that if the student makes one *mistake/fault* they will not necessarily fail.
5 Instead, they can improve their *grade/level* in the next piece of work they do.
6 Many students like this form of testing because it is less *stressful/agitating* for them.

4 Now answer these questions.

1 How similar or different is the English education system to the one in your country?
2 Describe the way in which students qualify for university in your country. What is your opinion of the system?

Speaking
Interactive communication

In the last part of the interview you will have to discuss a series of questions with your partner. The questions will all be on the same topic. One of the criteria you are assessed on is 'interactive communication'. This involves being able to keep a conversation going by:

- responding to what the other speaker says e.g. 'Yes, that's a good point ... '
- expressing your own opinion or making a new point e.g. 'It seems to me that ... '
- inviting a response from the other speaker e.g. 'What do you think ... ?'

1 Read the question below and discuss some ideas with a partner.

How far do you think that formal written exams are a good way of measuring progress?

2 Now listen to two English speakers discussing the question. Which point of view do you agree with?

3 Listen again and note any useful expressions you hear under the following headings.

- Acknowledging an opinion before disagreeing
- Disagreeing
- Agreeing
- Asking for opinions

4 Read the question below and discuss your ideas with a partner.

To what extent do you agree that continuous assessment is the best way of testing students?

Writing

▶ Paper 2, Part 1 (proposal)

For the compulsory task in Paper 2, Part 1 you may be asked to write a **proposal**. A proposal uses a similar format to a report, with headings, but whereas a report focuses on a past or present situation, the focus of a proposal is on making recommendations for future action or further discussion. These recommendations will form the longest and most important part of the proposal. In a Part 1 proposal you have to present, develop and evaluate different points of view. (In a Part 2 proposal you will generally focus on one point of view.)

1

1 Read the following writing task.

> **TASK**
>
> You have read the extract below, which is part of a letter sent to the local newspaper. You decide to write a proposal to put to the school authorities, making suggestions about how the curriculum and facilities could be improved.
>
> (300–350 words)

> I've been extremely disappointed in the way in which my son has been let down by a narrow-minded attitude towards his education. His strengths lie in practical areas, but he has to study academic subjects. Surely there is no place in the modern world for outdated subjects like history? Should they not be replaced by useful vocational training such as accountancy – and by life skills? I for one resent the time and money spent on teachers and would rather see more facilities and training for the modern world.

2 To start you thinking about the topic, interview a partner about your own school and ways in which you could improve the syllabus. Make notes under the following headings.

- Current situation and problems
- Recommendations for change with reasons
- Conclusion summarising advantages of changes suggested

2 Read the following proposal which was written in answer to the task. Note down any ideas that are different from your own.

Proposal to up-date the school curriculum

Current situation

The school curriculum currently covers a wide range of subjects, including traditional areas such as history and Latin. Although exam results in these subjects are generally good, they cost the school a great deal in teacher salaries and provide only paper qualifications. They also take time away from more practical subjects such as information technology, which are vital in today's world.

Recommendations

Current research indicates that educational needs are changing, and that children need to be better prepared for the modern world. So we've got to make drastic changes to the curriculum to take into account these needs.

Firstly I suggest that subjects such as Latin and history are a waste of time. Some people say they train the mind, developing understanding of cause and effect, but I feel that the information they provide will be useless in later life. These qualities could be more effectively developed in other ways. I therefore propose that these subjects should be dropped from the curriculum, saving money which could be diverted into other areas.

If it is felt that students need to develop more effective life skills, I propose that we should set up links with local businesses, which would give students more useful experience than pure academic study can provide.

While I do not agree that there is little need for teachers, I do feel that there is a place for developing the skills of independent study. I would like to put forward the idea of developing an area dedicated to self-study. I reckon it would be a good plan to use money saved by the reduction in the number of subjects studied to finance this.

Conclusion

We always have to remember that the school must maintain its reputation as one of traditional excellence while moving into the modern world. The proposals outlined above will achieve this result by providing a more up-to-date curriculum and resources which will be perceived by teachers, pupils and parents as sensible preparation for life after school. I hope that you will think about these ideas a lot.

(349 words)

3 You must use the information you are given for the task in Exercise 1 to give you ideas for your writing. Read the extract given in the task again and compare it with the proposal.

1 What ideas in the extract have been used in the proposal?
2 How do the introduction and the conclusion link to the extract?
3 What other ideas have been added by the writer in the proposal?

4 How many points has the writer made in the recommendations section of the proposal? Underline the phrases used to introduce each new point.

5 A proposal should be written in a formal style throughout. The underlined expressions used in the proposal on page 35 are too informal. Choose more formal expressions from the box below to replace them. You do not need to use all the expressions.

> ... these proposals will be given due consideration ...
> ... clearly pointless ...
> It is vital ...
> It would seem sensible ...
> I therefore recommend that we should ...
> I propose that radical changes should be made to ...

6 Read the following writing task.

TASK
You have read the extract below from a report written following an inspection of your school. Your principal has now been offered funding to address some of these problems and has asked students to provide suggestions for how the money should be spent. You decide to write a proposal responding to the points raised and expressing your views.

(300–350 words)

> ... student motivation throughout the institution is generally high, and there was evidence of learning taking place. However, the facilities available to both students and teachers are outdated and uninspiring. There is little for students to do outside the classroom and nothing to tempt them to stay in the building for longer than necessary. The environment is not conducive to the full learning experience which should be the benchmark of the 21st century.

1 Discuss your ideas with a partner and make notes for your proposal, using the headings in Exercise 1. Remember to use the information given in the extract.
2 Write your proposal. Remember to use a formal style and to order your points clearly using a variety of phrases.
3 Check your proposal for accuracy, style and length.

1 Complete these sentences by putting the verbs in brackets into the correct form.

1 Since starting her degree, Molly wishes she .... greater attention during maths lessons at school. (*pay*)

2 If you .... me earlier that you haven't got a computer, I .... you to do those calculations. (*tell*) (*not ask*)

3 It's high time students in this school .... to study subjects relevant to the world of work. (*begin*)

4 If only my teachers .... me running this company – they .... totally amazed. (*see*) (*be*)

2 Complete the second sentence with three to eight words so that it has a similar meaning to the first sentence, using the word given. Do not change the word given.

1 Could you help me tackle this problem?
   deal
   I'd be grateful .... this problem.

2 I regret that my education has left me so ill-equipped for real life. **prepared**
   If .... for real life.

3 She never passed any exams, as far as I know.
   knowledge
   To .... no paper qualifications.

4 He'd better abandon all hope of promotion.
   thoughts
   He should .... promoted out of his mind.

5 What is the point of all this research?
   aid
   What is .... of?

6 The scriptwriter said that she'd invented the whole plot herself. **thought**
   The scriptwriter said that she'd .... help.

7 None of us expected to have a test yesterday.
   blue
   Yesterday's test .... for us all.

8 It's difficult for some people to express their feelings. **words**
   Putting .... is difficult for some people.

3 Read the text below. Use the word given in capitals at the end of some of the lines to form a word that fits the space in the same line.

When people enjoy whatever they are doing, they report some (0) *characteristic* feelings **CHARACTER**
that distinguish the (1) .... moment from **PLEASURE**
the rest of life. The same types of feelings are reported in the context of playing chess, climbing mountains, playing with babies, reading a book or writing a poem. They are the same for young and old, male and female, American or Japanese, rich or poor. In other words, the nature of enjoyment seems to be (2) .... We call this state of **UNIVERSE**
(3) .... a flow experience, because many **CONSCIOUS**
people report that when what they are doing is (4) .... enjoyable, it feels like being carried **SPECIAL**
away by a current, like being in a flow.

At present, (5) .... few students would **LAMENT**
recognise the idea that learning can be like that. But if educators invested a fraction of the energy on (6) .... the students' enjoyment of **STIMULUS**
learning that they now spend in trying to transmit information, we could achieve much better results. Once students' (7) .... is engaged, once they **MOTIVATE**
can be (8) .... to take control of their own **POWER**
learning and provided with clear (9) .... on **FEED**
their efforts, then they are on their way to a lifetime of self-propelled (10) .... of knowledge. **ACQUIRE**

4 This picture is being considered for the cover of a brochure advertising holiday courses for young people. Say why young people might want to go on a holiday course and decide if this is a suitable picture for the cover of the brochure or not.

3 The moving image

Speaking

1 Discuss the following quotations. What common theme links them?

> 'The telephone has too many shortcomings to be seriously considered as a means of communication. The device is inherently of no value to us.'
>
> *Western Union internal memo, 1876*

> 'Who the hell wants to hear actors talk?'
>
> *H. M. Warner, Warner Brothers, 1927*

> 'The wireless music box has no imaginable commercial value.'
>
> *Business response to appeal for investment in radio during the 1920s*

> 'Television will never be a serious competitor for radio because people must sit and keep their eyes glued to a screen; the average American family hasn't time for it.'
>
> *The New York Times, 1939*

> 'I think there is a world market for maybe five computers.'
>
> *Thomas Watson, chairman of IBM, 1943*

2 Imagine you could talk to one of the people quoted. Explain how wrong their prediction was, using evidence from today's world.

3 What do you think has been the greatest advance in the media in the last ten years? What changes could occur in the next ten years?

Listening
▶ Paper 4, Part 3

1 Look at the advertisements. Which of these films were made in Hollywood? What features would you expect to find in a 'typical' Hollywood film?

2 You will hear an extract from a radio programme in which a film critic, Dan Sheldon, is interviewed about Hollywood and the part it has played in the film industry. Before you listen, read the multiple-choice questions below.

1 After the early French documentaries, film-makers became interested in
    A illusion and reality.
    B the effect of movement.
    C adapting stories for film.
    D manipulating plot.

2 The use of mass production techniques in films led to
    A further technological developments.
    B the establishment of Hollywood.
    C the rise of the studio system.
    D the development of specialised genres.

3   The speaker says colour was different from sound because
   A   its impact on film-making was more gradual.
   B   it was not accepted by some film enthusiasts.
   C   its arrival was associated with a particular film.
   D   it was more technologically complex.

4   According to the speaker, what stopped the decline in Hollywood films?
   A   the development of cheaper means of production
   B   the introduction of new genres
   C   the identification of a younger audience
   D   the rise of video

5   The speaker suggests that in the future
   A   film stars will be less remote.
   B   the viewer will be more directly involved.
   C   there will be more film 'packages'.
   D   new film genres will develop.

3   Now listen and choose the answer (**A**, **B**, **C** or **D**) which fits best according to what you hear.

4   Discuss these questions.

1   Can you think of a film you have enjoyed recently that was not made in the USA?
2   How important is the film industry in the country where you live, and what kinds of film are produced?

5   **Say it again**

Re-express the following sentences using the word given, without changing the meaning.

1   Everyone knows the Hollywood sign and what it represents.   **stands**
2   Cinema began with the development of the cinematoscope.   **when**
3   It wasn't until the 1950s that colour really arrived.   **didn't**
4   People completely lost interest in silent movies.   **longer**

Reading

▶ Paper 1, Part 2

1 Discuss the following questions.

1 Are there any programmes being shown on television in your country which you think are objectionable or dangerous?
2 Who, if anyone, should be responsible for controlling what is shown on television?
3 What changes would you like to see in the types of programmes shown on television?
4 Do you think that the main function of cinema and television should be to inform, or to entertain?

2

1 Read quickly through the four extracts on this page and pages 41 and 42 to get a general idea of what they are about. Then write one of the following titles above each of the extracts.

Mass production movies
Where are movies going?
Professionalism in broadcasting
A new lease of life

2 Which extract is:

a) a film review written in colloquial English?
b) an extract from a novel written in literary English?
c) an argument expressing a strongly held personal belief, written in a style which is mainly formal?
d) a magazine article written in a style which is a mixture of formal and informal?

3 Read the extracts again and answer the questions that follow each one.

Extract 1

At eighty-three years old, Baby Kochamma had a new love. She had installed a dish antenna on the roof of the Ayemenem house. She presided over the World in her drawing room on satellite TV. The impossible excitement that this engendered in her wasn't hard to understand. It wasn't something that had happened gradually. It happened overnight. Blondes, wars, famines, football, sex, music, coups d'état – they all arrived on the same train. They unpacked together. They stayed at the same hotel. And in Ayemenem, where once the loudest sound had been a musical bus horn, now whole wars, picturesque massacres and Bill Clinton could be summoned up like servants.

And so, while her ornamental garden wilted and died, Baby Kochamma followed American NBA league games, one-day cricket and all the Grand Slam tennis tournaments. On weekdays she watched *The Bold and The Beautiful* and *Santa Barbara*, where brittle blondes with lipstick and hairstyles rigid with spray seduced androids and defended their empires. Baby Kochamma loved their shiny clothes and the smart bitchy repartee. During the day disconnected snatches of it came back to her and made her chuckle.

(This text is set in Southern India.)

1 Find more formal terms in the extract for the following expressions.

1 she had put
2 she ruled
3 caused
4 hard (adj)

2 Read the sentence beginning 'Blondes, wars, famines …' in lines 6 to 7. In this metaphor, the writer uses the image of a train's arrival to make a point about her main topic.

- What *actually* 'arrived' at Ayemenem?
- Does the metaphor suggest that this arrival was gradual or sudden?
- What other ideas are suggested here by the image of the train and its passengers?

3 Choose the best answer (**A**, **B**, **C** or **D**).

1 In the first paragraph, the writer emphasises the effect of television by
  A giving examples of its use.
  B listing the changes it caused.
  C comparing it with something else.
  D contrasting it with something different.

2 When watching television, Baby Kochamma is amused by
  A the dialogue.
  B the clothes.
  C the plots.
  D the events.

Extract 2

Broadcasters can exploit ignorance, apathy and cruelty; more and more do. To describe objections to all this as 'do-goodery' is to take refuge in misguided slogans so as to avoid embarrassing interrogations. No programme is ever justified by the answer, 'but they enjoyed it.' So does a cat playing with a dying sparrow. 5 The tendency to meet such charges with a ribald dismissal is yet another instance of moral bankruptcy, of the rotten 'give the punters what they want' spirit.

One has to return in the end to 'professionalism', which arises from respect for the medium, its themes, its listeners and 10 viewers. It emerges from mutual respect and support of one's peers, the sense of working honestly towards a common end, a constant to'ing and fro'ing of skilled judgements. We are back with the need for a clear eye, not a squint.

In the light of all the irrelevant pressure under which 15 broadcasters work today, it is remarkable how much good work is produced. Excellent programmes there are, as good as they ever were. Appalling programmes there are also, worse than ever before.

1   Which of the following words have a positive implication in the extract? Which are used negatively?

exploit	do-goodery	ribald
bankruptcy	professionalism	skilled
clear	squint	

2   Answer the following questions about the structure of the extract.

1   Does 'they' (line 5) refer to
 a) the broadcasters?   b) the actors?   c) the audience?
2   Does 'such charges' (line 7) refer to accusations of
 a) making programmes which are cruel and immoral?
 b) being cruel to animals?
3   'the punters' (line 9) is a colloquial expression with a negative implication. Does it refer to
 a) the broadcasters?   b) the actors?   c) the audience?
4   Is 'the medium' (line 11)
 a) broadcasting?   b) criticism?

3   Answer the following questions about the use of metaphor and image.

1   'with the need for a clear eye, not a squint' (line 15)
 a) If you have a squint, do you look at people directly or sideways?
 b) Which way of looking suggests truth? Which suggests deceit?
 c) In this metaphor, a clear eye and a squint suggest the difference between ....
2   'a cat playing with a dying sparrow' (line 6)
 a) Is the cat aware of good and evil?
 b) Why is the cat playing with the sparrow? What will happen at the end of the 'game'?
 c) Do we feel sympathy for the cat or the sparrow?

 d) If we think about TV programmes involving cruelty, is the writer comparing the cat to the audience or the programme makers?

4   Choose the best answer (**A**, **B**, **C** or **D**).

1   The writer is concerned that some broadcasters
 A   inflict their own moral values on viewers.
 B   make programmes based on unacceptable values.
 C   provide viewers with misleading information.
 D   are not aware of the needs of the public.

2   The writer feels that
 A   broadcasters have a moral responsibility to their audience.
 B   clearer guidelines are needed for broadcasters.
 C   professionals should have more power to make decisions.
 D   clear standards exist which should be followed.

Extract 3

Cinema is an art born from a technology. And the future of the movies is as bound up with technology as its short past has been. The last century saw innovation and obsolescence at a frantic pace, affecting every element of the 5 medium – sound, colour, 3-D. But movie history is also a graveyard of formats and processes, of treasures mutilated, junked and lost. Even what we think of as the canon of imperishable films is physically vulnerable, drowned by brackish tides of 10 decaying chemicals.

Film has already outlived a number of death threats, notably from its unruly kid brothers, television and video. Now Hollywood techies are working around the clock to create synthetic 15 actors – pure special effects in human form, free of all the flaws of human actors – their imperfect complexions, their tantrums, their agents. Before too long the first actorless feature film will make its appearance, with a huge surge of publicity and 20 interest. And then things will carry on pretty much as before. The need for human faces, for stars to identify with, is too central a part of film's appeal to be abandoned.

1   Which of the following words are formal and which are informal/colloquial? Suggest a more formal term for each of the informal words.

movies	obsolescence	techies	aspire
mutilated	junked	carry on	kid

2 Answer the following questions about the use of metaphor and image.

1 'the canon of imperishable films ... drowned by brackish tides of decaying chemicals' (lines 9–11)
   a) 'Brackish' is usually used to describe impure water. Which two other words in this metaphor relate to liquid?
   b) Are chemicals regarded as solid or liquid here?
   c) What is the connection between old films and decaying chemicals? Why might decaying chemicals be harmful for films?

3 Choose the best answer (**A**, **B**, **C** or **D**).

1 The writer is concerned that
   A film-making is influenced too much by technology.
   B film-makers are interested in novelty rather than quality.
   C we may be losing some classic films forever.
   D newer media are likely to supersede film.

2 The writer says that the 'Hollywood techies' will
   A produce actors that people can identify with.
   B never be able to produce perfect actors.
   C save film-making through the use of special effects.
   D have little long-term effect on film-making.

Extract 4

Although Jackie Chan has only been known to the general public for a few short years, it seems like he's been around for ever. That's because he has now made 3,500 films, many without having to re-feed the cameraman's parking meter. Chan makes movies faster than most people can make change, which is astonishing considering the number 5 of bones he has broken in his career. In the time it will have taken to write this review, he will have made another three movies. Jackie Chan is more than a movie star. He is an entire industrial sector.

One of the things that makes Jackie Chan movies so appealing is their fabulously cheesy quality. Shot on shoestring budgets in out-of- 10 the-way locales with no stars and wafer-thin plots, films like *What's My Name?* are basically just an excuse for Chan to clamber up and down the facades of tall buildings and ride motorcycles atop speeding locomotives. The basic plot-line is set up immediately, and then the stunts begin: niceties like subplots, character development or actual acting are 15 dismissed out of hand. Although the films are filled with fight sequences, the combat tends to be of a decidedly cartoonish variety, with little blood and few mutilations. This makes the films suitable for viewing by all age groups and genders, though Chan's biggest fans are young men.

Primitive yet clever, the average Jackie Chan movie is the celluloid 20 equivalent to the average pop song: dumb but entertaining. They are what they are.

1 Answer the following questions about the writer's language and tone of voice.

1 Find four examples in the first paragraph where the writer uses exaggeration. What is the point being made by all four statements?
2 'cheesy' (line 10) is a colloquial word meaning cheap and low quality. Is it used here in a positive or negative sense?
3 Find expressions in paragraph 2 which mean:
   a) very cheaply
   b) weak story-lines
   c) not even considered
   d) very unreal.
4 What word in paragraph 2 suggests that to Jackie Chan subplot, character and acting are unimportant details?

2 Choose the best answer (**A**, **B**, **C** or **D**).

1 What makes Jackie Chan films special, according to the writer?
   A their unusual locations
   B their cheapness
   C their realistic use of violence
   D their unsophistication

2 The overall tone of the review is
   A critical.
   B ironic.
   C neutral.
   D respectful.

Language Focus: Vocabulary
Fixed phrases and idioms

Fixed phrases and idioms may be tested in Paper 1, Part 1 and Paper 3, Parts 1, 3 and 4. You will also find these phrases help to make your speech and writing more fluent.

1   Match the sentence halves. The expressions in **bold** form fixed phrases with the pattern noun + *of* + noun.

1   The film's release caused **a surge**
2   I didn't get **a wink**
3   Everything he told her was **a pack**
4   She showed great **presence**
5   Whether it's right or wrong is **a matter**
6   When he met her, she showed **no sign**

a)   **of opinion** – there's no definite answer.
b)   **of mind** in the emergency.
c)   **of publicity** in the press.
d)   **of lies** – he made it all up.
e)   **of recognition**, but just walked past.
f)   **of sleep** all night – the baby kept crying.

2   Read the statements 1–7, and answer the questions a)–g) below, which all include idioms with noun + *of* + noun.

1   'I can't go on like this – if I don't have a holiday, I'll collapse!'
2   'I didn't think about it – I just got on a plane and went!'
3   'I think there may be a new treatment for this type of illness.'
4   'I really wish I hadn't insulted him – it's just that I was so angry.'
5   'I've won a free holiday for two in Hawaii.'
6   'You only just made it – another few minutes and he would have drowned.'
7   'I feel so much better since I had the operation.'

a)   Who acted on the spur of the moment?
b)   Who's at the end of her tether?
c)   Who arrived in the nick of time?
d)   Who has provided a ray of hope?
e)   Who spoke in the heat of the moment?
f)   Who's been given a new lease of life?
g)   Who's had a stroke of luck?

3   Complete the sentences below with a suitable phrase from the box and make any necessary structural changes. The sentences all follow the pattern verb + noun + preposition. Use the preposition in the sentence to help you choose the right phrase.

| draw the line | put one's back | shed light |
| have a go | make sense | spare a thought |

1   If we really .... into it, we could be finished by tonight.
2   The instructions are so complicated I can't .... of them at all.
3   I'd like to .... at running my own business.
4   His explanation did little to .... on the mystery.
5   I believe in freedom of choice, but I .... at letting children choose whether or not to go to school.
6   Not everyone is as lucky as you – .... for those who are out of work.

4   Read the text below and decide which answer (**A, B, C** or **D**) best fits each gap. All the gapped expressions here are fixed phrases with prepositions.

Bert vs Mrs Colly

Soon after his seventieth birthday, Bert ran into a (1) .... of bother with his next-door neighbour. He never told us exactly what had happened, just saying that it was all a (2) .... of nonsense; all we knew was that he'd had what he called a 'misunderstanding' with his neighbour, Mrs Colly, and as a result she'd taken him to court. Bert decided to have a (3) .... at conducting his own defence and although he had no legal training, he made short work of the prosecution. The judge said he was satisfied there wasn't a grain of (4) .... in the accusations, and that Mrs Colly must have taken (5) .... of her senses, since she didn't have a shred of evidence to support her accusation. The case was widely reported in the local press, and Bert was made out to be something of a hero. But the whole thing (6) .... years on Bert, and his neighbours never regarded him in quite the same light again. As for Mrs Colly, she moved away soon after that, and we never did find out the truth about the 'misunderstanding'.

1   **A** piece   **B** spot   **C** point   **D** lump
2   **A** pile   **B** collection   **C** matter   **D** load
3   **A** stab   **B** kick   **C** brush   **D** hit
4   **A** right   **B** reality   **C** accuracy   **D** truth
5   **A** loss   **B** leave   **C** lack   **D** left
6   **A** set   **B** made   **C** put   **D** added

5   Find out if these statements are true about your partner.

1   I like to do things on the spur of the moment.
2   I tend to jump to conclusions without thinking first.
3   I would draw the line at lying to help a friend.

Language Focus: Vocabulary
Dependent prepositions

Some questions in Paper 1, Part 1 and Paper 3 require knowledge of the particular prepositions that must follow certain verbs, adjectives and nouns. For example:

- Jenny was praised by the Principal **for** her outstanding contribution.

  congratulated

  The Principal *congratulated Jenny **on** her contribution,* which he said was outstanding.

1 Adjective + preposition

1 Adjectives with related meanings are often followed by the same preposition. Match each of the prepositions in the box to one set of adjectives A–F.

about	at	from	of	on	to

A bad   hopeless   efficient   adept

B similar   applicable   preferable   contrary

C anxious   happy   worried   curious

D dependent   reliant   intent   keen

E different   apart   distinct   exempt

F indicative   typical   illustrative   characteristic

2 Most of the expressions above can be followed by both noun and gerund. For example:

- *He's hopeless at* **maths**.
- *He's hopeless at* **doing** *maths problems.*

Which group of expressions can only be followed by a noun?

3 Complete the following sentences with an appropriate adjective + preposition combination from Exercise 1.1.

1 I'm absolutely .... parking, even with a little car like this one.

2 No-one should be .... prosecution if they have committed a crime.

3 He was very .... what she had been doing the previous evening, and asked her a lot of questions.

4 It's absolutely .... her to leave everything until the last minute!

5 Unlike young animals, children remain totally .... their parents for many years.

6 Fortunately the event was a great success, ... our expectations.

7 She's not very .... being the first person to test the equipment – she says it's a bit risky.

8 These rules are not .... members of the club.

2 Noun/verb + preposition

Nouns, verbs and adjectives which share the same root are often, though not always, followed by the same preposition. Complete each pair of sentences below with a noun or verb related to the adjective given in brackets, and the appropriate preposition. (Sometimes no preposition is needed.)

1 (*dependent*)
I'm concerned by his .... other people to solve his problems.
I'm concerned by the fact that he .... other people to solve his problems.

2 (*indicative*)
According to these figures, there is no .... any increase in profits.
These figures do not .... any increase in profits.

3 (*applicable*)
Your .... this post should be submitted as soon as possible.
You should .... this post as soon as possible.

4 (*characteristic*)
The main .... living creatures are the abilities to grow and reproduce.
Living creatures are .... the ability to grow and reproduce.

5 (*different*)
There is very little .... this car and the original model, except that this one is much more expensive.
This new car hardly .... the original model, apart from being much more expensive.

6 (*preferable*)
I think my .... would be .... a salad rather than a cooked meal today.
I think I'd .... a salad .... a cooked meal today.

7 (*involved*)
His .... the robbery is beyond doubt.
It is certain that he was .... the robbery.

8 (*contributory*)
The director made an enormous .... the success of the film.
The director .... enormously .... the success of the film.

Exam Focus
▶ Paper 3, Part 1

In Paper 3, Part 1 you have to complete a text with fifteen gaps. One word is needed to fill each gap. You need to think about:

- word combinations such as collocations, fixed phrases and phrasal verbs
- structural items such as auxiliary verbs, prepositions, pronouns and articles
- conjunctions and linking words, e.g. *despite*, *unless*.

1 Read through the whole of the text below, ignoring the gaps for the moment. Then choose the best phrase to complete this summary of the text.

Developments in television technology
A mean we have lost our national identities.
B could lead to a widening of cultural values.
C are threatening the movie business.

Television used to act (0) .... a uniquely unifying national phenomenon. Never before (1) .... so many people had so common (2) .... core of shared cultural experiences. People might not know the names of their next-door neighbours, (3) .... they probably watched many of the same programmes.

(4) .... days, however, with the vast expansion of television programming, everyone can watch (5) .... different, just as each Internet user can explore a different selection of websites. Even so, programmes aimed at international markets generally (6) .... to be less popular (with the partial exception (7) .... those from America) and people still often choose to watch their own national programmes. In (8) ...., if television develops along similar (9) .... to the movie business, with a few blockbusters attracting vast international audiences, people may even (10) .... up watching a narrower range of programmes. But (11) .... patterns of viewing habits develop, television will almost certainly become a personal (12) .... of equipment, more (13) .... a mobile phone than a communal source of entertainment. Armed (14) .... a credit card and a remote control, viewers will be able to pick their programmes from wherever they choose. Television will then have become truly global. (15) ...., perhaps, will the cultural values it instils.

2 Now go through the text and fill in the answers that are immediately obvious. Don't fill in anything you are not sure of at this stage because you need to keep an open mind when you look back at the gap.

3 Go through the text again and fill in the remaining words. You should always read through the whole sentence carefully when you fill in a gap, as clues for the missing word may occur later. Consider whether the word you need is singular or plural, positive or negative. Use these hints to help you if necessary.

Hints
1 auxiliary verb
2 determiner
3 conjunction
4 determiner
5 indefinite pronoun
6 verb followed by infinitive, meaning 'to do something often'
7 preposition depending on the preceding noun
8 part of a linking expression
9 part of a fixed phrase meaning 'in a similar way'
10 part of a phrasal verb
11 determiner
12 part of a fixed phrase
13 adjective used as part of a comparison
14 preposition depending on previous participle
15 adjective referring back to previous sentence

4 Read through the completed text to check that:

- the text as a whole makes sense
- tenses, plural forms and noun/verb agreement are all correct
- there are no spelling mistakes.

Here is a procedure to follow for this task.

- Read the text for general understanding.
- Read it again and fill in only the answers that are immediately obvious.
- Go back and work out the remaining answers.
- Read it once more to check accuracy and ensure that the completed text makes sense.

Note: This is a similar technique to that recommended for Paper 1, Part 1.

Language Focus: Grammar
Participle clauses

1 Read the short film reviews below and discuss these questions.

1 Which of the films have you seen? How far do you agree with the reviewer?
2 Which film would you most/least like to see? Why?

Jurassic Park. By extracting the blood from a prehistoric mosquito preserved in amber, scientists are able to develop living dinosaurs. Billionaire John Hammond masterminds an epic theme park for the dinosaurs, but before revealing his secrets to the public, he invites a small group of people to visit. Big mistake …

Spielberg drew on a budget of $60 million for the film, creating an astonishing range of prehistoric creatures that move, breathe and attack like the real thing. Although the human characters are less convincing, it has to be said that the film is an exhilarating and often intensely frightening experience.

Robin Hood Prince of Thieves. Opening with a man having his hand cut off in Jerusalem, this film hurtles back to England and never stops. Witchcraft, comic villains and large-scale battles fill the screen until your head aches. Kevin

Costner comes over as an unsympathetic Rob… not thinking twice about putting an arrow throug… a colleague's hand, and the rest of the cast a… equally unconvincing. Another overblow… overscored, overbudgeted Hollywood excess sto…

Heavenly Creatures. Exploring th… emotional experience that makes a murderer, Ne… Zealand director Peter Jackson charts the tr… story of two schoolgirls, Pauline (played … Melanie Lynskey) and Juliet (played by Ka… Winslet, outstanding in her debut fi… performance). Both were bright, imaginative gi… who were trapped in a provincial world that w… stifling them. Seeking to escape from it throu… the power of their imaginations, they resorted t… murder to preserve their unique universe. Th… intensity of the young actresses' performances a… the superbly realised fantasy sequences make thi… memorable film.

2

1 Rewrite the following sentences using participle clauses, as in the examples below. (Participle clauses are clauses in which a finite verb – i.e. a verb with a tense – is replaced by an *-ing* or *-ed* participle.)

EXAMPLES:
Before he reveals his secrets to the public, John Hammond invites a small group of people to visit.
Before revealing his secrets to the public,
John Hammond invites …

Spielberg drew on a budget of $60 million for the film, and as a result he created an astonishing range of prehistoric creatures.
Spielberg drew on a budget of $60 million for the film,
creating an astonishing range …

1 This film opens with a man who is having his hand cut off in Jerusalem. It then hurtles back to England and never stops.

....

2 Kevin Costner comes over as an unsympathetic Robin, since he doesn't think twice about putting an arrow through a colleague's hand.

....

3 New Zealand director Peter Jackson explores the emotional experience that makes a murderer and charts the true story of two schoolgirls.

....

4 They were seeking to escape from it through the power of their imaginations, so they resorted to a murder.

....

2 Now compare your sentences with the reviews. (More than one option may be possible.)

3 Which of the sentences 1–4 describes:
- simultaneous events?
- events in rapid sequence?
- an event and its reason?

► Grammar reference p. 213

3   Complete the second sentence with three to eight words so that it has a similar meaning to the first sentence, using the word given. Do not change the word given. You will need to use a participle clause in each case.

1   Please read the instructions carefully before you use this appliance.   **making**
Before ....
this appliance, please read the instructions carefully.

2   When I had another look at the film script, I was impressed by its quality.   **through**
On ....,
I was impressed by its quality.

3   He started his journey early but he still didn't get there on time.   **off**
Despite .... late.

4   They made him wait for three hours, then finally let him in.   **kept**
He was finally admitted after having ....
.... for three hours.

5   We were bowled over by the news as we hadn't thought we would win an Oscar for the film.
expected
Not ....
an Oscar for the film, we were completely bowled over by the news.

6   This car will give you many years of service if you care for it properly.   **after**
Properly .... ,
this car will give you years of service.

Improving your writing

The exercises in this section will help you to improve your writing in these areas:

- consistency and appropriacy of style and register
- effect on target reader.

1   **Consistency and appropriacy of style and register**

The writer of the following extract is using an inappropriate mix of formal and informal language.

> She was my teacher for one year. I can tell you our relationship wasn't at all warm: I used to be a pain in the neck and she would try to calm me down by getting me out of the classroom. But the most important thing I learned from her was not to stand in her way if she had a bad day; she could be extremely petulant.

Look at the two rewrites A and B below. Which version could be:

- part of an informal letter to a friend?
- part of a formal essay or article to an unknown reader?

Underline the words and phrases in each rewritten version which helped you to decide.

A
> She was my teacher for one year and our relationship was far from warm. My behaviour in class was difficult for her to accept, and she would try to calm me down by telling me to leave the classroom. But the most important thing I learned from her was not to stand in her way when she was in a bad mood as she could be extremely irritable.

B
> She was my teacher for a year and I can tell you, our relationship was pretty bad. I suppose I was a pain in the neck, and she'd try to calm me down by getting me out of the classroom. The main thing I learned was to keep out of her way if she was having a bad day - she could be really awkward.

2   **Effect on target reader**

The reader of the letter below might be offended as the information is given too directly. Rewrite the letter to make it more acceptable.

> Dear Peter
> Thank you for your letter inviting me to be a guest speaker for your society. However, the date which you suggest is very inconvenient for me. I am not free at all in May. Please try to arrange a date in June or July instead.
> Yours sincerely

Hints
1   **Content**
Give more details to explain why you can't come in May.
Mention that you're looking forward to speaking to/meeting Peter.

2   **Language**
Use some of the following words and expressions:
*rather   unfortunately   I'm afraid   If possible
I wonder if you could   I would be happy to
I hope this doesn't inconvenience you*

Language Focus: Grammar
Inversion

1 Read the pairs of sentences below and tick the sentence in each pair which is more emphatic. Underline the structural differences between the sentences.

1 a) People have <u>never had</u> such a common core of experiences before.
b) <u>Never before have</u> people had such a common core of experiences.

2 a) Nowhere else in the world will you find scenery like this.
b) You won't find scenery like this anywhere else in the world.

3 a) You must not leave your baggage unattended at any time.
b) On no account should you leave your baggage unattended at any time.

4 a) I didn't realise how cold it was until I went outside.
b) Not until I went outside did I realise how cold it was.

5 a) Only recently did they get the chance to visit the city.
b) They only got the chance to visit the city recently.

► Grammar reference p. 214

2 Rewrite these sentences using standard word order to make them less emphatic.

1 Nowhere in the world are people free from the influence of television.
People are ....

2 Not since the printing press has there been an invention which so radically affected society.
There ....

3 Rarely do you find a family without a television set these days.
You ....

4 Seldom can busy parents resist the temptation to use the television as a childminder.
....

5 Not only does television discourage conversation, but it also encourages anti-social behaviour, some claim.
....

6 However, not a single case of violence have researchers found that could be directly linked to a television programme.
....

3 *hardly/no sooner*

In these examples the underlined expressions indicate that two actions take place in rapid succession.

1 They had <u>hardly</u> finished cleaning up the mess, <u>when</u> their parents arrived home.
2 The car had <u>no sooner</u> arrived <u>than</u> it was surrounded by journalists.

Note: *when* introduces a time clause. The expression *no sooner ... than* is a comparative.

1 Combine the sentences below using the words in brackets. You will also need to make some changes in the tenses used.

1 She got on the bus. She realised she had left her money at home. (*no sooner*)
2 The game began. It started to pour with rain. (*hardly*)
3 They got to know one another. She was offered a job in the USA. (*hardly*)
4 He settled himself down in front of the television. The phone rang. (*no sooner*)

Inversion of the subject and verb may be used with these expressions to increase the dramatic effect.

1 <u>Hardly</u> had they finished cleaning up the mess when their parents arrived home.
2 <u>No sooner</u> had the car arrived than it was surrounded by journalists.

2 Rewrite sentences 1–4 above, using inversion.

4 **Writing practice**

Rewrite each of the sentences using inversion and the word(s) in brackets.

1 The minute she left, the meeting broke up. (*No sooner*)
2 Immediately after solving one problem, I was faced with another. (*Hardly*)
3 The colour of that jacket suits you, and it fits you perfectly. (*Not only*)
4 The minute he set eyes on her, he fell in love. (*No sooner*)
5 You must remember to pay that bill, whatever you do. (*On no account*)
6 He did not start to feel ill until after the meal. (*Only when*)

► Exam Maximiser

Writing

▶ Paper 2, Part 2 (review)

In Paper 2, Part 2 you may have to write a **review**. This could be a review of a book, a film, a play or a place open to the public such as a restaurant or a hotel. The review will usually include some kind of evaluation and may also involve discussion of wider issues related to the topic.

1

1 Read the following writing task.

> **TASK**
>
> You are a student on a film studies course and have recently seen a remake of an old film. You saw the original film earlier in the course. Write a review of the new film for your college journal, saying what you think the problems might be in remaking films for modern audiences and how successful such remakes can be.
>
> (300–350 words)

2 Here is a possible structure for a film review.

- Introduction of topic
- Description of film
- Evaluation of wider issues
- Conclusion

2 Read the first part of the review below, which describes *Psycho*, a film originally made in 1960 by Alfred Hitchcock and remade in 1998.

1 Underline an example of a participle clause.
2 What is the purpose of the second paragraph?

Alfred Hitchcock's classic thriller *Psycho*, originally shot in black and white, created a sensation when it was first shown in cinemas; its simple plot was filmed with consummate skill. Has the remake added anything to the original?

The story itself is still straightforward and little has been changed to script or plot. Marion, the victim, steals money from her employer. Driving away, she runs into bad weather and books into the Bates Motel. She is murdered in the shower. The Bates family secret is exposed and the murderer is revealed. Remaking the film was costly for the film studios – and was it worth it?

3 Read the list of ideas below. Choose those you might expect to be included in the second part of the review, which assesses the problems of remaking old films for modern audiences.

- values or historical perspective of original film possibly out of date
- original script possibly old-fashioned
- difficulties for directors in finding a new approach
- audience expectation of graphic special effects
- colour versus black and white

Discuss what problems these ideas might cause for film-makers and audiences. What examples would you choose to include to support your ideas? Would you add any other ideas to the list?

4 Read the second part of the review. Were any of your ideas included?

Remakes are actually quite popular, perhaps because studios can make money by cashing in on previous successes, or because remakes allow older audiences to wallow in nostalgia. However, they are not always successful and the new *Psycho* is a case in point. It is more colourful and more high-tech than the original – yet it has lost its impact. To me the original film seemed much fresher. Why is this? It may be that because the original film is more than thirty years old, moral attitudes towards such things as theft and even murder have changed. The new version did not move me. Then, old films are not always suitable vehicles for the sophisticated special effects demanded by modern audiences. *Psycho* is a clear example of this. The original shower scene was terrifying, yet the only effect used was a shadow on the shower curtain. Could that simple shadow be bettered by more graphic effects? Clearly not – as the disappointing remake shows. Sadly, the expectations of modern audiences blind them to the value of simple story-telling and they overlook the subtleties of older films. This is not to say that films should never be remade, but watching the original *Psycho*, my eyes were opened to the craft of older films and the limitations of special effects.

Personally I doubt whether Hitchcock's version can ever be improved. After forty years, Hitchcock's *Psycho* remains absolutely terrifying. It is as perfect a film as one could want.

(347 words)

5 Read the whole review again, and answer the following questions.

1 What is the main point of each paragraph? Does the review match the structure suggested above? Justify your answer.

2 What two reasons does the writer give for old films being remade?

3 What problems does the writer suggest there might be in remaking old films?

4 What evidence does he provide from *Psycho* to support his ideas?

6

1 What technique does the writer use in paragraphs 1, 2 and 3 to involve the reader and introduce new issues?

2 Underline two words or phrases used by the writer to introduce his own opinion.

3 Is the writer in favour of remakes of films in general? Discuss his ideas in relation to any films that you have seen. Do you agree with him?

7

1 Read the following writing task.

> **TASK**
>
> You have recently seen a film that depended very much on the use of technology and special effects for its impact. Write a review of the film, evaluating the use of technology and special effects in films in general and this film in particular, and giving your opinion about this type of development.
>
> (300–350 words)

2 To start you thinking about the topic, discuss the following questions.

1 What film will you write about?
2 What types of special effect are used in modern films? Think about some of the following:

- setting
- costumes and make-up
- computer animation
- music and sound effects
- special filming techniques.

How effectively were they used in the film you saw and how much did they actually contribute to the film?

3 What is your overall opinion of the use of such technology in films? Who does it appeal to? Does it improve the quality of films?

8 Using the structure suggested in Exercise 1, write your review. Remember to include:

- a brief overview of the film you have chosen
- a description and evaluation of the way in which technology and special effects contribute to modern films, giving examples from the film you saw
- your own opinion on the use of these developments.

1 Find and correct the errors in the following sentences.

1 Contrary from what you might expect, I have in fact completed my assignment.
2 Not once he has asked me whether I agree with his ridiculous scheme.
3 I'm prepared to keep quiet about what I know, but I draw a line at lying.
4 She's adept in finding plausible excuses for not doing as much work as she should.
5 Not only have you my evening ruined, but you've offended my friends as well.
6 With maturity, we are less inclined to conform in the expectations of our peers.
7 Only now I am free to do what I want with my life.
8 Whether you're ready or not, filming will start tomorrow as scheduling.
9 This supposedly comic story is singularly lacking of humour.
10 There are means and ways of evading taxes, but I wouldn't advise you to try any of them.

2 Think of one word only which can be used appropriately in all three sentences.

1 Audiences prefer to see films .... in exotic locations.
Their new single .... to the top of the charts.
A spasm of pain .... down his arm.

2 My .... is that the plan will never work, but I could be wrong.
She waited until the whole of the castle was in .... and then took a photograph.
The pictures are currently on .... in the local art gallery.

3 They were .... on a diet of bread and potatoes.
He slowly .... his arms above his head.
The participants .... a number of questions at the meeting.

4 The film company supplied an information .... for the sponsors.
She didn't trust him when she discovered he had told her a .... of lies.
The dealer shuffled the .... and dealt the cards.

5 Although it's not very high, it's a .... wage for the job.
A .... number of people came along to the meeting.
I think it's only .... to say that she didn't know all the facts.

6 The driver escaped with just a few .... on his face.
The writer was annoyed that so many .... had been made to the script.
The recession means that .... in pay are inevitable for many workers.

3 Talk about the photos.

1 Discuss the different media pictured.
2 Which of the media pictured do you think has had the greatest effect on modern life? Why?
3 Which one do you think will have the most long-lasting effect? Why?
4 Imagine that you are choosing things to put in a time capsule for future generations. The time capsule is called 'The dawn of the 21st century – when real communication broke down'. Which aspects would you choose to highlight, what would you put in the capsule, and what lessons would you want people in the future to learn from them?

4 The hard sell

Speaking

1 Look at the company logos. Can you identify the companies? What products do they sell?

2

1 Think of some consumer products you have bought recently, such as an item of clothing, a CD, electrical equipment, etc. Which of the factors in the list below influenced your choice? Can you add any other factors to the list?

- brand name
- brand loyalty (you had bought the same brand before)
- a friend's recommendation
- pressure from your peer group
- advertising
- price
- accompanying special offers or gifts

2 Compare and discuss your answers with other students.

3 What are the advantages and disadvantages of advertising for:

a) the consumer?
b) the manufacturer or producer?

4 What do you consider makes a good advertisement?

3 Work with a partner. Together choose one of the following prompt cards and discuss the topic, using the three suggestions to help you. Make notes of your ideas.

> What do you feel makes a good advertisement?
>
> - concept
> - medium
> - approach

> How far do you agree that TV advertisements are better than the actual programmes?
>
> - originality and creativity
> - words and music
> - settings and locations

4 You are going to read a newspaper article about the way people perceive advertisers and advertisements.

1 Read the article and decide whether the writer's attitude towards advertisements is generally positive or negative.

2 Now answer the questions below, which focus on the main ideas in the article.

1 How does the writer describe advertisers? Underline the four adjectives he uses in the first paragraph. Are these positive or negative words? What evidence does he give for his attitude?
2 What constraints do advertisers have to take into account when making advertisements?
3 What does the writer say about the difference between television programmes and good advertisements?

I've worked in the business, on and off, for more than a decade, and have consistently found advertising workers to be more scrupulous, meticulous, exacting and professional than in any other area of broadcasting. While TV stations nowadays are increasingly embracing the stack-'em-high-and-sell-'em-cheap philosophy, the better advertising agencies are still creating commercials constructed with an attention to detail, a level of craftsmanship and a per-frame budget rarely encountered outside a Hollywood studio.

More astonishingly, the people who create these gems are simultaneously performing incredible feats of balance behind the scenes. They have to make an ad that's safe enough to pass the ultra-strict regulations of the Advertising Standards Authority (unlike programme-makers, they can't use nudity, swearing or violence to attract attention), yet stimulating and witty enough to captivate viewers. Also, it has to be distinctive, it has to satisfy the client (who usually just wants the product name repeated as often as possible), and it has to fit into exactly twenty-nine seconds of airtime.

As the digital age begins to fragment the televisual monolith into hundreds of tiny stations, the communality of viewing is vanishing beyond recall.

But, because they are shown right across the spectrum of channels, commercials are proving to be the one exception to that rule. That's why, although the question 'Did you see that programme about ... ?' will increasingly be met with blank stares, a witty and original ad will still be watched and remembered by everyone.

5 Look back at the prompt card you chose in Exercise 3. Using your notes and any additional ideas from the article, prepare a two-minute talk with your partner. Then present your talk to the rest of the class.

6 In Paper 5, Part 2 you will be given one or more pictures and asked to complete a task with your partner. You will not have to describe the picture or pictures in detail.

1 Work in pairs. Look at the pictures below. Choose two of them. Discuss why the people might be shopping in those places and the ways in which shopping patterns are changing generally.

2 Compare your ideas with other pairs.

3 Complete the following task.

You have been asked to advise a marketing company which is promoting products aimed at people of your own age. Using all the pictures to help you, discuss ways in which patterns of shopping are changing and which trends in shopping are most relevant to people of your generation.

7 Discuss the following questions.
1 How important are possessions to you?
2 What are your favourite possessions, and why?
3 Do you think that people generally are too materialistic?
4 Can you think of any evidence to support the idea that we would all be better off without money and material possessions?

Exam Focus

▶ Paper 3, Part 5

In Paper 3, Part 5 you have to read two texts on related topics, answer **two comprehension questions** on each text and write a **summary** using information from both texts.

Comprehension

To answer the comprehension questions successfully, you need to be able to:

- identify the effect of the writer's choice of words
- recognise stylistic devices such as formal and informal language, image and metaphor
- understand patterns of reference in the text, e.g. pronoun use.

1

1 The following texts are about children and advertising. What type of information do you expect to find in the texts?

2 Read the opening and closing lines of both texts to get a general idea of the content and style. Do the texts give one point of view, or more than one?

3 Read quickly through the texts and match the following headings to the paragraphs.

Text 1
Writer's conclusion (para. ....)
The origins of advertising to children (para. ....)
Why children are vulnerable (para. ....)

Text 2
Why regulation is needed (para. ....)
The basic question (para. ....)
Evidence that there is a problem (para. ....)
The argument against regulation (para. ....)

Text 1

Marketing people say that the big sell to the tinies began for them with the invention of the child-carrying supermarket trolley. Their most powerful weapon in the fight to sell is sitting right under the nose of the parent, bored, seeking attention and absolutely bound to spot anything whose packaging features a logo or a cartoon character seen regularly on the television. But many of the items in these packages are foods and soft drinks with high fat and sugar contents which are not particularly good for children. 5

It takes until the age of about six for the young consumer to understand the difference between an advert and a programme on the television, and even longer to appreciate what the ad is trying to do. Even then, the child does not necessarily care. Keeping in with the peer group is much more important at that age, and marketing managers are well aware of this. If they can start a craze with, for example, collectable toys given away in packets of cereal or crisps, sales of that product will probably go through the roof. 10 15

Such marketing is aimed at a very impressionable age group, and although companies claim that it is the responsibility of parents to monitor what their children eat, drink or play with, it may be that the time has come for a little more social responsibility to be shown by those people who are exploiting children for their own financial gain. 20

---

2 Read the texts again and answer questions 1–4 with a word or short phrase. You do not need to write complete sentences.

1 Explain in your own words what 'their most powerful weapon in the fight to sell' refers to. (line 3)
(HINT: *This question tests your understanding of the word 'weapon', which is used metaphorically here. What subject would you normally expect for the verb 'is sitting' in this context?*)

2 Explain in your own words exactly what it is that the child cannot yet appreciate at the age of six.
(HINT: *At six, the child can understand the difference between an advert and a TV programme. What can't he understand? Remember you have to explain this in your own words.*)

Text 2

A growing number of senior figures in advertising are rebelling against the official industry line that 'if it's legal to sell, it should be legal to advertise'. They are prepared to say in public what they have hitherto only said in [5] private: that advertisers deliberately encourage children to pester their parents to buy products they don't need and can't afford. Peter Mead, chairman of one of the UK's biggest advertising agencies, is one of them. 'It's a [10] personal decision,' he said. 'I remember once watching a child nagging his father for a present he clearly couldn't afford and felt how painful that must be.'

Much of the debate about advertising to [15] children centres on whether or not they are able to work out that the advertiser is working to an agenda, and not merely spreading the good news about a toy or fizzy drink as a matter of public service. Many in the industry [20] are now prepared to argue that this is expecting too much, even of the media-wise 21st-century brat.

'I believe in commercial freedom. But it is obvious that children are not able to strike a [25] free and informed bargain with advertisers, which is why I personally believe they need extra protection,' says one account director.

But Lional Stanbrook, legal affairs adviser at the advertising association, doesn't agree. [30] 'Pester power is not a real issue. It has been manufactured by special interest groups. It is insulting to suggest that children can't deal with ads,' he says.

3   Who and what is referred to in the phrase 'how painful that must be'? (line 13)
(HINT: *This is a reference question. You need to work out what 'that' refers to, and who is implied to be feeling pain.*)

4   Explain in your own words what the writer means by 'children are not able to strike a free and informed bargain with advertisers'. (line 25)
(HINT: *Read further in the text for a simpler expression of the same idea, but remember you must explain the ideas in the quoted section in your own words.*)

Summary

To do the summary task successfully, you need to be able to:

- identify the focus of the task
- find the correct information in the texts
- identify when the information or opinions given in the two texts are the same or different
- re-express this information as a well-constructed paragraph of 50–70 words, using your own words as far as possible.

3   The first step when doing the summary is to make sure you have understood what information is required.

1   Read the following summary task and underline the key words.

In a paragraph of between 50 and 70 words, summarise in your own words as far as possible the arguments for regulating advertisements aimed at children.

2   Which of the following should you include? Tick **one** only.

- justification given for advertising for children
- specific names of people and their opinions
- types of advertisement shown to children
- places where advertisements are shown to children
- general dangers of advertising to children
- your own opinion

4   The next step is to find the information in the texts.

1   Read through the texts again and underline the answers to the following questions.

Text 1

Why might supermarket advertising have harmful effects on children's health?
What two things do children have difficulty in understanding?
How are the companies being irresponsible to children?

Text 2

Why do children pester their parents?
What is the basic question in the debate about advertising?

2   Look at the last two paragraphs in text 2. Is the information given here new, or supporting detail for points already made?

5 The next step is to make notes. This is a very important stage. It will help you to:

- decide whether points made in the two texts are the same or different
- express the ideas in your own words
- rewrite the ideas within the limit given.

You should always end up with 4–6 main points.

1 The notes below are the main points from text 1. The underlined words have been changed. Find the words in the original text and compare them.

Text 1

things advertised may be bad for children

_young children can't _see the difference_ between adverts and _ordinary television_ programmes_

older children _don't understand or care about the purpose of_ advertisements

advertisers are _taking advantage of_ children _to make money_

Text 2

....

....

....

---

2 Now read text 2. One point from text 1 is repeated in text 2. Tick this point in the notes above. One new point is made in text 2. Make brief notes on this point in the final box above. Try to use your own words.

6

1 Look at the notes and decide if you want to re-order them or not. Then write out the notes as a connected paragraph. Leave plenty of space for corrections and amendments.

2 Now compare your paragraph with the following one. Underline the extra point that has been added from text 2. Is the order of points the same as in the notes above and if not, why do you think it has been changed?

There are many reasons why advertisements aimed at children should be regulated. One argument against allowing advertising aimed specifically at children is that the things advertised may be bad for them. Young children can't see the difference between advertisements and ordinary television programmes. Older children may not understand or care about the purpose of advertisements. Advertising may lead children to try to persuade their parents to buy things which they can't afford. It seems wrong that advertisers are taking advantage of children's lack of understanding in order to make money.
(90 words)

7 The paragraph above has good content and organisation, but it is too long and the ideas are not very well linked.

1 Look at the improved version below. Find an example of:

- something which has been deleted because it does not give essential information
- an expression which has been changed in order to use fewer words
- a linking word which has been added.

~~There are many reasons why advertisements aimed at children should be regulated.~~ One argument against allowing advertising aimed ~~specifically~~ at children is that the things advertised may be bad for them. Young children can't distinguish ~~see the difference~~ between advertisements and ordinary television programmes while older ~~Older~~ children may not understand or care about the purpose of advertisements. Advertising may also lead children to try to make ~~persuade~~ their parents ~~to~~ buy things ~~which~~ they can't afford. Finally, It seems wrong that advertisers are taking advantage of children's lack of understanding in order to make money.

(76 words)

2   However, the paragraph is still six words too long. Read through the edited version and find examples of the three techniques used in Exercise 7.1. Then discuss ways in which it could be further shortened to 70 words or fewer.

3   Now look back at your own paragraph.
Check that the points are well ordered (they need not be the same as in the model above) and that your paragraph includes linking words to make the organisation clear. Count the number of words. If there are too many, reduce the length using the techniques discussed in Exercise 7.1.

8   Read through your own paragraph once more and check that the grammar, spelling and punctuation are correct, and that it is legible and easy to read.

Exam Strategy

It is important for your summary to be tidy and legible. You will lose marks if it is difficult to read. It is best to write on alternate lines in order to leave yourself space to make any necessary corrections tidily and clearly. If your summary looks untidy and you have time, you may wish to make a final copy.

Here is a procedure to follow for this task.

- Read the instructions. They will tell you the general topic linking the two texts.
- Read the opening and closing lines of each text to get a general idea of the content and style.
- Read through the first text at normal speed to understand the main ideas.
- Look at the two comprehension questions on the first text and reread all or part of the text again in order to find the answers. (If the question is on a specific section of the text, you will usually be told where to look.)
- Repeat these steps with the second text. **Note**: One question may ask you to compare ideas from both texts.
- Read the summary task and underline the key words.
- Go through each text again and underline the relevant information.
- Make brief notes of the main points. Use simple English, trying not to repeat the vocabulary used in the text. If the same point is made in both texts, only note it once. You should have 4–6 key points. If you have fewer than four, you have probably omitted some necessary information.
- Without looking back at the texts, write out your notes as a connected paragraph.
- Check the length of your paragraph. Count the number of words. If your paragraph is too short, check again that you have included all necessary information. If it is too long, shorten it by removing repetition or unnecessary words.
- Check that your grammar, spelling and punctuation are accurate.

Language Focus: Vocabulary
▶ **Paper 1, Parts 1 and 2**

1 The following techniques can be used for effect in written advertisements:

- exaggeration
- humour
- irony
- repetition
- unusual collocations
- unusual use of words.

Think of any examples of these techniques in advertisements you have seen.

2 Read the following text and decide which answer (**A**, **B**, **C** or **D**) best fits each gap. Then identify any examples of the techniques discussed in Exercise 1.1. How effective do you think this advertisement is?

When fitting your new Bose speakers you'll find your old system will (1) .... in very handy. The new Bose speaker system (2) .... old approaches to stereo sound to history. (3) .... the traditional pair of boxes that only produce stereo at one (4) .... point, our technology delivers open, spacious high-fidelity sound with incredible realism. Bose fills your room with sound, not speakers. Two tiny, easily positioned cubes, 40% smaller than their predecessors, yet with even better performance, (5) .... with the hideaway Acoustimass bass module to reproduce a natural balance of reflected and direct sound throughout the listening area. So now you and your friends can experience powerful, distortion-free bass with stunning (6) .... in the higher frequencies. Close your eyes and you could be in the front row at a performance. Audition the Acoustimass 5 speaker system at your Bose dealer. Then you'll know that there are better things to do with your speakers than listening to them.

1 **A** get   **B** go   **C** come
   D move
2 **A** consigns   **B** develops   **C** constrains
   D suggests
3 **A** As well as   **B** Instead of   **C** In addition to
   D Equivalent to
4 **A** fixed   **B** stationary   **C** rigid
   D secure
5 **A** associate   **B** merge   **C** combine
   D unify
6 **A** lucidity   **B** clarity   **C** sensitivity
   D simplicity

2

1 What packaging techniques do manufacturers use to make their products more interesting and attractive to consumers? Think of some examples of products with effective packaging.

2 Read the following text and decide which answer (**A**, **B**, **C** or **D**) best fits each gap.

The history of packaging

The appearance of a product has always affected what people think of it. The Romans recognised wine and water from the shape of their earthenware (1) .... In the sixteenth century, goods in paper wrappers with their producer's signature on the outside became a way of authenticating the quality of the product. Then a nineteenth-century tea merchant did a (2) .... trade when he began putting his tea into sealed bags rather than selling it (3) .... With technology and changing lifestyles, packaging has (4) .... First, it became more sophisticated – canning in mid nineteenth-century America, the mass production of cardboard later in the century, and the cheap manufacture of plastics in the last century – (5) .... ensuring more widespread use. Then changing social conditions guaranteed its place in our culture. The rise of the self-service supermarket, for example, meant that goods needed to (6) .... more for themselves, with no jolly Mr Cornershop to help the housewife make her choice.

1 **A** cisterns   **B** cases   **C** casks   **D** containers
2 **A** blazing   **B** roaring   **C** ripping   **D** glowing
3 **A** loose   **B** free   **C** alone   **D** untied
4 **A** intensified **B** duplicated **C** protracted **D** proliferated
5 **A** thereby   **B** therewith   **C** thereupon   **D** therein
6 **A** cope   **B** look   **C** speak   **D** show

3 Read the text again and find the reasons why packaging has become such an important part of marketing. Do you think that the writer is in favour of modern packaging or against it?

3   Discuss the following questions.

1 What influences you most when you are choosing a product, the advertising or the appearance of a product?
2 Can you think of any particular products that use more packaging than is necessary? Why do you think manufacturers use packaging to such an extent? What problems can this cause?
3 Can you think of any other ways in which modern technology is affecting methods of advertising and marketing goods?

Listening

▶ Paper 4, Part 1

In Paper 4, Part 1 you have to listen to four short extracts and answer multiple-choice questions. Each question will only have three answers to choose from, and you will hear both monologues and dialogues. You will hear each extract twice.

Before you listen to each extract, read through the questions. They will help you to focus on what to listen for in each extract. This may be:

- attitude and inference
- gist and detail.

Remember, for any Listening task, always read through the questions before you listen, so that you can try to anticipate what you are going to hear.

 1 Listen to the recordings, and for questions 1–8, choose the answer (**A**, **B** or **C**) which fits best according to what you hear. If you are unsure of the answer, mark the ones you think are wrong. Then listen again to complete and check your answers.

Extract One

You hear a marketing executive talking about her job.

1 The woman regards her job as
 A creative.
 B stimulating.
 C worthwhile.

2 What is the woman doing when she talks about ice-cream?
 A summarising procedures
 B comparing processes
 C describing opportunities

Extract Two

You hear a boy talking to his mother about a jacket he has bought.

3 The mother is upset because the jacket is
 A damaged.
 B poor value.
 C old-fashioned.

4 She is concerned because her son
 A does not save any of his money.
 B only thinks about his appearance.
 C is untidy and careless.

Extract Three

You hear two people talking about a picture in a fashion magazine.

5 The woman says that nowadays models are expected to
 A look cheerful.
 B be under twenty.
 C eat a balanced diet.

6 The two speakers agree that these days people are too concerned with
 A their own appearance.
 B imitating celebrities.
 C the latest fashions.

Extract Four

You hear part of a radio talk about market brands.

7 What is the speaker doing in this extract?
 A describing beliefs
 B criticising ideas
 C explaining causes

8 The speaker mentions Coca-Cola as an example of a brand which is
 A long-established.
 B highly influential.
 C widely known.

2

1 Read the statement below and fill in the gaps with words from the box.

price	product	promotion	place

The marketing mix

To meet customers' needs a business must develop the right (1) .... to satisfy them, charge the right (2) ...., get the goods to the right (3) .... and make the existence of the goods known through effective (4) ....

2 Work in groups. Think of a product you all buy regularly, such as an item of confectionery, a magazine, etc. Decide how effective the marketing mix for your selected product is by discussing these questions.

- Does the product meet the requirements of the customers for whom it is intended?
- Is the price right?
- Can consumers get it when and where they want it?
- Is it well advertised?

Language Focus: Grammar
Emphasis (preparatory *it*)

1

1 Read through the text below and underline all the examples of the pronoun *it*. Think about how each one is used.

Paul stood up and looked out over the beach towards the sea. It was noon, and the sun was directly overhead, blazing down on the blue sea and the rows of sunbathers. Far away on the horizon he could just see the big yacht. He followed it with his eyes until it disappeared over the horizon, then picked up his bag and started to walk slowly back towards the road. It was not going to be easy to accustom himself to living an ordinary life after the last two weeks. He found it incredible that only the previous day he had been sitting on that same yacht. Now it was easy to see that Juliana and Carlos had never really regarded him as a friend. They had been amused by him, but that was all.

2 Now match the examples you have underlined to the following uses of *it*.

1 *It* referring back to something that has already been mentioned.
2 *It* acting as a preparatory subject, referring forwards to a phrase later in the sentence.
3 *It* acting as a preparatory object, referring forwards to a phrase later in the sentence.
4 *It* acting as an 'empty' or 'dummy' subject, it does not refer to any word or phrase in the text.

2 It as preparatory subject

This structure is often used to postpone the subject of a sentence to a later position, especially if the subject is a long phrase. It may also be used to place important or new information at the end of the sentence.

Underline the words or phrases acting as subject in the following sentences. Then rewrite each sentence replacing the subject with *It* and make any other structural changes necessary. Decide which version sounds better, and why.

1 For the young consumer to understand the difference between an advert and a programme on the television takes until the age of about six.
2 Monitoring what their children eat, drink or play with is the responsibility of parents.
3 Advertising should be legal if selling is legal.
4 That children are not able to strike a free bargain with advertisers is obvious.
5 To suggest that children can't deal with ads is insulting.

3 It as preparatory object

As well as replacing a subject, *it* may replace the object, for similar reasons.

Underline the clause in each sentence which *it* refers to. Then rewrite each sentence without using *it*. You will need to change the structures used in two of the clauses.

1 I find it enjoyable working here.
2 Parents may consider it easier to give in to their children's demands.
3 We owe it to him that the campaign has been a success.

4 Introductory *it* can be replaced by other structures which may change the focus of the sentence without changing the meaning.
Look at the way the following sentences have been rewritten. Underline the words that have been changed or added.

1 It is the responsibility of parents to monitor what young children watch on TV.
Monitoring what young children watch on TV is the responsibility of parents.

Parents are responsible for monitoring what young children watch on TV.

2 It would be a good idea to introduce a code of advertising practice.
To introduce a code of advertising practice would be a good idea.

The introduction of a code of advertising practice would be a good idea.

3 I find it amazing that he won.
I find the fact that he won amazing.

I find his victory amazing.

▶ Grammar reference p. 214

Language Focus: Register

In the Proficiency exam you will be expected to deal with spoken and written texts in a variety of registers, and to use appropriate registers in the different Writing tasks.

1   Read the introduction to a magazine article about the fashion designer Stella McCartney, then answer the question below.

Stella McCartney is the daughter of Paul McCartney of the famous pop group, the Beatles. She studied fashion design and after her graduation in 1995 she was almost immediately made head of a Paris fashion house at the young age of 25. Some felt that this rapid success was due in part to the influence of her father. But in fashion, talent is more important than influence.

Do you think the article will be mainly about
a) Stella's relationship with her father?
b) her career as a fashion designer?
c) something else?

2   Read the two texts A and B below, and discuss the following questions.

1   What information do the texts give you about Stella McCartney?
2   Which text is more like spoken English? Which is more like written English? What features helped you decide?
3   Why do you think the writer uses direct quotations in text A and not in text B?

A

Despite the fame, it's the most normal family I know and it's close – we all love each other so much, and get on so well. My parents have always told me I was great.

At the weekend I was down in the country at their place baking cookies and I was a bit stressed out about work and dad came up to me and said 'Stella, just stop for a minute and look at me and remember you are a lovely girl.' My dad's so funny – he'll say, 'So, Stella, I think it's kilts with tassels this season, what do you reckon?' Oh dear, I wish I hadn't told you about that – I want to hold back my private life.

What's funny is that in his interviews people have started asking him about me. The first time I realised that my dad was incredibly famous was when he performed a concert in Rio in front of 20,000 people. Suddenly it dawned on me. Actually, my dad is the coolest dude alive.

B

Her 1995 graduation show featured top models Kate Moss and Naomi Campbell, while other students were relying on friends to model. Although this made her unpopular, she is unrepentant. Somewhere in this irresistibly photogenic young woman is the talent of a modest, diligent worker who asks that we swallow our vague sense of injustice and look at how eagerly she has beavered, how hard she has tried.

She was the only student at college to use a thimble because, dissatisfied with the tuition in tailoring, she enrolled for evening lessons with an old Savile Row* friend of her father's. The dedicated work ethic is partly explained by a fear of being dismissed as a rich girl dilettante. Partly, too, it is the influence of parents who made it clear from the start that their children would be expected to make their own way. And finally it is the knowledge, boldly stated, that genius alone would never be enough.

Savile Row: London Street famous for its expensive tailors' shops

3 Most written English texts, especially newspaper and magazine articles, are neither very formal nor very informal in style, but somewhere in between. The degree of formality depends on the target reader, the reason for writing, and the type of publication.

Look at the table of features that distinguish formal and informal written English.

1 Complete the table by adding the following information in the appropriate place.

- use of inversion for emphasis, e.g. *Should you need further information . . .*
- personal tone with use of first person
- may not be clearly or logically organised
- impersonal tone, avoidance of first person
- use of active verbs
- full forms used, e.g. *It is, does not*
- repetition of individual words, e.g. *it was really really hot*

2 Underline examples in texts A and B.

4

1 Read text A again. Think of an alternative for each colloquial word or expression you underlined. For example:
stressed out – worried

2 Rewrite the text in a more formal written style. Use the following framework to guide you.

> **D**espite being so . . . , my family is as normal as any other. We are . . . and . . . . My parents have always made me feel . . . .
>
> One weekend, . . . them in the country. I was feeling . . . . Then, while I . . . , my father tried to . . . , telling me . . . .
>
> It is interesting that my father is now being asked . . . . It was not until I . . . that I realised . . . .

Feature	Informal	Formal
1 Choice of vocabulary	colloquial and slang expressions phrasal verbs	formal expressions; one-word verbs of Latin origin; abstract nouns
2 Tone	(1)	(2) ....
3 Personal/impersonal structures	(3)	use of passive and impersonal constructions, e.g. *It is said that...*
4 Contractions/full forms	contractions used *It's, doesn't*	(4) ....
5 Sentence patterns	short sentences or long sentences with several main clauses joined by *and* or *but*	complex sentences with subordinating conjunctions, e.g. *although*; use of participle clauses
6 Emphatic structures	Use of cleft, e.g. *What's odd is that he actually came.*	(5) ....
7 Punctuation	use of dashes and exclamation marks for emphasis; use of commas to link clauses where conjunctions are normally needed	correct use of commas, use of semi-colons; use of parentheses or dashes for explanatory insertions
8 Coherence and cohesion	(6)	clear organisation sign-posted by linking words; repetition of or rephrasing of vocabulary items throughout a text (lexical cohesion)
9 Stylistic devices	(7)	deliberate repetition of a structure; rhetorical questions

Writing

▶ Paper 2, Part 2 (formal letter)

In Paper 2, Part 2 you may have to write a **formal letter**. For this type of task it is very important to:

- think about the purpose of writing and the target reader
- use a style, tone and register suitable for the task
- use a consistent register – you will lose marks if you mix registers in your answer.

1 You are going to write a letter of complaint about an advertisement you have seen. First, read the information below about the UK Advertising Standards Authority and discuss these questions.

1 What is the function of this organisation?
2 Is there a similar organisation in your country?

ASA

The Advertising Standards Authority was set up in 1962 and acts independently of both the advertising business and the government to make sure that the millions of advertisements that appear in the UK each year are:

 legal   decent   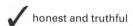 honest and truthful

The Authority safeguards the public by applying the rules contained in the British Codes of Advertising and Sales Promotion to all advertisers. The Codes stipulate what is and is not acceptable in newspapers, magazines, poster and direct marketing sales promotion, cinema, video and electronic media. Advertisers who break the Codes' rules risk receiving damaging adverse publicity and they will be refused space to advertise.
In addition to the Codes' general rules, advertisements are subject to the following requirements:
- They should contain nothing that is likely to cause offence on the grounds of race, religion, sex or disability.
- They should contain nothing that condones or is likely to provoke violence or anti-social behaviour.
The ASA handles around 10,000 complaints each year.

WR|TE
One letter is all it takes

2 Read the following case study and discuss these questions.

1 On what grounds do you think the complaint was based?
2 Do you think complaints 1 and 2 were upheld or not upheld? (You can check your answers on page 238.)

Complaint: Objections were raised to a trade press advertisement. The advertisement showed a picture of a nuclear power plant alongside pictures of sheep grazing on green fields and a man fishing in a pond. The complainants challenged:

1. the implication, in the claim that "BNFL* can transform old nuclear installations into land that can be used again" and the picture, that land used for nuclear installations could be re-used for any purpose; and

2. the claim "... we've perfected ways to deal with all types of nuclear waste."

Adjudication:

BNFL: British Nuclear Fuels plc

British Nuclear Fuels

⊞ BNFL

3 Work in pairs. **Student A**, look at the advert on page 234. **Student B**, look at the advert on page 236. Take turns to describe your advert to your partner. The adverts are intended to be shocking. How do you react to them?

4 Think of some advertisements that you have seen recently in your national press, in magazines, on posters or in the cinema. Describe them to a partner. Your partner should decide if any of them could be accused of breaking the ASA requirements described on page 63.

5 Any formal letter should normally follow a similar pattern. Put the sections below into the order you think they should appear in a letter. (Each section should have a separate paragraph.)

- [ ] any requests for action or information
- [ ] clarification of situation
- [ ] further details, if necessary
- [ ] reason for writing

Note: In the exam you don't need to include addresses, unless the task specifically asks you to.

6 Read the following writing task. How many parts does it have? Look back at Exercise 5. Which section of the letter will each of these parts come in?

TASK

A company has put up a large advertising hoarding in your local town centre. The advertisement seems to you likely to provoke unacceptable behaviour. Write a letter of complaint to your local council, explaining why you object to it and what you would like them to do about it.

(300–350 words)

7 Read the following letter, which was written in answer to the task, and answer these questions.

1 What kind of advert is the writer complaining about?
2 What is the reason for his complaint?
3 What does he want done?
4 How does he conclude the letter?
5 Are the tone and register appropriate to the task? Are they consistently maintained?

Dear Sir,

I am writing to complain about the car advertisement currently being displayed on the hoarding outside the main post office in the centre of town.

The advertisement shows a car speeding away from a set of traffic lights, with the caption, '0-100 in under 10 seconds'. I feel that this claim is misleading and irresponsible. For a start, there is so much traffic on the roads these days that it is extremely unlikely that anyone could reach a speed of 100 kilometres per hour in a town. The advertisers also seem to have forgotten that there are speed limits on most roads. In my view, this type of advertising only encourages drivers to break the law.

Furthermore, the advert suggests that the best cars are the fastest cars and places undue emphasis on the power of this car in particular, implying that its best feature is its speed. I would argue that this can only encourage those people who buy the car to drive fast in order to maintain that image. However, we all know that speed kills, and more often than not it is the innocent pedestrian who is the victim of the speeding driver. Don't you think car companies should behave responsibly and try to reduce fatalities on our roads by giving safety a better image?

May I request that you have this advertisement taken down as soon as possible? While I have no objection to cars being advertised, I feel strongly that this type of advertising should not be allowed. I have already written to the company concerned, requesting that they remove this advertisement from their campaign and giving them my reasons in detail. I enclose a copy of this letter for your information.

I look forward to hearing from you.

Yours faithfully,

Sam Broadbent

Sam Broadbent
Encs.*

Encs: short for 'enclosures'
(301 words)

8

1   A letter of complaint is usually written in a formal style, and it clearly states the writer's point of view. Underline the formal phrases or set expressions used by the writer of the letter to indicate his own views.

2   Now underline the expressions that mean the following.

1   on show at the moment (para. 1)
2   giving the wrong impression (para. 2)
3   makes something seem too important (para. 3)
4   cut down the number of deaths (para. 3)
5   I don't mind about ... (para. 4)

9   Read the following writing task. What do you need to include?

TASK

You have seen a commercial on your local television station which appeared during a children's programme. You feel that an advertisement of this type is not suitable for showing on children's TV. Write a letter of complaint to the television company, explaining why you object to it and what you would like them to do about it.

(300–350 words)

10   Plan your letter before you write. How many paragraphs will it have? What will each contain?

11   Write the letter. Make sure you state your point of view clearly and use a consistent tone and register. After you have written your letter, exchange it with a partner. Evaluate each other's work and suggest improvements.

1 Choose a suitable word or phrase from the box to fill each of the gaps in the following letter.

accordingly	as a result	because of this
better still	first of all	for example
furthermore	in addition	last but not least
what's more		

Dear Mr Perkins,

I wish to bring to your attention some problems which I encountered at your hotel when you were absent.

(1) ......, when I booked I clearly stated that we required one double and two single rooms on the same floor. When we arrived, we were informed that this was impossible and (2) ..... that it should not have been promised, as all single rooms are on the top floor.
(3) ......, I had explained when booking that we are vegetarians and I was reassured that there is always a vegetarian option on the menu.
(4) ......, I did not request special dietary arrangements. To our horror, we discovered that the vegetarian option is always the same and (5) ...... we had baked aubergine three times in two days.
(6) ......, the dining-room staff were extremely slow and forgetful. (7) ......, it took three requests to get a simple jug of iced water! (8) ......, I must inform you that the manner of your deputy was far from polite when these matters were raised with her.

Our stay was by no means the pleasant experience we had anticipated and (9) ...... I feel that at least an apology, or (10) ..... a refund, is due to us.

Yours sincerely,

Jack Lawrence

Jack Lawrence

2 Complete the second sentence with three to eight words so that it has a similar meaning to the first sentence, using the word given. Do not change the word given.

1 Will it matter for this job that she can't drive?

                                                     inability

   How much of a handicap .... this job?

2 In the circumstances, learning French quickly was essential. **given**

   It .... the circumstances.

3 Being market leader is the long-term aim of the company. **ultimate**

   It is the .... market leader.

4 Of course, the price has to be right. **saying**

   It .... has to be right.

5 Marketing executives usually earn a lot of money. **highly**

   Marketing .... general.

6 It is easy to aim advertising at children. **targets**

   Children .... for advertisers.

7 It really wasn't necessary for you to apologise at all. **totally**

   Your .... really.

8 Our late arrival didn't matter as the concert didn't start on time. **unimportant**

   The fact .... as the concert didn't start on time.

3 Read the text below and decide which answer (**A**, **B**, **C** or **D**) best fits each gap.

Shopping heaven?

Had a bad week? What you need is a little retail therapy. Meet up with your friends for a quick trip to the shops, make a few (1) .... buys, collect a few shiny carrier bags with trendy logos and you'll be feeling better in no time. Has the boss been getting at you? A pair of designer shoes will soon put things into (2) .... Have you had a row with your family? A few new CDs and you can put them out of your mind. And you don't even need to worry about money – the shops are (3) .... over themselves to give you credit. Shopping is our fastest-growing leisure activity – the feel-good (4) .... we've all been looking for. The problem is, of course, that for too many people shopping is a quick (5) .... but not a solution – and with mounting credit card bills they're in danger of ending up trapped in a vicious downward (6) .... of debt from which there finally seems to be no escape.

	A	B	C	D
1	instant	instinct	impact	impulse
2	shape	order	dimension	perspective
3	going	looking	falling	working
4	factor	feature	element	item
5	repair	cure	fix	remedy
6	pattern	circle	ladder	spiral

5 A life of crime

Speaking

1 Look at the pictures. They all show different aspects of crime and criminal behaviour. Discuss what aspects of crime they show, and decide which you find the most disturbing.

2 Interview a partner using the questions below. Compare your experiences.

Have you or has someone you know ever ...
1 been the victim of a crime?
2 witnessed a crime?
3 reported a crime to the police?
4 been called to give evidence in a court of law?
5 been called to do jury service?

3 Discuss the following questions.

1 What types of crime are most/least common in your country?
2 Are crime rates rising or falling in your country? Why do you think this is?
3 Why do you think people turn to crime?
4 Do you think that criminals are born or made?

Exam Focus

▶ **Paper 1, Part 3**

In Paper 1, Part 3 you have to read a text from which some paragraphs have been removed, and replace the missing paragraphs in the correct places. In order to do this, you need to be aware of the way in which the ideas or events in the text are organised, as well as of words and expressions which link one part of the text to another.

Here is a procedure to follow for this task.

- Read through the gapped text quickly to get a general idea of its subject-matter and style. Do not read the jumbled paragraphs at this stage.
- Read through the text again carefully. When you get to a gap, look through the eight jumbled paragraphs and make a note of any that seem possible. Don't worry if you have several possibilities at this stage. Remember to look both backwards and forwards.
- Read through again and choose the best paragraph for each gap.
- Check that you have not used the same paragraph in two different places.
- Finally, read through to check that the text as a whole makes sense.

1 You are going to read an extract from a novel. Seven paragraphs have been removed from the extract. Choose from the paragraphs **A–H** the one which fits each gap. There is one extra paragraph which you do not need to use.

I put on my costume – dark jeans, black T-shirt, a pair of Adidas trainers. From a drawer in my mother's dressing table I took a pair of thin black leather gloves. They were a tight fit and smelled faintly of perfume. I had the two canvas bags, one folded inside the other, along with a torch and some old newspapers.

1 ....

And when at last I did reach the window I'd targeted, I found that the stone sill was much higher than it appeared from the road. It was level with my heart, so I had to balance the canvas bag on it and hoist myself up after, taking care not to knock the bag off. I found the latch, raised the sash, slid over, pulling the bag after me. Suddenly I was inside.

2 ....

The house felt alive, not unwelcoming. After a few minutes or so my eyes got accustomed to the darkness. I sensed the proportions of the room I was in. It seemed big, an open area, with width on either side of me and dark patches, doorways I imagined, leading to other rooms beyond.

3 ....

Through an archway there was another room, disappearing around a corner. The torch created one half of a dining table and the ribbed backs of two or three chairs. A floor lamp sprang up, with a tasselled shade. I turned off the torch and waited again. Everything had a glow, as if the objects themselves were a source of light, not just reflecting the little that came from outside through the opened curtains. There was no moon. I took down the carriage clock, the ornaments, and wrapped them in sheets of newspaper so they wouldn't break when I put them in the bag. I hadn't thought at all about what I was going to steal. A house such as this contained a near infinity of objects. Which were valuable and which were not?

4 ....

I moved, making my feet quiet, stealing with an almost tender care, and went through a door into much thicker darkness where I had to turn on the torch again. This was the hallway, high, with a wooden parquet floor and wood panels all around. A wide staircase was on my left. I left behind the one bag I'd already filled and took the stairs two at a time, swinging myself around on the banister at the landing. I was upstairs. A door was open on the right. With the torch I went quickly in. This was a bedroom, the master bedroom, where Mr and Mrs Robinson slept. There was a double bed with a plain walnut headboard. There was a tall chest of drawers and a dressing table above which a mirror bounced back light. Most of all there was a confusion of smells: of make-up and perfume, of musty clothes, of sleep.

5 ....

Across the landing was a room like my own – a boy's room. Clothes were heaped on a chair. Socks were strewn on the floor, and the faces of the members of the Leeds United team of the 1970s looked down from the wall.

6 ....

The next room was that of Denise herself and I thought I might like to stay there forever. The fragrances here were lighter, more delicate, and the room seemed airier. A window was open a few inches at the bottom, letting in a breeze and odours from the night. The bed was made. A teddy bear and hand-stitched cushions were on one side of it, pushed up against a wall. There was a bookshelf with lots of the same books my sister had – *Jane Eyre*, *Gone with the Wind*. There was another jewellery case and, on a table, a vase, made from glass that was opaque and grainy when I touched it. I pressed my lips against Denise's pillow.

7 ....

I had to be professional. I'd started off well enough downstairs but up here, in the bedrooms, I'd been thrown.

A

I turned on the torch. Its beam discovered a fireplace and a mantelpiece with a glinting carriage clock and ornaments on top. A mirror flashed light back at me and as I moved the torch those objects vanished while new ones came up out of the darkness. A little round table with dimpled edges. An armchair.

B

I turned into another room, also on the left. This one was neat and tidy, almost unlived in. The curtains were open and I was careful about not letting the beam of the torch strike the darkened windowpanes. Here I am, I thought. I'm a burglar, being a burglar.

C

The curtains were drawn, the carpet thick and soft – the whole impression was cosy, old fashioned, as of a nest lived in by people much older than myself. I swept up the silver dressing table set. There was a case of jewels on top of the chest of drawers with rings, earrings, chains and brooches all caught together, a knot of treasure. That went straight into the bag.

D

I hadn't counted on the flower beds – wide flower beds, thick with rose bushes. Lovely to sniff, not so easy to wade among with the canvas bags held high above my head.

E

There was an impression of silence, of space, of a thick pressing darkness that – even though pierced by me a moment before – was already settling back all around. Somewhere there was a tick of a clock, counting time at a much slower beat than once a second, or so it seemed. I felt the empty house with my nerve ends: old stone surrounding an atmosphere that asked, politely, that I disrupt it as little as possible, even if I was a thief.

F

I didn't know how long I'd been in there. I'd lost all track of time. I had to fight against this feeling, the wonderful strangeness of being in a place so familiar in some ways, so like home, yet so utterly strange, as if I'd walked straight into a fairy-tale.

G

Moving through to the dining room it was the shiny silver things – candlesticks, a cigarette box, a fruit dish – that caught my attention. I was a hero, stumbling on a dragon's hoard. I was a trout, tempted by the hook.

H

There was a collection of tarnished Victorian pennies. He kept his in a saucer; at home mine were piled in a tubular red container that had once held cough sweets for my grandfather.

2 Read the completed text and underline the parts which helped you to replace the missing paragraphs.

Which of the following strategies did you use?

- You looked for specific words, or synonyms, in the paragraphs next to one another.
- You made a visual image of the house and its rooms.
- You noticed details such as whether the torch was on or off.
- You thought about the main focus of the description of each room.
- something else (what?)

3 Discuss the following questions using evidence from the whole text.

- What is unusual about this burglary?
- What kind of person is the narrator?
- Why do you think he is breaking into the house?

4 What may the consequences of this type of crime be for

- the victim?
- the thief?
- the community?

Language Focus: Grammar
Modals and related expressions (1)

1 Read the following text, which is an extract from a website advising the public how to avoid burglaries. What advice did Mr and Mrs Robinson **not** follow? (See text on pages 68–69.)

Netsite:

Beat the burglar

Most burglaries are committed by opportunist thieves. In two out of ten burglaries <u>they don't (1) even have to use force</u> – they get in through an open door or window. Reduce the risk of burglary happening to you by making sure you've taken these simple precautions.

▸ Look at your home through the burglar's eyes – are there places where they could break in unseen?

▸ Have you fitted strong locks on your doors and windows? Would thieves have to make a lot of noise by breaking glass in order to get in?

▸ Even small windows such as skylights or bathroom fanlights need locks – a thief can get through any gap larger than a human head.

▸ Check for weak spots – a low or sagging fence, or a back gate with a weak lock.

▸ Patio doors should have special locks fitted top and bottom unless they already have a multi-locking system.

▸ Buy a chain and fit it to your front door. When strangers ask if they can enter the house for any reason, e.g. to read meters, always check their identity before you let them in.

! Remember that consideration must be given to the safety of the house's occupants as well as to protecting the house from thieves. For example, in case of fire, bars mustn't be fitted to upper floor windows unless there is another way of escape.

2

1 Underline and number eight phrases containing modal verbs and semi-modal verbs in the text in Exercise 1. The first one has been done for you.

2 Now match each phrase to one of the following functions.

obligation	necessity
prohibition	lack of necessity (1)
advice	permission
opportunity/free choice	ability

3 Read the following sentences and match them to the phrases you have underlined in the text. Decide whether the meaning is the same or different. The first one has been done for you.

1 Thieves are prohibited from using force.
   Different: 'don't have to' means 'it's not necessary'.

2 When strangers ask for your permission to enter the house, check their identity.

3 Remember that it is advisable to consider the safety of the occupants.

4 You are not obliged to fit bars to upper floor windows.

5 Patio doors are able to have special locks fitted.

6 Are there places where they have the opportunity to break in unseen?

7 Would thieves need to make a lot of noise to get in?

8 A thief has the opportunity to get through any gap.

4 The text above refers to the present time. Look at the phrases you have underlined and, wherever possible, change them so that they refer to the past. Which one cannot be changed to the past? Why not?

3 Find and correct the mistakes in the following sentences.

1 You needn't to come with me if you don't feel like it.
2 We needn't have gone to work last Monday, so we went to the beach.
3 You mustn't help me, but you can if you want to.
4 The child was struggling in the deep water but fortunately his mother could rescue him just in time.
5 You didn't need to do that – I could manage on my own.
6 You hadn't to give him that tip – the service was awful!

▶ Grammar reference pp. 215–216

4 Instead of using modal verbs, we can express obligation, advice, etc. in other ways. Read the following examples and match them to the functions in Exercise 2.2. Underline the phrases that helped you. Try re-expressing them using an appropriate modal verb.

1 All students are required to attend the fire drill at 5.00 p.m.
2 I don't recommend going on your own, especially at night.
3 It's entirely up to you whether you stay or go.
4 She's quite capable of managing on her own.
5 Students are not to use dictionaries in the exam.
6 Please feel free to browse – you are under no obligation to buy.
7 You'd be better off getting a taxi – the buses are always full.
8 You've got to have a good head for heights to do that job.
9 Hadn't you better go home? Your family will be looking for you.
10 I didn't quite manage to finish the job on time.

5 Use of English: Paper 3, Part 4

Complete the second sentence with three to eight words so that it has a similar meaning to the first sentence, using the word given. Do not change the word given.

1 You'd be better off doing what he suggests without arguing.   **advice**
I recommend .... argument.
2 Was formal clothing actually necessary for all the guests?   **wear**
Did .... formal clothing?
3 In that country there was no compulsory military service.   **do**
You .... in that country.
4 She is not to play in any further matches this season.   **banned**
She ....
.... any further matches this season.
5 He's already proved he can manage on his own.   **capable**
He's already proved himself ....
.... help.
6 It's not necessary for you to decide immediately. **up**
You don't .... now.
7 I think exams should be voluntary for students. **have**
I don't think .... exams.
8 He couldn't have escaped from them if he hadn't run so fast.   **only**
He .... he ran so fast.

Use of English
▶ **Paper 3, Part 1**

1 Read the title, then the rest of the text quickly without filling in any of the gaps to get a general idea of what it is about.

Rules, laws and norms

Any discussion of criminal behaviour requires understanding of the difference (0) ....*in*.... meaning between *rules*, *laws* and *norms*. Rules (1) .... be unwritten, or formal and written. The rules of dress or of how we eat are unwritten guides. (2) .... contrast, the rules of a factory, for example safety regulations, are usually (3) .... down and serve (4) .... strict regulators of behaviour.

Laws are perhaps the (5) .... example of written, formal rules and are decided upon by powerful and influential groups in society. In order to ensure that everyone adheres (6) .... the laws, there are specific penalties, including fines or imprisonment, for those (7) .... guilty of (8) .... them. Unlike other rules, (9) .... as rules of dress or of grammar, laws can always be enforced by agencies (10) .... the police and the courts.

A norm is a very much (11) .... general term; it is an expected code of behaviour shared by (12) .... of a social group. Norms can be thought of as unwritten rules, for (13) ...., that one should respond appropriately to a 'good morning' greeting. They are part of the culture of a society and are (14) .... on from one generation to the (15) .... over time.

2 Now fill in each gap, following the procedure recommended on page 45.

3 Discuss.

Laws are not universal. They change over time, and from one place to another. Can you think of:

• a law that used to be enforced in your country, but which no longer exists?
• a law which is enforced, but which you think should not be?
• a law which does not exist, but which should exist?

Listening

▶ Paper 4, Part 4

In Paper 4, Part 4 you have to listen to a conversation and decide whether a list of statements reflects the views of one or both of the speakers.

To do this type of question you need to listen for:

- the stated facts
- the attitudes and opinions of the speakers
- whether they agree with one another or not.

You may also need to understand colloquial or idiomatic language.

1 Read the following information about Angus and Rick, who are both convicted offenders.

Angus comes from Glasgow but ran away to London when he was 15. He is now 17. He has convictions for breaking and entering, and petty theft.

Rick is 17 and has always lived in London. He has been in trouble with the police on and off since he was 11. He was recently convicted of petty theft and minor assault.

2 Discuss which of the following types of treatment you think would be appropriate for Angus and Rick.

> prison   probation   psychiatric treatment
> young people's detention centre   counselling
> something else (what?)

3 You will hear Angus and Rick discussing their experiences of Community Service. Before you listen, read through the list of statements below. What can you predict about the content of the Listening? What do you think Community Service involves?

1	The influence of friends led him astray.	1
2	Community Service is preferable to prison.	2
3	Community Service was sometimes physically demanding.	3
4	Community Service led to further conflicts with those in authority.	4
5	Community Service work can be rewarding.	5
6	The experience has changed him.	6

4 Now listen to the recording. Indicate which of the opinions are given by each speaker. In each box, write either:

    A (Angus)
or **R** (Rick)
or **B** (both Angus and Rick)

5 Listen again to check and complete your answers.

6 What is your opinion of Community Service as a method of dealing with criminals?

7 Say it again

Re-express the following sentences from the Listening text, using the word given.

1 I thought I could make a new start.   **over**
2 Lots of people say it's a soft option.   **choice**
3 I really hit it off with him.   **got**
4 I can't wait to get away from London.   **looking**

Speaking

1 You are going to hear an English teenager, Neil, discussing the question below. Before you listen, read the question and think about what you would say.

On the basis of what you have read and heard so far in this unit, which of the views of punishment below would you agree with? Give reasons.

1 An eye for an eye, a tooth for a tooth.
2 We need punishment as a deterrent to stop people offending.
3 The legal justice system should aim to rehabilitate offenders, not take revenge on them.

---

 2 Listen to the recording. Which view of punishment does Neil argue for? Is your opinion the same as his?

 3 Now listen again and tick the expressions Neil uses from the list below.

a) I think (that) ...
b) It seems to me that ...
c) The main argument for ...
d) However, the argument against this ...
e) As well as that ...
f) So let's look at the alternatives ...
g) Another related point is that ...
h) Finally, the idea that ... seems to ...
i) Some people think that ...
j) All in all, I suppose ...

4 Notice how Neil deals with each point.

1 He gives his opinion.
2 He gives arguments for and against.
3 He discusses the alternatives and gives reasons for rejecting them.
4 He summarises – by restating his original opinion.

Which of the expressions above could be used at each of these stages?

2 Work in groups or pairs. Each of you should choose one of the following crimes. Using the model you have heard to help you, give your views on which punishment you think is most appropriate, together with your reasons for rejecting the alternatives. The other student(s) should listen carefully and then say if they agree or not.

Crimes

1 A teenager hacks into an airline company's computer system and deliberately introduces a virus.
2 A man is attacked by muggers on the subway, defends himself with a gun and shoots his assailants dead.
3 A small business is caught selling pirated CDs.

Punishments

* long prison sentence/short prison sentence
* community service
* fine
* caution (a formal warning)

3 Work with a new partner. Use the prompt card below and prepare a two-minute talk. Then practise the talk with your partner.

How far do you agree that rehabilitation is more effective than punishment?

* feelings of victims
* effect on criminals
* effects on society

4 Write a paragraph summarising your views on rehabilitation and punishment, using some of the expressions from Exercise 1.

Language Focus: Grammar

Modals and related expressions (2)

1 Agatha Christie (1890–1976) is one of the best-known crime writers of the 20th century. Have you read any of her books or seen a film based on any of them? What was it about?

2 Look at the poster below. What happened to Agatha Christie in December 1926?

BERKSHIRE CONSTABULARY,
WOKINGHAM DIVISION.
9th. December 1926

MISSING

From her home "Styles" Sunningdale in this Division.
Mrs. Agatha Mary Clarissa CHRISTIE
(WIFE OF COLONEL A. CHRISTIE)

AGE 35 YEARS, HEIGHT 5 ft. 7 ins., HAIR RED (Shingled), NATURAL TEETH, EYES GREY, COMPLEXION FAIR, WELL BUILT.

DRESSED—Grey Stockingette Skirt, Green Jumper, Grey and dark Grey Cardigan, small Green Velour Hat, may have hand bag containing £5 to £10. Left home in 4 seater Morris Cowley car at 9.45 p.m. on 3rd. December leaving note saying she was going for a drive. The next morning the car was found abandoned at Newlands Corner, Albury, Surrey.

Should this lady be seen or any information regarding her be obtained please communicate to any Police Station, or to
CHARLES GODDARD, Superintendent,
WOKINGHAM.
Telephone No. 11 Wokingham.
PRINTED AT THE "BERKSHIRE GAZETTE" OFFICES, PEACH STREET, WOKINGHAM.

3

1 Look at the information about Agatha Christie and then read to the conversation between two policemen concerning her disappearance. What three possible explanations do they come up with?

Agatha Christie had left the house the night before. Her husband was away for the weekend. She had seemed depressed and had gone upstairs and kissed her baby daughter goodnight. The following day her empty car was found in a ditch not far from her house. But there was no sign of Mrs Christie. The police started a search, but over a week later they had got no further.

A: She must have been driving too fast, and lost control.

B: Yes. She might have hit her head as her car went into the ditch and lost her memory … she could still be wandering around somewhere.

A: But she couldn't possibly have been wandering around for over a week without being found.

B: You know, I think it might not have been an accident at all. Things weren't right between her and the Colonel. He may know more than he's saying … there could be another woman involved.

A: Yes, the Colonel might conceivably have had more to do with it than he's admitting. He could well be implicated in her disappearance.

B: Or, of course, Mrs Christie may have engineered the whole thing. She does specialise in mysteries, after all.

A: In that case we could end up being accused of wasting the tax-payers' money if we carry on looking much longer. This search must have cost a fortune already.

2 Read the dialogue again and underline all the phrases including modal verbs. Number them 1–12. Match each phrase to the appropriate explanations below.

The speaker
a) is sure this happened.
b) thinks it is possible this happened.
c) thinks it is possible this didn't happen.
d) is sure this didn't happen.
e) thinks it is possible this is the case or will happen.

► Grammar reference p. 216

3 What do **you** think was the most likely explanation for the mystery? Check your ideas by referring to page 236.

4 Other ways of expressing degrees of likelihood

1 Underline the expressions used to express degrees of likelihood in the sentences below. Notice that similar expressions may use two different structures.

1 It's highly unlikely that he'll go.
2 She is highly unlikely to have finished.
3 There is a strong/faint possibility that he'll be caught.
4 There's every chance/likelihood of him being chosen.
5 It is bound/certain/sure to happen.
6 The chances are that he'll come.
7 I bet he'll be late.
8 I doubt if she'll agree./It's doubtful that she'll agree.
9 There's not much chance that the sun will shine/of the sun shining.
10 I can't see him agreeing to that.
11 The odds are against him succeeding.
12 The chances/prospects of success are good.

2 Re-express the following sentences using the word given and appropriate expressions from Exercise 4.1.

1 Our team should win the Cup easily. (*chances*)
   The chances are that our team will win the Cup.
2 He could very well have been the murderer. (*possibility*)
3 I'm afraid we may not arrive in time for the start of the film. (*doubt*)
4 It must have been Peter you saw last night. (*bound*)
5 I don't think they will have solved the mystery. (*chance*)
6 I don't think anyone can have survived the crash. (*highly*)
7 I suppose they might decide to double our salaries, though it's unlikely. (*faint*)
8 I don't think Anna would get married secretly. (*agreeing*)

Use of English
▶ Paper 3, Parts 2 and 1

1 Read the text below quickly to get the main idea. Do not try to fill in the gaps yet. What is the writer's main point?

2 Now read the text again. Use the word given in capitals at the end of some of the lines to form a word that fits in the space in the same line.

3 Finally, read through the text again to check that the words you have added make sense.

DO STATISTICS TELL THE WHOLE STORY?

Once confidently regarded as reflecting the level of crime in society, (0) ...*criminal*... statistics are now interpreted with caution. Such statistics are based only on notifiable (1) .... which have been reported and recorded. But not all of these are reported by the public, so there are (2) .... in what is actually recorded. It has been suggested that routinely compiled statistics seriously under-record some types of crime such as (3) ...., petty theft and domestic violence.

The (4) .... of a court case, and whether a conviction is actually recorded or not, also depends on a complex mix of ingredients. And changes in police (5) .... or even simple human (6) .... can sometimes mean no record is made of a crime.

Some would argue, therefore, that the criminal statistics we have are less a picture of the (7) .... of crime than an (8) .... of what the authorities actually find it (9) .... to police, and also a reflection of the kinds of offences that tend to end up in court and result in convictions. Nevertheless, after a period of criticism and (10) .... , the use of criminal statistics has been regaining broad acceptance.

CRIME

OFFEND

ACCURATE

VANDAL

COME

PROCEED
ERR

INCIDENT
INDICATE
MANAGE

CERTAIN

2 Can you think of any more examples of crimes that may go unrecorded? Why is this and what is the effect?

3 Methods of crime detection have improved enormously since Agatha Christie wrote her detective novels. Nowadays the police can use a number of techniques to help them, including:

- forensic evidence (blood, hair, fingerprints)
- DNA fingerprinting
- psychological profiling
- geographic profiling.

What do you know about these techniques?

4 Now read through the cloze text opposite without trying to fill in any of the gaps yet. How was the robber 'caught' by his jeans?

5 Fill each gap in the text with one suitable word.

6 Read through the text again and check and justify your answers with a partner.

7 Do you foresee any danger in the development of sophisticated techniques such as the ones mentioned in this section? Which of the statements below would you agree with?

'With improved techniques at their disposal for the detection of crime, the police can ensure that law-abiding citizens no longer need go in fear of their lives and property.'

'The development of ever more sophisticated techniques for surveillance and detection increases the likelihood that innocent people will be harassed and possibly wrongly convicted and imprisoned.'

Robber caught by his jeans

When gang member Charles Barbee woke (0) ....*up*.......... one morning and considered (1) .... to wear for the first of two bank robberies he had planned, he made a crucial mistake. He slipped (2) .... his jeans – a decision which was (3) .... put him in jail for 64 years.

Barbee was caught by surveillance cameras while (4) .... out the robbery, and (5) .... he wore a mask to disguise his face, his jeans were clearly visible on the photograph. Later, police arrested him on suspicion of (6) .... committed the crime, but had to release him (7) .... to lack of evidence. However, they passed a pair of Barbee's jeans on to a team of forensic scientists, (8) .... noticed the distinctive lines worn into their fabric. Enlarging the photograph (9) .... by the surveillance cameras and comparing the (10) ...., they found over two dozen features matching Barbee's jeans to (11) .... worn by the suspect in the photograph – (12) .... evidence to convict Barbee of the crime.

'Jeans (13) .... usually be identified more easily than any other type of clothing, because their owners tend to keep them until they are (14) .... out,' says a member of the forensic team.

The jeans analysis (15) .... since been used in hundreds of trials in the US.

Language Focus: Vocabulary

Collocations

1 Read the following newspaper extract and discuss the question below.

US murder rates collapse

New York City is heading for a remarkable achievement: the lowest number of murders since 1964. Its rapidly declining murder rate is part of a nationwide trend towards lower crime figures and in particular a rapid decline in murders in the big cities.

Which of the following do you think could be the main reason for the decline in crime rates?

- zero-tolerance policy (no crime is ignored)
- introduction of closed-circuit TV
- improved detection rates
- better economic conditions
- more effective rehabilitation of offenders
- more visible police presence

2   Discuss the following questions.

1   What types of crime are most/least common in your country?
2   Are crime rates falling or rising in your country?
3   What explanation can you suggest for this?

3   Collocations tested in Papers 1 and 3 may be general, or related to a particular topic. The words below have been taken from a newspaper article about developments in video surveillance.

1   Match the words in columns A and B. Then complete the gaps in the text below with the phrases.

A (adjectives/nouns)	B (nouns)
a) closed-circuit TV	analysis
b) police	cameras
c) sophisticated	records
d) recorded	incidents
e) time-consuming	technology

A verb phrases	B noun phrases
f) building	accurate matches
g) make full use of	a project
h) involved in	massive drops in crimes
i) claims to produce	a bridge
j) have reported	the system

Big brother is watching you

Cities using (1) .... to monitor their streets (2) .... such as muggings and assaults. However, the recordings from such cameras require (3) .... to be of use. But a new type of system known as Virtual Interactive Policing (VIP) could change all that. VIP uses (4) .... to enable officers to scan a crowd or street and automatically cross-match the faces against a database of photographs of offenders. It (5) .... within seconds.

In order to (6) ...., the Police Foundation is (7) .... to bring together (8) .... and databases from private sources such as bank and building society security cameras. (9) .... between the private systems and police records will make it possible to search for a criminal's involvement in thousands of (10) ....

2   What are the advantages of a system like the one described above? Can you think of any dangers if such systems become widely used?

4

1   Read the following text ignoring the gaps for the moment. Which of the ideas in Exercise 1 is it related to?

Going for zero

For many years, it appeared impossible to halt the rising crime rate in New York City. Then it was decided to (1) .... a zero-tolerance policy, whereby no infringement whatsoever of law and order would be passed over by the authorities. So the police started (2) .... down on people committing even the most trivial (3) ...., such as jumping over the subway turnstile instead of buying a token, or selling goods in the street without a licence. To many people's amazement, once this policy had been in force for a few months, the crime rate (4) ...., and very noticeably. This was not just for trivial offences, but even for more serious crimes. Why? The first reason was that people noticed that the law was being (5) .... even in small things, which acted as a deterrent overall. And the second reason for the fall was that almost every (6) .... turnstile-jumper, every unlicensed street vendor turned out to be wanted for a whole slew of other crimes. Simple when you think about it.

1	A adopt	B make	C install
	D foster		
2	A hitting	B thrashing	C pushing
	D cracking		
3	A offences	B crimes	C proceedings
	D infringements		
4	A reduced	B fell	C diminished
	D shrank		
5	A applied	B enforced	C asserted
	D oppressed		
6	A trapped	B caught	C retained
	D detained		

2   Decide which answer (**A, B, C** or **D**) best fits each gap. In each case you need to choose the word which best collocates with another word or phrase in the text. Underline the words in the text which helped you to decide.

3   What minor crimes do the police tend to ignore at present in your own town or city? What do you think the effects of a zero-tolerance policy would be?

Writing

▶ Paper 2, Part 2 (proposal)

In Paper 2, Part 2 you may be asked to write a **proposal**. You will be given a task and an audience, but you will need to use your own ideas in the proposal.

1 Which of the following are true of a proposal?

- It is written in an informal style.
- It gives facts.
- It makes suggestions.
- It includes direct speech.
- It uses headings.

2

1 Read the following writing task.

> ### ■ TASK
>
> Your local neighbourhood has been having problems with petty crime, and your local radio station has started a campaign to try to do something about it. It has invited listeners to send in formal proposals on ways of reducing crime; these will be considered in a panel discussion on air, voted on by listeners, and the best one sent to the council.
>
> Write your proposal, identifying the main problems leading to crime in your area and making formal recommendations for improving the situation, with reasons.
>
> (300–350 words)

2 Underline the three parts of the task and add them as headings to the table below.

3 Discuss what ideas you might include under the three headings in the table. Think about ways of:

- improving leisure facilities
- expanding the police force
- providing help with security
- improving video surveillance
- getting through to children and teenagers.

4 Write your ideas in the table under the headings.

3

1 Read the following proposal, which was written in answer to the task.

> ### Introduction
>
> There are two main problems in our area related to crime which need to be addressed. The proposals outlined below would go some way to improving the situation.
>
> ### Main problems
>
> One of the biggest problems in our region is vandalism. This may be because there is a high density of population, and much overcrowding. When people live too close together they can become angry and frustrated, and they may take this aggression out through vandalism. The proliferation of crime among young people is also very worrying; even schoolchildren are being lured into crime by older children.
>
> ### Recommendations
>
> - I would suggest that the problem of vandalism can be addressed through video surveillance. Cameras should be set up in affected areas, enabling the vandals to be identified. This would make them think twice before attacking property. The expense should be borne by the town council.
>
> - Dealing with young criminals is more complex. One solution might be to extend the work of the local police, and encourage them

2   Compare the ideas in the proposal with your own.

1   How many problems does the writer mention? What are they? Add any new points to the table in Exercise 2.2.

2   What recommendations does the writer make, and how does he justify his recommendations? Add the points he makes to the table.

to mix with the community on a regular basis. If the police visited schools regularly, talking to the children and becoming better known to them, they would become more visible and so be a more effective deterrent. The police should also become a more visible presence in the city generally by walking rather than driving around the streets.

● Another possible way of dealing with the problem of young children and crime is related to the idea that a great deal of crime is actually caused by out and out boredom. There is certainly very little for children to do in the evenings around here. I propose that money be set aside to provide leisure activities for young people. It should also be used to pay for helpers to set up these activities, which should be organised and supervised.

Conclusion

All three measures suggested here will require some financial outlay by the local authority. However, I feel that were they to be implemented, there would be a noticeable reduction in crime across the whole community.

(340 words)

4

1   Read the proposal again. Find formal expressions that mean the same as the phrases or sentences below.

1   The council ought to pay for this.
2   The police would discourage people from committing crimes.
3   Someone should watch the children while they play.
4   If someone took these measures …

2   Underline the modal verbs in the proposal. Which ones are most frequent? Why do you think this is?

3   Underline an example of the subjunctive in the last paragraph of the third section. What effect does this have on the tone of the proposal?

5

1   Read the following writing task.

TASK

You are taking part in a project to involve unemployed young people in a range of activities. A committee has been set up to consider possible ideas, which may involve voluntary work, leisure or educational activities. The committee have asked you to write a proposal for the local council describing and justifying three activities the project could undertake, and suggesting possible sources of funding.

(300–350 words)

2   Underline the three parts of the task, and make a table with headings. Discuss what you might include in each part of the table, and make notes on your ideas.

3   Decide which ideas to propose, and why.

4   Plan your proposal using the headings from your table.

Remember that:
● the main part of the proposal will be your recommendations
● you need to give reasons for these.

5   Write your proposal and exchange it with a partner. Check that:
● your partner has completed all parts of the task
● the sections are clear and that the longest part contains the recommendations
● the style is formal.

1 Multiple-choice lexical cloze

For questions 1–6, read the text below and decide which answer (**A, B, C** or **D**) best fits each gap.

The moment of truth

It seemed as if I had been waiting at the back of the crowded hall for hours as item after item was produced and sold. Finally the auctioneer announced Lot 64 and held up the small dark painting in its ornate gilded (1) .... He looked around the room impassively as he invited (2) .... This was the moment I'd been waiting for. My heart began to (3) .... as the amounts rose higher and higher. Five hundred pounds, six hundred pounds – the tension in the room was (4) .... Suddenly I was on my feet. I heard myself shout 'One thousand pounds!' A (5) .... of faces turned to look at me as people gasped in astonishment. The auctioneer paused, looked round the room and, seeing no further signals, brought his hammer down with a crash to confirm the sale. Feeling weak at the knees I sat down again, (6) .... with relief.

1	**A** structure	**B** shell	**C** frame	**D** border
2	**A** bids	**B** sales	**C** purchases	**D** bets
3	**A** strike	**B** pound	**C** drum	**D** throb
4	**A** accumulating	**B** multiplying	**C** mounting	**D** soaring
5	**A** sea	**B** carpet	**C** cloud	**D** spread
6	**A** overpowered	**B** overcome	**C** overtaken	**D** overdone

2 Open cloze

Read the text below and fill each space with one suitable word.

The trouble with school

In the (0) ..*first*.. few years at school all appears to (1) .... very well. There is much concern, (2) .... the part of the teachers, with high educational standards, and the children, even those who are (3) .... from being socially privileged in other ways, seem eager and happy. However, by the (4) .... the children reach adolescence, the promise of the early years frequently remains unfulfilled. Many leave school (5) .... having mastered those basic skills which society demands, let (6) .... having developed the ability to exercise any sort of creative intelligence.

There is (7) .... denying that, in spite of the enlightened concern of our primary schools with happiness, schooling (8) .... or other turns into a distinctly unhappy experience for many of our children. Large (9) .... of them emerge from it well (10) .... that they are ill-equipped (11) .... life in our society. So then they either regard (12) .... as stupid for failing or else, quite understandably, they regard the activities at (13) .... they have failed as stupid. In (14) .... event they want no (15) .... of them. How can we justify a long period of compulsory education which ends like that?

3 Word formation

Use the word given in capitals at the end of some of the lines to form a word that fits in the space in the same line.

TV violence and young children

Claims that the increasing (0) *depiction* of violence on television has a damaging effect on children and young people have led to (1) .... concern on the part of some people over the amount of time children spend watching TV, which in some cases may exceed the time spent at school.

One group of (2) .... investigated the possibility that TV might have an imitative dimension, i.e. that children copied what they saw. However, the results of this study remained (3) .... and further research indicated that the 'normal' child brought up in stable family (4) .... was generally likely to be unaffected by the depiction of violence on TV, but that the unstable child often found fact and fictionalised violence almost completely (5) .... Another study suggested that, while viewing one programme was not likely to have a (6) .... effect on any but the most disturbed children, young children who were (7) .... exposed to violence might be provided with inappropriate role models for solving conflicts. More recent research has (8) .... this link between (9) .... exposure to TV violence and aggressive behaviour in children, but has not (10) .... that this correlation means that one actually causes the other, and so the debate continues.

	DEPICT
	CONSIDER
	~~IMITATE~~ RESEARCH
	CONCLUDE
	STANCE
	DISTINCT
	SIGNIFY
	REPEAT
	FIRM
	TERM
	STABLE

4 Gapped sentences

For questions 1–6, think of one word only which can be used appropriately in all three sentences.

1 Hugh had .... to be a doctor for seven years, but wasn't sure he wanted to be one.
They have dogs in the airport that are specially .... to sniff out explosives.
The firemen .... their hoses on the burning factory, but it was too late.

2 I couldn't really .... to what he said because it was so far from my own experience, so I kept quiet.
I would like to .... this point to something that was mentioned earlier.
She's a conscientious worker, but she finds it difficult to .... to people.

3 She leads a very .... and varied life, although sometimes she finds there's not enough time in the day.
In the photograph Hilda was wearing a .... skirt and a patterned blouse.
Brad's all right, but he's a little too .... of himself sometimes.

4 Caroline has really made progress with her maths – this year she's been moved to the top .... at school.
Steve opened the window and a .... of cold air immediately rushed into the room.
On the video recording, they could see a .... of visitors passing through the exhibition hall.

5 The atmosphere in the room was very .... and she went over to open a window.
There was a look of resentment in her eyes which was .... to hatred.
There are .... links between the school and local industries.

6 She really needs to find a new .... for all her energy or she'll end up very frustrated.
You can change the .... if you don't like the football.
The management needs to open some sort of .... of communication with the workers.

5 Key word transformations

Complete the second sentence with three to eight words so that it has a similar meaning to the first sentence, using the word given. Do not change the word given.

1 Tom is always being criticised by my grandfather because he's so untidy.   **fault**
My grandfather is always ....
.... of his untidiness.

2 It is a shame he has to start his journey before his friends arrive.   **set**
I wish he ....
the arrival of his friends.

3 The moment the witness started to speak, the lawyer interrupted her.   **begun**
No ....
the lawyer interrupted her.

4 You needn't have paid to register.   **pay**
There was .... fee.

5 I can't tell you if it's a good buy or not as I don't know anything about computers.   **idea**
Not ....
advise you whether to buy it or not.

6 He told them that the trial would almost certainly continue for another week.   **likelihood**
He said ....
continue for another week.

7 Far fewer people buy this product now than in the past.   **demand**
There has been a sharp ....
.... this product.

8 She never considered the possibility of living alone.   **mind**
It never .... her own.

6 This picture was considered for a campaign poster to deter young people from turning to crime. Discuss the issues suggested by the picture and decide whether it should be used or not.

6 Bright lights, big city

Speaking

1 The photos on this page were selected to promote the following cities. Can you identify the cities?

- Berlin
- Bilbao
- Kuala Lumpur
- Jeddah
- New York
- Hong Kong

2 Discuss these questions.

1 What image of the city does each photo convey? For example:
- cosmopolitan and sophisticated
- a place where history lives
- bustling and dynamic
- futuristic
- green and clean
- cultural.
2 Which picture do you find most striking? Why?
3 Which city would you most like to visit or live in? Why?

3 You have to choose a picture to be used on the cover of a controversial new book entitled *Cities of the future – the good and the bad news*. None of the pictures above was chosen.

1 Discuss which issues you think the book may present, and why the pictures shown were not chosen.

2 Make suggestions for a suitable picture for the book's cover, to reflect your ideas of the issues presented in the book.

4 Discuss the following questions.

1 Are cities becoming more or less popular places to live in your country? Why?
2 What do you think makes a city a good place to live in?

5 If you were asked to submit a photograph to promote your own town, city or region, what image would you choose? What image do you think your parents or grandparents would have chosen 25 years ago – the same as you, or something different?

Exam Focus
▶ Paper 4, Part 3

In Paper 4, Part 3 you have to listen to a passage involving two speakers, for example, a conversation or an interview, and answer five multiple-choice questions. Each question will have four options **A–D**. You will hear the passage twice.

As well as testing your understanding of main ideas and the details of what you hear, the questions may also test your understanding of the attitudes and opinions of the speakers, either stated or implied. The questions generally follow the order of the passage; the last question may test global understanding.

Here is a procedure to follow for this task.

- You will have one minute after the instructions are read to read through the five questions.
- During the **first** listening, eliminate the answers you're sure are wrong.
- During the **second** listening, choose the correct answer. (If you're not sure, put something.)

1 You will hear a conversation between two friends, one of whom lived for many years in Jeddah, a city in Saudi Arabia. For questions 1–5, choose the answer (**A**, **B**, **C** or **D**) which fits best according to what you hear.

Follow the recommended procedure and use the hints to help you choose the correct answer.

1 When the speaker first arrived in Jeddah, there were no
   A large commercial buildings.
   B cars in the city centre.
   C modern buildings.
   D tall buildings.
(HINT: *Statements and questions containing negatives can be confusing. Try underlining any negatives in the stem so you don't overlook them when answering the question.*)

2 The speaker was relieved that
   A more goods were available in the market.
   B unsafe buildings were pulled down.
   C some buildings were restored.
   D there were no tourists.
(HINT: *You need to think about the speaker's attitude. The statements are all true, but the speaker only indicates she is relieved about one of them.*)

3 One problem she had was that
   A her friends lived far out of town.
   B social life was family-based.
   C it was difficult to find her way around.
   D there was no telephone or public transport service.

(HINT: *You will hear the information needed for the answer before you are told that it was a problem. Don't worry. You can check this type of question the second time you listen.*)

4 After she had been in Jeddah for some time, there were more
   A outdoor facilities for families.
   B air-conditioned shops in the city centre.
   C social facilities for teenagers.
   D restaurants on the sea coast.
(HINT: *The distractors may be partly true and partly untrue. Each of the answers in this question gives two pieces of information. You need to check that both pieces of information are correct in the answer you choose.*)

5 Overall, what was the speaker most conscious of during her time in Jeddah?
   A its sense of history
   B its beauty
   C its rapid development
   D its variety
(HINT: *The word 'overall' tells you that you need to think about the meaning of the whole passage, not just the last section.*)

2 In multiple-choice listening activities you need to be able to match phrases in the recording with the items on your question paper and then decide if the meanings are the same or different. To analyse your answers, look at the extracts from the tapescript and the notes on page 235.

3 **Say it again**

Re-express these sentences from the Listening text, using the framework given.

1 Although it was a port, you weren't all that conscious of the sea.
   Despite ...., you weren't all that conscious of the sea.
2 The whole city expanded at an amazing rate.
   The rate .... amazing.
3 They'd planted trees and bushes along the central reservation.
   The central reservation .... trees and bushes.
4 I'll always remember the atmosphere of the old town.
   The atmosphere .... in my memory.

4 Think of ways in which the place where you live has changed in recent years. Do you consider these changes to be for the better? Why/Why not?

Language Focus: Vocabulary

1 Phrasal verbs with *up*

Complete the sentences below using an appropriate verb from the box in the correct form. Then match the meanings of the particle *up* to the definitions below.

shoot	end	spring	start	speed	do

1 I was offered a job for ten weeks and .... up staying ten years.
2 Before long, office blocks and multi-storey hotels were .... up all over the place.
3 Later on, an ambitious programme of restoration was .... up.
4 The old houses were .... up and their original features restored.
5 Extensive shopping malls were .... up in the new suburbs.
6 It was a very interesting time to live through, like seeing history .... up.

The particle *up* can:
a) suggest increase, or progress to a higher position, e.g.: *turn up* (the volume), *bring up* (children).
b) intensify the meaning of the verb, adding the idea that the action has been completed, e.g.: *cut up, smash up, sell up*. In this case the particle can often be omitted.

2 Phrasal verbs with *down*

Complete the sentences below using an appropriate verb from the box in the correct form. What two general meanings or functions can you suggest for the particle *down*?

get	fall	go	stand	pull	let	put	break

1 The lifts in this building are always .... down.
2 The street has several neglected old buildings that look as if they're about to .... down.
3 All this waiting about is really .... her down.
4 This neighbourhood has really .... down in the last few years.
5 The villagers felt that they had been .... down when the council cut the bus services.
6 They were forced to .... down the old theatre as it was unsafe.
7 He had to .... down as candidate for Mayor when it was discovered he'd been involved in fraud.
8 Our neighbour's dog had to be .... down after it attacked the postman.

3 Verbs with *way*

A number of verbs are typically used in the following pattern.

- *The motorists managed to **edge their way** carefully through the old, narrow streets.* (Listening text)

Complete the following sentences with an appropriate verb from the box in the correct form. Use each verb once only.

find	inch	talk	worm	force	make

1 After the picnic, we slowly .... our way home across the fields.
2 She remembered bitterly how he .... his way into her confidence and then betrayed her.
3 He slowly .... his way along the window ledge, holding on for dear life.
4 The President has finally gone too far – he'll never manage to .... his way out of it this time.
5 The thieves seem to have .... their way in through the window.
6 We'll never .... our way back in the dark without a map.

4 Collocation

1 Read the text below and decide which answer (**A**, **B**, **C** or **D**) best fits each gap.

The population of the city is (1) .... rapidly, and this is leading to an unprecedented demand for housing. Unfortunately, this is having a knock-on effect in other areas. Public (2) .... such as gas and electricity are already severely over-stretched, and road (3) .... throughout the city are deteriorating and in desperate need of repair. Other issues are being raised by the boom in building work, notably the question of the preservation of historically important sites. A number of (4) .... beautiful buildings have already been pulled down to make way for living accommodation, and recently the destruction of a historic area of the city centre was only (5) .... averted after a series of organised protests. In order to preserve our cultural heritage, it is vital that we should (6) .... funds to preserve and restore our historic public buildings and cultural monuments while still endeavouring to provide housing and services for the city's increasing population.

1 A expanding   B stretching   C developing
  D broadening
2 A features   B services   C facilities
  D functions
3 A layers   B coatings   C tops
  D surfaces
4 A acutely   B considerably   C exceptionally
  D drastically

5   A closely   B narrowly   C purely
    D positively
6   A make   B develop   C exploit
    D raise

2   The exercise above practises six different types of collocation. Identify these patterns, e.g. verb + adverb.

3   How far does this text apply to your own home town?

5   Use of English: Paper 3, Part 3

Think of one word only which can be used appropriately in all three sentences.

1   He had an operation to .... his hearing but unfortunately it was only partially successful.
    The police were called in to .... order.
    Some states in the USA may decide to .... the death penalty for serious crimes.

2   There has been a .... decline in manufacturing output.
    They have been in a .... relationship for some time now.
    Try to keep the camera .... while you take the picture.

3   They want to .... the land and have submitted plans for a housing estate.
    We hope to .... these ideas in a further seminar.
    Scientists hope to .... new drugs to treat the diseases of old age.

4   My computer is out of .... at the moment so I can't e-mail you.
    If he doesn't repay the loan they are threatening legal ....
    The police need to take .... to deal with violent crimes.

5   For the first time, she noticed the .... on her father's face.
    They made the children stand in four ....
    The dresses he designs closely follow the .... of the body.

6   The smoke from the fire .... in the air for days.
    I .... around for an hour, then got tired of waiting.
    I .... on tightly as the motorbike roared round the corner.

Language Focus: Grammar
The passive

1   Read the following text. Can you guess which city is being described? What time period do you think it refers to?

Most of the City streets were cobbled. (1) Only a line of posts reserved the rare sidewalks for pedestrians. Sometimes the road surface sloped down to a central drain; (2) rubbish usually blocked this.

Main streets were prone to traffic bottlenecks; at least no modern City driver has had to face a drove of turkeys (3) which someone is driving to their last home in City storehouses. (4) Narrow alleys barely wide enough for two pedestrians to pass punctuated side streets.

Sign boards hung from almost every house; in theory they were supposed to be nine feet off the ground, to give room for a man on a horse to pass underneath. (5) Sometimes an elaborate code conveyed their meaning. An elephant showed where (6) people could buy combs of ivory and other materials. Adam and Eve offered apples and other fruit.

Householders had a duty to hang out a candle or a lantern from dusk until nine o'clock during the winter. However, from the frequency with which (7) City regulations had repeated this duty since the fourteenth century, one can only suppose that (8) people did not generally observe it. Mostly the City streets were ill-lit or dark.

City authorities had tried for centuries, with only partial success, to discourage 'noxious' trades from operating in the City, their main market. Even when these trades obeyed the rules and stayed away from the City, (9) the wind blew air-borne pollution in from across the river.

2   The text above has been adapted. In the original, the numbered sentences and clauses were written using the passive. Rewrite them as you think they were, using an appropriate passive form. Decide whether it's necessary to include the agent or not. Then read the information on the next page.

3 Uses of the passive

Read this information about the uses of the passive and look at the passive sentences you wrote for Exercise 2. Can you give further examples from the text for any of the uses described?

In English, the new or most important information in a sentence is usually placed towards the end: this is where we normally expect to find it. Complex phrases or clauses should also be placed towards the end, otherwise the sentence can sound awkward.

Using the passive allows us:

1 to focus attention on the *action* by putting it in the end position. We may do this because the agent (the person or thing that actually did the action) is unknown ('someone'), unimportant, or obvious, or because we deliberately want to avoid saying who did the action. Compare:
   An elephant showed where people **could buy** *combs of ivory and other materials.*
   An elephant showed where combs of ivory and other materials **could be bought**.

2 to focus attention on the *agent* by moving it from the beginning to the end of the sentence or clause. Compare:
   Only a **line of posts** *reserved the rare sidewalks for pedestrians.*
   The rare sidewalks were reserved for pedestrians only by a **line of posts**.

3 to put long complex phrases at the end, and avoid awkwardness. Compare:
   Narrow alleys barely wide enough for two pedestrians to pass *punctuated side streets.*
   Side streets were punctuated by ***narrow alleys barely wide enough for two pedestrians to pass***.

4 to make previously given information the subject or topic of the sentence or clause. Compare:
   … from the frequency with which City regulations had repeated **this duty** *…*
   … from the frequency with which **this duty** *had been repeated in City regulations …*

Because it is less personal, the general effect of the passive is to give a statement or text a more formal, objective style. It is therefore frequently used in factual accounts, reports, etc.

▶ Grammar reference p. 217

4 Imagine you live in the city described in the text in Exercise 1. The city authorities have asked for recommendations on ways of improving life for the citizens.

1 Read the following suggestions. What word can be removed from the underlined clauses without changing the meaning?

I recommend <u>*the streets should be widened*</u> *in order to reduce congestion.*

I propose <u>*that more pavements should be built*</u> *so that people aren't forced to walk on the road.*

I suggest <u>*large fines should be introduced*</u> *to discourage manufacturers from polluting the atmosphere.*

The verbs *suggest, recommend, propose, insist, demand* and *urge* are often followed by a *that*-clause + modal *should*. In more formal English, *should* may be omitted. For example: *I suggest (that) large fines be introduced.* Here, the verb *be* is in the subjunctive form.

▶ Grammar reference p. 217

2 Use the prompts below to make more suggestions with the passive. Add a reason.

1 I suggest ....
   (*rubbish/collect/more frequently*)
2 I recommend that ....
   (*underground drains/build*)
3 I propose that ....
   (*city centre/pedestrianise*)
4 I demand that ....
   (*fines/introduce/litter*)
5 I urge that ....
   (*street lighting/install*)
6 I insist that ....
   (*heavy industry/ban*)

5 Work with a partner. Think about the place where you live. Recommend changes that could improve life for a) the people who live there b) tourists visiting the area. First, discuss what you think:

1 could/can't be done.
2 should/shouldn't be done.
3 is likely/unlikely to be done.

Then decide on three major recommendations.

6 Use of English: Paper 3, Part 4

Complete the second sentence with three to eight words so that it has a similar meaning to the first sentence, using the word given. Do not change the word given.

1 She has never been allowed to go there by herself.   **let**
   They ....
   .... her own.

2 If they catch anyone dropping litter in Singapore, they immediately make them pay a fine.   **fined**
   In Singapore anyone caught ....
   .... spot.

3 They have not yet made up their minds where to locate the concert hall.   **location**
   No decision ....
   .... the concert hall.

4 This scheme will help young people become better qualified.   **additional**
   Young people ....
   .... through this scheme.

5 I observed that a thick layer of mud covered the man's boots.   **caked**
   I could see ....
   .... mud.

6 There should have been no action without prior consultation.   **before**
   People should ....
   .... taken.

7 Someone must have seen the thieves escaping with the jewels.   **making**
   The thieves ....
   .... with the jewels.

8 If the new stadium had been built, this would have greatly improved the club's reputation.   **boosted**
   The club's reputation ....
   .... of the new stadium.

Speaking

1 Read this information.

attersea Power Station, which served London with electricity for over fifty years, is one of the city's best-loved landmarks. One of the largest brick buildings in the world, it was built in the 1930s and continued to function until it was finally closed in the 1980s. The building lay empty and neglected for years, despite protests from those who regarded it as part of England's architectural heritage. Finally the Central Electricity Generating Board announced a competition inviting the public, including schools and local residents, to suggest a use for the building. Suggestions included a theme park, a sports centre, an entertainment complex, a film production centre and an art gallery. Latest plans for the site are

Which suggestion do you think won the competition? Why?

2 You have been invited to take part in a similar competition to consider the renovation and redevelopment of a building in your own town or city. Your proposal should cover the following areas.

• the ways in which you think the building could best be used
• any objections which might be made about the project, e.g. from people living or working in the surrounding areas, and how these might be overcome
• the overall benefit your proposal would bring to the community

Work in groups to prepare your proposal and be ready to present it to the rest of the class.

3 Listen to each other's presentations. Then vote to decide the winning proposal.

Use of English

▶ Paper 3, Part 5

1 The picture shows a vision of a city of the future by an artist living in the 1930s. Imagine you could go back in time and talk to the artist about his predictions.

- Which parts of his vision have come true?
- Does anything in his vision look old-fashioned to you?
- What other developments in modern city life could you tell him about?

2

1 You are going to read two texts about city development. Read the first paragraph of the text below. How many of the features mentioned there are illustrated in the picture?

Text 1

Imagining cities of the future was a favourite 20th-century sport. Film directors, novelists and architects all practised it, dreaming up with remarkable consistency gleaming towers
5 joined by skyways, aeroplanes and helicopters flitting between them like aerial buses, and buildings and people looking ever more uniform.

Now the city of the future has become the
10 city of the present, and it turns out that a few things were overlooked. If the metropolis of the 21st century does indeed have some large shiny blank buildings, it also includes such things as a theme park in the 15-year-old city
15 of Shenzen, China, where Sydney Opera House, the Grand Canyon, the Eiffel Tower and other great monuments of the world are reproduced at reduced scale.

For, as the future-gazers failed to spot, the
20 industry that is shaping the city in the 21st century is entertainment. Once the urban role models were the skyscrapers of Manhattan. Now it is Las Vegas, with its recreations of Egypt, medieval England, New York, Venice,
25 Paris, and ancient Rome. Las Vegas is the fastest growing city in the United States and is spawning imitations from Malaysia to Italy. It is the American city most people in China would like to visit.
30   And across the developed world entertainment is becoming ever more intimate with its good friend shopping, to create malls that look like theme parks and theme parks where you can do a lot of shopping.

2 Skim the whole of the first text. What does the writer think is the main factor influencing city development?

3 Answer the following questions based on text 1. You don't need to write complete sentences.

1 According to the writer, how accurate were 20th-century ideas about future cities and why?
2 Which phrase in paragraph 2 echoes the view of the city of the future suggested in paragraph 1?

Text 2

For some city planners, the attempt to create an authentic, localised environment seems doomed as large firms gobble up everything from coffee shops to dry cleaners. The taking over of the traditional shopping street by the big
5 chain stores means that our cities are becoming increasingly standardised and that the very existence of the independent merchant is under threat. To this picture, electronic commerce is now adding yet another dimension as consumers are presented with greater choices, convenience, and lower prices
10 on the internet. Some observers believe that the 'chaining' of shops and services, coupled with the growth of cyberspace, will soon reach such a level that shopping districts will no longer be able to provide the social and cultural glue holding together the local community.

15 For our cities to continue to have a role in the future, perhaps something else must be offered. Many cities see cultural and arts-related activities – museums, theatres, ballet, and video production – as potential sources of urban recovery. In the USA, Cleveland's Rock and Roll Hall of Fame – won after fierce
20 competition with other, arguably more attractive locales – has given the city a new public image.

But although a library, concert hall, or art museum can lure visitors on special occasions, only the marketplace can create a true permanent central place. Without retailing, the commercial
25 justification for the city centre and the High Street will have been lost. Ultimately, in order to survive, a revived city centre will have to combine a sense of community and uniqueness with a strong commercial appeal.

4 Skim the second text. What two general aspects of city development does it focus on?

5 Answer the following questions based on text 2.

1 What phrase in text 1 links with the idea in line 5 of text 2 that cities are becoming 'increasingly standardised'?
2 Explain in your own words what the writer is referring to as 'social and cultural glue'. (line 13)

6 Read the following summary task carefully. Remember the procedure recommended in Unit 4, page 57.

> In a paragraph of between 50 and 70 words, summarise in your own words as far as possible the main trends in city development described in the texts.

- Underline the key words in the summary question.
- Identify the information you need in the texts. (Remember that you are not summarising all the information given in both texts.)
- Make short notes of the main points.
- Decide on the best order for the information.
- Write your summary, basing it on your notes.
- Count the words, check and amend as necessary.

You should have about four main points in your notes for this particular summary.

Language Focus: Vocabulary
Metaphor

1 Read the following examples. The words in italics are being used metaphorically. Answer the questions about their meaning and effect in the sentence.

1 You could walk around without getting *mown down* by traffic. (Listening, p. 83)
   a) Which of the following things can be mown? the grass/a beard/a lawn
   b) What does the metaphor suggest about the traffic and the pedestrians?
2 Tempers used to get *frayed* looking for places in the suburbs. (Listening, p. 83)
   a) What normally frays? What does it look like when it has frayed?
   b) What does the metaphor suggest about the way the person is feeling?
   c) What's the difference in meaning between 'they lost their tempers' and 'tempers became frayed'?
3 ... gleaming towers joined by skyways, aeroplanes and helicopters *flitting* between them ... (text, p. 88)
   a) What usually 'flits'? What type of movement does the verb suggest?
   b) What does the choice of verb suggest about the tone of the article? Is the writer being entirely serious?
4 Las Vegas ... is *spawning* imitations from Malaysia to Italy. (text, p. 88)
   a) What is the literal meaning of 'spawn'?
   b) Does the use of this verb have a neutral, positive or negative connotation in the context?

2 Read the postcard below.

1 What city do you think the writer could be describing? What are her three main impressions of the city? How does she feel about it?

Dear Monica,

I'm here at last and I can't tell you how great everything is. It's a huge city – you can't imagine the size of some of the skyscrapers! Everything round them is dwarfed and when you're on the 50th floor looking down the people are just like ants. Everyone and everything is in a hurry – the streets are swarming with people all day long, and it can be really difficult to push your way through the crowds. And the noise – it's never quiet, and police sirens are wailing all night. It's all so exciting, I'm so glad I'm here!

See you soon,

Love, Christine

2 Find three examples in the postcard of verbs used metaphorically. What are the usual meanings of these words? What do they suggest when used in this context?

3

1 Choose a verb from the box which can complete both gaps in the sentence pairs below. There are three extra verbs which you don't need to use. You may need to change the form.

screech	crawl	fly	freeze	melt
squeal	stampede	surge	fight	

1 a) The soldiers .... their way over the bridge.
   b) People .... their way onto the buses.
2 a) The children .... into the playground, shouting and yelling.
   b) Terrified by the noise, the cattle .... across the plain.
3 a) The bird .... angrily as the cat approached the nest.
   b) The car brakes .... as the car stopped just in time.
4 a) The baby was .... across the room on all fours.
   b) The road was jammed with cars .... along at a snail's pace.
5 a) The car tyres .... as he raced round the corner.
   b) The children .... in delight when they heard they had a holiday.
6 a) As night fell, the crowd .... away.
   b) The sun came out and gradually the ice ....

2 In which of the above sentences, a) or b), is the verb used literally, and in which is it used metaphorically? What is the effect of the metaphor in each case?

3 Now write similar pairs of sentences for the three remaining verbs from the box.

4 Work with a partner. Write sentences using some of the metaphors from this section, and others that you know, that could be included in a description of:

1 a famous landmark in your town/country.
2 rush hour in your town.
3 the crowd at a big public event.
4 your home town in 2050.
5 a car chase in a big city.

EXAMPLE: *The older buildings are dwarfed by the gleaming new skyscrapers which tower above them.*

Language Focus: Grammar
Relative clauses (1)

1   Read the information about Curitiba, a city in southeastern Brazil. How has it solved its transport problem? How does the situation in Curitiba compare with your home town?

The Curitiba experience

Curitiba in southeastern Brazil has earned an international reputation for good city management with its innovative programmes for public transport, industrial pollution control and waste recycling. One of Brazil's fastest growing cities, it has avoided many of the problems that usually go with rapid expansion. Early in its development, Curitiba adopted a plan for linear growth along radial axes, using the areas in between for green space and leisure facilities as well as for industrial and housing development.

Curitiba has few traffic jams, despite having more cars per capita than any other Brazilian city except Brasilia. Roads running along the structural axes include special 'busways', which provide rapid transport of people to and from the city centre. A sophisticated bus system has been developed, featuring red express buses, green inter-district buses and yellow 'feeder' buses. There are regular services, which are closely linked, so that it is easy and quick to switch from one route to another. A single fare operates for all journeys within the city limits, with tickets interchangeable on all routes.

The transport network is managed by a city authority which lays down operating rules, sets timetables and routes, and monitors performance. The buses themselves are run by private companies, licensed by the city authority. The bus system Curitiba opted for is far cheaper in terms of capital cost than underground metro or light rail. It is a simple transparent system and it works – some 75% of commuters travel by bus. (In Sydney, by contrast, over 60% go to work by car; in Los Angeles, 90%.)

Another innovation has been the preservation of green space. During the last 20 years, green space per capita has increased one-hundredfold, which is all the more amazing given that this increase took place during a period of rapid population growth.

A key factor in Curitiba's civic development has been its mayors, whose enthusiasm and persistence have been maintained for over 20 years. But as they have always stressed, it is ultimately the people themselves to whom the city belongs.

2

1   Read the article again and underline seven examples of relative clauses introduced by a relative pronoun. Number the examples 1–7. Decide which ones are a) non-defining or b) defining.

2   Read the rules below. Which of these rules are true of a) non-defining relative clauses b) defining relative clauses c) both? Write ND, D or *both* next to each rule. For each rule, find one example from the text.

1   The clause gives essential information and cannot be omitted. ....
2   It may refer back to the whole of the previous clause. ....
3   We use commas to separate the clause. ....
4   The relative pronoun immediately follows the noun it refers to. ....
5   The relative pronouns *who* and *which* can both be replaced by *that*. ....
6   The clause can be introduced by *whose*, *where* and *when*. ....
7   The original subject does not stay in the clause – it is replaced by the relative pronoun. ....
8   When a preposition is necessary, it can go at the beginning or end of the clause, depending on formality. ....

► Grammar reference p. 218

3   Identify the mistakes in the following sentences and correct them.

1   New York is one of the cities that I would most love to visit it.
2   He took a pamphlet from one of the folders that they were on the table.
3   The house where I lived in was very big.
4   We met a really interesting man, the name of who I've unfortunately forgotten.
5   The man was very interesting that gave the talk on local history.
6   The people are using public transport are not very satisfied.

4   In which of the sentences below can the relative pronoun be omitted?

1   The bus system which Curitiba opted for is far cheaper than underground metro.
2   London's underground system, which the city set up over 100 years ago, originally used steam trains.
3   The house which I used to live in has been demolished.

► Grammar reference p. 218

Language Focus: Grammar
Relative and participle clauses (2)

1 Sentence relatives

1 Read the following examples and underline the prepositional phrases used with a relative. What type of relative clauses are they used in?

1 Stricter controls on energy use may be introduced, in which case taxes will inevitably rise.
2 The Clean Air Act was introduced in Britain in the late 1950s, since when air quality has greatly improved.

2 Combine these sentences in the same way.

1 Curitiba invested heavily in public transport. As a result, pollution was greatly reduced.
2 We are expecting a full report in April. At that time we will make our decision.
3 A five-point action plan was agreed. Since then many improvements have been made.
4 People started arguing. At that point, I left.

2 With quantifiers

1 The relative pronouns *whom*, *whose* and *which* are often used after quantifiers such as *all of*, *the majority of*, *some of*, *both/neither of*, etc. For example:

1 I have two brothers, *both of whom* live abroad.
2 The city bought a fleet of garbage trucks, *only three of which* were still in service five years later.

2 Combine these sentences in the same way.

1 Mrs Carr was delighted. Four of her children had already won prizes.
2 A lot of people came to the meeting. I didn't know most of them.
3 The Lottery makes a lot of money. Only a small proportion of it goes to charity.
4 The City has had two mayors in the last ten years. Both of them were excellent.

3 Participle clauses

1 Compare these pairs of sentences.

1 a) People who live in small villages have close ties with their neighbours.
  b) People *living in small villages* have close ties with their neighbours.
2 a) Children who are brought up in cities cope well with the stresses of urban life.
  b) Children *brought up in cities* cope well with the stresses of urban life.

The clauses in italics are participle clauses in which a relative pronoun and verb are replaced by a participle. Which type of participle clause has an active meaning? Which type has a passive meaning?

2 Re-express the following sentences from the text on page 91 using full relative clauses instead of participle clauses.

1 Roads running along the structural axes include special 'busways'.
2 A sophisticated bus system has been developed, featuring red express buses.
3 The buses are run by private companies, licensed by the city authority.

3 Which words can you remove from the relative clauses in the following examples without omitting any information? How are these examples different from those above?

1 The first walk begins in Placa de Catalunya, which is the nerve centre of the city.
2 The square is bordered on all sides by splendid old buildings, which are now banks and stores.
3 The bank, which is already the tallest building in the city, is about to be extended.

▶ Grammar reference pp. 218–219

4 Rewrite the following extract from a guidebook, replacing the relative clauses with participle clauses where possible.

Originally, Las Ramblas was nothing more than a river-bed which marked the outer limits of the 13th-century city walls. A promenade was formed which ran parallel to the walls, through which various entrances allowed access to the town. In the course of time, these walls ceased to serve their defensive function and were destroyed. All along the Rambla, houses, hospitals and colleges were built, which formed the splendid promenade we see today. In the centre are stalls which sell flowers, birds and animals or newspapers and magazines, whilst further down are pavement cafés and stands that sell craftwork. There are also street performers, Tarot card readers and portrait artists, who are usually surrounded by curious onlookers.

5 Choose **one** of the following tasks.

1 Write a paragraph for a guidebook describing a part of your village, town or city in such a way as to make it attractive to a visitor.

2 Write a paragraph for a report on city development projects describing a problem in your town or city.

▶ Exam Maximiser

Writing

▶ Paper 2, Part 2 (report)

In Paper 2, Part 2, you may be asked to write a
report. You will be told what the report should be
about, and who it is for.

A report:

- is normally written for a particular purpose in a
  business or work situation
- deals with facts
- may contain recommendations for action
- normally uses headings for each section
- is written in an impersonal, neutral to formal style.

For this type of task, it is very important to:

- organise your report carefully, using headings as a
  guide
- ensure your ideas are supported with evidence.

1 Read the newspaper headlines below. What
main problems are they highlighting?

Gridlock Imminent As Traffic Piles Into City Centre

Pollution Levels Rise To Record Heights

Demands For Better Public Transport From Residents

2

1 Read the following writing task.

> **TASK**
>
> ▌As part of your Urban Studies course, you have
> attended a presentation of proposed changes
> to ease traffic congestion in your town centre.
> Write a report for your tutor on the plan,
> giving your opinion of the proposals and
> making recommendations to improve them.
>
> (300–350 words)

2 To start you thinking, discuss any problems that
traffic congestion causes where you live, and any
measures that have been taken to ease them.

3 Read the following report, which was written in answer
to the task. Are any of the problems mentioned similar to those
you discussed? What solutions are proposed? What are the
advantages and disadvantages of the proposed solutions?

Background information
Castleford is a historic city founded over 600 years
ago, and now has a population of 300,000. The city
has recently been suffering severe traffic
congestion. The Town Planning Officer held a meeting
on May 21st to discuss the situation and to suggest
measures to deal with it.

Problems
The city has narrow winding streets, many of which
are one-way only. Offices, shops and entertainment
facilities attract large numbers of people into the
centre at all hours. As a result, there is a steady
stream of traffic, causing jams at peak times and
raising pollution levels, a situation which is both
frustrating and unhealthy.

Suggested changes
It was suggested that the city centre be
pedestrianised, and all private vehicles be banned.
Large underground car parks should be built at three
entry points into the traffic-free zone. From these
entry points, special shuttle buses would run at
regular intervals to convey people around the
centre. Shop deliveries would only be made at night,
on a rota basis. In addition, improved public
transport services from the suburbs would encourage
people to leave their cars at home.

Comments and recommendations
In my view, the proposals have much to recommend
them. The main stumbling block, however, is the
total cost. It was not stated how this money was
to be raised. Presumably there would be high car
park charges, in which case people may be less
inclined to use them. The result could be congestion
caused by parked cars in the streets outside the
traffic-free zones.

While I support the proposal in general terms,
I recommend that it be implemented in stages.
Initially, public transport to and from the suburbs
should be improved, and charges for parking in the
city centre should be increased. This would
immediately ease the pressure of private cars. Car
parks and shuttle buses should then be introduced in
phase two. This would both spread the cost and make
the whole proposal more workable.

(326 words)

4 The writer planned his report carefully by preparing an outline. Read the report again and fill in the missing information in the notes.

Background information
Castleford founded 600 yrs ago; population 300,000
Meeting held by TPO on May 21 to discuss ....

Problems
1   old town
*   — narrow streets, some one-way only*
2   ....
*   — constant traffic, rush-hour jams*
*   — pollution*

Suggested changes
1   .... town centre
2   ....
3   three .... + shuttle buses
4   night deliveries
5   ....

Comments / own recommendations
Comment: main problem = ...
Recommendations: phased implementation:
Phase 1 — .... public transport
*   — increase ....*
Phase 2 — ....

5 Look through the report again and find examples of the following features of more formal language.

- passive and impersonal structures
- the subjunctive
- complex sentences (i.e. with more than one clause)

6

1   Read the following writing task and underline the key words that tell you what information you have to include.

TASK
Your local authority is planning to develop the area you live in to provide better sports, leisure and other facilities. Young people have been asked to contribute their ideas. As secretary of the local Youth Community Organisation, you have called several meetings to establish the main problems and opportunities facing your area. Write a report summarising your findings, identifying the most urgently needed changes and making recommendations for achieving these.

(300–350 words)

2   Read the extracts from conversations you had at your meetings. What problem does each refer to?

'Kids have nowhere to play football, so they play in the street.'

'The neighbourhood would be much more attractive if they'd just deal with the litter.'

'There are some wonderful old buildings around and they're just decaying — why don't they renovate them and use them?'

'The library only opens three times a week, and it has no money to buy new books — it's a real shame!'

3   Using some of the ideas above and adding any more of your own, write an outline for your report using the headings below.

Background information
Main problems and opportunities
Most urgent changes needed
Recommendations

7 Exchange your outline with a partner and evaluate each other's work.

- Are the points clear and supported by evidence?
- Is each point in the most appropriate part of the report?

8 Now expand your outline into the final report.

1 Rewrite the following sentences, using passive forms to avoid using the words in italics.

1 *They*'re constructing a bypass to relieve city centre congestion.
2 I think *they* ought to have done that years ago.
3 Unfortunately, *it*'ll only prevent a small proportion of the traffic jams.
4 *They* shouldn't have given permission for the developers to build all those blocks of flats.
5 *They*'ve built over all the open spaces.
6 *No-one* gave any consideration to the need for access roads.

2 Join each of the following pairs of sentences by using a relative or participle clause.

1 I recently attended a meeting. The purpose of the meeting was to discuss the modernisation of the swimming pool.
2 The pool was constructed in 1968. In those days little thought was given to the matter of access for wheelchair users.
3 Some disabled people use the pool now. Only a small number of them could attend the meeting.
4 We all agreed there should be a ramp as well as steps. The ramp should lead up to the entrance doors.
5 It should be possible to get a government grant to pay for the ramp. If that proves to be the case, we'll have enough money to re-paint the changing rooms.
6 We all agreed that the meeting had in fact been very useful. We hadn't been particularly keen to attend it.

3 Use the word given in capitals to form a word that fits the gap.

1 The .... of green spaces is important for city planners. PRESERVE
2 The city expanded .... quickly. BELIEVE
3 The mayor instigated an .... programme of restoration. AMBITION
4 Street performers may be found in city centres, surrounded by crowds of .... LOOK
5 Traffic jams create high levels of .... in motorists. FRUSTRATE
6 City planners have shown great .... in their desire to improve city life. PERSIST

4 Read the text below and decide which answer (**A**, **B**, **C** or **D**) best fits each gap.

I'm very much a country person at heart and not a city dweller at all. I was (1) .... in a village and even though I've now worked in the city for many years, I always find it a great relief to get out of the (2) .... and bustle of the city crowds every evening. (3) .... to work every day certainly isn't very pleasant but for me it's infinitely (4) .... to actually staying in the city. I value my peace and quiet. And when I get out of the train every evening into the fresh air and stillness, there's no (5) .... in my mind that the inconvenience is well worth it. I just feel so much better. The journey distances work and stress and this means that I can (6) .... my batteries ready for the onslaught of the next day.

1	A reared	B raised	C nurtured	D bred
2	A hustle	B hurly	C rustle	D rush
3	A migrating	B shuttling	C commuting	D tripping
4	A desirable	B preferable	C favourable	D advisable
5	A uncertainty	B hesitation	C doubt	D query
6	A rekindle	B recharge	C restore	D redo

5 Complete the second sentence with three to eight words so that it has a similar meaning to the first sentence, using the word given. Do not change the word given.

1 The mountains surrounding the camp site made my little tent look very small. **dwarfed**
My little tent ....
.... surrounding the camp site.

2 The students demanded the immediate abolition of the regulations. **be**
The students ....
.... immediately.

3 He borrowed the money from his father so that he could buy the old house and restore it. **up**
He wanted to ....
.... so he borrowed the money from his father.

4 The new one-way system has not been entirely successful up to now. **partial**
The new one-way system ....
.... far.

5 Independent shops may not survive the growth of supermarkets. **threat**
Independent shops ....
.... the growth of supermarkets.

UNIT 7 The living planet

Language Focus: Vocabulary

The environment

1 You are going to read a text about environmental change.

1 Look at the photos and describe what is happening. What environmental issue does each one illustrate?

2 Read the introductory paragraph below and fill in the gaps with words from the box.

resources	destruction	ecology
environment	habitats	

2 Read the next part of the text and identify the key environmental issues being described. Then use words and phrases from the box below to fill in the gaps.

We have come to the end of a millennium of relentless and accelerating (1) .... of the world around us. While human creativity and technology have blossomed, we have steadily been destroying the (2) .... of the planet on which we depend for our survival. The sad fact is that every day the diversity of life on Earth gets poorer because of our overuse of (3) .... and our disregard for the riches of nature. Ecologically, our natural (4) .... provide services without which life on the planet would become impossible. When we tamper with the (5) ...., it is not just nature which suffers. Our own way of life is under threat.

Since the industrial revolution, man has burned ever larger quantities of (6) ...., first coal and then oil, with the result that the composition of the atmosphere has started to change. Burning these fuels produces (7) .... such as carbon dioxide, which act in the atmosphere like glass in a greenhouse and trap the heat of the sun – this is known as the (8) .... The overall global temperature has already begun to rise. Global warming is expected to lead to extreme (9) ...., with more frequent floods, droughts and heat waves. No person, animal, bug or bird will be unaffected.

In addition to greenhouse gases, industrial processes produce poisonous substances which can be virtually impossible to dispose of safely. If these (10) .... are buried in underground storage sites, there is the danger that they may (11) .... into lakes and rivers, with serious long-term effects on living organisms. Emissions from industrial plants, such as sulphur, can also enter the atmosphere, where they can cause damage to the (12) .... around the planet. They may also fall back to Earth as (13) .... and destroy plants and trees. All these are examples of types of (14) .... that could be prevented.

acid rain	changes in climate	fossil fuels
gases	greenhouse effect	pollution
ozone layer	toxic wastes	leach

3   Now read the continuation of the text. Fill in the gaps with words from the box below.

We drain (15) .... near rivers and coastal areas to create land for building. Through (16) ...., the large-scale cutting down of trees, the (17) .... that allow species to survive are changed and the amount of land available for (18) .... decreases. Some species are so reduced in number that they are in danger of (19) .... At this stage they are known as an (20) .... and are only one step away from total (21) ....

We are now beginning to manipulate nature in new ways, without thought for the possible consequences. Technology now allows us to create (22) .... of plants which are resistant to diseases and which can survive extremes of temperature or salinity (salt content). The danger of this process of (23) .... is that producing new plants or other (24) .... like bacteria may bring disaster as well as apparent advantages, as experience has already shown.

So, with the new millennium, we need a new beginning, a fresh start. We need to reverse the major threats to our environment. Above all, we need to understand that we cannot go on consuming and polluting with no thought for tomorrow.

deforestation	wildlife
ecosystems	endangered species
extinction	genetic engineering
living organisms	dying out
wetlands	strains

4   In technical texts, the writer often helps the reader to understand difficult words or concepts by giving examples or definitions, describing causes and effects, using synonyms, and so on. In this sentence from the text, two examples of 'fossil fuels' are given, which explain the meaning of this term.

'Since the industrial revolution, man has burned ever larger quantities of fossil fuels, first coal and then oil,...'

With a partner, discuss what methods the writer has used to help the reader understand the following concepts.

1   emissions
2   deforestation
3   salinity
4   genetic engineering

5   Work in pairs. Without looking back at the text, take turns to explain the following concepts to your partner.

1   the greenhouse effect and global warming
2   industrial pollution
3   species loss
4   genetic engineering

Language Focus: Grammar
Cause and result

1   Join these sentences using the words in brackets. Make any changes necessary. Then check your answers by referring back to the text you have read.

1   Every day the diversity of life on Earth gets poorer. We are overusing resources and disregarding the riches of nature. (*because of*)
2   Man has burned ever larger quantities of fossil fuels, first coal and then oil. The composition of the atmosphere has started to change. (*result*)
3   Some species are very reduced in number. They are in danger of dying out. (*so ... that*)

2   Now rewrite the following sentences beginning with the words given, making any changes necessary.

1   The number of private cars has increased enormously, and this is a key factor in global warming.
    A major cause of global warming is the
    ....
2   The Earth's temperature is rising and, as a result, the polar ice caps are melting.
    The polar ice caps are melting as a result of ....
3   As sea levels rise, there is an increased incidence of flooding.
    One effect of the ....
4   Sea levels may rise even more and cause whole countries to disappear.
    Sea levels may rise to such an extent ....
5   Toxic waste is being dumped in the sea with the result that many fish and sea mammals have died.
    Many fish .... due to ....
6   The spread of deserts is linked to deforestation and farming methods such as irrigation and excessive grazing.
    .... have led to ....

3   Choose an environmental issue that you think is particularly relevant to your country. Answer the following questions.

1   What are the specific effects of the problem on your country? Give examples.
2   What is being done to improve matters? Is it enough, or should more be done? What?
3   What is likely to happen if nothing is done?

In Paper 1, Part 4 you have to read a text and answer seven questions, choosing the correct answer from four options. Here is a procedure to follow for this task.

- Read through the text to get an overall impression of what kind of text it is (e.g. fiction or non-fiction) and what it is about.
- Look at each question or stem – **not** the four options – and find the answer or completion in the text.
- Read the options and find the one that is closest to the information in the text.
- Read the text again and check all your answers.

Using this procedure, choose the answer (**A**, **B**, **C** or **D**) which you think fits best according to the text.

1 The case of the barndoor skate is particularly significant because

A it disappeared relatively quickly.

B its disappearance was not noticed.

C it is a well-known species.

D it is almost extinct.

(HINT: *All the answers give information that is mentioned in the text, but only one answer fits the question stem correctly. Here you are reading for the main idea in a paragraph.*)

Tearing up the map of creation

1 A big fish is about to swim away forever. The barndoor skate, Raja Levis, seems close to extinction. In 1951 research ships found it in ten per cent of all trawls in the Atlantic Ocean off Newfoundland. Over the last 20 years, none at all have been caught there. The fish grows to a metre across, not something you would miss if you were looking out for it. But nobody was. If something the size of a barn door could slip away without being missed, the fate of little known species is likely to be worse.

2 The things that make life possible are barely visible. Laboratory experiments based on small, artificial worlds keep demonstrating that diversity is life's strongest card. The recycling of air and water and plant nutrients is the business of little creatures most of us never notice. The food we eat, the medicines we take and the tools we use have been fashioned for us by

500 million years of evolution. Yet we know practically nothing about most of them. All the evidence is that humans are extinguishing other life forms on an epic scale. But there are probably only about 7,000 experts – they are called taxonomists – on the whole planet with the authority to distinguish species one from another. Most are in the wrong places. And few have been getting much encouragement. Without them we cannot even begin arguing.

3 The enormous task of identifying and classifying the species that exist on our planet was begun in 1758 by Carolus Linnaeus, the great Swedish taxonomist. Over the next 240 years, French and British natural historians followed suit, establishing a local habitation and name for each of about 1.7 or 1.8 million species. With no central catalogue or inventory, the same species was sometimes recorded under one identity in one country and under an entirely separate name in another, but even when these double entries were taken out, the number was still about 1.4 million.

4 Then researchers began to look a little harder. They spread nets under trees, dusted them with insecticide and counted just the arthropods* (including insects) that fell out. The numbers astonished them. When they reached 50,000, they started to get alarmed: by that reckoning there might

be 20 million species to be described, rather than two million. What was true for the Amazon rainforest turned out to be equally true for coral reefs, mangrove swamps and the great plains of Africa.

5 But taxonomists are oppressed by something darker than the task of counting. What is going on now is described, quite calmly, as 'the sixth great extinction'. The fossil record shows a pattern of evolution and extinction, with species continuously evolving, flourishing and expiring as individuals are born, develop and die. Imposed on this hubbub of appearance and disappearance is a series of dramatic happenings: mass disappearances, followed by new beginnings, at least five times in the past 500 million years.

6 The last of these was 65 million years ago, when a 10-kilometre asteroid whacked into the Yucatan in Mexico. The change now is less dramatic but no less significant. According to some theorists, half of all the creatures with which humans share the planet could be on the verge of extinction, about to steal away into the eternal night simply because their homes are being destroyed. By man. The world's dwindling tropical forests could be losing creatures at a conservative estimate of 27,000 a year – three creatures an hour. While the precision of these figures is disputed, the truth behind them is not. Crude counts confirm that

2 'Without them we cannot even begin arguing.' (para. 2) What does the writer suggest we should be arguing about?
   A the number of different species we are destroying
   B the chances of species surviving in different places
   C the difference between laboratory experiments and the real world
   D the work that should be done by taxonomists

(HINT: *This question tests both reference – who or what does 'them' refer to in the sentence quoted – and implication. For both these you need to look back through paragraph 2.*)

many of the big mammal groups and a tenth of all flowering plants could be about to disappear, and a tenth of all birds on the planet are seriously endangered. But 99 per cent of creation is less than 3 mm long. Most of the smaller species will be gone before scientists ever find out they were here.

7 There is a case for biodiversity: everyone recognises it. A landscape without birds and wild flowers is poorer. There could also be billions of dollars worth of useful, exploitable knowledge to be gained from almost unknown creatures. Why do barnacles not grow on starfish? Because the starfish secrete a natural anti-fouling paint. Why do arctic fish not freeze? Because they have an antifreeze fluid to keep blood circulating. Last year Cornell scientists calculated that if humans had to pay for the services they received free from nature – pollination, water purification, crop pest control, that sort of thing – the bill would be $2.9 million million annually.

8 Our fellow creatures are a kind of map of creation. Their preservation is clearly both a duty and a matter of naked human self-interest. But biodiversity cannot be preserved unless it can be understood, and it cannot be understood unless its components are identified. In the meantime, our massacre of these species could have baleful consequences for Planet Earth.

* *e.g. crabs, spiders, insects*

3 One drawback of the first inventories of species was that
   A lack of cross-checking led to inaccurate figures.
   B language problems led to confusion over names.
   C the same species were recorded in different countries.
   D different species were sometimes classified as similar.

(HINT: *Several answers may be true on their own but only one completes the stem correctly.*)

4 What is the writer's main point in paragraph 4?
   A Most new species are in remote parts of the world.
   B Research procedures may damage the environment.
   C The majority of species are still to be classified.
   D Some species have been insufficiently studied.

(HINT: *This question tests your understanding of implication. All the statements could be true, but only one develops the line of argument.*)

5 What does the writer say in paragraphs 5 and 6 about the 'sixth great extinction'?
   A It is part of a natural cycle.
   B It is more serious than the previous one.
   C It threatens the survival of the human race.
   D It is destroying known and unknown species.

(HINT: *Do not allow your own opinions to mislead you. You need to check carefully to find out what is wrong with the three distractors.*)

6 Why does the writer mention starfish and arctic fish in paragraph 7?
   A They are threatened by pollution.
   B They benefit the environment without costing anything.
   C They have features which humans could exploit.
   D They are examples of biodiversity.

(HINT: *In this type of question, all the answers could be true, but only one reflects the writer's purpose in this part of the text. Which explanation gives the general point that the writer is making?*)

7 What is the general tone of this article?
   A concerned   B objective   C critical   D despairing

(HINT: *Here you need to think about the overall impression given of the writer's attitude to the topic. Remember that you are evaluating the writer's attitude, not your own. You should consider both the content and the language used.*)

Exam Strategy

- Remember that the questions are in the same order as the information in the text.
- Don't be distracted by your own opinions or knowledge of the subject: the questions can all be answered from information given in the text.
- Don't be put off by new words. Ignore them if they aren't important, or use the context to work out the meaning.

Language Focus: Vocabulary

1 Style and register

You may find it useful to refer to the table on page 62 for the following exercises.

Find words and phrases in the text on pages 98–99 which mean the same as the words in italics in the following sentences. Are the words in the text formal, informal or literary?

1 The fish is not something you would miss if you were *searching* for it. (para. 1)
2 How could something so large *quietly disappear* without being missed? (two expressions – paras. 1 and 6)
3 Diversity is life's *biggest advantage*. (para. 2)
4 There are only about 7,000 taxonomists *who can tell one species from another*. (para. 2)
5 When the researchers reached 50,000, they started to get alarmed: *according to these calculations*, there might be 20 million species to be described. (para. 4)
6 But taxonomists *are worried by something more serious* than the task of counting. (para. 5)
7 Species are continuously *developing, growing and dying*. (para. 5)
8 65 million years ago a 10-kilometre asteroid *hit* the Yucatan in Mexico. (para. 6)
9 *Not everyone agrees these numbers are accurate.* (para. 6)
10 The result of this rapid loss of species could *be extremely serious* for the planet. (para. 8)

2 Word formation

1 Find the following words in the text. What part of speech (noun, verb or adjective) is each word in the text? What other forms of the word are possible?

1 grows (para. 1)
2 diversity (para. 2)
3 nutrients (para. 2)
4 distinguish (para. 2)
5 habitation (para. 3)
6 verge (para. 6)
7 precision (para. 6)
8 exploitable (para. 7)

2 Use an appropriate form of each word to complete the sentences below.

1 It is difficult to make .... measurements of the numbers of endangered species.
2 It should be possible to .... the riches of nature without destroying it in the process.
3 Many species may seem .... from one another to the non-specialist.
4 Most parts of Europe were once .... by wolves and bears.
5 The gradual .... of species is a process which has occurred over millions of years.
6 Their claim that we shall soon have classified all existing species .... on the ridiculous.
7 Warm, damp conditions may encourage the .... of harmful bacteria.
8 Young children need .... food if they are to grow up strong and healthy.

3 Fixed phrases: with prepositions

Fixed prepositional phrases may be tested in Paper 1 and in Paper 3. Look out for such phrases in your reading and make a note of them.

1 Rewrite the following sentences using the phrase in brackets. Make all the necessary changes to the rest of the sentence. Remember that if a verb follows a preposition, it will always be in the *-ing* form.

1 Half of all the creatures on the planet are about to become extinct. (*on the verge of*)
2 The bear has been wiped out in most countries of the European Union other than France and Spain. (*with the exception of*)
3 The government is setting up more nature reserves to try to save the remnant populations of these animals. (*in the hope of*)
4 He got the job because he had had so much experience with animals. (*on the strength of*)
5 The government does not understand what ordinary citizens need or want. (*out of tune with*)
6 With her tutor's help, she came to be recognised as a leading talent in her field. (*under the guidance of*)

2 Now rewrite these sentences. This time you only have the key word.

1 Fair-skinned people are more likely to get skin cancer from over-exposure to the sun. (*risk*)
2 The charity appeal did very well. (*response*)
3 The police suspected that he had broken into the building, and arrested him. (*suspicion*)
4 High production rates are often achieved only when the quality of the work is reduced. (*expense*)
5 Mary was short and plump, and was very different from her mother, who was tall and willowy. (*contrast*)
6 The medal was awarded to the retiring mayor for his services to the town. (*recognition*)

Listening

▶ Paper 4, Part 2

1   Read the following headlines. What do you think the problem is?

END OF A WAY OF LIFE

COD WARS INTENSIFY

What happened to all the fish?

2   You will hear a radio documentary about fishing. Before you listen, read the gapped sentences below. What do you think the programme will focus on?

In the past, the sea around Cape Bonavista was .... (1) in the world.

Since 1992, ... (2) has been almost completely forbidden.

Bill was unhappy about the effect of the distant water fleets on .... (3) levels.

One effect of the new methods of fishing was that .... (4) were damaged.

Now the traditional .... (5) is rapidly disappearing.

Fish farming does not help numbers of .... (6) to return to their former levels.

Another fishing community is surviving by using a scheme which involves .... (7) the fish.

This scheme allows enough fish to swim up the river and .... (8).

During an 'opening', ... (9) is permitted in the bay.

3   Now listen and complete the sentences with a word or short phrase. Your answers must fit the grammatical structure of the sentence.

4   Listen again to complete and check your answers. Finally, check that what you have written is grammatically correct and that you haven't made any spelling mistakes.

5   What does the report you have just heard suggest about our ability to reverse the pattern of extinctions of the last 1,000 years? Do you agree?

6   Say it again

Re-express the following sentences from the Listening text, using the framework given.

1   The traditional life of the local fishermen is soon going to be a thing of the past.
   The local fishermen are ....
   .... of life.

2   The local people have come up with an answer.
   The problem ....
   the local people.

3   When the salmon are ready to reproduce they come to the river mouth.
   The salmon ....
   about to reproduce.

4   The decline of the world's fisheries is not inevitable.
   It is possible for us ....
   declining.

Language Focus: Grammar
Conditionals (2)

1 Hypothetical conditions

These may refer to the past, present or future. The hypothetical result does not always relate to the same time period as the condition.

1 Read the examples below and underline the verb forms. Think about what time period – past, present or future – each refers to.

1 If government fishing quotas had been observed, fish stocks would not have collapsed.
2 If humans had to pay for the services they received free from nature, the bill would be $2.9 billion annually. (text, p. 99)
3 If efforts hadn't been made to protect wild salmon stocks at Bristol Bay, Alaska, the salmon industry would no longer exist today.
4 If mankind were less shortsighted, we would not have done so much damage to the environment.
5 More species might have become extinct if environmental groups were not so active.

2 Which sentences have:

a) an *if*-clause referring to the present, and a result in the present?
b) an *if*-clause referring to the past, and a result in the past?
c) an *if*-clause referring to universal time (past/present/future), and a result in the past? (two examples)
d) an *if*-clause referring to the past, and a result in the present?

▶ Grammar reference p. 219

2

1 Think of as many **present** results as you can for each of the following hypothetical past conditions.

1 If the sea had not been over-fished, ...
... *stocks* **would still** *be abundant.*
... *species which feed on fish* **would not be threatened.**
2 If the car had not been invented, ...
....
3 If I'd been born ten years earlier, ...
....
4 If it hadn't been for my parents, I ....
....

2 Think of as many **past** results as you can for each of the following hypothetical conditions.

1 If species such as the panda or elephant were less appealing, ...
... *less effort* **would have been** *put into saving them.*
... *they* **might have become** *extinct by now.*
2 If people had a greater awareness of environmental problems, we wouldn't have
....
3 If I were Prime Minister/President of my country, I would have ....
....
4 If I were rich, ...
....

3 Open conditions

These describe events that are a real possibility. Various verb forms are possible, and time references can be mixed, as with hypothetical conditions.

1 Underline the verb forms in each clause in the following sentences and complete the notes.

1 If something the size of a barn door *could* slip away without being missed, the fate of little-known species *is likely to be* worse. (*could* + future)
2 If you stand on the tip of Cape Bonavista, Newfoundland today, you can look out on the remnants of the richest fishery on Earth. (present + ...)
3 If the world's waters are pure for humans to drink but contain no fish, then we haven't really solved our environmental problems. (........................ + ...)
4 If we are to avoid the catastrophic effects of global warming, we must take action now. (........................ + ...)
5 In the past, if men didn't find animals to kill, they went hungry. (........................ + ...)
6 If it will help, I will join an environmental group. (........................ + ...)

▶ Grammar reference p. 219

2 Which of the completions a)–c) are grammatically possible? Tick all the possible options.

1 If people continue to hunt tigers,
   a) they will have become extinct in ten years.
   b) our children may never see one.
   c) they must have died out by now.
2 If prehistoric tribes chose to settle in villages,
   a) they would have been able to grow crops.
   b) they couldn't survive by hunting alone.
   c) they needed to domesticate animals.
3 If he went to the meeting yesterday,
   a) we'll hear all about it tomorrow.
   b) he had heard the news.
   c) he's probably still considering what to do.
4 If you'll bring some food to the party,
   a) I can do the rest.
   b) you'll have done your share.
   c) I'll bring something to drink.
5 If you're going to make a fuss,
   a) we won't do it.
   b) we've done something about it.
   c) we'd better not do it.

4 Inverted conditionals

Read the following sentences. Which of the versions in each group a) sounds more formal b) makes the event sound more unlikely?

1 a) If you see a rhino, ...
   b) If you should see a rhino, ...
   c) Should you see a rhino, ...
   ... run for your life
2 a) If we had realised the danger, ...
   b) Had we realised the danger, ...
   ... we would never have gone there.
3 a) If you study the proposals carefully, ...
   b) If you were to study the proposals carefully, ...
   c) Were you to study the proposals carefully, ...
   ... you might notice some technical problems.

► Grammar reference p. 220

5 Implied conditions

The following sentences illustrate other ways of expressing conditions. Underline the structures or expressions introducing the conditional clause, then rewrite the sentences using *if*.

1 Destroy the processes of nature, and you can expect untold damage to the world we inhabit.
2 Suppose we could see into the future, would that shock us into changing our behaviour?
3 I'm prepared to go along with the idea, as long as you promise not to tell anyone.
4 But for his intervention, the situation would have got much worse.
5 Assuming that you are reasonably fit, you should be able to go on the walk.
6 You shouldn't have any problems, provided you've got the instruction booklet.
7 I hope they take credit cards – otherwise I'll have to find a bank.
8 Don't move an inch, or I'll shoot!
9 Without government action, unemployment will continue to rise.

► Grammar reference p. 220

6 Use of English: Paper 3, Part 4

Complete the second sentence with three to eight words so that it has a similar meaning to the first sentence, using the word given. Do not change the word given.

1 If the traffic isn't too heavy, we should get there in an hour. **provided**
   It should only ....
   .... the traffic isn't too heavy.
2 You can expect years of low-cost heating for your house if you invest in our new solar powered system. **look**
   Invest in our new solar powered system ....
   ....
   years of low-cost heating for your house.
3 If it hadn't been for the bad weather, we'd have made a lot more money. **profit**
   We'd have ....
   .... it not been for the bad weather.
4 There might be trouble if you let anyone know that information. **yourself**
   You'd better ....
   .... there might be trouble.
5 If his friends hadn't helped him, he'd never have managed. **without**
   He'd never ....
   .... his friends.

Listening

▶ Paper 4, Part 1

1 Read the information and answer the questions below.

The WWF (World Wide Fund For Nature) and Greenpeace are well-known environmental campaign groups in the UK. The WWF was established as the World Wildlife Fund in 1961 to raise funds from the public for conservation of particular species, for example the Giant Panda, and habitats. Greenpeace is an international environmental pressure group, operating a policy of non-violent direct action supported by scientific research.

What similar environmental campaign groups exist in your country? What are their aims? What kind of activities are they involved in? Are you a member of such a group? Why/Why not?

2 You will hear four different extracts about the environment. There are two questions for each. Before you listen to each extract, look through the questions to get an idea of the focus of that extract. (In the exam, the extracts will be on different themes.)

Listen to each extract and choose the answer (**A**, **B** or **C**) which fits best according to what you hear. Then listen again to complete and check your answers.

Extract One

You hear part of an interview with a member of an environmental group.

1 The speaker says that one of her group's achievements has been to
   A give out information.
   B make companies more responsible.
   C reduce levels of toxic waste.

2 The overall attitude of the speaker is
   A positive.
   B encouraging.
   C patronising.

Extract Two

You hear two friends talking about different ways of protecting the environment.

3 What do the speakers disagree about?
   A the importance of recycling
   B public understanding of environmental problems
   C the effects of using public transport

4 What is the woman's attitude towards saving fuel?
   A It's as effective as recycling.
   B It has other advantages.
   C It's easy to do.

Extract Three

You hear part of a lecture about the effects of a green project in a developing country.

5 The speaker suggests that the project failed because
   A the farmers depended too much on technology.
   B the wrong type of crop was grown.
   C the land was farmed too intensively.

6 What was the long-term effect of the irrigation project?
   A Poor farmers suffered the most.
   B Rice could no longer be grown.
   C Rich farmers lost all their money.

Extract Four

You hear part of a television advertisement for a charity organisation.

7 What does the advertisement ask people to do?
   A Join a large organisation.
   B Give money regularly.
   C Help the work of sponsors around the world.

8 The advertisement emphasises how much
   A the children are suffering.
   B money is needed.
   C effect sponsorship can have.

3 Say it again

Re-express the following sentences from the Listening text, using the framework given.

1 We've made far more progress than anyone would have predicted.
   No-one would ....
   .... progress.

2 The companies are not only responsible to their shareholders, but to society in general.
   The companies are responsible to ....
   .... their shareholders.

3 If we recycle paper, fewer trees will be cut down.
   As ....
   .... trees will be saved.

4 The output of rice had almost tripled.
   They had produced ....
   .... rice as before.

Speaking

1   Selection

1   Work in pairs. Look at this list of practical measures which individuals can take to help preserve the environment and the world's natural resources. Discuss what each measure can achieve, then choose the five measures you feel are the most effective. Add at least one more idea of your own.

- recycle paper
- travel by public transport
- don't accept plastic packaging
- insist on organically produced food
- turn off the lights when you leave a room
- don't use disposable products
- ride a bicycle
- use natural ventilation instead of air conditioning

2   Now discuss how easy or difficult the measures above would be to bring into your life.

2

1   Work with a partner. Read the two prompt cards below and choose one each. Using the ideas that you discussed in Exercise 1 and the prompts on the card to help you with further ideas, plan a two-minute talk.

> What do you think people can do most easily to improve the environment?
>
> - financial constraints
> - time constraints
> - family constraints

> What changes should be made to people's lifestyles to safeguard our planet's future?
>
> - individual/governmental responsibility
> - trade/workplace
> - transport/energy

2   Listen to your partner's talk, and make comments. Then present your own talk to your partner.

3   Discuss the following questions.

1   What effect do you think countries working together could have on environmental issues?
2   What worries you most about the situation in your own country?
3   What do you feel most positive about? Why?

Use of English

▶ Paper 3, Part 1

1   Look at the picture. Do you know anything about the bird that's illustrated? Why do you think it is important?

2   Read the text to see if your ideas were right.

3   Fill each gap in the text with one suitable word.

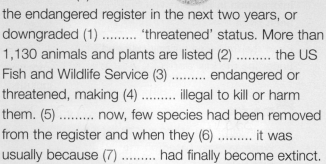

America's big bird is back

The American bald eagle is top of a list of recovering species which are likely either to be (0) *taken* off the endangered register in the next two years, or downgraded (1) .... 'threatened' status. More than 1,130 animals and plants are listed (2) .... the US Fish and Wildlife Service (3) .... endangered or threatened, making (4) .... illegal to kill or harm them. (5) .... now, few species had been removed from the register and when they (6) .... it was usually because (7) .... had finally become extinct.

As America's national bird, the bald eagle has been protected (8) *in* .... various ways since 1940. The eagle, (9) .... is not really bald but looks it because of the white feathers on its head, is found only in North America. It appears on the national coat of arms and on (10) .... sorts of everyday items, including the dollar bill, and has been the (11) .... of attention in the argument (12) .... the best way to protect endangered species. Its numbers had been reduced to (13) .... than 500 by the use of pesticides that affected (14) .... reproductive system, but (15) .... are now more than 5,000 nesting pairs in the continental US and the numbers are growing at 10 per cent a year.

Writing

▶ Paper 2, Part 1 (essay)

For the compulsory task in Paper 2, Part 1 you may be asked to write a discursive **essay**, based on information which will be provided in written form, possibly supported by diagrams. Depending on how the task is worded, you may need to:

- present both sides of an argument in a balanced discussion
- present one point of view, giving supporting evidence.

In this section you will see the best way to plan your writing and organise your ideas for presenting a balanced discussion.

1   You need to understand exactly what the question asks you to write about, and how to use the information in the text you have been given.

Read the following writing task and underline the key words.

TASK

Your tutor has asked you to write an essay based on the title below.

'Protecting the environment is the most important problem facing the world today.'
How far do you agree with this opinion?

(300–350 words)

To help you to focus your ideas, your tutor has given you part of an e-mail posted on the website of a radio station. It was written in response to a documentary broadcast by the station the previous week on medical advances.

---

2   Read the extract from the e-mail, and answer the questions below.

Subject: The world has lost its way

The world has lost its way. No-one seems to be addressing the real issues facing us today. Media companies like yours deal with the same 'fashionable' topics time after time – health and the latest medical discoveries, scares about the population – but these are muddying the waters and obscuring the central issue. Shouldn't you be devoting more air time to the real problem – how we can protect our environment?

1   Should you:
   a) write about all the different ways of protecting the environment?
   b) omit the environment and only write about the other problems facing the world today?
   c) discuss whether the environment or a different problem (or problems) is the most important in the world today?
2   What information from the e-mail do you need to use in your answer? What other global problems would you choose to include?

3

1   Read the following essay, which was written in answer to the task. What information has the writer used from the e-mail? What other issues has she included? Would you have chosen the same problems to write about?

2   Now answer these questions.

1   What is the purpose of the introduction? How has the writer attempted to draw the reader into the discussion?
2   In what order are the issues introduced?
3   Underline the linking expressions used in paragraphs 2, 3 and 4. Which organisational pattern has the writer used?
   a) a list of specific examples
   b) contrasting and conceding points
4   What is the writer's opinion about these issues in paragraphs 2, 3 and 4? How important does she consider them to be?
5   In what way(s) is the issue of the environment different, according to the writer?
6   The writer has discussed the issue that she considers most important last. What is the reason for this?
7   What is the purpose of the conclusion?

A

The modern world faces many major problems to which there are no easy solutions. These include unemployment, health, over-population and of course the environment. All have a bearing on all our lives, but is the environment really the most important?

If people are unemployed, they are unable to earn money and it is a fact of life that without an income it is difficult to live. Of course, work provides more than financial support; it gives people self-esteem and pride. Unfortunately, technological developments and other factors mean that the job market is shrinking world-wide and young people have reduced prospects for work. Although this is certainly a major threat to people's well-being, it needs to be addressed by individual governments rather than globally.

Health is clearly an important concern that affects both individuals and the planet as a whole. Even though many illnesses have been eradicated, others remain a threat, and the overuse of antibiotics has led to the development of resistant strains of bacteria. Nevertheless, on the whole, general health is improving, and in the developing countries medical aid programmes are already working towards creating a healthier population.

Over-population has implications for all of us, and improved general health means that people are living longer. However, as with health, there are already programmes in place implementing measures to deal with not only a rising population, but an ageing population.

So what about the environment? There are urgent issues that need to be faced, including global warming, pollution and the loss of species. Unlike the other issues discussed, there is no clearly discernible global move to deal with these problems. Also, unlike the other issues, changes in the environment have a direct impact on the whole planet. Climate change and destruction of ecosystems could endanger all life on the planet if not dealt with quickly and at an international level.

In conclusion, other problems primarily affect only the quality of life, whereas environmental issues affect the actual existence of life itself. It is clear, therefore, that protecting the environment is the most important problem facing the world today.

(348 words)

4 Read essay A again, and complete the following outline in note form.

Introduction
Statement of topic: *The world faces many problems.*
Plan of development: *Unemployment, health, over-population, environment.*

First supporting paragraph
Issue 1: *Unemployment*
Details: *Need work to live, for self-esteem; but local issue, not global.*

Second supporting paragraph
Issue 2: ....
Details: ....
....
....

Third supporting paragraph
Issue 3: ....
Details: ....
....
....

Fourth supporting paragraph
Issue 4: ....
Details: ....
....
....

Closing paragraph
Conclusion: ....
....
....

5

1   Now read the following extracts from another essay written in answer to the same task. In what way is the organisation of the essay different?

B

There are many important issues facing the world today, including unemployment, health and overpopulation. Whether these issues are more important than environmental problems is debatable.

The growth in unemployment is a serious problem world-wide. It has partly been caused by improvements in technology as well as changing economic factors, which together mean that the job market is shrinking. While unemployment can of course have a devastating effect on the quality of life of individuals, an environmental issue such as the burning of fossil fuels is potentially more serious. It has resulted in global warming, causing climate change which could threaten the existence of entire nations. Is full employment worth this risk?

From this it must be clear that protecting the environment is the most important issue facing the world today. We ignore it at our peril. If we look after the houses we live in as individuals, why do we not take care of the larger house we all share?

2   Now use information from essay A and your own ideas to complete the following outline of essay B.

Introduction
Statement of topic: *Many important issues facing world today.*
Plan of development: *Unemployment, health, over-population.*

First supporting paragraph
Issue 1: *Unemployment*
Details: ....
Environmental issue 1: ....

Second supporting paragraph
Issue 2: ....
Details: ....
Environmental issue 2: *Depletion of the ozone layer*

Third supporting paragraph
Issue 3: ....
Details: ....
Environmental issue 3: ....

Closing paragraph
Conclusion: ....

3   Both approaches are acceptable for an exam answer. However, one is more focused and more complex than the other. Decide which one, and give your reasons.

6

1   Read the following writing task.

TASK

Your tutor has asked you to write an essay based on the title below.
'Generally the future of mankind looks bright. Those who argue otherwise are being unnecessarily pessimistic.'
How far do you agree with this opinion?

(300–350 words)

To help you to focus your ideas, your tutor has given you an extract from a magazine article about the future.

So there is no point in trying to improve matters at this stage – it is too late. The march of technology, overpopulation, and environmental problems have all contributed to a downward spiral which is unstoppable. Some people may try to bury their heads in the sand and pretend that improvements in these areas have made a difference – but what evidence is there for this?

2   Underline the key words in the task.

3   Read the information in the magazine extract and decide what points you want to cover in your essay.

4   Jot down some ideas. What evidence can you think of to support your ideas?

5   Decide how to organise your essay and complete an outline based on essay A or B in Exercises 4 and 5.

7   Now write your essay, making sure that you support your ideas with plenty of evidence.

8   Exchange your essay with a partner. Evaluate each other's work. Use your partner's comments to help you improve your essay.

1 Rewrite the following sentences beginning with *If*. Make any changes necessary.

1 They built that chemical factory and our local river is now polluted.
2 Environmental scientists tested the water so people realised how dangerous it was.
3 The scientists published the results of their tests and prevented people from becoming ill.
4 The authorities might have ignored pollution hazards, had they seen the chance of creating jobs.
5 With authorities who refuse to investigate, it's up to us to find out the truth.
6 Clean up the environment and our quality of life will improve.

2 Use the word given in capitals to form a word that fits the gap.

1 It was difficult to provide accurate .... of all species. IDENTIFY
2 Man and nature are ...., totally dependent on each other. SEPARATE
3 Scientists are studying patterns of .... EVOLVE
4 A reliable system of .... was not easy to set up. CLASSIFY
5 Scientific reports are generally written in a very .... tone. PERSON
6 There may be some dangers that are not immediately .... APPEAR

3 Read the text below and decide which answer (**A**, **B**, **C** or **D**) best fits each gap.

It is a sad but true fact that only an environmental catastrophe will actually cause people to think about how they behave – and where their responsibilities (1) .... Merely selling 'green' items in trendy recycled paper bags with environmental logos clearly displayed will not do the (2) .... The problem is bigger than that. Many animals are already threatened as their traditional (3) .... disappears, and many valuable and interesting species are in (4) .... of becoming extinct. Naturalists are still battling to save (5) .... species, even though it is already too late for some, but they will be fighting a losing battle if they are not supported by the population as a whole. It is difficult to know how to (6) .... this message through to the people who most need to hear it.

1 **A** stay	**B** go	**C** lie	**D** stand
2 **A** work	**B** trick	**C** task	**D** duty
3 **A** ecosystem	**B** environment	**C** nature	**D** habitat
4 **A** risk	**B** danger	**C** verge	**D** brink
5 **A** endangered	**B** embattled	**C** imperilled	**D** jeopardised
6 **A** put	**B** reach	**C** get	**D** relay

4 This picture was suggested as the promotional poster advertising a TV documentary about conservation issues, but it was rejected. Talk about the issues raised by the picture, say why you think it was rejected, and suggest an alternative image for the poster.

8 A sporting chance

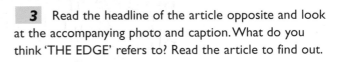

Language Focus: Vocabulary
Sport

1 Describe the activities shown in each photo. In what ways are the people involved taking risks?

2

1 Look at the lists of factors below. Choose the factors which are most and least important for each of the activities shown in the photos, giving reasons.

skill	mental qualities
muscular control	strong nerves
sense of balance	courage
co-ordination	determination
sense of timing	self-control
	trust
	sensitivity

technology	fitness
special clothing	regular training
and equipment	special diet
back-up support	individual fitness
safety checks	programme
	genetic traits
	individual body
	chemistry

2 Can you add any other factors which may be important?

3 Read the headline of the article opposite and look at the accompanying photo and caption. What do you think 'THE EDGE' refers to? Read the article to find out.

4

1 Find **one** phrase from the article which illustrates each of the following ideas.

- the skill of the windsurfer, e.g. '...*he swoops down the front of the wave*'
- the nerve of the windsurfer
- the quality of the technology and equipment involved

2 Match each of the verbs in the box below to one of the following subjects. Then check your answers by referring to the text.

a) the windsurfer   b) the sail   c) the sea

heaves	powers	accelerates
catapults	hums	leans
rises	snaps	spins
swoops	twists	splashes

3 Which verb(s) in the box suggest(s):

1 very rapid, powerful movement?
2 an upward movement?
3 a circular movement?
4 movement accompanied by sound?

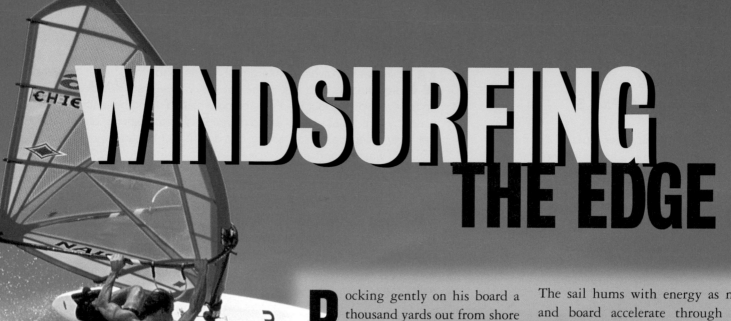

WINDSURFING
THE EDGE

Catapulted by wind and wave, a windsurfer experiences the thrill of staying in control aboard one of the most high-tech machines there is.

Rocking gently on his board a thousand yards out from shore on the blue-grey waters of the Pacific, Rich Foster is waiting for a wave. Or rather, the wave. Then the sea slowly heaves itself skyward, rising into a mountain of water. Foster leans well back into his harness and as his sail snaps into a tight aerodynamic curve, the wind's energy surges down through his body and into the shark-like board below.

To gain momentum, he swoops down the front of the wave, the nose of the board slicing through the water, and then turns back to power up the steepening cliff.

The sail hums with energy as man and board accelerate through the foamy wave-crest and catapult skyward. Day-Glo sail and board form a pyrotechnic display against the blue sky.

Foster spins and twists in the air, a quick barrel-roll before board and rider splash down safely into the sea to wait for the next wave. Once again he's escaped being thrown into the craggy embrace of the many rocks fringing this Hawaiian beach. For this is windsurfing at the edge: the edge of your skill, the edge of your nerve, and the cutting edge of technology.

---

5 Work with a partner.

1 Choose one of the photos you discussed in Exercise 1. Use some of the verbs in the box below to help you describe more accurately the type of movement or activity involved.

dive	drive	flash	grasp	hurtle
leap	plummet	shoot	spin	strike
sweep	swerve	wheel	whirl	strain

2 Write a caption for your photo similar to the one used with the picture of the windsurfer. Use these prompts to help you.

Photo 1: nerves/to the limit/racing cyclist/into a corner/last lap/gruelling race

Photo 2: heart pound/striker/swerve round defender/shoot into net/best goal/season

Photo 3: grasp partner/under arms/lift/whirl round/fast spin

6 Interview a partner about his/her attitudes to sport and risk, using these questions as a guide.

1 What is your favourite sport, either as a spectator or participant?

2 What skills and training does it need? Is any special equipment required? Which of the factors in Exercise 2 are most important?

3 What do you think are the main benefits of sport?
- builds team spirit
- provides the chance of fame and fortune
- builds confidence
- promotes health and fitness

4 What do you think is the attraction of sports that are physically dangerous?

5 What drives some people to push themselves to 'the edge' of their skill and nerve?

Reading
▶ **Paper 1, Part 3**

1   What other types of risk may people take in addition to sport? Which of the following high-risk activities do you think you might like to try one day? Which would you never want to try? Why?

- riding on a 'state-of-the-art' roller-coaster
- exploring an undeveloped area of the world
- gambling on the stock exchange
- resigning from a safe job to set up your own business

2   You are going to read an extract from a book written by a young couple who recently travelled by canoe up a remote river in South America. The extract is narrated by the woman.
Why might the following qualities be needed for such an expedition? Can you suggest any more?

- ability to keep your head in a crisis
- a sense of humour
- physical strength
- a high level of fitness

3   Read the text quickly and answer the following questions. Do not look at the jumbled paragraphs on page 113 yet.

1   What is the main event described in the text?
2   Are the events described in chronological order? If not, how are they ordered?

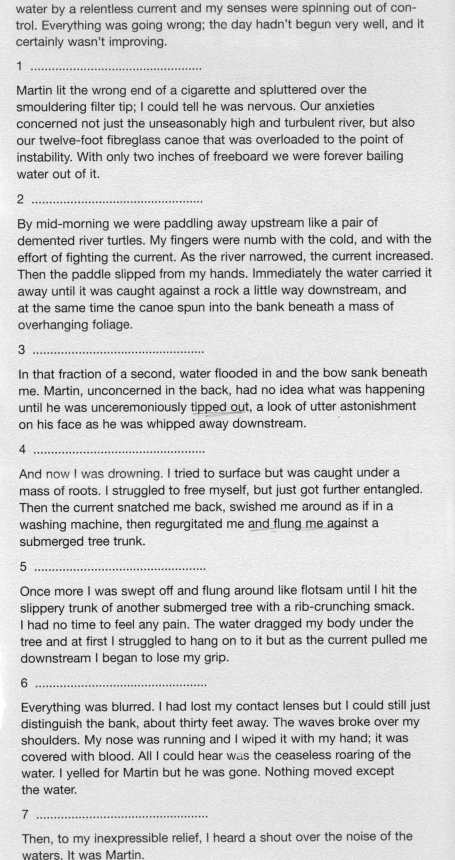

While I was drowning I thought of Martin, and wondered if he were drowning as well. But in the urgency of my predicament there was no time to worry about it – I was being whisked along beneath murky water by a relentless current and my senses were spinning out of control. Everything was going wrong; the day hadn't begun very well, and it certainly wasn't improving.

1 ....

Martin lit the wrong end of a cigarette and spluttered over the smouldering filter tip; I could tell he was nervous. Our anxieties concerned not just the unseasonably high and turbulent river, but also our twelve-foot fibreglass canoe that was overloaded to the point of instability. With only two inches of freeboard we were forever bailing water out of it.

2 ....

By mid-morning we were paddling away upstream like a pair of demented river turtles. My fingers were numb with the cold, and with the effort of fighting the current. As the river narrowed, the current increased. Then the paddle slipped from my hands. Immediately the water carried it away until it was caught against a rock a little way downstream, and at the same time the canoe spun into the bank beneath a mass of overhanging foliage.

3 ....

In that fraction of a second, water flooded in and the bow sank beneath me. Martin, unconcerned in the back, had no idea what was happening until he was unceremoniously tipped out, a look of utter astonishment on his face as he was whipped away downstream.

4 ....

And now I was drowning. I tried to surface but was caught under a mass of roots. I struggled to free myself, but just got further entangled. Then the current snatched me back, swished me around as if in a washing machine, then regurgitated me and flung me against a submerged tree trunk.

5 ....

Once more I was swept off and flung around like flotsam until I hit the slippery trunk of another submerged tree with a rib-crunching smack. I had no time to feel any pain. The water dragged my body under the tree and at first I struggled to hang on to it but as the current pulled me downstream I began to lose my grip.

6 ....

Everything was blurred. I had lost my contact lenses but I could still just distinguish the bank, about thirty feet away. The waves broke over my shoulders. My nose was running and I wiped it with my hand; it was covered with blood. All I could hear was the ceaseless roaring of the water. I yelled for Martin but he was gone. Nothing moved except the water.

7 ....

Then, to my inexpressible relief, I heard a shout over the noise of the waters. It was Martin.

4 Now choose from the paragraphs **A–H** the one which fits each gap. There is one extra paragraph which you do not need to use. Underline the sections of the text which helped you to decide on the order.

A

It wasn't meant to be like this. One of us wasn't supposed to die. It was just another trip, like the others. It was supposed to be fun, an adventure. That's what we did it for, wasn't it? It was dangerous of course, and we'd often talked about getting killed. Usually we joked about it, confident it wouldn't happen to us.

B

I hung onto a branch, water up to my chest. I caught a fleeting glimpse of brightly-coloured equipment floating away, then the branch broke and I was sucked under water.

C

'Let's put our lifejackets on,' said Martin, and I was eager to comply. Lifejackets were things we normally used as pillows: sometimes we inflated them to sit on; this day, well into our fourth South American river trip, would be the first occasion we'd used them for their intended purpose.

D

The single overwhelming need was to get my head out of the water and breathe again. Surfacing briefly I managed it, seeing at the same time that I was a long way from the bank. Back in the depths, brilliant blue lights flashed in my head before I surfaced again, this time to discover that my lifejacket was now so tightly wrapped around my neck and face that I could see nothing.

E

The next thing I saw was the canoe floating upside-down next to me. I clutched at it, trying to right it. It turned, but with a mass of slimy green muck on it, and sank under the weight.

F

Then, driven by fear, I made a last effort and hauled myself up onto the tree to a position of relative safety, with my head and shoulders above water and my legs wrapped tightly round the trunk, and looked around.

G

Unfortunately we'd parked in a residential area and the alligator whose exit we'd blocked chose that moment to emerge, suddenly and violently like a cannon-ball shooting out straight under the boat, tipping it sideways.

H

Early that morning, in the second week of our journey, we'd emerged from our jungle camp to survey the river. Downstream stretched the miles of rapids and fast water we'd struggled up the previous day. Upstream there was no visible end to more of the same.

5 The writer uses carefully chosen words to describe her feelings and sensations during the canoe accident.

1 Find six verbs in the paragraphs beginning *And now I was drowning* and *Once more I was swept off* which have the current or the water as their subject. What do all these verbs have in common?

2 Choose the word that gives the most dramatic effect in the sentences below. Justify your choice.

1 The boat *spun/went* into the bank.
2 The water was *dark/murky*.
3 I was *pulled/sucked* under the water.
4 I *tried/struggled* to hang on.
5 I *hauled/pulled* myself up.
6 All I could hear was the *noise/roaring* of the water.
7 Then, to my *great/inexpressible* relief, I heard a shout.

6 Although this extract describes a dangerous and frightening situation, the writer occasionally uses irony and humour to make her point.

1 Find a phrase in the opening paragraph where understatement is used ironically.

2 Find two examples in the rest of the text (main section and paragraphs A–H) where the writer adds humour by using images or expressions which would be more appropriate in an urban setting.

Exam Focus
▶ **Paper 3, Part 3**

In Paper 3, Part 3 you are given six sets of three separate sentences, each with one gap. For each set, you have to find one word which can fill all three gaps. The word will always be in the same form and will always be used as the same part of speech.

This question tests your knowledge of collocations. There will be more than one possible answer for each individual sentence but only one word will be possible in all the three gaps. You should check your answer carefully with all three sentences. Never base your answer on only one sentence.

The best way to prepare for this question is to record vocabulary in phrases rather than single words.

1

1   Read this example. What part of speech is the missing word? Can you guess what the word might be?

I got a lot of .... out of that coat.
The carpet is showing signs of ....
The shop has a new range of casual .... for men and women.

2   Now look at the dictionary definition on page 236 and check your answer.

3   Underline the three sections in the dictionary definition that relate to the three sentences. How many other uses can this word have?

2   Think of one word only which can be used appropriately in all three sentences.

Here is a procedure to follow for this task.

- Read through the three sentences. If you think of a possible word to fill the gaps, do not write anything until you have read all the sentences and you are sure that it fits all three contexts.
- If you cannot immediately think of a suitable word, check what part of speech is required, e.g. noun, verb or adjective. You will probably already know the main meaning of the word, but you may not recognise it immediately in these contexts. Look carefully at the other words in the sentence and see if they suggest any collocations.
- If you still can't think of a possible word, leave the question and go back to it later.

1   She really wanted him to join the company and she got her .... – though later she regretted it.
The registry office and the hotel where the reception was to take place were a long .... apart, so we had to organise transport.
Gloria thought that working as a make-up artist might be a .... of getting into films.

2   I'm sorry, I didn't .... what you said – could you repeat it, please?
They tried as hard as they could, but didn't manage to .... up with Susie and her friends.
As she sorted out the children's clothes, she would sometimes .... herself wishing she was somewhere else entirely.

3   My grandmother was strict, but the advice she gave me was always ...., and I did my best to follow it.
She tossed and turned for several hours and then towards morning she fell into a .... sleep.
The bodywork of the car appears to be quite ...., but the engine definitely needs replacing.

4   She's .... to find out about it one day – we can't keep it a secret forever.
He was legally .... to report to the police once a week, but did not always fulfil this requirement.
The planes .... for the disaster zone were well equipped with medicine and supplies.

5   When she picked the rose, a thorn went into the .... of her thumb, and she fell into a deep sleep.
Can you look in the top drawer in the kitchen and see if you can find a .... of string?
Her parents had arranged a formal .... for her eighteenth birthday, although she'd have preferred to go to a club.

6   The sailors feared the storm would .... before they got safely back to harbour again.
If we have a cheap holiday this year then we won't have to .... into our savings.
I don't expect the news of the discovery will .... for a few more days.

3   How many of the words above would be the same in all three contexts in your own language?

4   Now work in pairs. You are going to make up similar questions for one another.

Student A look at page 237.
Student B look at page 239.

▶ Exam Maximiser

Language Focus: Grammar
Emphasis

1 The words *so* and *such* can be used to intensify adjectives and nouns.

1 In informal contexts, *so* and *such* are stressed, and the sentences have the force of exclamations. Say these sentences aloud with the appropriate stress.

1 It was **such** a relief to know he was safe.
2 The party was **such** fun!
3 The results were **so** disappointing, weren't they?
4 I'm **so** worried about the test.

2 More formally, *so* and *such* are used with clauses of result, as in the following examples.

1 The hotel was so noisy that I couldn't sleep.
2 His performance was so impressive that they offered him the leading role.
3 She felt such anger that she was unable to speak.
4 He gave such a moving speech that the audience was in tears.

2 We can make sentences 1–4 in Exercise 1.2 above more emphatic by using inversion. More than one alternative is possible. Complete the sentences below, which show the different options.

Sentence 1
a) So .... was the hotel ...
b) Such was the .... in the hotel ...
... that I could not sleep.

Sentence 2
a) So .... was his performance ...
b) So .... a performance did he give ...
c) So .... were they by his performance ...
... that they offered him the leading role.

Sentence 3
a) Such .... did she feel ...
b) So .... did she feel ...
... that she was unable to speak.

Sentence 4
a) Such ....
b) So ....
c) So ....
... that the audience was in tears.

What do you notice about the use of *a* in the sentences you have completed?

► Grammar reference pp. 220–221

Use of English

1 Look at the photo. Describe the situation. How do you think the person is feeling?

2 The extract below was written by a climber who had to make an important decision during a difficult climb. Read the text, ignoring the gaps for the moment. What decision did he have to make and what effect did it have on him?

The Fight for the Summit

At 1.30 on May 12 1988, the British mountaineer Stephen Venables was confronted (0) ..*with*.... an agonising dilemma. (1) .... an epic, month-long ascent of the Kangshung face of Everest, he had reached the final staging point before the summit itself. He was hours (2) .... schedule, close to exhaustion and utterly alone, his companions (3) .... fallen far behind. He knew that (4) .... he did decide to push (5) ..*on*...., he would have to (6) .... a night on the mountainside in plunging temperatures, (7) .... frostbite almost inevitable and his very survival (8) .... stake.

As he wondered (9) .... to continue or turn back, Venables saw the final section of the summit ridge, recognising it (10) .... the photograph taken by the (11) .... climbers ever to reach the summit during the British ascent in 1953. Venables later said that (12) .... was the mythology of the place and a chance to become part of it (13) .... willed him on. He arrived on the summit two hours later, waiting just ten minutes (14) .... starting his descent. He (15) .... indeed suffer frostbite, and almost died as he struggled back to base camp. Later he had three toes amputated – but resolved to carry on climbing.

3 Fill each of the numbered blanks in the text with one suitable word. Then read the completed text again to check that it makes sense. Compare and justify your answers with a partner.

4 Can you think of a time when you had to make an important decision that could have had serious consequences? Tell the class about it.

Speaking

 1

1 Look at the list below of people who can benefit from involvement in sport. Choose two groups of people from the list and discuss:

- what their involvement might be
- how they benefit
- how their involvement can be increased.

young children   investors   manufacturers
professional sportsmen and women   sponsors
scientists   fans   spectators

2 Choose two more groups and discuss how they may be exploited through their involvement in sport. Discuss:

- who exploits them
- how this is done
- how this exploitation could be reduced or prevented.

 2

1 Read the prompt card below. Discuss what ideas you could use in a talk in answer to the question. Then plan your talk, using the prompts to help you if necessary.

> How far do the benefits of being involved in sport outweigh the disadvantages?
>
> - types of involvement
> - types of sport
> - social issues

2 Practise your talk with a partner.

Listening

▶ Paper 4, Part 3

1 Simon Clifford taught at a primary school in the north of England. Then his career took a surprising turn. Before you listen, read through the statements and options and discuss what you think happened.

1 Simon felt that the Brazilian players he saw
   A were very skilful.
   B played fairly.
   C were surprisingly unconcerned about money.
   D adapted well to new situations.

2 How did Simon get money for his visit to Brazil?
   A from teaching
   B from football coaching
   C from his publisher
   D from a bank

3 'Football of the hall' developed
   A through the influence of an Englishman.
   B in order to make use of handball courts.
   C because of lack of space.
   D to allow more intensive practice.

4 What affects the type of training in Brazil?
   A The ball doesn't bounce.
   B The ball is heavier.
   C The ball is easier to kick.
   D The ball is easier to pass accurately.

5 Simon is determined that soon Brazilian training methods will
   A be adopted by professionals.
   B lead to major changes in the game.
   C become policy in England.
   D be used by English children.

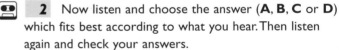 **2** Now listen and choose the answer (**A, B, C** or **D**) which fits best according to what you hear. Then listen again and check your answers.

3 Say it again

Re-express these sentences from the Listening text, using the framework given.

1 He happened to be sitting in the row behind me.
   Quite ....
   .... sitting in the row behind me.
2 It doesn't have the same bounce.
   It .... way.
3 We've got the book under way.
   We've .... already.

Language Focus: Vocabulary
Phrasal verbs and idioms

1 Phrasal verbs with *take*

The verb *take* is used to form a number of phrasal verbs. What does the phrasal verb in this sentence mean?

- *Football **took over** his life.*
  (Listening text)

Fill in the missing particle in the following sentences and explain the meaning of each phrasal verb.

1 Training took .... so much of his time that his social life suffered.
2 I listened to the speech carefully but I still couldn't take it ....
3 Were you really taken .... by that old trick?
4 Glen has taken .... painting now that he has more spare time.
5 Her career really took .... after she was spotted by a talent scout.
6 Does he realise how much extra responsibility he's taken .... in his new job?
7 The old cinema has taken .... a new lease of life since its renovation.
8 I took .... Paul as soon as I met him.

2 Fixed phrases with *take*

Rewrite the following sentences using the word given as part of a phrase with *take*. Use the pattern verb + noun + preposition.

1 Students are encouraged to participate in as many activities as possible.   **part**
....

2 The report was rewritten to include the new evidence.   **account**
....

3 I disagree with your analysis of the causes.   **issue**
....

4 She felt sorry for the children walking in the rain and gave them a lift to school.
    pity
....

5 The weather was good so she painted the shed.   **advantage**
....

3 Phrasal verbs used metaphorically

Phrasal verbs frequently have a metaphorical meaning which may be related to the original meaning of the verb, as in this example.

- *I decided to **branch out** from teaching and start up my own business.* (Listening text)

What usually 'branches'? What do you think the phrasal verb means? In each of the sentences below, underline the phrasal verb. Then decide which of the phrases in italics fits the meaning of the verb.

1 The sports authorities didn't exactly <u>bend over</u> *backwards/ a long way* to help him.
2 The New Zealand rugby player Jason Lamba has bounced back *after a serious illness/and retired from the game*.
3 I leapt at *the chance/the hope* to get a ticket for the match.
4 The government played down *the danger of war/the members of the opposition*.
5 All the family rallied round *to help us/to get what they could from us*.
6 Your report skates over the main issues, instead of *ignoring them/discussing them in depth*.
7 They stumbled over the answer *quite by chance/as the result of years of work*.
8 It's too big a job for us to tackle on our own – let's try to rope in *our plans/some of our friends*.

4 Read the text below and decide which answer (**A, B, C** or **D**) best fits each gap.

New ideas achieve
dramatic turnaround

After the team lost three games, the manager signed up a new coach who (1) .... an ingenious method for improving the players' fitness – he brought (2) .... a system of rewards for good performance. Before any kind of exercise athletes do special exercises to warm (3) .... The coach made these exercises competitive, setting the players against each other head to head. The club was able to (4) .... a deal with the sponsors of the team to provide prizes for the winners, for which the sponsors themselves would (5) .... the bill. The new approach worked like a dream. In next to no (6) .... there was a dramatic improvement in the team's results. The coach himself gained such a good reputation from his methods that he was head-hunted by another club and moved on to further his career. ■

	A	B	C	D
1	hit upon	hit out	struck up	struck off
2	in	about	through	on
3	down	in	up	through
4	hit	thrash	knock	strike
5	stand	foot	shoulder	bear
6	time	period	term	moment

Use of English

▶ **Paper 3, Part 5**

1

1   You are going to read two texts about the use of drugs to improve performance in sport. Before you read the texts, decide which of these statements you agree with. Give your reasons.

'There have been such wonderful advances in technology, training techniques and diet that athletes should make use of as many as they can. It's only common sense.'

'Sportspeople should rely only on their own natural biology and physiology. If they use any other aids, they are cheating and not competing fairly.'

2   Now read through the two texts quickly. Are they giving similar or opposite points of view? Which writer has similar views to your own?

2   Read text 1 again carefully and answer the questions with a word or short phrase.

1   What does the writer feel is the key to progress in sport?
2   What phrase used later in the text has a similar meaning to 'a sport of immense attrition'? (line 24)

3   Read through text 2 and answer these questions in the same way.

1   Explain the significance of 'a level playing field' (line 26) in this context.
2   What idea in the last paragraph illustrates the final point that using drugs is cheating?

4   Think back to your discussion of the statements in Exercise 1. Discuss these questions.

1   Have the arguments put forward in the texts caused you to change your mind?
2   Can you think of any further arguments for your point of view?
3   Can you think of any situations in which the opposite point of view might be justifiable?

Text 1

"The debate falls into the same category as recreational drugs. From the Prime Minister down we are forbidden to discuss such things. Everybody just goes around in a state of ignorance without the requisite research or education. The great danger at the moment is not to professionals – who are, on the whole, well looked after – but kids going into cycle races who might feel it is OK to take a bit of EPO (Erythropoietin, which increases the oxygen absorbed in the blood) with no idea of what it is. That's why I feel the high moral tone everyone takes is not actually helping anyone.

As for the argument that it ruins sport, that is totally unrealistic. Do we want to go back to the Olympic ideal as represented in the film *Chariots of Fire*? No. People don't want sport to grind on at the same level. Technology in every sense, in training and nutrition, has come a long way since then and using it makes sense. Flo Jo [Seoul Olympics gold medallist Florence Griffiths-Joyner who died in 1998] was a tremendous success. She was obviously worth a hundred other runners.

Look at cycling. For top class professionals it is a sport of immense attrition. What you're doing in one long stage in the Pyrenees is like riding from Brussels to Paris and climbing the height equivalent of a small mountain in the Himalayas. It is devastating on the human body and the necessity of restoring and resuscitating the body is looked at very carefully. Participants would be the first not to want to take things which are going to cause their joints to seize up or their livers to fail. These people do not want to die young and can see the implications of what they are taking."

James Waddington, writer and cycling expert

5

1   Read the following summary task. Underline the key words.

> In a paragraph of between 50 and 70 words, summarise in your own words as far as possible the dangers described in the texts of removing all restrictions on the use of performance-enhancing drugs in sport.

2   Read texts 1 and 2 again. Underline and number the main points related to the dangers of using drugs in sport. Although only one of the texts suggests that drug use should be banned, they both admit that the use of drugs can cause problems to some people.

3   Make notes, using your own words as far as possible.

4   Look at your notes carefully. Does each one make a new point? (One point is made by both texts. You will need to recognise this point.) What is the best order for the points?

5   Write out your notes as a connected paragraph.

6   Check that:

- you have made four clear points about the dangers of unrestricted drug use. (It is probably best to put each point in a separate sentence.)
- the number of words is between 50 and 70.
- you have organised and linked your ideas clearly.
- your grammar, spelling and punctuation are accurate.

6   Compare your paragraph with the one below.

This paragraph is well organised, the ideas are well linked together, and it is within the specified limit. However, only three of the four necessary points have been included, and one sentence is completely irrelevant. Decide which point has been omitted (it is a point from text 1) and which sentence is irrelevant. Then replace the irrelevant sentence with a new sentence giving the necessary information. Make sure that the paragraph remains within the 70-word limit.

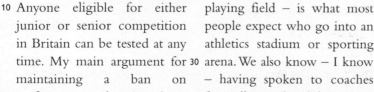

The use of performance-enhancing drugs can physically damage the body and may be responsible for a rise in sports-related illnesses. Competitors must therefore be tested, and banned from sport if found to be using drugs. Drug use removes the social value of sport, making players depend on artificial substances rather than their own skill. If success depends only on such chemicals, the whole purpose of sport will be destroyed. (69 words)

Text 2

"I was the first athlete to address the Olympic Committee in 1981 when I called for the life ban of 5 competitors that used drugs. Then I joined the Sports Council and as vice-chairman set up the out-of-competition testing that is now common. 10 Anyone eligible for either junior or senior competition in Britain can be tested at any time. My main argument for maintaining a ban on 15 performance-enhancing drugs is that free, open and pure competition remains an essential social value. We either 20 have sportspeople who are faster, fitter and stronger than the rest, by natural means and with recourse only to their natural biology and physiology, or we go down the road where 25 success lies in the hands of the chemists. Fairness – a level playing field – is what most people expect who go into an athletics stadium or sporting 30 arena. We also know – I know – having spoken to coaches from all over the globe, we are getting more than a casual correlation between some of 35 the illnesses seen in sports and some of the methods being used to improve performances.

Using drugs is like climbing the wall of the football ground 40 without paying. You've got to pay your dues and that means hard work. Having entered the moral maze and said all that, you still can't get away from 45 one simple fact – using drugs is cheating."

Sebastian Coe, Olympic gold medallist

Language Focus: Vocabulary
Prepositions and particles

1 Re-express the following sentences using the words in brackets **and** an appropriate preposition. Don't change the word in any way.

1 Performance-enhancing drugs must be banned if we are to retain the social value of sport. (*ban*)
2 Cycle riding in the Pyrenees is like climbing a mountain in the Himalayas. (*equivalent*)
3 If we permit the use of drugs in sport, it could end up being controlled by scientists and businesspeople. (*hands*)
4 Most people are not told about the effects of these drugs. (*ignorance*)
5 Professional cyclists recognise the need to restore and revitalise their bodies. (*necessity*)
6 Sportspeople should depend on their own natural body systems and nothing else. (*recourse*)
7 Some sports illnesses are linked to the use of performance enhancers. (*correlation*)
8 These types of drugs are very dangerous for children. (*danger*)
9 Sportspeople who take drugs should not be allowed to take part in any further competitions. (*banned*)

2 Complete the following sentences with appropriate phrasal verbs from the box in the correct form. The meanings are given in brackets.

get away from	get away with	get down to
get on with	get out of	get round to
get through to	get up to	

1 Doing exercise takes up time, and many people just never .... it. (*make time for*)
2 Professional sport is a hard way to make a living, and sportsmen have to train hard and really .... it. (*concentrate*)
3 The children are making a lot of noise – I'll go and see what they're .... (*do something bad*)
4 Susan usually .... her colleagues. (*has a good relationship*)
5 Why don't you try to .... that meeting tomorrow and play tennis with me instead? (*avoid*)
6 I don't know how they .... paying such low wages. (*avoid being caught*)
7 We're .... the main issue in this discussion. (*talking about irrelevant things*)
8 It's difficult to .... some people how much training top athletes really have to do. (*make people understand*)

Writing
▶ Paper 2, Part 2 (formal letter)

In Paper 2, Part 2 you may be asked to write a **letter** with a narrative focus, describing an event and making a point arising from it. In this type of letter it is important that the narrative is focused on the point you want to make and that the events are vividly described.

1

1 Read the following writing task and underline the key words.

> **TASK**
> You have recently spent a day in a theme park with some friends. During the visit something happened which upset you, and which you feel was the fault of the park organisers. You also feel that it could be a danger to others visiting the park. Write a letter to the organisers describing the incident and expressing your concerns.
>
> (300–350 words)

2 Think about the task.
- What kind of events might be upsetting?
- What action might you want the organisers to take?
- Will the letter be formal or informal in style?

In this type of task it is easier if you can write about something you have experienced personally. If you cannot think of anything yourself, then imagine yourself in a situation from a film or a TV show to help you with ideas.

2 Read the letter on page 121, which was written in answer to the task, and discuss the following questions.

1 How far is the content similar to your own ideas?
2 Which paragraph contains the most vivid description and why?

3 Underline the formal expressions used by the writer to:
- introduce the incident
- express concern over wider implications
- call for action.

Dear Sir,

   I am writing to express my concern over one of your attractions, which I believe to be highly dangerous.

   Yesterday I visited Funland with friends. Having tried several rides, I decided to go on the 'Super Circuit Ride'. As you know, this comprises three circles of seats shaped like spacecraft, cars and bikes. In contrast to other attractions such as the roller-coaster, there were no warning signs and I therefore assumed that the ride would not pose any risk.

   Without the slightest hesitation I sat on a 'motorbike' on the outside ring, which, unlike other seats, had no restraining bars. At first I did enjoy myself, but, as the roundabout gathered speed, I found that the motion was throwing me outwards. Hanging on to the handlebars with all my strength, I could still feel myself being pulled off. I was utterly terrified that at any moment I would be flung out into the crowds. I realised that I was in dire straits. I shouted desperately at the attendants, who either couldn't hear me or chose to ignore me. Gripping desperately with my legs, and staying totally focused on sheer survival, I prayed that I would have enough strength not to let go.

   I was immensely relieved when the roundabout eventually slowed down, but when it finally stopped, I was shaking so much that I could hardly stand and needed help from my friends.

   I told the attendants that the roundabout was extremely unsafe, but they just laughed, claiming it was all 'part of the fun'. I was so shaken that I had to get a taxi home. This morning my legs are badly bruised from gripping the motorbike so tightly.

   I personally cannot understand how a major tragedy has not yet occurred. If someone with less strength than me – a young child, for example – had been in my place, I am in no doubt whatsoever that they would have been thrown off the roundabout. I would urge you to review the safety procedures for this attraction before it is too late.

Yours faithfully,

(344 words)

4 The writer has set the scene of the incident very carefully.

1 What is the writer concerned about? What information is given to support these concerns?

2 How does the writer emphasise the danger of the situation?

5 Answer the following questions.

1 Find the words or phrases that the writer uses to describe:
- ways of holding on (× 2)
- ways of being thrown off (× 2).

2 How do you know that the writer was afraid? Underline the words that tell you.

3 How does the writer show the force needed to stay on the ride?

4 Choose the word that gives the most dramatic effect to the sentences below.
  a) The roundabout *whirled/turned* round rapidly.
  b) I *hung/held* on to the bar.
  c) I *screamed/called* to the attendants.
  d) The incident *upset/unnerved* me.
  e) I felt *afraid/petrified* on the ride.

6 You will be assessed on the range and appropriacy of sentence structures you use. One way in which you can extend your range and make your writing more vivid is through using participle clauses (see page 46).

1 Rewrite the following sentences using a participle (*-ing*) clause.

1 After I had tried several rides, I decided to go on the 'Super Circuit Ride'.
2 I hung on to the handlebars with all my strength, but I could feel myself being pulled off.
3 I gripped on desperately with my legs and prayed that I would have enough strength not to let go.
4 They just laughed, and claimed it was all 'part of the fun'.

2 Now compare your answers with the original version on page 121. What is the effect of using the participle clauses?

7 The writer emphasises some points by using an intensifying word or expression.

1 Match the words below. Then check your answers with the text.

| slightest | highly | immensely | extremely |
| utterly | badly | | |

| terrified | hesitation | relieved | dangerous |
| bruised | unsafe | | |

2 Think about different ways to make the following sentences more emphatic by adding a word. Check your answers with the letter on page 121.

1 I cannot understand the point.
2 At first I enjoyed myself.
3 I am in no doubt that it is true.

8

1 Read the following writing task.

> **TASK**
>
> You have recently been to an event organised by your local community which was attended by large numbers of people. You feel that the event was badly organised and potentially dangerous. Write a letter to the authorities describing the event and expressing your concerns.
>
> (300–350 words)

2 Plan and write your letter.

1 Complete each of the following sentences with one of the words from the box below.

aback	away	between	behind	down
for	in	of	on	through	to	up

1 If everyone's ready, I think it's time we got .... to some serious practice.

2 He found there was a strong correlation .... diet and stamina.

3 She was somewhat taken .... by the team's reaction to her speech.

4 He was advised to take .... a less strenuous sport after his accident.

5 A bout of flu meant I had fallen .... in my training schedule.

6 We roped .... our parents to help and the sports pavilion was soon as good as new.

7 No-one should remain in ignorance .... the dangers such activities may hold.

8 Is it right to expect the manager to take .... extra responsibilities at such a critical time?

9 I've tried persuasion and punishment, but I just don't seem to be able to get .... to him.

10 Tests reveal that some players have recourse .... drugs to enhance their performance.

11 They really shouldn't be allowed to get .... with such behaviour.

12 He was too young to be eligible .... the full marathon, but won the junior one easily.

2 Think of one word only which can be used appropriately in all three sentences.

1 The doctors can .... malaria with drugs if these are available, but there are often shortages.
I'm fed up with your attitude – you seem to .... everything I say as a joke.
I'll give you the information, but please .... it as confidential.

2 There's no need to write down every .... word I say, just put the main points.
The report confirms that smoking is the .... most important cause of lung cancer.
He was disappointed that he didn't get a .... reply to his advertisement.

3 Her main .... at that time was tennis, although she later gave it up.
I think this book will be of particular .... to you, given its subject matter.
The financial statistics don't take account of the .... rate over the past year.

4 When I got to work I found a huge bunch of flowers .... on my desk.
The court will be .... until all the evidence has been heard.
I spent half the morning .... in a traffic jam, and so I got to the meeting in a bad temper.

5 She could just see the shadowy .... of a man's body approaching through the mist.
You need to think about the grammatical .... of the word as well as its meaning.
Judging by their past ...., they should have a good chance of winning the cup.

6 They had a meeting with a delegation .... by the former chairman.
The letter was .... 'confidential', so she didn't read it.
They've .... off several major crises since they took office.

3 Read the text below and decide which answer (**A**, **B**, **C** or **D**) best fits each gap.

My Son

As a child I was never any good at sport, so when my youngest son (1) .... out to be a natural athlete, I was unprepared for the thrill his sporting achievements gave me. And they are beneficial to him in ways that I would never have predicted. (2) .... a start, his skills bring him instant friends wherever he goes. Bouncing his basketball with obvious talent, he has only to walk onto an outdoor (3) .... in an unfamiliar town and other boys hail him, 'Wanna play?' Boys twice his age (4) .... him onto their teams, big kids with attitude (5) .... his style, then invite him to play one on one. He's popular, he's confident, and his success at sports seems to (6) .... to his success in other school activities. For me it's a whole new perspective on life skills – but for him his talent is invaluable.

1 **A** came **B** turned **C** stood **D** made
2 **A** As **B** At **C** For **D** With
3 **A** court **B** pitch **C** field **D** course
4 **A** conscript **B** join **C** mobilise **D** recruit
5 **A** annotate **B** research **C** scrutinise **D** scan
6 **A** bring **B** add **C** increase **D** help

The mind's eye

Speaking

1

1 Close your eyes and try to recall in detail the events of the last dream you can remember. Why do you remember it? Have you ever had a similar dream before? How did it make you feel?

2 Work with a partner. Can you identify some typical features of dreams? For example:

- The events don't follow any logical sequence.
- You can do things that you can't do in real life.

2

Now discuss the following general statements about dreams. Which ones do you agree/disagree with? Can you give examples to support any of the statements?

'Dreams are just random thoughts and memories which don't have any special meaning.'

'Our dreams are symbolic – the things we dream about have special meanings which can be interpreted.'

'When we dream, our unconscious mind is working out the day's unresolved problems.'

Reading

In the vocabulary and reading questions in Paper 1 and comprehension questions in Paper 3, Part 5, you have to show how the effect of the text depends on the writer's use of language and also deal with vocabulary that may be unfamiliar to you. The following exercises will help you with these skills.

1

The following text is an extract from a novel, and describes a dream and how it affected the dreamer. Read the text carefully to find out what happened in the dream.

The dream came to her again, but this time it was different. Cassie no longer tried to run, allowed herself instead to drift, as though carried by some invisible, intangible force towards Tan's Hill.

The woman waited, blue dress swirling around her, arms outstretched as if welcoming her. Cassie turned from the Greenway and began to climb the hill. This time she didn't fight to reach the top. She seemed able, by sheer force of will, to rise easily and effortlessly up the slope. In her head, she could hear a voice calling to her. 'Cassie! Caa-ssie!'

For an instant Cassie tried to hurry, felt the resistance return and forced herself to relax, to give in to the strange current drifting her slowly towards her destination. She could see the woman clearly now, though she stood with her back to Cassie, face turned away. Cassie approached, reached out towards her. 'I'm here.' The woman turned, outstretched arms ready to embrace, fingers extended as though she couldn't move from that spot, couldn't quite reach out far enough to draw Cassie to her.

'Cassie …' The voice was soft, whispering inside her head. Cassie reached out again, longing to touch, to make that last effort to contact, but her feet seemed to be sliding backwards. Looking down, she saw her body, her legs being extended, stretched, as though something were pulling her down from the hill, but her will to be there kept her hands reaching, her upper body still and untouched. For a

2

Without looking back at the text, say which details of the story you remember most vividly. What words or expressions can you remember that contributed to the effect of these parts of the story?

3

Discuss these questions. Read the extract again if necessary.

1 Who could the woman be? What might she want from Cassie?
2 What are the main emotions conveyed by the story? For example: fear, loss, sadness, joy.
3 What type of novel do you think the extract is from?
   a) romantic fiction
   b) a children's novel
   c) science fiction
   d) a ghost story for adults
4 How might the story continue in the next paragraph?

moment, Cassie found herself examining this strange phenomenon. Some part of herself knew she was dreaming, wondered which particular cartoon this ridiculous effect was from. Some other part of her mind railed against the distraction it offered, ordered her to look back at this strange woman, reach out that little bit further, hold tight.

A slight gasp made her turn. She stared horrified as the woman, mouth open now in some parody of a scream, hands thrown abruptly above her head, was sucked down, swallowed whole and alive into the hill itself.

There were seconds when Cassie could not act; she fell forward as though drawn by the other's momentum. Then, as though someone at the other end of herself, that part where her feet disappeared down the hill, had given a sudden jerk, she felt herself retracting rapidly, body and legs compressing, squashing back into their original form. Cassie hung on, trying to dig her fingers into the grassy slope, but there was no purchase. The dew-dampened grass came away in her hands. Her nails dug into the earth, only to be torn away again by the urgent pulling on her ankles.

Cassie woke with a sudden jolt as though falling from a great height. She lay still, trying not to waken Fergus, then on a sudden impulse, held her hands in front of her face, inspecting them closely. Somehow, she was not surprised to find still-damp mud caked beneath her fingernails.

4   There may be words in the extract that you don't know but would like to understand and learn.

1   Use context clues to help you work out a synonym or definition for the following words.

1   intangible (para. 1)
(CLUE: *If you can't see it, do you think you can touch it?*)
2   (force of) will (para. 2)
(CLUE: *Look for another occurrence in paragraph 4.*)
3   to long (para. 4)
(CLUE: *What does paragraph 3 tell you about Cassie's attitude to the woman?*)
4   to rail (para. 4)
(CLUE: *What does the preposition 'against' suggest?*)
5   parody (para. 5)
(CLUE: *Can we hear the woman?*)
6   momentum (para. 6)
(CLUE: *What has happened to the woman that could draw Cassie towards her?*)

2   What other words are new to you? Can you work out their meaning or do you need to use a dictionary?

5   Now answer these questions, which focus on details of the text and use of language.

1   What differences between Cassie's previous dream and this are indicated in the first two paragraphs?
2   Which two words in paragraph 3 continue the idea of 'an invisible force' in paragraph 1?
3   What detail about the woman's voice in paragraph 4 supports the idea that this is a dream?
4   In paragraph 4, Cassie is aware of two things at the same time. Explain what they are.
5   Why does the writer mention cartoons in paragraph 4?
6   What does 'it' refer to in the last sentence of paragraph 4?
7   What is suggested by the verbs 'sucked down ... swallowed' in paragraph 5?
8   Find three words in paragraph 6 which continue the image of the cartoon-like movements introduced in paragraph 4.
9   What kind of movement is suggested by the words 'jerk' and 'retracting' in paragraph 6? What other words helped you understand their meaning?
10   Do you think Cassie feels shaken by her dream? Why/Why not?

Language Focus: Grammar
Comparisons with *as if/as though*

1   The writer makes a number of comparisons introduced by *as if/as though* to describe the events in the dream, for example:

- *She allowed herself to drift **as though carried** by some invisible force.* (para. 1)

1   How many more examples can you find? Underline them. What is their effect?

2   In the example, the subject and auxiliary verb have been deliberately omitted from the clause. Can you put them back in? What form will the verb be in? Do the same with the other examples where subjects and auxiliary verbs have been omitted.

2   Write a paragraph describing a dream – it could be one you've had, or you could make it up. Your dream should convey one of the following:

- fear   • loss   • peace   • freedom

Language Focus: Grammar
Verb patterns (-ing and infinitive)

When two verbs follow one another, the second may be an infinitive with *to*, a bare infinitive or an *-ing* form. Sometimes the first verb can (or must) have an object.

1 How much do you know?

1 Fill in the gaps using the correct form(s) of the verb in brackets. In which sentences are two alternative forms possible? Does a change of form affect the meaning or not?

1 In her dream, Cassie began .... the hill. (*climb*)
2 She longed .... the woman standing at the top. (*touch*)
3 She felt the woman wanted her .... closer. (*come*)
4 A part of her mind ordered her .... tight. (*hold*)
5 She found herself .... this strange phenomenon. (*examine*)
6 She tried .... her fingers into the grassy slope. (*dig*)
7 A slight gasp made her .... (*turn*)
8 She saw the hill .... the woman. (*swallow up*)
9 For days afterwards, she kept .... the dream. (*remember*)
10 She didn't look forward to the dream .... (*come back*)

2 Complete the table with examples from sentences 1–10.

Patterns	Examples
• Verb + *to* infinitive	*she longed to touch (2)*
• Verb + *-ing*	....
• Verb + *to* infinitive or *-ing*	
a) little change in meaning	....
b) a change in meaning	....
• Verb + object + bare infinitive	....
• Verb (+ object) + *to* infinitive	*she wanted her to come (3)*
• Verb + object + *to* infinitive	....
• Verb (+ object or genitive) + *-ing*	....
• Verb + object + *-ing*	....
• Verb + object + bare infinitive or *-ing*: some change in meaning	....

▶ Grammar reference pp. 221–222

2 Verb + infinitive

Verbs followed by an infinitive often refer forward to the future. Continuous, passive and perfect forms of the infinitive are all possible:

• *He pretended to be working.*
• *She expects to be promoted soon.*
• *I hope to have finished this by tomorrow.*

Rewrite the following sentences using an appropriate infinitive form.

1 I hope that I will make a million by the time I'm 30.
2 It seems he has put on weight. (He ...)
3 She resolved that no-one would ever take advantage of her.
4 They pretended that they had not met before.
5 It appears that he is living off his inheritance. (He ...)

3 Verb + -ing form

Verbs followed by an *-ing* form often look back to an earlier action or state. Passive and perfect *-ing* forms are possible. A perfect *-ing* form is used to emphasise that one action happened before another. It may be replaced by a *that*-clause + perfect tense, e.g.:

• *She denied having been followed.*
• *She remembered having had the dream before.*
• *She remembered that she had had the dream before.*

Rewrite the following sentences using an *-ing* form or *that*-clause. Which sentence can't be rewritten using an *-ing* form without adding an extra word? Why?

1 The man denied having been anywhere near the scene of the crime.
2 I admitted that I had forgotten to lock the door behind me.
3 I often regret not having been made to study history.
4 Did I ever mention that I worked on a ship once upon a time?
5 I remembered that I had seen her at the party the previous weekend.
6 I remembered that she had been at the party.

4 Adding an object

Choose the correct option or options to complete each sentence. More than one is possible.

1 I hope
   a) to go soon.
   b) him to go soon.
   c) that he and I will go soon.
   d) to have gone by tomorrow.

2 I want
   a) to see that film.
   b) him to see that film.
   c) that I will see that film.
   d) that he sees that film.

3 He promised
   a) to finish it.
   b) me to finish it.
   c) me that he would finish it.
   d) that his secretary would finish it.

4 The robbers told
   a) everyone to lie down.
   b) that they would shoot.
   c) us that we were hostages.
   d) we had to keep quiet.

5 We have applied
   a) for her to do the course.
   b) for to do the course.
   c) to do the course.
   d) that she will do the course.

6 The doctor advised
   a) her to stay in bed.
   b) staying in bed.
   c) her staying in bed.
   d) her that she should stay in bed.

7 We heard
   a) the orchestra to play as we arrived.
   b) the orchestra playing as we arrived.
   c) the orchestra play several new pieces.
   d) that the orchestra played several new pieces.

8 I appreciate
   a) your inviting me.
   b) you inviting me.
   c) that you invited me.
   d) it that you invited me.

5 Writing: error correction

Read through the following text, which describes a dream. The writer has made nine mistakes with verb patterns. Find the mistakes and correct them. In some cases, more than one answer may be possible.

The Dream

Sylvia dreamed she was in a strange house, sitting in a room filled with white furniture. She had never seen the room before, but it felt familiar. Gregor was next to her, but he didn't speak. She remembered to have arranged for him staying in this house while she went away on a long journey. She suggested them looking round the house, hoping him to like it. He got up, still without speaking, and slowly, hand in hand, they walked down a long corridor between white walls towards a closed door.

She didn't want it that he should be unhappy, but she knew that she had to go on the journey. At the same time she felt guilty – why had she failed informing him earlier that she had to go? Had she intended deceiving him? But she knew the answer. He would never have let her to leave on her own.

She turned and looked at him, then let go of his hand and left him standing there as she walked on towards the door. She dreaded to open it, not knowing what would be on the other side. But as she approached, it slowly swung open by itself.

 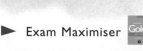

Exam Focus

▶ Paper 4, Part 2

In Paper 4, Part 2 you have to complete gaps in sentences. You need to listen for specific information and the speaker's stated opinions. You only need to write a word or a very short phrase (2–3 words) for each answer. The words you need to add must fit the grammar of the sentence and be spelled correctly. They will be in the Listening text, and you will not need to change their form. However, the words in the rest of the sentence will probably be different.

1 Look at the photos. What do you know about the American actor Christopher Reeve?

 2 You will hear an extract from Christopher Reeve's autobiography, about a man in a situation similar to his own. For questions **1–9**, complete the sentences with a word or short phrase.

Here is a procedure to follow for this task.

- Before you listen, read through all the sentences.
- Look at the words before and after the gap, and decide what kind of information is missing.
- Write only a short word or phrase in the gap.
- Check and complete your answers on the second listening.
- Finally, check grammar and spelling.

In Reeve's film, a paralysed man ⬚ **1** that he can go sailing.

Gradually, these trips come to seem ⬚ **2** to him.

He thinks the nurse is wrong about the reason for his ⬚ **3**

His wife starts to believe that he is recovering from his ⬚ **4**

He sets sail one evening intending to ⬚ **5** on board his ship.

But he turns back because of his ⬚ **6**

He gives ⬚ **7** to the old man.

In this way he gains a ⬚ **8** on which to build his life.

Reeve is ⬚ **9** since his family supported him early on.

3 To analyse your answers, look at the extracts from the tapescript and answer the questions on page 237.

▶ Exam Maximiser

128

Language Focus: Grammar
Emphasis (cleft sentences)

- *It was sailing **that** he loved most in the world.*
- ***What** he was tempted to do **was** to sail away and never return.*
- ***All** he wanted to do **was** to be in his boat, sailing down the path of the moon.*

1 Cleft sentences with *It + be*

This structure can be used to emphasise almost any element of a sentence. It often implies a contrast with a previous statement.

1 Re-express these sentences using standard word order. Which part of the sentence has been emphasised?

1 It was sailing that he loved most in the world.
2 It was in December that we first met.
3 It's my sister who does most of the cooking in the family.
4 It's learning about a new culture that's the most important thing for me.

2 Rewrite these sentences to emphasise the different parts.

Rick took his cousin out for a meal last night.
1 It was *Rick* that *took his cousin out*, (not Steve).
2 It was ...., (not his girlfriend).
3 It was ...., (not for a drink).
4 It was ...., (not the night before last).

3 Which part of the sentence **can't** be emphasised using this structure?

▶ Grammar reference p. 222

2 Cleft sentences with *What* and *all*

This structure can focus on the object, the verb, or on the whole sentence.

1 Rewrite the following sentences without using a cleft structure.

1 Football is what he really loves.
2 What is happening nowadays is that everyone is trying to do more work in less time.
3 What they're doing now is advertising.
4 What we've never done is ask the children what they think.
5 What I am enjoying is the social life.
6 All he wanted was to have a car of his own. (*Use 'just'*)

2 In which of the sentences 1–6 is the cleft structure focusing on a) the object? (3 sentences), b) the verb? (2 sentences), c) the whole phrase? (1 sentence).

3 Rewrite the following sentence in five different ways.

Scientists are looking for a cure for the common cold.

▶ Grammar reference p. 222

Watch Out!

1 What she did was feel afraid. ✗
2 What she did was phone the police. ✓

What types of verbs **can't** be used in this structure?

---

3 Other ways of introducing cleft sentences

We may use a general word such as *person, thing, reason,* to introduce a cleft sentence, e.g.:

- *The only **person who** knows the answer is John.*
- *The **reason (why)** I came was to meet Sarah.*

Complete the following sentences by writing a suitable general word in each gap. Use the context to help you.

1 The .... where I saw him first was in a crowded restaurant.
2 The .... who introduced us was his girlfriend at the time.
3 The .... that I noticed first was his beautiful smile.
4 The next .... that I saw him was a year later, on January 31.
5 The .... I remember the date so well is because he asked me to marry him.

4 Complete the sentences below, giving true information. Then take turns to read your sentences to a partner, giving reasons for each one.

1 What I most enjoy is ...
2 What really annoys me is when ...
3 All I want to do when ...
4 ... is playing computer games.
5 The reason I ... was to ...
6 The place where I'd like to be right now is ...

Use of English
▶ Paper 3, Part 1

1 Look at the photograph. What are these people doing? How do you think they do it? Can you think of other feats which appear physically impossible?

2 Look through the text but don't try to fill in the gaps yet.

1 Underline the topic sentence. How does this relate to the title?

2 The rest of the text gives supporting evidence for the topic sentence. Three sets of examples are given. Underline them. Find the sentence which tells you what these cases all have in common and underline it.

3 Fill each gap in the text with one suitable word. Then compare and justify your answers with a partner.

4 Always check your completed text again to ensure that it makes sense. To help you with this, decide which of the following statements are true, according to the writer.

1 We can change the world around us through visualisation.
2 Some people can vary their body temperature by imagining themselves in different situations.
3 Picturing himself running for a train caused one man's heart-beat rate to increase.
4 Anyone who wants to achieve changes must consciously try to change their body state.
5 Visualising an achievement before doing it can create success.

5 Discuss these questions.

1 Can you give any other examples of ways of controlling the physical processes or reactions of the body?
2 Discuss some ways in which your state of mind could affect your performance in the following areas:
   • sport • exams • illness.
3 What could you do to help yourself in each case?
4 Can you add any other areas in which mental state is important?

Mind over matter

The control (0) ...*that*... our mind can have (1) .... the physical processes of our body has been well documented. In a large (2) .... of cases, people have shown that (3) .... are able to use the power of their imagination to produce measurable physical changes. One man (4) .... change the temperature of two areas of skin on the palm (5) .... his hand, making (6) .... hotter and the other colder. He did (7) .... by picturing one part of his hand being burned by a hot flame and the other being frozen by ice. Another man was able to raise or lower his heart-beat rate by imagining (8) .... running for a train or lying in bed. He even used (9) .... imagination to control pain (10) .... he was at the dentist by visualising the pain (11) .... an orange-red thread that he could make smaller and smaller (12) .... it disappeared completely. Once trained to achieve the right mental state, people can even walk barefoot over red hot coals (13) .... suffering any injury. (14) .... all these cases, rather than trying to change the physical processes of their bodies directly, those involved use visualisation in (15) .... to produce the required effect.

Language Focus: Vocabulary

Expressions with *come*

1   Use of English: Paper 3, Part 2

1   Read the text below. What is it about?

So can our mind be used to help us to achieve less physical goals such as (1) .... shyness or achieving success in business? Of course it can! It's (2) .... itself. What you have to do at the (3) .... is first define what you want to achieve and then imagine the situation in which your (4) .... has been achieved. It comes down to this. Once you can (5) .... the (6) .... of your goal, your (7) .... mind accepts that the goal is possible, and it can then work out (8) .... ways and means by which you can get there in (9) .... This process can throw up (10) .... solutions that the rational mind would never have come up with.

1 COME	**2** SIMPLE	**3** SET	**4** OBJECT
5 VISUAL	**6** ATTAIN	**7** CONSCIOUS	**8** VARY
9 REAL	**10** EXPECT		

2   Complete the text with the correct form of the words given in capitals. You may need to add a prefix and/or an appropriate ending.

3   Work with a partner. Discuss how the technique described in the text could be helpful in the following situations.

* overcoming exam nerves
* learning to overcome a particular fear, e.g. of insects, or the dark
* dealing with an important interview

2   Three-word phrasal verbs with *come*

Read the following examples of phrasal verbs from the text in Exercise 1. Notice that each verb is followed by two particles.

* *It comes down to this.*
* *... solutions that the rational mind would never have* **come up with**.

Fill in the missing particles in the following sentences.

1   I can't come .... a better explanation for how people can walk on hot coals.
2   In the interview she came .... cool, calm and collected.
3   Now you've said that, I'm starting to come .... your way of thinking.
4   I feel really ill – I must be coming .... flu.

5   If I eat crab, I come .... a rash.
6   What it comes .... is a straight choice – a well-paid but stressful job, or a badly-paid job with no stress.
7   The President came .... heavy criticism when he admitted having lied.
8   Those who claim to have special mental powers may come .... considerable prejudice and opposition.
9   My membership comes .... renewal next April.
10   She came .... a really stupid remark in the middle of the meeting.

3   Use of English: Paper 3, Part 4

Complete the second sentence with three to eight words so that it has a similar meaning to the first sentence, using the word given. Do not change the word given.

1   People legally become adults at the age of eighteen in Britain.   **come**
   In Britain, people don't .... are eighteen.
2   Finally, everything worked out well.   **came**
   It .... the end.
3   He finally accepted the situation, although he was concerned.   **terms**
   Despite his .... the situation.
4   It wasn't until the second half that the game started getting exciting.   **life**
   The game .... the second half.
5   'You ought to tell the truth about the incident,' he said.   **clean**
   He advised us .... about the incident.
6   Just use whatever is available.   **hand**
   Whatever .... will be OK.
7   The ball rolled downhill and stopped behind the tree.   **rest**
   After .... behind the tree.
8   In spite of his efforts, his plans failed.   **nothing**
   His plans .... he tried hard.

Reading

▶ **Paper 1, Part 4**

1 You are going to read a text about a man who wants to find a cure for his mentally and physically disabled daughter. First, read through the extract and answer the following question.

What is your impression of Miss Whittaker?

a) She is a dangerous woman with strong powers.

b) She is a sincere woman with real but limited powers.

c) She is a convincing fraud with no real powers.

The faith-healer

I suppose I'm expecting somebody thin, drawn, spiritual, mysterious, perhaps dressed in black. Instead I am greeted by a woman who surprises me by her likeness to my mother when she was younger.

'You must be Mr Crawley. Do come in. Is this your little girl?'

Miss Whittaker's dumpy body is dressed cheaply and sensibly in patterned skirt and synthetic pink sweater. I am disappointed. Far from a mysterious place of healing, her flat might be any of the more middle-class variety one sees when visiting colleagues from work: stuffy, cleanly-kept, unexciting. Photographs of relatives and so on. Catching a faint twinkle in her clear eyes I realise that she is aware of, and rather amused by, my sense of disappointment. She is intelligent.

She walks me through to a small back bedroom where floral curtains and a mass of potted plants are allowing only a dim green light to filter onto spartan furnishings; divan bed, armchair, chair, bookcase. There is none of the supernatural bric-a-brac I had imagined. Perhaps it's not going to be the performance I expected.

'No, don't tell me anything, Mr Crawley. No medical details, please. It only interferes. Just lay her on the bed then, will you.'

'Do you want me to undress her?' I ask.

'No, no, you just relax and sit in the armchair for a little, will you?'

She waits for me to move away and then goes to the bed and strokes Hilary's hair. Immediately the child quietens and begins to gurgle softly.

'What a pretty little girl,' Miss Whittaker murmurs. 'What a pretty pink ribbon Mummy has put in your hair. What pretty clothes. Someone's mummy and daddy think a lot of them, don't they? Someone's a very lucky little girl.'

Curiously, she is right. We do think a lot of her.

I sit in the chair watching the woman's squat back. Hilary is lying quite still and calm, despite the strange place, the strange voice. This is very unusual. A good sign. So, do I sense the faintest ray of hope? It's quickly quelled. How can this woman even know what's wrong with my daughter?

Kneeling on a cushion, Miss Whittaker runs her small podgy hands the length of the child's body, letting them slide lightly over her clothes. Minutes pass. She has stopped talking now, her hands move back and forth, not hypnotically or even rhythmically, but more with a questing motion, stopping here and there, hovering, moving back, coming quietly to rest: on her head for a full minute, above her knees, her ankles, which below her socks, I know, are fierce with scars. Hilary lies still, eyes blindly open, breathing soft. She doesn't even move when a plump hand covers her face, gently pressing the eyelids. Leaning over her, Miss Whittaker blows very lightly on her forehead. Then repeats the whole rigmarole.

I watch, biting a nail. Fifteen minutes. It's hard keeping still, frankly. I fidget. I feel tense. It's farcical. For of course, now I'm here, I don't expect anything. In the end I would have done a lot better by myself and Hilary if I'd gone to St James's Park. Shirley* would think I'd lost my marbles.

Another ten minutes before at last Miss Whittaker rises slowly to her feet, then sits on the bed and strokes Hilary's hair in what is now an entirely normal way. Immediately the child begins to smile and gurgle again.

'Poor little lovey.' Then she turns to me. She says: 'Well, apart from some small irritation or infection which I may have been able to help, your child is really perfectly healthy, Mr Crawley, and beautifully, beautifully innocent. Don't you see how her smiles shine?'

What? Is the 'session' over? Is that her verdict? But she holds up a hand to stop my protest. 'As for the question of what she is, I mean the form in which she was sent into this world, I'm afraid it is far, far beyond my humble powers to alter that.'

After a moment's awkward silence in this dimly-lit room, I decide the best thing to do is cut my losses. Only £12.50 after all. A joke. I stand up to go, reaching for my wallet.

She smiles her sad smile, so similar to any sympathetic, middle-class smile an older woman might give you waiting in a long queue at a supermarket or post office. And she says calmly:

'Perhaps I could help you, though, Mr Crawley.'

'I'm sorry, I beg your pardon.'

'Perhaps I could help you more than your child.'

Shirley is the narrator's wife.

2 Choose the answer (**A, B, C** or **D**) which fits best according to the text.

1 Why is the narrator disappointed when he meets Miss Whittaker?
  A   He had expected someone more exotic.
  B   He had hoped for more evidence of supernatural powers.
  C   He had hoped for more medical expertise.
  D   He had expected someone more intelligent.

2 Miss Whittaker realises that the little girl's parents
  A   are overprotective towards their child.
  B   have a disturbing effect on their child.
  C   constantly think about their child.
  D   care deeply about their child.

3 By her movements over the child's body, Miss Whittaker is trying to
  A   ease the child's pain.
  B   find where the problems are.
  C   send the child to sleep.
  D   impress the child's father.

4 How does the man feel as he watches Miss Whittaker?
  A   apprehensive
  B   impatient
  C   worried
  D   desperate

5 Miss Whittaker suggests that the child's disability
  A   should not be seen as a problem.
  B   is not as serious as her parents thought.
  C   has not affected her mental powers.
  D   needs specialist treatment.

6 What is the effect of the visit?
  A   Unknown to the man, the child's disability is cured.
  B   There is no real change in the child's condition.
  C   The man realises that he needs help.
  D   The man realises he has been cheated.

7 What impression does the extract give of the narrator?
  A   He is upset and arrogant, but cares about his child.
  B   He is more concerned about himself than about his child.
  C   He is clear-minded and not easily deceived.
  D   He is unaware of the suffering of his child.

3 Discuss the following questions about the text.

1 In what ways do you think the narrator might have needed help?

2 Do you think he was right to go to the faith-healer? Why/Why not?

Use of English

▶ **Paper 3, Part 3**

Think of one word only which can be used appropriately in all three sentences.

1 The doctor was unable to .... the child as he did not have the right drugs.
Attempts to .... unemployment have so far failed in spite of all their efforts.
In olden times people used to .... meat with salt to preserve it.

2 She passed her driving test at her first .... in spite of feeling nervous.
Do you think they'll really make a .... of this restaurant – it's not in a very good location.
Tommy, you've had your .... with the computer – now let Susie use it for a bit.

3 You can't argue – the rules are very .... on this point.
She says her skin is so .... because she drinks a lot of water.
From the top floor of the hotel you get a .... view of the bay.

4 When they arrived in the banqueting hall, they found a wonderful feast .... out in front of them.
She .... her hand on my arm to stop me going further.
The workmen had barely .... the foundations for the building when the project ran out of money.

5 My daughter's really hopeless with her possessions – she's lost her bus .... twice this week.
The expedition followed a narrow mountain .... through spectacular scenery.
She is delighted with her .... in geography as it was totally unexpected.

6 You can .... that book if you want – I've already read it.
I'm trying to cut his hair but he won't .... still – it's going to look terrible!
Frank used to .... the butcher's shop on Park Road but he's retired now.

Speaking

1 Which of the factors below have the greatest effect on you, either physically or mentally? Discuss each one and say how it can change the way you feel. Can you add any others?

> diet   leisure   relationships   environment   exercise

2 Read the prompt card below. Work with a partner. Discuss your ideas, and plan a two-minute talk based on the card.

> Do you agree that the strongest influence on our health is our mind?
> - lifestyle   ● money   ● people

3 Now listen to a student giving a two-minute talk based on the card above.

- What were her main points? Were they the same as yours?
- Did she make any points not related to the prompts?
- At one stage the speaker hesitated. What strategy did she use to keep going?

4 Listen to the student's partner giving feedback on the talk. Do you agree with her comments?

5

1 Now read the prompt card below. Working on your own, plan a two-minute talk based on the card.

> What do you think is the ideal environment to encourage a child's development?
> - physical   ● mental   ● financial

2 Ask your partner to listen to your talk and to give feedback on the main points you made and how well you made them.
If you run out of things to say, go back to the original question to help you focus on the main issue; use personal anecdotes or information to support your points; discuss related points that were not mentioned in the prompts.

6 Discuss the following questions.

1 How much do you think people in your country are aware of alternative medicine? Do you think this type of medicine is becoming more or less important? Why?
2 Do you think that life is more or less stressful nowadays?
3 What do you think is the greatest stress factor in modern life? Why?
4 What do you think people can do to relieve stress?

Language Focus: Grammar

do, give, have, make, take + noun phrase

English often uses a general verb such as *do*, *give*, *have*, *make* and *take* followed by a noun or noun phrase to replace a verbal construction, e.g.:

She **smiled** sadly. → She **gave** a sad smile.

He **works** very little. → He **does** very little work.

This structure may be less formal than the use of the related verb, e.g.:

I'll think about it. → I'll have a think about it.

In some cases there may be a slight difference in meaning, e.g.:

a) She chatted with him briefly. (unplanned)
b) She had a brief chat with him. (planned)

have and *take* are often interchangeable in this structure, e.g.

Let's have/take a break.

1 Rewrite the following sentences, using *do*, *give*, *have*, *make* or *take* + noun phrase. Make any other changes necessary.

1 She glanced at him fleetingly as she left.
2 I drank some water.
3 Let's rest for an hour.
4 He kicked the dog viciously.
5 I had to lecture to a group of 500 students.
6 She kissed him tenderly.
7 Who will volunteer to wash up?
8 In time, Peter recovered fully from his illness.
9 She affected him strangely. (*Be careful with the spelling.*)
10 Then Marie suggested something unusual.

2 Read the following story. Replace the verbs in italics using a verb + noun construction, as in Exercise 1.

Zoe (1) *frowned* worriedly. It was late at night, she was alone, and someone was following her. She could hear the footsteps coming closer as she walked down the dark street. She (2) *looked* behind her quickly and as she did so, the man who was following her turned his head away. 'He doesn't want me to see his face,' she thought in terror.

She started to run, and then (3) *cried out* as she tripped and felt herself falling. The next moment he had caught her up and was bending over her. She looked up and realised that she knew him – she'd met him at the club and (4) *danced* with him a couple of times that evening.

'I'm sorry,' he said. 'It's me, Philip. It was stupid of me. I wanted to see you got home safely. I didn't want to frighten you.'

Zoe was more concerned about her ankle. She (5) *groaned* as she tried to stand. 'I've twisted my ankle,' she said. 'You'd better try to find a taxi. And I'd like to (6) *suggest* something – if you want to see people home safely, it's not a bad idea to ask them first.'

Improving your writing

In Paper 2 one of the criteria your writing will be assessed on is organisation and discourse management. The exercises in this section will help you to improve your writing in this area.

1

1   The following extract is confusing because it is not logically ordered, and it is not always clear what the pronouns and other linking words refer to. Rewrite the extract as a paragraph of two sentences beginning as given and using phrases from the list in the box.

Famous people can influence the whole of society by their behaviour, because <u>people</u> accept them as a role model for their life. <u>It</u> means <u>they</u> are often considered to be the image of the <u>society</u>. <u>Therefore</u>, people dress, speak, and behave like the pop stars or the rich people.

and try to dress, speak and behave like them
may take them as role models for their own lives
can influence the whole of society by their
   behaviour
like pop stars or rich people
may become images of the societies they live in
since ordinary people

Famous people ....
....
....
....
This means that such celebrities ....
....
....

2   What words or expressions have been used to replace the underlined words in the original text?

2   The following extracts contain examples of problems in several of the areas described in the *Improving your writing* sections.

1   Choose the best option for each of the phrases in italics. What is wrong with the phrases you reject?

First of all, he *sensed which my aptitudes were/ understood what my strengths were* and encouraged me *to go for them/to develop them*. The fact that I have followed a profession *in which I can use my abilities fully/which commensurates with my abilities* is all due to his *advice/advisory*. His influence extends *furthermore/ even further*. His own mild nature *modified/smoothened* my character and calmed the aggressiveness and *arrogance/absoluteness* which characterises most teenagers. He taught me to forgive and appreciate people for *as much as they can be/what they are*, to be always patient and try to *read between the lines/be aware of others*.

2   The main problems in the following extract are inaccuracy of grammar and spelling and too much repetition of the word *friend*. Rewrite the extract, improving it as much as you can.

As a friend she is very loyal, she is very supportive and faithful, a person which you can count to be to your side whenever a problem arises. That is something I really need from a friend as it can make me fell safe, knowing that somebody apart from my family will be here for me at any time. I have acepted her as a friend because she has several times proved that she diserves to be called like this.

Language Focus: Vocabulary

Words with similar meanings

1

1 Read the following definitions from the Longman *Dictionary of Contemporary English*. What are the main differences in meaning between the verbs *heal*, *cure* and *treat*?

heal *v* 1 [I] if a wound or a broken bone heals, the flesh, skin, bone etc grows back together and becomes healthy again: *It took three months for my arm to heal properly.* 2 [T] to cure someone who is ill or make a wound heal.

cure[1] *v* [T] 1 to make someone who is ill well again: *The doctors did everything they could to cure her, but she died three months later.* 2 to make an illness disappear completely, usually by medical treatment: *an operation to cure a hernia problem.*

treat[1] *v* [T]
3 ► MEDICAL ◄ to try to cure an illness or injury by using drugs, hospital care, operations etc: *Nowadays malaria can be treated with drugs.*

2 Now use one of the verbs in the appropriate form to complete each of the sentences below.

1 At first Colin was .... for influenza, but then they found he actually had malaria.
2 Some types of cancer can now be completely .... if the disease is detected early enough.
3 I cut myself last week and it still hasn't .... – I'd better see a doctor.

2

What do you know about other types of treatment which don't depend on conventional medicine, such as:

- acupuncture?
- homeopathy?
- aromatherapy?
- hypnosis?

Would you ever be prepared to try any of these yourself?

Writing

▶ Paper 2, Part 2 (article)

In Paper 2, Part 2 you may be asked to write an **article** for a newspaper or magazine in which you narrate an event or describe a situation, and explain how it has affected you or what its results have been. In some cases you may be able to write a personal account, providing evidence for your ideas from your own life. If you do not have personal experience, then think of a friend, family member or film you have seen to give you ideas.

1

Read the following writing task.

> **TASK**
>
> Your local newspaper is running a series of articles on overcoming phobias. The editor has asked readers to write in with articles describing their own particular phobias and explaining how they dealt with them. You have decided to submit an article.
>
> (300–350 words)

1 Underline the key words in the task.
2 Should the style be formal or informal?

2

1 Read the introduction to the following article, which was written in answer to the task.

1 What was the fear that the girl faced?
2 Underline the sentence which introduces the topic of the article.

I had a happy childhood with plenty of friends and a loving family. I even enjoyed school work. However, I had one phobia that I couldn't overcome – I was terrified of heights.

2 Read paragraph 2, ignoring the instructions in brackets. Then answer the questions below.

It started when I was about five years old and it was totally irrational. For some reason my mind told me that being high was dangerous, and no matter how much I tried to persuade myself otherwise, I couldn't overcome the fear. When the rational side of my mind said 'Don't be stupid,' the irrational side would say 'Don't ignore the danger!' Whenever I was asked to do anything which involved heights I felt absolutely terrified. (Give details of how you felt.) Looking down, I felt as though I was going to fall. The fear affected my whole life. I couldn't stand on a ladder. I couldn't use escalators. (Explain how you felt when you tried. Use 'without -ing'.) I couldn't even visit anyone who lived in a flat higher than the second floor. (Describe how you felt when you did. Use 'without -ing'.)

1   What is the main idea of paragraph 2? Underline the topic sentence.
2   The paragraph would be more effective if it had more supporting detail. Look at the instructions in brackets. What details could you add?
3   What is the effect of the direct speech in this paragraph?

3   Read the next paragraph, ignoring the instructions.

> One day when I was about 12, I decided that I was going to overcome this fear. What I decided to do was attack the phobia in stages. I started by visualising myself managing in situations that normally caused the panic. For example, (describe the situation/s you visualised). The next step was the real thing. (Describe a real situation you deliberately faced.) It took time, and I had various setbacks. (Describe a setback.) However, gradually I got better and better. Once my mind realised that I was actually safe in these situations, it stopped telling me to be afraid.

1   What is the main idea of this paragraph? Underline the topic sentence.
2   Look at the instructions in brackets. What details could you add?

4   Read the last paragraph, ignoring the gaps.

> Now I can .... without .... I can .... without .... It has improved my confidence, because I overcame the difficulty alone, and although I will never be completely happy with heights, I can at least live with them.

1   Underline the main conclusion.
2   Now decide on suitable information to fill in the gaps. The paragraph should link back to earlier ideas in the article.

3

1   Write the article out, incorporating all the additional ideas you have thought of.

2   Exchange your completed article with a partner. Do you find the added detail convincing? Does it improve the article? How?

4

1   Read the following writing task.

> **TASK**
> Your local newspaper is running a series of articles on personal success. The editor has asked readers to write in with articles describing a success they have had and what the effect of the success has been. You have decided to submit an article.
>
> (300–350 words)

2   Plan what you are going to write, using the outline of the article in Exercise 2.

3   Exchange your outline with a partner, and comment on the ideas and structure.

5   Now write your article. Include:
- plenty of supporting detail
- reference to feelings and reactions
- vocabulary that conveys these feelings vividly
- emphatic structures such as cleft sentences, inversion and intensifying expressions.

1 Find and correct the errors in the following sentences.

1 All the students denied to have written the note.
2 There's nothing you can do which will make me to change my mind.
3 If you're caught driving without a licence, you risk to be heavily fined.
4 They were quite wrong to assume us all being in agreement with their proposals.
5 We were delighted when our school was chosen testing the new software.
6 I'm so upset that they all heard you to be rude me.
7 I had expected having heard from the selection committee by now.
8 The worried father had refused believing the doctor until he was shown the test results.
9 If you so dislike that I am in charge, you'd better ask to work with another group.
10 She absolutely dreaded to tell her father what had happened.

2 Use the word given in capitals at the end of some of the lines to form a word that fits the space in the same line.

Dealing with phobias

Do you feel hysterical at the thought of spiders? Do you start to shake if you think that you might have to touch cotton wool? It is estimated that between three to five million Britons suffer from such phobias, and the (0) *majority* of these people do not (1) .... any form of treatment. Most (2) .... fears begin in the first instance as mild forms of (3) ...., and only develop gradually into (4) .... phobias. They seem to be becoming increasingly frequent in all sections of society – perhaps because with the expansion of technology, people who are (5) .... to controlling their (6) .... with the push of a button panic when things go wrong. Men are less likely to suffer from such fears than women, but attempts by either men or women simply to (7) .... them can exacerbate the problem.

    Nowadays, however, phobias can be treated. The easiest option is prescription drugs, which effectively control the physical symptoms, but may have (8) .... side-effects. The other option is behavioural therapy, in which you gradually learn to (9) .... your fear through facing up to it. This is a safe and lasting (10) .... to drug treatment.

MAJOR
GO
RATION
ANXIOUS
BLOWN

CUSTOM
STYLE

REGARD

DESIRE

COME
ALTERNATE

3 Read the text below and decide which answer (**A**, **B**, **C** or **D**) best fits each gap.

Our perception of time

Distortions are commonplace in the brain's perception of the passing of time. In fact, there does not appear to be any direct monitoring of time by the brain. Research suggests that we seem instead to rely on our memory of how many events filled a particular period. Thus minutes, hours and days which contain (1) .... few events tend to be 'shrunk' by our memories, while action-packed times are 'magnified'. In other words, time might seem to (2) .... while we're bored, but our memories (3) .... just the opposite impression. This may help to explain why landmark events such as birthdays seem to come (4) .... faster each year. As we grow older, we either do less or we have fewer new (5) .... We therefore find ourselves thinking that our birthday has arrived sooner this year because the number of (6) .... events has been smaller than it was in the past.

1 A quite   B relatively   C rather
   D similarly
2 A pall   B dawdle   C drag
   D lag
3 A save   B note   C record
   D log
4 A about   B back   C through
   D round
5 A incidents   B experiences C actions
   D episodes
6 A interfacing B interposing C intervening
   D interfering

4 Talk about the photo.

What makes this photograph a good choice for the cover of a health magazine? Think about the image created by the picture and the possible lifestyle of the woman.

The world of work

Speaking

1 Work with a partner.

1   Choose one photo each to talk about. Say where you think the photo was taken and how the people might be feeling.

2   Discuss the different aspects of work and attitudes to work illustrated by the two photos you have chosen. Think about:
- the relationship between work and home life
- the different values of old and modern lifestyles.

3   Report back to the class and share your ideas about all the photos.

2 Imagine you are working on a project to assess different working situations around the world. Discuss which aspects of work you would want to include in the project, and which you feel are relevant to life today.

3 Do you think work means the same thing in different cultures? Think of other countries that you have read about, seen in films or visited. Do you think other factors might be more important than those you discussed in Exercise 1.2?

Use of English

▶ **Paper 3, Part 5**

1

1   Look at the following list of factors you might consider when choosing a job. Select five and rank them in order of importance for you. Compare your ideas with a partner and discuss the reasons for your choices.

- job security
- independence
- income
- status
- job satisfaction/self-fulfilment
- social life
- future prospects

2   How could you find out about these factors before applying for a job? Which factors might it be appropriate to ask about if you were being interviewed for a job?

3   What sort of information can an employer get from an interview apart from facts that could be gained from a letter of application or a CV?

4   How effective do you think interviews are as a means of selecting people for jobs?

2   Read the following texts on job applications and interviews. Which text is written in a more personal style?
Answer questions 1–4 with a word or short phrase. You do not need to write complete sentences.

Text 1

In today's job marketplace, the interview is increasingly a structured event, with each candidate being asked the same
5 predetermined questions, rather than a process guided by whatever questions happen to float into the minds of the panel. A growing number of interviews are also
10 situational, with candidates being asked questions such as 'What would you do if ...?', or 'How would you deal with a situation where ...?'. This approach lets
15 them provide practical examples of how they would tackle particular situations, whether or not they have had any direct experience of them. Despite their increasing
20 rigour, interviews are also generally becoming a lot less formal, reflecting the decreasing importance attached to hierarchy within organisations. It has been
found that despite all these 25 efforts to bring the interview process up-to-date, employers frequently make the wrong choice – but although the interview may be a highly unreliable predictor 30 of a candidate's suitability, it remains the centrepiece of most organisations' selection procedures.

From the point of view of the 35 candidate, there are important pointers towards maximising the possibilities of success at the interview stage. One of the most important is good preparation, 40 both in personal appearance and in knowledge of what the job entails. Confidence gained in this way will enable the candidate to feel at ease, and to avoid the traps of either 45 false modesty or overconfidence when answering questions in the interview.

1   What are the three main changes in the nature of the interview described by the writer?
2   What phrase in the first paragraph suggests that interviews are now more challenging for candidates?

Text 2

Barbara left university armed with a good degree in advertising and a desire to fulfil her dream of working in PR. But three months after sending scores of letters in response to adverts,
5 she was still looking for that elusive job.

Nowadays it's not just the traditionally popular professions like the media and law that are difficult to enter. To make sure you get noticed, you have to be prepared to pull out all the stops. And here's how you
10 can do it.

You should identify your skills and what you want out of your job. The core skills employers are looking for are communication, teamwork and IT skills; seek help with this from careers advisors and consultants.
15 Send out speculative letters, but make sure your letter stands out – you want the reader to stop and take notice. Once you reach the interview stage, beware of pitfalls that can trip you up. Your performance here is crucial. Blunders can cost you the job; make sure
20 you're well-versed in as many of the company's products and services as possible. Dress smartly but comfortably, as you will be judged in some respects by what you wear. When in doubt, dress conservatively. Appear confident, relaxed and in control at all times
25 – this is of primary importance – and remember to listen as well as talk. Communication is a two-way street – talk too much and you may miss clues concerning what the interviewer feels is important.

3 Explain in your own words why the writer has chosen to use the expression 'pull out all the stops' in line 9.
4 Which phrase in paragraph 3 links with the idea in text 1 of 'knowledge of what the job entails'?

3 In a paragraph of between 50 and 70 words, summarise in your own words as far as possible the advice given in the texts for the best approach to take when applying for a job. Look back at Unit 4 page 55 for advice on the procedure for summary writing. (You should look for four main points, with supporting detail.)

4 In interviews, a candidate showing over-interest in the salary or perks of a job is often regarded with suspicion. What reasons can you think of for people wanting to work, other than financial ones?

Language Focus: Vocabulary
Compound adjectives

In Paper 3, Part 2 you may need to use compound adjectives. For example:

Make sure you're ..... *well-versed* ..... in the company's products.

1 Combine the following words to make three compound adjectives in each group.

1	red	narrow	one
	minded	sided	haired
2	ill	widely	ready
	known	made	advised
3	well	labour	smooth
	talking	meaning	saving
4	trouble	full	five
	page	free	scale

2

1 Match groups 1–3 above to one of the following patterns:

a) adjective/adverb/noun + present participle
b) adjective/number/noun + noun + *ed*
c) adjective/adverb + past participle

2 What different patterns can you see in group 4?

3 Complete the following sentences using compound adjectives, including a form of the word given in capitals.

1 I had to write a ....
essay in just three hours.   FIVE
2 She may be ....,
but she seems to end up annoying a lot of
people.   MEAN
3 Don't you think that's a rather ....
.... argument? What about the
other point of view?   SIDE
4 I would say that you'd be ....
to resign without having found a new job.
                                                               ADVICE
5 He's certainly a ....,
but I don't trust what he says.   SMOOTH
6 Working couples often buy ....
meals for the evening.   MAKE

Listening
▶ Paper 4, Part 2

1 Look at the advertisement below, produced by a charity dedicated to the needs of children around the world. What point is the advertisement making?

Andrew is 12.
He practises football every evening.

Ali is 12.
He sews footballs every day.

2 You will hear an interview with Joanne Waters, who works for a children's charity. Before you listen, read the sentences below and try to predict what kind of information is missing.

On her fact-finding trip Joanne was investigating the problem of .... (1)

Children may be employed to make .... (2)

It's important to consider .... (3) before taking action.

Banning the .... (4) of goods produced by children could harm them.

Joanne's charity wants to .... (5) the production of sports goods by children.

The charity started investigating work conditions by talking to .... (6)

The children appreciated having work that was .... (7) and could be done at home.

The charity wants to begin by banning .... (8) jobs.

Joanne also recommends checking children's .... (9) regularly.

3 Now listen and complete the sentences with a word or short phrase. Then check and complete your answers on the second listening.

4 Discuss these questions.

1 How far do you agree with the following statement in the light of the information you heard in the interview?

'Consumers should boycott all products whose manufacture has involved the use of child labour.'

2 Can you think of any arguments to **justify** young children working, apart from the need to make money?

5 In the interview, the speaker said: 'If children don't need to work, they can have the sort of life we think of as a child's life.'

1 What do you think the basic ingredients of a child's life should be?
2 If you were drawing up a list of children's rights to be applied internationally, what would you include?

Language Focus: Vocabulary
Adverb + adjective collocation

> Adverbs are often used to intensify the meaning of adjectives, for example:
>
> A: **Very hot** today, isn't it?
> B: Yes, **absolutely boiling**.
>
> The adverb you can use depends on the type of adjective that follows it.

1   Match the sets of adverbs 1–2 below to the three sets of adjectives A, B and C. Can you explain the reason for your answer?

1   very/extremely/incredibly/fairly/rather
2   absolutely/completely/totally

A   terrified/amazed/exhausted/ruined
B   large/important/old/happy
C   perfect/frozen/extinct

► Grammar reference p. 223

2   Some intensifiers collocate strongly with particular adjectives. Complete the sentences using intensifiers from the box.

> deeply   closely   entirely   highly   widely   wildly

1   The whereabouts of the exiled president remains a .... guarded secret.
2   English language newspapers are not .... available outside the main tourist centres.
3   The company employs a team of .... skilled designers.
4   I was .... moved by the experience of visiting the refugee camp.
5   We were not .... convinced by his arguments.
6   His description of the accident is .... exaggerated – it was far less dangerous than he suggests.

3   Work in pairs. Take turns to ask and answer the following questions. Use an adverb from box A and an adjective from box B in your answers.

Say what you think of:

- a film/play you have seen recently
- a well-known personality at home and/or abroad
- the public transport system in your country
- your first job/the worst job you have ever done
- your first day at secondary school
- the education system in your country.

A
deadly	extremely	fantastically	hopelessly
utterly	relatively	totally	incredibly

B
boring	conceited	competitive	dull
confusing	enjoyable	funny	good-looking
(in)efficient	progressive	rich	successful

4   Re-express the following sentences using the intensifier given in brackets, so that they mean almost the same. You will need to change the adjective used in the original sentence, and you may need to make other changes as a result.

1   The carpenters were very clever at their job. (*highly*)
2   The weather could not have been better. (*absolutely*)
3   They had no idea where they were. (*completely*)
4   I found the film absolutely terrifying. (*extremely*)
5   I was absolutely amazed when I heard I'd passed the exam. (*exceedingly*)
6   When her boyfriend left her she was extremely unhappy. (*utterly*)

► Exam Maximiser

Adjective + noun collocation

In the following sentences, only **two** of the three adjectives collocate with the noun. Cross out the adjective that doesn't collocate.

1   The *high/large/increasing* incidence of heart disease may be due to poor diet.
2   The pass rate in the exam is *higher/lower/smaller* in some areas than in others.
3   A *large/considerable/big* number of companies are reducing their workforces.
4   Tourism is the most *major/important/significant* source of income in the area.
5   We have invested *expanding/even greater/ever-increasing* sums of money in improving our equipment.
6   A *high/considerable/rising* ratio of pupils to teachers is bound to lead to falling standards in education.
7   This town has a *larger/greater/higher* proportion of older residents than its neighbour.
8   Counterfeit goods are being produced in *large/enormous/grand* quantities.

Collocation practice

1 Read the text below in which an air traffic controller talks about his job and decide which answer (**A**, **B**, **C** or **D**) best fits each gap.

LEARNING THE JOB

Air traffic controllers like me need specialist training. In America you have three months at the FAA's air traffic control academy, then after that there's a further one to five years' training on the (1) .... You need to know everything about how aircraft work. You have to understand how different aircraft will react when they're climbing, turning or landing – nothing about planes should be an (2) .... quantity. The qualities required of an air traffic controller are daunting. You need to think quickly and have (3) .... good anticipation. And you need to have an aggressive, confident personality. Planes might be a (4) .... second apart but you have to know from the moment you look at a situation that it will work. There has been a (5) .... increase in the (6) .... of air traffic in recent years, which adds to the stress of the job.

The most crowded (7) .... of sky in the world is the airspace above New York – every inch is being flown in by somebody. There's not even a (8) .... margin of error – we have to be spot on every time. We work in shifts of eight hours, with 30 minute breaks every hour and a half. We probably control around 70–80 planes an hour, which seems a heavy work (9) .... There's a (10) .... degree of stress in the job, but it's done by people who handle stress very well. We deal with it in different ways; we joke about it or moan a lot. To a (11) .... extent the best therapy is staying busy with the rest of your life. And the calibre of controllers in New York is (12) .... high.

1	**A** work	**B** job	**C** service	**D** shift
2	**A** unrevealed	**B** unfamiliar	**C** untested	**D** unknown
3	**A** utterly	**B** completely	**C** incredibly	**D** deeply
4	**A** mere	**B** plain	**C** sheer	**D** stark
5	**A** high	**B** wide	**C** massive	**D** mighty
6	**A** volume	**B** density	**C** extent	**D** rate
7	**A** plot	**B** block	**C** spot	**D** patch
8	**A** thin	**B** lean	**C** narrow	**D** minute
9	**A** amount	**B** load	**C** quantity	**D** ratio
10	**A** great	**B** wide	**C** broad	**D** high
11	**A** wide	**B** broad	**C** complete	**D** great
12	**A** totally	**B** pretty	**C** hardly	**D** downright

2 Read the text again. Underline the qualities the writer identifies as necessary for an air traffic controller.

3 What other qualities do you think tutors at the FAA academy would look for when accepting people for training as air traffic controllers?

Use of English
▶ Paper 3, Part 1

1 Look at the list below. Which would you be prepared to do as part of your job? Rank them in order of acceptability.

- move to live in another country
- work unsociable hours
- work overtime without extra pay
- live away from your family
- bring work home in the evenings
- spend hours commuting

2 Read the following text, ignoring the gaps. Why is Tadao Masuda unusual? Would you agree with his final statement?

The long journey home

You think you (0) ..*have*.... a difficult journey to work? You travel for over an hour, change trains, fight (1) .... crowds down tunnels and up escalators, and arrive crumpled and sweaty (2) .... face the day. Well, it (3) .... be worse. Spare a thought for Tadao Masuda. At first glance he does not (4) .... out in the crowds of blue-suited office workers swarming into central Tokyo (5) .... morning. Not until you learn that not only (6) .... he travel for three and a quarter hours to get there, but he spends the same time travelling home again. 'I can't (7) .... that I enjoy commuting, (8) .... then again, I don't feel it is time wasted,' he says. 'People who go out after work or sleep later in the morning are using their time (9) .... constructively than me. It gives me the (10) .... to have time for my own thoughts (11) .... interruptions. Travelling home in the evenings, I find that (12) .... many problems there were at work, I have forgotten them by the time I get home. It's my way of (13) .... rid of stress. To (14) .... you the truth, I regard (15) .... as rather a lucky man.'

3 Now fill each of the gaps in the text with one suitable word. Then discuss and justify your answers with a partner.

▶ Exam Maximiser

Language Focus: Vocabulary
Work

1   Read the following text. In each line there is a word or phrase used wrongly. Find them and correct them. Be prepared to explain why they are inappropriate.

The boss from hell

Before I went for my interview on the job with Cramer and Blake
Services, I talked to a few people and found out some informations
about the company. This strategy worked very effective as it gave the
impression that I was keen and committal and I was offered the job
by the personnel manager in the spot.
I was very delighted at first, but I soon discovered that my new
boss, Tom, worked totally hard, spending all his time in the office and
never leaving before 8 p.m. He expected the same grade of commitment
from his employees — the workload he expected every and each one of us
to carry was deeply unreasonable. He accused anyone who didn't work
overtime regularly of not making their fair share and letting the team down.
I decided to put up to the situation without complaining for a while
but lastly I felt I had to confront Tom. I told him I wasn't prepared to
work so hard for such a low salary. Tom said that I had large potential
and could easily get to the top if I was prepared to have an effort.
However, he thoroughly refused to reduce my workload and so in the
end I decided to hand out my resignation.
Just a week later I got another job in Cramer and Blake's main
competitors. Now I'm earning twice as high as my old boss, and my
job's twice as interesting. I work exactly as long hours — but I'm glad I
moved. I haven't got to the top yet — but I'm far on the way!

2   Read the text again and discuss the following questions.

1   What problems did the narrator have with his job?
2   Do you think his boss should have tried harder to keep him?

3

1   Work with a partner. Take turns to read the following statements to each other. Your partner should respond with an appropriate idiomatic expression from the list below. There are two possible responses in each case. (There are four responses you will not need to use.)

1   I've just started a fantastic job with an advertising agency – the money's great too.
    'You must be over the moon!'
2   It's a job that is very unpredictable – it means I often have to think quickly.
3   The fly in the ointment is – my boss works all hours. He never leaves the office before 8 p.m.
4   It wouldn't matter so much, but he expects all of us to do the same.
5   And there's another manager who's always ordering people about and setting us totally unreasonable deadlines.
6   I really like the job, but the workload is a problem. What do you think I should do?

a)   He has no right to work you so hard.
b)   Well, you could grin and bear it for the sake of the money.
c)   So he won't play ball.
d)   You must be thrilled to bits.
e)   Everyone has to pull their weight.
f)   So you have to think on your feet.
g)   A real slave-driver!
h)   Someone who likes to throw his weight around, huh?
i)   You must be over the moon! ✔
j)   He's a workaholic, then?
k)   It's all in a day's work.
l)   You could try making a fuss and standing up for your rights – it could work wonders.
m) So you've really got to be on the ball.
n)   He's obviously driving himself too hard.
o)   Obviously a good team player.
p)   It's hard to work with someone breathing down your neck, isn't it?

2   Check the meaning of the expressions you didn't use and suggest a context for them.

Exam Focus
▶ **Paper 1, Part 2**

In Paper 1, Part 2 you have to read four short extracts and answer two multiple-choice questions on each. The extracts will all be on the same theme but from different types of source, e.g. novels, newspaper or magazine articles, advertisements, essays, etc. The questions may focus on:

- main idea, detail, attitude and implication
- purpose of the whole extract or of sections of it
- text organisation (reference words, comparison, relation between main idea and examples).

Here is a procedure to follow for this task.

- Look at the instructions, the titles and the opening sentences of each extract to get an idea of the main theme and the types of text.
- Look at the first extract. Read it quickly to get a general idea of what it is about.
- Look back at the strategy for dealing with Paper 1, Part 4 multiple-choice questions suggested in Unit 7 page 98, and follow this if you found it useful.
- If you are unsure of the answer, mark the best possibility and go on to the other extracts. Don't forget to return and make a final decision later on.

1 You are going to read four extracts which are all concerned in some way with work. For questions 1–8, choose the answer (**A**, **B**, **C** or **D**) which you think fits best according to the text.

Voluntary Service Overseas

You have just graduated, or are about to graduate, with a degree in any Science discipline, Engineering or Maths. Countless opportunities lie ahead of you. So why not get off to a memorable start with VSO?

A VSO placement is an excellent way to widen your horizons before you immerse yourself in your career. Working in schools with a desperate need for your skills, you'll be making friends with people from a very different culture and gaining a valuable insight into your hidden qualities – a uniquely rewarding experience. And an impressive entry on your CV.

We will give you all the training you need. You will also be provided with air tickets, accommodation, medical insurance, a locally appropriate salary and other financial benefits.

To find out more, please contact our Enquiries Unit, quoting ref: NS/EM82, on 020 8780 7500.

---

1 What is the writer suggesting can 'get off to a memorable start'?
  A the reader's experience of a different culture
  B the reader's career in education
  C the reader's professional life
  D the reader's specialised training

2 What is the main argument used in the advertisement to attract applicants?
  A personal development
  B attractive financial package
  C the opportunity to use their skills
  D improving career prospects

CHANGING **JOBS**

Jobs for life are history. But while most people accept they may have to change employers several times during their working life, the majority still hold to the old adage that a cobbler should stick to his last. Most job moves are either in the same industry or in the same line of work.

That attitude is now being reappraised. Sticking to what you know could mean staying in a not very profitable rut. Taking your courage in both hands and making a fresh start can produce a rapid earnings boost. Equally importantly, starting a second career can help put the lid on an unhappy or unsatisfactory working life.

A small but growing number of employers are now starting to realise that all but the most technical skills are interchangeable – managing staff or dealing with customers is much the same whether you are involved in retailing or railways. And switching from controlling employees to controlling a process – or vice versa – is just one step further along the flexi-work road. But your success in getting out of a rut and into the fast lane will depend on the field you target. Don't expect to succeed with ease if you want to be a brain surgeon or a high-flying stockbroker.

3 What aspect of working life is changing at present?
  A the idea of jobs for life
  B the need to change jobs
  C the need to have training for specific skills
  D the idea of staying in the same field

4   What does the writer say is the alternative to being stuck in an unsatisfactory job?
   A   finding a more flexible working environment
   B   using your existing talents in a new area
   C   gaining a job which demands management skills
   D   retraining for a completely different job

The Bridge Builder

My father was a bridge-builder. That was his business – crossing chasms, joining one side of the river with the other.

   When I was small, bridges brought us bread and books, Christmas crackers and coloured pencils – one-span bridges over creeks, two-span bridges over streams, three-span bridges over wide rivers. Bridges sprang from my father's dreams threading roads together – girder bridges, arched bridges, suspension bridges, bridges of wood, bridges of iron or concrete. Like a sort of hero, my father would drive piles and piers through sand and mud to the rocky bones of the world. His bridges became visible parts of the world's hidden skeleton. When we went out on picnics it was along roads held together by my father's works. As we crossed rivers and ravines we heard each bridge singing in its own private language. We could hear the melody, but my father was the only one who understood the words.

   There were three of us when I was small, Philippa, the oldest, Simon in the middle, and me, Merlin, the youngest, the one with the magician's name. We played where bridges were being born, running around piles of sand and shingle, bags of cement and bars of reinforced steel. Concrete mixers would turn, winches would wind, piles would be driven and decking cast. Slowly, as we watched and played, a bridge would appear and people could cross over.

5   Which of the following ideas is central to the writer's description of bridges?
   A   mystery
   B   connection
   C   distance
   D   beauty

6   What was the children's attitude towards the bridges?
   A   They were interested in how they were made.
   B   They wanted the things the bridges provided for them.
   C   They accepted them as an integral part of their life.
   D   They were proud to be involved in making them.

Dicing with death?

When asked what it's like living each day with danger, most people in high-risk jobs say the same. They don't think about it. Steeplejack Andrew Fontaine knows it's time to get back down to the ground when his ladders start to sing. 'It's a ghostly sound,' he says. 'It happens when the wind gets up and starts blowing through the steps in the ladders and the lashings that are holding them on. The noise travels right up and down the ladders. The minute you hear it sing, you know that you've got to get down, and quick. If you're up a 100-metre steel chimney, you can find yourself moving half a metre with every blast of wind. After a while, no matter how strong you are, it becomes physically impossible to hang on. You just let go – and you're gone. But I don't consider what I do dangerous – I take great care to eliminate all possible risks beforehand. Everything gets inspected and tested. There's no in-betweens in this business. You either do it properly or you're dead.'

Steven Moore, a diving engineer, is another worker for whom danger is an ever-present but a largely ignored silent partner. 'Even when you're working under an oil rig, the problem's not the diving, it's what's going on around you. Pipes can burst, seals can blow and things that are being loaded onto the rig have a tendency to get dropped on your head. But the regulations have got so tight now there's very little danger any more.'

7   Andrew Fontaine says that the 'singing' of his ladders
   A   can affect the stability of the ladders.
   B   tells him they are not properly secured.
   C   may be a warning that he has climbed too high.
   D   occurs before the ladder starts to sway violently.

8   Which of these situations is described semi-humorously?
   A   being on a ladder inside a steel chimney
   B   finding mechanical problems on oil rigs
   C   being hit by falling objects underwater
   D   falling off a ladder in high winds

2   **Where do you think each of the extracts above might have appeared? Which one did you enjoy reading most and why?**

147

Language Focus: Grammar

Future forms

1

1 Read the text below. What main point is the writer making about the workplace of the future?

The workplace of the future

Forget science fiction, future workplaces could resemble images from centuries past.

Ask any IT or telecommunications firm what the office of the future is going to be like and you are likely to get a realistic but fairly short-sighted answer, mainly because they need to sell the products at their disposal now. However, ask a crystal-gazing professor and he or she will have a wider grasp of the concept.

Professor Jeremy Myerson, who runs a 'Tomorrow's office' course at de Montfort University predicts: 'Thanks to modern technology, we will have gone back to a more natural pre-industrial, pre-modern way of life by the mid-21st century. The modern office is inflexible, structured and encased by technology. But as communication equipment shrinks, we'll be able to carry round all the information we need in something as small as a credit card. Open-plan, desktop and computer-linked systems will become things of the past. And going to work in these weird buildings that we call offices will seem as quaint as chucking sewage into the street.'

One leading IT services provider believes that we will become less and less dependent on the office concept itself. Technology will have disposed of cables and offices. Like our ancestors, we will be making all those important business transactions in coffee houses. Twenty years on, we won't need vast numbers of people working in large offices, so we can move back to the coffee table to do our business. What we all need to ask ourselves though is: will we want to work office-less, will we be able to take on the sociological implications, whatever they might be?

2 Underline all the examples you can find of verb forms referring to the future. Which form is used:

a) to make a general prediction?
b) for prediction probably based on present evidence?
c) for a repeated activity around a point in the future?
d) for an action that will be finished before a point of time in the future?
e) for an action that will fairly certainly take place?
f) to indicate future ability?

3 How would you answer the question in the last paragraph of the article? What are the possible 'sociological implications' referred to?

▶ Grammar reference p. 223

2 *will / be going to*

Fill in the gaps with the correct form of *will* or *be going to*. Can you add any uses to the list in Exercise 1.2?

1 It seems inevitable that the nature of office work .... be changed by recent developments in technology.
2 My husband hates commuting, so he .... apply for a new job nearer home.
3 It's nine o'clock already! I .... late for work.
4 Since everyone appears to be here, I .... ask the Divisional Manager to give his report.

3 *will be doing/will have done/will have been doing*

1 Fill in the gaps with the correct form of the verb in brackets. Can you add any more uses to the list in Exercise 1.2?

1 Things we take for granted, like notebooks .... (*most likely disappear*) by the middle of the 21st century.
2 Maybe in fifty years' time we .... (*spend*) our days entirely at home.
3 However, people .... (*travel*) to work for a few more years yet.
4 My plane arrives at 11.00 a.m. tomorrow. You'll be able to recognise me easily – I .... (*carry*) a red briefcase.
5 By the end of this month, we .... (*work*) on this project for ten years.

2 Which time expressions are used with which tense forms? Group them into categories.

4   Write five sentences making predictions about your partner without talking to him/her. Use the phrases in the box and a future tense. Then read out your predictions to your partner. Does he/she agree?

> this weekend   by this time next year
> in a couple of years   in ten years' time
> by the time you are fifty   quite soon

5   Other ways of referring to the future

1   Underline the ways of referring to the future used in the following sentences.

1   Guidelines for improved working conditions are to be introduced shortly.
2   I was wondering if you might like to buy a ticket for the school concert.
3   She looks as if she's on the point of losing her temper.
4   The committee is due to meet tomorrow.
5   They're quite likely to turn round and tell us it was all our fault.

2   Which of the sentences above suggests:

a)   something fairly certain to take place?
b)   a formal arrangement?
c)   something which should happen because a time has been fixed for it?
d)   something which may not have been planned, but is going to happen almost immediately?
e)   a polite and rather tentative request?

6   Fill each of the gaps with a suitable word or phrase.

1   By next April Jenny .... to Mike for ten years.
2   According to the doctor, Mandy is .... to have the baby a week tomorrow.
3   She's not very .... pass unless she works harder.
4   I was on .... giving up on him when he finally showed up.
5   This time next week I .... my new job.
6   Will you .... Tessa to the office party, or Bob?
7   New regulations concerning company cars .... introduced by the government, according to reports.
8   If we win the election, we .... all this campaigning in vain.

7   Tenses in time clauses

- *As communication equipment **shrinks**, we'll be able to carry round all the information we need in something as small as a credit card.* (text, p. 148)

1   Read the examples below and complete the chart.

1   I'll start work as soon as I finish university.
2   After I've finished university, I plan to go abroad.
3   I have always forgotten my problems by the time I get home. (cloze text, p. 144)
4   You lucky thing – while we're working our fingers to the bone, you'll be lying on a beach.
5   By the time he retires, he'll have been working for the company for thirty years.
6   I'll do it when I can find the time.

main clause (tense)	link word	subordinate clause (tense)
will	as soon as	present simple

2   Fill in the gaps in the following paragraph with an appropriate verb form.

Kate and Mickey are doing a four-year degree course in fashion design and marketing. As soon as they (1) .... qualified, they (2) .... to set up their own company, designing and making children's clothes. When they (3) .... into business, they (4) .... from home and sell the clothes by mail order. However, once they (5) .... to make a profit they (6) .... to their own premises and take on extra staff. Later on, as their business (7) ...., they (8) .... into producing clothes for babies and toddlers. With luck and hard work, they (9) .... their own factory and a chain of shops all over Europe by the time they (10) .... thirty.

8   Interview a partner about his/her career plans. Ask questions like these.

1   Where do you see yourself in ten years' time?
2   What do you hope to have achieved in your career by the time you are 30/40/50?

Writing

▶ Paper 2, Part 2 (report)

1 In Paper 2, Part 2 you may be asked to write a **report**. Which three of the following are **not** features of report writing?

A report:
- deals with facts
- includes interviews and direct quotes
- is written for a particular audience
- may contain recommendations for action
- normally uses headings for each section
- uses adjectives for dramatic effect
- is written in an impersonal, formal style
- uses set phrases and passive forms
- uses irony and rhetorical questions.

2 Read the writing task and underline the key words.

> ### TASK
>
> You have been asked to help your college to improve its facilities for helping college leavers with careers advice. Write a report for the new careers officer on any facilities that exist at present, assessing their usefulness and making recommendations for ways in which they could be improved.
>
> (300–350 words)

3 Discuss the following points in groups. If you are already in work, think back to the school or college you attended.

1 Does your school or college
   a) offer a careers advice service? How helpful is it?
   b) arrange work experience opportunities for the students in local companies or organisations?
2 Do you know where to find out information about job opportunities? What information do you think you might find helpful when you make your choices?

4 Listen to a former student talking about her problems in finding work and what could have helped her make better choices. As you listen, answer the questions below by writing notes.

1 Why did the speaker have an unsatisfying job after leaving school?
2 What does she think would have helped her and why?

5 Using your own ideas or ideas from the Listening text, write an outline for your report using headings suggested by the task. Remember to add an introduction giving background information (see Unit 6, page 93). The sections may be of different lengths; if there are few existing facilities, then your section for recommendations will be longer.

6 A, B and C are extracts from introductions to reports written in answer to this task.

1 Which one do you think is the best? Why?

A I think it's absolutely terrible that there isn't any solid information to help us make career choices - there's nothing to give us exciting ideas and I haven't a clue how to go about finding out what to do. So what can the school do to help? 'It's a big problem,' say the teachers, 'but it's nothing to do with us.'

B There are many more opportunities available for accessing data and data banks now than in the past, and I think the school should make full use of these. Why not use the information that's there? After all, someone put it there! So this report will describe interviews with different people giving their opinions and then try to assess the best way forward - if there is one.

C There are about 200 school leavers each year who should be given the best possible advice on their future careers. This means that they need well-presented, clear, up-to-date information on opportunities open to them. This report will examine existing facilities, assess the best way of improving them, and make recommendations for future action.

2 Can you find examples of features not usually included in reports in the two introductions you rejected?

7   In the middle section of the report you will have to assess the value of current facilities. Read the notes below and turn them into full sentences, using appropriate linking words and phrases.

> 1   Only 2 computers available, constantly in use: v. frustrating for students needing careers information.
>
> 2   Not many careers books in library; out of date, so not v. helpful.
>
> 3   Librarian v. knowledgeable: tries to provide good service, but v. busy, not always available.
>
> 4   Reps. from local companies visit, give information: vital, helps us to learn about real life.
>
> 5   Weekly careers sessions after school run by a teacher: inconvenient, few students go. Has potential: better if time changed.

8

1   Underline the linking expressions in the sentences below. How do they connect the ideas?

1   I had no help at all and as a result I ended up in a dead-end job.
2   My friend said she spent a week with a local company and in this way she found out about opportunities that she had no idea existed.

2   Combine these sentences in as many ways as you can. Use a subordinate or relative clause, or an appropriate linking expression.

1   Setting up connections with local firms enables students to learn about work. They make fewer mistakes when they come to choosing their career.
2   I feel that the best way forward is to set up a formal system for advice. This makes the scheme an integral part of the school curriculum.
3   There is no opportunity for students to talk about their ambitions. They never have a fair chance to realise them.
4   My friend found careers information in her library. She could make a reasoned choice.
5   Students should be able to visit a company they are interested in. They get a good idea of what the job entails.

3   In which section of the report could the ideas in the sentences above be used?

9   Look at the pairs of sentences below, which could form part of the final section of the report. Which one is most appropriate for this type of writing? Why?

1   a) The school has got to make changes to the current library set-up.
   b) The school should look at ways of changing the current library layout.
2   a) If the computers were linked to a job information database, this could provide a major resource for school leavers.
   b) If we could all get into a job information database on the computers, we'd be able to use it as a resource.
3   a) I think they've got to present everything really clearly, with ways of getting in touch with possible employers.
   b) The information should be presented as clearly and simply as possible, preferably with instructions on ways of contacting potential employers.

10   Now write your report.

> **Exam Strategy**
>
> When you write a report, remember:
> DO
> • keep your points clear and concise: your target reader is busy.
> • use headings to organise the information and make it easy for the reader to follow.
> • use a neutral to formal register, and use it consistently.
> DON'T
> • begin and end your report like a formal letter.

6–10 Progress check

1 Multiple-choice lexical cloze

For questions 1–6, read the text below and decide which answer (**A, B, C** or **D**) best fits each gap.

The origins of the calendar

We take the mechanism of the calendar for (1) .... Passing through years, months, weeks, hours, minutes and seconds we seldom think about where these things came from, or why we have chosen to divide time one way and not another.

It has not always been so. For thousands of years the effort to (2) .... time and to create a workable calendar was one of the great struggles of humanity, a conundrum for astronomers, mathematicians, priests and anyone else who needed to count the days until the next harvest, to calculate when taxes were due or to (3) .... out the exact moment a sacrifice would be made to appease an angry god. A case can be (4) .... that science itself was first sparked by a human compulsion to comprehend the passing of time, to wrestle down the forward motion of life and impose on it some (5) .... of order. And the effort to organise and control time continues (6) .... today. We are a people of the calendar in a way that our ancestors who tilled fields and lived and died according to natural cycles would never have comprehended.

1   **A** normal   **B** granted
    C read   **D** given
2   **A** allot   **B** calculate
    C measure   **D** adjust
3   **A** figure   **B** count
    C divide   **D** lay
4   **A** shown   **B** given
    C made   **D** defended
5   **A** definition   **B** sense
    C implication   **D** denotation
6   **A** unappeased   **B** unalleviated
    C unabashed   **D** unabated

2 Open cloze

Read the text below and fill each space with one suitable word.

The climb of my life

Dave moved fast while I wobbled along behind. He was unaware that I (0) _had_..... no snow and ice experience in the Alps, and I didn't tell him in (1) .... he chose not to climb with me. But my fear evaporated with the dawn, replaced with a mixture of wonder and delight (2) .... being on this stupendous mountain. (3) .... we climbed higher I knew that we were going to succeed. There was (4) .... reason why I (5) .... believe this but I did. I had never before had (6) .... an exultant feeling. I stood (7) .... the foot of the huge north wall and knew unquestionably that I (8) .... climb it, and that this was exactly (9) .... I should be and exactly what I should (10) ....

I climbed in a daze of excitement, revelling (11) .... the deepening abyss (12) .... me and the walls (13) .... granite and ice thrusting up to the summit cornices far (14) .... Darkness fell, and we made our camp, shivering in the cold night. When the eastern sky slowly changed (15) .... black to blue and a streamer of gold spread across the horizon, I knew that this would be the greatest day of my life.

3 Word formation

Use the word given in capitals at the end of some of the lines to form a word that fits in the space in the same line.

Urban rubbish tips – haven for wildlife

To many of us, the rubbish tip is just the end of the road for (0) _unwanted_. articles, but these heaps of refuse are places where life can begin (1) .... for many species. Although they may seem to be unlikely havens, rubbish tips support an (2) .... large and (3) .... number of plants and animals, including some species that are seldom seen (4) .... in Britain. They are among the few places where common species can be seen side by side with the more exotic: wild flowers, cultivated blossoms and even subtropical vegetables may all thrive there.

Urban rubbish tips are relatively recent phenomena, (5) .... in the nineteenth century when the populations of towns increased dramatically. In the current method of (6) ...., known as controlled tipping, the rubbish is deposited in shallow layers, each covered by a layer of soil. Sites chosen for tipping are usually those considered (7) .... for building or agricultural (8) ...., and include such places as heathland and marshes.

Being set apart in this way, the rubbish tip is an ecological island – it has conditions quite different from those of the (9) .... land, and therefore has its own (10) .... plant and animal communities which can live largely undisturbed by human activity.

WANT
NEW

ASTONIS
VARY
ELSE

ORIGIN

DISPOSE

SUIT
DEVELO

JOIN
CHARAC

4 Gapped sentences

For questions 1–6, think of one word only which can be used appropriately in all three sentences.

1 She was just .... off to sleep when there was a loud knocking at the door.
Snow was .... across the road, making driving increasingly difficult.
She was aware that they were .... apart but couldn't see how to save their relationship.

2 It was quite a .... to reach the castle, which was built on a rocky hill.
After a steady .... , the price eventually levelled off at $5 a litre.
The speed of her new album's .... up the charts has been sensational.

3 The president won the election by a very .... majority, thanks to the hard work of his campaign team.
Unfortunately, the company takes a very .... view of market possibilities.
Peter had a .... escape from drowning when his boat capsized and flung him into the water.

4 The ships .... their catch at the harbour in the early hours of the morning.
She's .... a plum job with the BBC – she's really delighted.
After three years of wild living he .... up in serious debt and had to sell his house.

5 It's .... to read the small print at the end of legal documents.
I believe that the .... difference between man and apes is the awareness of time.
The village has retained its .... character in spite of the new developments.

6 The full details of the case were not printed in the newspapers out of .... for her family.
With .... to your proposal, I regret that I am as yet unable to make a decision.
His decisive handling of the crisis won him the .... of his peers.

5 Key word transformations

Complete the second sentence with three to eight words so that it has a similar meaning to the first sentence, using the word given. Do not change the word given.

1 You can buy these gadgets almost anywhere nowadays.
widely
These gadgets ....
.... nowadays.

2 She was about to leave when her friend finally arrived.
setting
Just as she was on ....
.... her friend finally arrived.

3 The weather was so appalling that we came home from our holiday early.
cut
It was such ....
.... short.

4 All that's involved is signing a few papers.
just
All you ....
.... a few papers.

5 We owe the fact that we won the tournament entirely to the coach.
due
Our victory in the tournament ....
.... the coach.

6 There is beginning to be a noticeable rise in the sea level.
happening
What ....
.... is beginning to rise noticeably.

7 Would any students wishing to participate please inform me immediately.
part
Any students who ....
.... me know immediately.

8 As soon as he arrived home, he went to the fridge.
made
On ....
.... the fridge.

6 This picture was taken by a photographer trying to capture the 'feel' of city living. Discuss what issues he was thinking of when he took the photograph and suggest other pictures he could have taken.

11 The monster in the machine

Speaking

1 Look at the photos.

1 In pairs or groups, choose two of the examples of technology illustrated, and think of as many ways as you can in which they:

- make life easier or more pleasant
- may be dangerous to individuals or to the environment
- may develop in the future.

2 Without the technology we take for granted, how would everyday life be different? Think of a normal day, and describe how it would change if you had to manage without any help from technology.

2 Which of the following qualities do you think humans share with animals such as dogs, horses and chimpanzees?

- intelligence
- feelings and emotions
- creativity
- a moral sense

Which of these qualities do you think a computer might have in the future?

Listening

▶ **Paper 4, Part 1**

1 You will hear four extracts about technology. The sentences below summarise some of the information you will hear. Work with a partner. In each sentence, only two of the three verbs given are possible. Cross out the verb which is inappropriate.

1 Nowadays, computers can *work/function/manage* independently of humans.
2 Computers can *operate/store/run* machinery and data bases.
3 They can *manage/monitor/supervise* manufacturing processes.
4 They can *calculate/store/hold* information in data banks.
5 They can *have/do/perform* increasingly complex calculations.

 2 Now listen, and for questions 1–8, choose the answer (**A**, **B** or **C**) which fits best according to what you hear. Remember to read the questions that relate to each extract before you listen to it.

Extract One

You hear two friends talking about technology.

1 The man and woman agree that technology is
  A taken for granted.
  B fashionable nowadays.
  C sometimes irrelevant.

2 What is the woman's view of machines?
  A They are essential for our survival.
  B They are taking over our lives.
  C They have encouraged progress.

Extract Two

You hear part of a talk on the radio on the use of computers.

3 The speaker thinks computers are potentially dangerous because they may
  A limit freedom of choice.
  B take away jobs.
  C control information.

4 What is the speaker's main concern about the future?
  A people misusing data
  B people being superseded by machines
  C people losing the ability to think

Extract Three

You hear two friends talking about the influence of science fiction on technology.

5 The man says automatic doors were
  A thirty years ahead of their time.
  B not thought possible by scientists.
  C first seen in science fiction.

6 The woman thinks science fiction writers are
  A unoriginal.
  B unprofessional.
  C hardworking.

Extract Four

You hear an author talking about his new book on the radio.

7 The writer thinks that the study of the paranormal used to
  A follow scientific methods.
  B be more wide-ranging.
  C have more status.

8 Science has become
  A more tangible than it used to be.
  B as exciting as the paranormal.
  C more accepting of the paranormal.

3 Check your answers with a partner. Then decide which extract the ideas in Exercise 1 relate to most closely.

4 Discuss the following questions.

1 What ideas were common to all the extracts?
2 Can you think of any gadgets that haven't caught on, e.g. wristwatch TVs? Why did they fail?

5 Say it again

Re-express these sentences using the framework given.

1 It's often used for marketing.
  What .... marketing.
2 The existence of the paranormal hasn't been proved yet.
  The existence of the paranormal ....
  .... be proved.
3 Today this is no longer the case.
  This .... more.
4 This open-mindedness has ended now.
  They used .... but they aren't now.

...Look, No hands!
FUTURE2012

Reading

▶ **Paper 1, Part 3**

1 What do you know about Frankenstein? Try this quiz.

1 The story of *Frankenstein* was written by
  a) a Hollywood screenwriter.
  b) a 19th-century woman novelist.

2 Frankenstein was
  a) a monster.
  b) a scientist.

3 The monster was made from
  a) parts of dead bodies.
  b) pieces of spare machinery.

4 The story explores
  a) the distinction between man and machine.
  b) the effects of being rejected.

2 Now read the first two sections of the gapped text (not the jumbled paragraphs) and check your answers.

3 You are now going to read the whole article, which discusses whether machines could ever have human qualities. Seven paragraphs have been removed from the article. Choose from the paragraphs **A–H** the one which fits each gap. There is one extra paragraph which you do not need to use.

One of the high points in Mary Shelley's gothic novel *Frankenstein* is when the tragic creature cobbled together from cadavers comes face to face with its human creator Victor Frankenstein, the real monster of the story.

1 ....

This heart-wrenching declaration exposes a paradox about the hapless creature. Frankenstein built his creation from spare parts, so in one sense it is just a machine. Yet the creature instinctively understands himself as human, something more than a machine.

2 ....

Nearly two centuries later the same question has surfaced again. And today the question is being asked not of some fictional creature but of machines in various states of creation that promise to have human-like senses and to be conscious, at least in some form. Theologians and computer scientists are starting to wonder if any of these machines might ever be said to have a soul. If so, would such a soul be like a human being's, or something altogether different?

3 ....

Between these two poles stretches a continuum of opinion. For example, Jennifer Cobb, a theologian and author of a forthcoming book on theology and cyberspace, says that today's

computers are about as alive as viruses – but 'along with a little bit alive comes a little bit of soul,' she says. 'If the day comes when computation becomes so complex as to express emotions, then they will have quite a bit more soul. It's an infinite resource with infinite potential.'

4 ....

Artificial intelligence researchers are already dabbling with emotional machines, and computers that could become conscious of their surroundings and of themselves. One of the most ambitious of these projects is Cog, a talking robot designed in human form that will be capable of exploring the world through sight, sound and touch. The project team hopes that Cog will be able to discover the world the way a human baby does, and will thus come to understand things as a child does.

5 ....

Yet how would we tell if a computer developed a soul? It might not be enough for a computer to look, behave and think like a human. It might also involve a more complex definition, such as the possession of a sense of moral responsibility, or sense of self. Of course, a sense of moral responsibility could be programmed into a computer. But what if a silicon-based being were to develop a morality of its own – its own

conscience? What would that be like?

6 ....

Alternatively, a computer could be 'cloned' so many examples of the same 'being' could exist. What would that do to the machine's conception of itself and others? We just don't know what ethics would be like for a computer – we barely know how to imagine such a thing.

7 ....

But this is not necessarily so. From Shelley's nineteenth-century monster to today's real-life robots, complex entities have a habit of taking on a life of their own.

F Constant rejection has finally led it to commit murder. Yet when it first became conscious it was not evil. 'Believe me,' it says in anguish, 'I was benevolent; my soul glowed with love and humanity.'

G It is interesting that we are happy to consider the Frankenstein creation in terms of what its thoughts are or the fact that it has self-will. But this is fiction. Whether or not a machine is conscious, and whether we can prove it, is a fascinating philosophical exercise, nothing more, nothing less.

H Opinions tend to fall between two extremes. Many people want to draw an unbreachable divide between humans and machines, insisting that however smart a computer might become it could never have a soul. On the other hand, some artificial intelligence researchers insist that humans are just complex machines, so why wouldn't a silicon-based machine also have a soul? For these scientists, a soul would be simply an emergent property of a very complex system.

A It could be different from the human variety. Take death, for example. A computer with a back-up tape might not see death as a big deal. Think about how different life would be if we had back-up tapes.

B The story raised the issue of whether or not something manufactured would have a soul – that mysterious entity which is the very essence of humanness, the thing that links us irrevocably to God.

C For Philip Clayton, a theologian and philosopher, such an idea goes against the grain of much religious thinking. But he agrees that, in the future, as machines become more like humans, the distinction between them could become blurred. 'On what grounds would we withhold souls from computers when they inhabit humanoid robotic bodies, accept visual input, give output with human voices and function comfortably in many social contexts?' he asks.

D Stories such as *Frankenstein* suggest that the things we humans create are often much more than the sum of their parts. Many people imagine that if we built something, we would know all about it.

E If it lives up to expectations, it will express emotions. Eventually, they argue, it's surely going to be able to say, 'I'm afraid,' or 'I'm bored,' and mean it. And if it does say such things – and mean them – then is it so far-fetched to wonder if it would have a soul?

4 Read the complete text again to check that it makes sense. Why do you think the unknown is often portrayed as threatening?

Exam Strategy

In a non-fiction text you need to think about the logical development of the argument. The missing paragraphs may develop a line of argument from what goes before or give an opposing idea.

Use of English

▶ **Paper 3, Part 1**

1 Read through the following text quickly without filling in any gaps. Find answers to these questions.

1 What social problem is mentioned in the first paragraph?
2 How can the 'robot room' help?

ROBOT ROOM TENDS TO THE SICK

Since more women are now working after marriage in Japan, there is no-one at home to (0) ...*look*... after the sick and elderly. To address this problem, Japanese scientists have begun work (1) .... a robotic room (2) .... occupants need never lift a (3) ...., since they have interactive computer-controlled devices catering to their (4) .... need.

The room holds a special bed containing pressure sensors monitored (5) .... a central computer, (6) .... a record to be made of the position and movement of the person in the

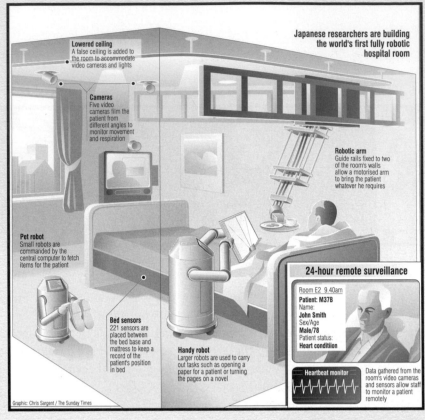

Japanese researchers are building the world's first fully robotic hospital room

Lowered ceiling A false ceiling is added to the room to accommodate video cameras and lights

Cameras Five video cameras film the patient from different angles to monitor movement and respiration

Robotic arm Guide rails fixed to two of the room's walls allow a motorised arm to bring the patient whatever he requires

Pet robot Small robots are commanded by the central computer to fetch items for the patient

Bed sensors 221 sensors are placed between the bed base and mattress to keep a record of the patient's position in bed

Handy robot Larger robots are used to carry out tasks such as opening a paper for a patient or turning the pages on a novel

24-hour remote surveillance

Room E2 9.40am
Patient: M37B
Name:
John Smith
Sex/Age
Male/78
Patient status:
Heart condition

Heartbeat monitor   Data gathered from the room's video cameras and sensors allow staff to monitor a patient remotely

Graphic: Chris Sargent / The Sunday Times

bed. Five video cameras also keep the patient (7) .... constant surveillance.

As (8) .... as keeping a watch over the patient's condition, the room provides other (9) .... of help. If the patient wants to watch television, he need (10) .... point at it and the television will turn (11) ....

on. A robotic arm can pick up objects the patient is pointing at and bring them to his bedside. In (12) ...., 'pet' robots are now (13) .... developed to keep the person company. (14) ...., the team warns that more research is needed (15) .... the robotic room could be trusted to guard our loved ones.

2 Now fill each gap in the text with one suitable word.

3 Discuss these questions.

1 Many countries have a growing proportion of elderly people. What problems is this likely to cause?
2 Is this an issue in your country? If so, what solutions are being discussed to deal with the problem?
3 Medical advances may soon increase life expectancy dramatically. Do you think this is a good thing? What age would you like to live to?
4 How would you ideally like to spend your old age?

4 **Vocabulary:** idiomatic expressions

1 The following idiomatic expressions involving parts of the body are usually only used in the negative. Match each one to the appropriate explanation a)–e).

1 He didn't move a muscle.
2 He didn't turn a hair.
3 He didn't lift a finger to help.
4 He didn't put a foot wrong.
5 He didn't have a leg to stand on.

a) He didn't make any mistakes.
b) He didn't do anything.
c) He remained totally still.
d) He stayed completely calm.
e) He had no proof or evidence.

2 Think of situations when each expression above would be appropriate, for example:

Number 1: He's a spy or a thief. He was in someone else's room when they came back unexpectedly – he hid behind the curtains and didn't move a muscle so as not to be discovered.'

Language Focus: Grammar
Reflexive pronouns

* *... the television will turn itself on.*
(cloze text, p. 158)

1   Which of the following sentences contain incorrect uses of reflexive pronouns? Put a cross next to them. How does the use of reflexive pronouns compare with your language?

1   The monster created by Frankenstein regarded itself as human.
2   Forbes got up, showered himself and went down to breakfast.
3   As they approached the gloomy old house, the door slowly opened itself.
4   She prides herself on her immaculate apartment.
5   Shall I make ourselves a cup of coffee?
6   This is no time to lose control! Pull yourself together!
7   Hearing footsteps on the stairs, I quickly hid myself behind the curtains.
8   The bad weather spoiled their plans for a picnic, so they had to content themselves with a meal in a restaurant.
9   You'll wear yourself out if you carry on working seventy hours a week.
10   He finds it hard to concentrate himself on his work.
11   The girls devoted themselves to looking after their sick mother.
12   Why don't you resign yourself to the fact you're never going to be a famous inventor?

2   Look at these pairs of sentences. What's the difference in meaning when the verb is used with a reflexive pronoun?

1   a) Genetic differences may explain why some people develop cancer.
     b) That's not what I meant. I probably haven't explained myself very clearly.
2   a) She sat down to compose a letter of complaint to the holiday company.
     b) She was so angry that she needed to compose herself before she could start writing the letter.
3   a) New technology is being applied to almost every industrial process.
     b) You will never do well if you don't apply yourself at school.
4   a) He dedicated his first book to his wife.
     b) He has dedicated himself to helping the poor.
5   a) I'm perfectly willing to lend you the money.
     b) His new novel lends itself perfectly to being made into a film.

6   a) There's not much to distinguish her from the other students in terms of ability.
     b) She distinguished herself by achieving the highest sales in the company.
7   a) He said he wouldn't mind helping me with my tax return if I needed it.
     b) He didn't mean to snap her head off, but he just couldn't help himself.
8   a) That coat suits you down to the ground.
     b) A: 'I think I'd rather not go out tonight.'
        B: 'Suit yourself.'
9   a) I'm sorry about last night – I behaved like a child.
     b) Did the children behave themselves while I was away?
10   a) The family were finally reconciled after years of silence following the argument.
     b) He reconciled himself to the idea of moving to another town.

3   **Use of English:** Paper 3, Part 4

Complete the second sentence with three to eight words so that it has a similar meaning to the first sentence, using the word given. Do not change the word given.

1   She told us to take whatever we liked from the fridge.   **help**
    She said we ....
    .... from the fridge.
2   There's no need for them to make a final decision yet.   **commit**
    They don't need ....
    .... later.
3   It wasn't your fault that you lost the game.
                                                                                              blame
    You shouldn't ....
    .... the game.
4   The politician was anxious not to get involved in the scandal.   **distance**
    The politician wanted ....
    .... the scandal.
5   You have to be firm or they will just exploit you.
                                                                                              assert
    If you ....
    .... just be exploited.
6   Whether you come or don't come is up to you.
                                                                                              suit
    You .... or not.

▶ Grammar reference p. 224

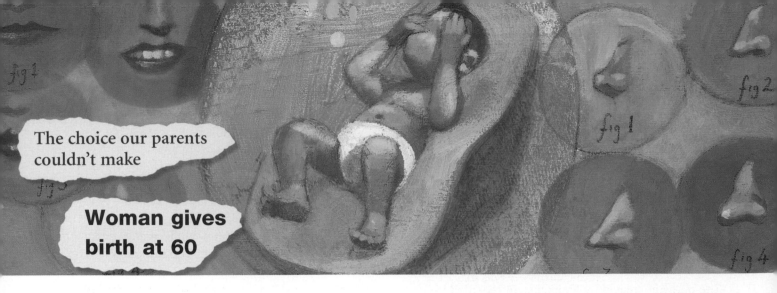

The choice our parents couldn't make

Woman gives birth at 60

Listening

▶ Paper 4, Part 4

1

1   Which of the following medical procedures are suggested by the illustration and headlines?

- choosing the sex of your child
- choosing the physical appearance of your child
- fertility treatment for older women
- cosmetic surgery
- the conception of a child after the death of one of the parents
- the creation of a child with identical characteristics to another person

2   Some of the medical procedures listed above are already possible, and some are likely to be possible in the near future. Do you think that they should:

a) never be allowed?
b) be allowed in special circumstances?
c) be generally available to those who want them?

 2   You will hear two friends, Jessica and Will, discussing a television documentary about medical advances. Before you listen, look through the list of opinions below. Which of them relate to the topics in Exercise 1? Which are new topics?

1	Cosmetic surgery can be acceptable at any age.	☐ 1
2	Children's toys may establish false standards of beauty.	☐ 2
3	People should be allowed to pay for cosmetic surgery if they want to.	☐ 3
4	It's acceptable for older women to be given fertility treatment.	☐ 4
5	Nowadays men and women share child-care more equally.	☐ 5
6	Multiple births may lead to problems for the children and families.	☐ 6

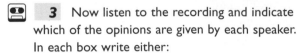 **3**   Now listen to the recording and indicate which of the opinions are given by each speaker. In each box write either:

   J (Jessica)
or **W** (Will)
or **B** (both Jessica and Will)

Then listen again to check and complete your answers.

4   Discuss this question.

How far do you agree that the developments discussed in the Listening are 'flying in the face of nature'?

5

1   Read the prompt card below and prepare a two-minute talk. Do not give the talk yet.

> How far do you agree that people worry too much about their appearance nowadays?
>
> - health
> - media
> - peer pressure

 2   Listen to a student giving his talk. What is his main problem?

3   Discuss what he could have done to improve his talk. Think about:

- speed
- use of own examples
- use of own ideas.

4   Now practise your talk with a partner. Give each other feedback on the areas listed above.

Language Focus: Grammar
Future forms with modal verbs

1 Read the examples below and decide whether the modal auxiliary verb suggests:

a) a fairly certain prediction.
b) a future possibility.
c) an implied condition.
d) a strong suggestion.

1 I don't think that cosmetic surgery *should* be completely forbidden.
2 I *will* probably go bald early, like my father did.
3 It *could/may/might* even happen before I'm thirty if I'm really unlucky.
4 In that case, I *might/may* have a hair transplant.
5 However, I *would* never wear a toupee.

2 In the following extract, an expert predicts what he thinks will be possible in the field of medicine in the year 2020. Complete the sentences using the verbs in brackets with an appropriate modal verb where necessary.

> I think 'spare-part surgery' using animal organs (1) *may well have become* (well/become) a routine procedure for transplants by 2020. Current concerns about animal organs transmitting diseases to humans are likely (2) .... (resolve) by then. Of course, any transplants of animal organs that took place (3) .... (need/precede) by very careful tests to make sure the organ did not contain harmful micro-organisms.
>
> By that time, however, instead of using animal organs, people who know they may need transplants in the future (4) .... (have oneself cloned) instead. Their clone's organs (5) .... (use) as spare parts for transplant surgery. Many people see this as a horrendous development which (6) .... (not allow) to happen. But history shows us that once technological developments become possible they (7) .... (always take up) by people in the long run, however much we may try to prevent this.

3 Discuss these questions.

1 What 'horrendous' consequences do you think cloning humans could have?
2 What justification could be given for human cloning other than its use in spare-part surgery? What benefits could it bring in future?

▶ Grammar reference p. 224

Language Focus: Vocabulary

1 Idiomatic expressions

The expressions in the following sentences all contain verbs or phrases to do with holding, touching or moving in some way. Fill in the gaps using words from the box in the correct form.

blow	grasp	grip	hit	hold
move	pinch	push	put	squeeze

1 I can't .... my finger on exactly why, but I just don't trust her somehow.
2 His failure to get promoted was a severe .... to his pride.
3 She has a good .... of abstract concepts.
4 The country people in that area .... fast to their traditional way of life.
5 The story was so sad, it .... me to tears.
6 The loss of his job has .... him very hard – he feels he's lost his identity.
7 The doctor's very busy today, but if it's really urgent I'll try to .... you in.
8 We're a bit .... for time – you'd better get a move on or we'll be late.
9 Try to get a .... on yourself – you won't help by getting upset.
10 I haven't got much time but I can fit your appointment in at a ....

2 Collocation practice

• *It's really **flying in the face of nature**.* (Listening text)

For each of the sentences below, write a new sentence as similar as possible in meaning using the word given. For each sentence, use a collocation or idiom with the words *nature/natural/naturally*.

1 The country is rich in raw materials such as coal and iron. **resources**
2 She learns languages without really trying. **come**
3 The police thought he had died as a result of illness. **causes**
4 If you've got a minor illness, it's best to let your body cure itself. **course**
5 She's not bad-looking but she spends a fortune trying to look even better. **improve**
6 The explosion wasn't due to any human cause. **disaster**
7 I got her to help by pointing out it was a good thing to do. **appeal**
8 Most people automatically fasten the seatbelt when they get into a car. **second**

Reading

▶ **Paper 1, Part 4**

1

1 The following are all positive qualities which parents may wish their children to have. Which four would you wish for a child of yours? Rank these four in order of importance. What others would you add to the list?

- beauty
- a calm and friendly personality
- energy and determination
- a brilliant scientific mind
- physical strength and co-ordination
- originality and creativity

2 Discuss the four qualities you chose with a partner. Do you think these qualities are:

- inherited from one or both parents?
- developed through a good education?
- enhanced by a healthy environment?
- encouraged by difficult circumstances?
- related to national background?

2 The text opposite is from a book for the general reader by Lee Silver, a Professor of Genetics at Princeton University, USA. In the book the author discusses possible future uses of genetic engineering.

Read the extract and answer the following questions.

1 What is the main idea stated in paragraph 1?
2 What general uses for genetic engineering does the writer suggest in paragraphs 2 and 3?
3 Paragraph 4 refers to genetic enhancements. What enhancements are mentioned in paragraph 3?
4 What is the main idea of paragraph 5?
5 Which words introduce the contrast in focus between paragraphs 5 and 6?

3 The questions below focus on the details and implications of the text. Choose the best option (**A**, **B**, **C** or **D**) to answer the questions.

1 According to the writer, what has been 'left to chance in the past'? (para. 1)
  A The ways in which parents may benefit their children.
  B The genetic compatibility of potential parents.
  C The social and environmental factors affecting children.
  D The qualities and characteristics that children inherit.

Genetic engineering – the unimaginable face of the future?

1 If we now know enough to be able to make changes in the genetic material that we hand on to our children, why not seize this power? Why not control what has been left to chance in the past? Social and environmental influences already control many other aspects of our children's lives and identities. We do not quarrel with the use of orthodontics to straighten teeth, or good nutrition and education to enhance intelligence. Can we really reject positive genetic influences on the next generation's minds and bodies when we accept the rights of parents to benefit their children in every other way?

2 It seems to me inevitable that genetic engineering will eventually be used. It will probably begin in a way that is most ethically acceptable to the largest portion of society, to prevent babies inheriting conditions that have a severe impact on the quality of life, such as heart or lung conditions. The number of parents needing or desiring this service might be tiny, but their experience would help to ease society's fears, and geneticists could then begin to expand their services to prevent the inheritance of genes leading to other disorders that have a less severe impact, or an impact delayed until adulthood. At the same time, other genes could be added to improve various health characteristics and disease resistance in children who would not otherwise have been born with any particular problem.

3 The final frontier will be the mind and the senses. Here, genetic engineering could have enormous benefits. Alcohol addiction could be eliminated, along with tendencies toward mental disease and antisocial behaviour like extreme aggression. People's senses of sight and hearing could be improved, allowing for new dimensions in art and music. And when our understanding of brain development has advanced, geneticists will be able to provide parents with the option of enhancing various intellectual attributes as well.

4 Is there a limit to what can be accomplished with genetic enhancements? Some experts say there are boundaries beyond which we cannot go. But humans have a tendency to prove the experts wrong. One way to

2 Genetic engineering may first be applied to disabilities affecting babies because
  A this would prevent so much suffering.
  B this would be the least controversial use.
  C the greatest long-term benefit would be provided.
  D the social consequences are so severe.

3 Once genetic engineering is accepted, it may be used to
  A improve the mental capabilities of unborn children.
  B extend understanding of how the brain works.
  C bring a new realism to art and music.
  D cure people with alcohol-related problems.

identify types of human enhancements that lie in the realm of possibility – no matter how outlandish they may seem today – is to consider what already exists in the living world. If another living creature already has a particular attribute, then we can work out its genetic basis and eventually we should be able to make it available to humans. For example, we could provide humans with a greatly enhanced sense of smell like that of dogs and other mammals, and the ability to 'see' objects in complete darkness through a biological sonar system like the one that allows bats to find their way in the dark.

5▶ In the longer term, it might be possible to identify the genetic information which allows creatures to live under extreme conditions here on Earth – like the microscopic bacteria that live in scalding hot water around volcanic vents on the ocean floor, far removed from light and free oxygen, and other creatures that use a biological form of antifreeze to thrive in sub-zero temperatures around Antarctica. One day it may even be possible to incorporate photosynthetic units into human embryos so that humans could receive energy directly from the sun, just like plants. Such genetic gifts could allow these genetically modified humans to survive on other planets in the solar system, where they could in turn use genetic engineering to further enhance the ability of their own children to survive in their chosen worlds.

6▶ In the short term, though, most genetic enhancements will surely be much more mundane. They will provide little fixes to all of the naturally occurring genetic defects that shorten the lives of so many people. They will enrich physical and cognitive attributes in small ways. But as the years go by over the next two centuries, the number and variety of possible genetic extensions to the basic human genome* will rise dramatically – like the additions to computer operating systems that occurred during the 1980s and 1990s. Extensions that were once unimaginable will become indispensable – to those parents who are able to afford them.

* The total of all the genes that are found in one living thing

4 Looking further into the future, the writer suggests that human attributes
   A could be transferred to other living creatures.
   B could be improved with genetic information from other creatures.
   C should not be interfered with beyond certain limits.
   D can only be enhanced with characteristics from other humans.

5 He suggests that genetic engineering may ultimately allow humans to
   A live under the ocean.
   B reproduce with creatures from other planets.
   C produce energy by using the Sun.
   D live and reproduce in inhospitable conditions.

6 In the final paragraph he implies that genetic engineering
   A should only be used to deal with genetic defects.
   B will be affected by computer technology.
   C may not be used to benefit everyone equally.
   D will one day be taken for granted by everyone.

7 Is the writer generally
   A enthusiastic about future developments in genetic engineering?
   B concerned about the implications of future developments?
   C hopeful that there will be rapid developments in the near future?
   D disappointed by the limited advances already achieved?

4 Vocabulary: word formation

1 Look at the following words from the text. What part of speech (noun, verb or adjective) is each word in the text? What other forms of the word are possible?

1 genetic (para. 1)   7 tendency (para. 4)
2 ethically (para. 2)   8 attribute (para. 4)
3 inheriting (para. 2)   9 provide (para. 4)
4 expand (para. 2)   10 modified (para. 5)
5 addiction (para. 3)   11 enhancements (para. 6)
6 intellectual (para. 3) 12 defects (para. 6)

2 Use an appropriate form of six of the words above to complete the sentences below.

1 Governments should make .... for controlling developments in genetic engineering.
2 Some people are very wary of the kind of genetic .... being made to food nowadays.
3 If .... genes are inherited, these may cause problems either in childhood or later on.
4 Once I start eating chocolate I can't stop – I find it's really ....
5 The new novel is an .... version of a short story he wrote years ago.
6 I think it's very .... to use animals in experiments to test cosmetics.

3 Discuss this question.

Which specific developments discussed in the text do you consider acceptable, and which are unacceptable or incredible?

Exam Focus

▶ Paper 3, Part 4

In Paper 3, Part 4 you have to rewrite eight sentences using a given word, to produce a sentence similar in meaning to the original. You will be given the beginning and end of the new sentence. You must use between three and eight words, including the word given, and you must not change the form of the given word.

Read the example below.

Their house will take them three years to renovate.

doing

They won't *have finished doing up* their house for three years.

In this case you need to change the tense and verb used, and think of a phrasal verb meaning *renovate*.

Here is a procedure to follow for this task.

- Read the original sentence carefully for meaning.
- Look at the key word and try to see how it relates to the original sentence.
- Look at the beginning and ending of the new sentence and see how the key word could fit in.
- Decide what other changes you need to make, e.g. tense change, adding a preposition, changing the form of a word. (Remember that you **can't** change the form of the key word.)
- Check that you have
  – included all the necessary information
  – included the key word, in its original form
  – written between three and eight words, including the key word
  – not made any grammar mistakes
  – not made any unnecessary changes (e.g. to tenses)
  – not changed the meaning of the original sentence.

1 Find the mistakes in the following transformations and correct them.

1 The original film was totally different from the new version.
bears
The new version *does not bear any resemblance to* the original film. ✗

2 Everyone in the office knew that he didn't like the manager.
common
His *dislike is common knowledge* in the office. ✗

2 For questions 1–8, complete the second sentence so that it has a similar meaning to the first sentence, using the word given. **Do not change the word given.** You must use between **three** and **eight** words, including the word given.

1 The government has changed its policy completely since the election.
undergone
The government's policy ....
.... since the election.

2 Lots of people have complained about last night's programme.
floods
There ....
.... about last night's programme.

3 You should get this checked immediately.
lose
You should ....
.... this checked.

4 The brochure didn't say anything about extra charges.
reference
There was ....
.... in the brochure.

5 The information revolution began when the first printing press was made.
invention
It was ....
.... started the information revolution.

6 The authorities should do something to reduce traffic congestion.
high
It's ....
.... reducing traffic congestion.

7 No-one knew anything about the matter.
shed
No-one ....
.... the matter.

8 They should not make any major changes in the near future.
term
Any changes made ....
.... only be minor.

Writing

▶ Paper 2, Part 1 (essay)

In Unit 7 you wrote a balanced essay presenting two sides of an argument. In this unit, you will write an **essay** presenting one side of an argument only.

1   Read the following writing task.

> ### TASK
>
> You have collected the headlines below as part of a class project on the effects of technology on modern society. For the project, your tutor has also asked you to write an essay about the problems created by society's increasing use of technology.
>
> Write your essay.
>
> (300–350 words)

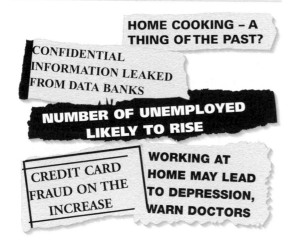

2   In the Paper 2, Part 1 essay question, you will be given some input on which to base your essay. With a partner, look at the headlines above and decide:

• what technological issue each headline relates to
• how the problems could be grouped together and ordered in an essay
• what details you could include to support your main points
• what sort of information would be given in the first and last paragraphs of the essay.

3   Read the following essay, which was written in answer to the task and answer the questions below.

> Technology plays an increasingly important part in our daily lives. While many technological developments may be beneficial – in the field of medicine, for instance – there are many others whose effects are less positive. We may find examples of these in the world of work, in the home and in the whole area of freedom and privacy.
>
> In the world of work, technological advances have had various negative effects. The development of robotics has meant that in industries such as car-manufacturing robots are replacing people. They work faster and more accurately and they don't need breaks. As a result, industrial workers see job opportunities dwindling further and unemployment levels rising. In addition, more and more people are working from home using personal computers, which means that they lose the stimulus that comes from working in direct contact with other people and may feel isolated.
>
> Another example of the negative effect of technological change can be found on the domestic front, in the home. In my view, technological developments such as the microwave are devaluing traditional home-making skills like cooking.
>
> Finally, there are the implications of information technology for freedom and privacy. More facts about individuals are being stored in data banks, which may be accessed through networks of computers. This creates an ever-increasing risk of accidental or deliberate leaking of private details. Every day more information is collected by banks, credit card companies, consumer organisations and so on – and who is there to keep an eye on what happens to it? It is certainly convenient to store information in this way, but I feel it could lead to long-term problems. There may be other hidden dangers – theoretically, could a 'thinking' computer start to use the data against us?
>
> To sum up, I believe that we must be very careful with technology. While it has clear advantages, there is also the danger that it could turn on us and we could find ourselves the victims of our own success.

(327 words)

1   Has the writer included all the ideas suggested by the headlines?
2   Has the information been presented in the same order, or have the points been re-ordered?
3   What is the main topic of each paragraph? Underline the sentence that tells you.
4   What specific information is given to support each main point? Which point lacks sufficient support? What evidence can you think of to support it?

4

1 Read the following writing task.

> **TASK**
>
> You have collected the headlines below as part of a class project on the ways in which natural processes are being modified as a result of advances in science. For the project, your tutor has also asked you to write an essay about either the advantages or disadvantages of such modifications.
>
> Write your essay.
>
> (300–350 words)

> **CROP YIELDS SHOW DRAMATIC INCREASE AS PESTS REDUCED**

> **AVERAGE LIFESPAN SOON TO BE OVER EIGHTY**

> **TRANSPLANT PATIENT CELEBRATES TENTH ANNIVERSARY OF OPERATION**

> **GENETICALLY MODIFIED CORN REDUCES THREAT OF FAMINE IN ARID ZONES**

> **NEW ORGANS SOON TO BE GROWN IN LABORATORIES, CLAIM SCIENTISTS**

> **'DESIGNER BABIES' – WILL THE 21ST CENTURY SEE THEM?**

2 Look at the headlines above and use the questions in Exercise 2 to plan your answer to this task.

5 Read the two opening paragraphs below. Which one relates best to the writing task in Exercise 4 and states the main idea of the essay most clearly?

A
> *There have been so many scientific advances over the last decade that it is difficult to remember them all, but the most dramatic have been connected with changing nature. Scientists can now do this in many ways, and the effects of this, both good and bad, can be seen everywhere in society.*

B
> *There have been many scientific advances over the last decade, but the most dramatic are related to our increasing ability to modify nature. Developments in the fields of medical science, genetics and agriculture have brought a wide range of benefits for both individuals and society.*

The supporting paragraphs of your essay should reflect the plan of development given in the introduction. (See Unit 7, p. 106.) How many supporting paragraphs would you write following on from Introduction B above?

6 Read the following sentences. What topic areas do they relate to? Combine them using a different linking word or expression each time.

1 There are more chemical sprays being used. Crops have fewer diseases.
2 People live longer but still age in appearance. Many want cosmetic surgery to improve their looks.
3 Hereditary illness may be eradicated. This would mean that the population would be healthier.
4 Immunisation programmes are more effective. Some infectious diseases are being brought under control.

7 You may want to show awareness of the alternative point of view in your conclusion, but you should always finish by reinforcing your own argument. Choose the best conclusion for the writing task in Exercise 4.

A
> *All in all, it is clear that there have been so many advances in scientific knowledge that we can change nature in almost every area of our lives. Who knows what the future will bring?*

B
> *To sum up, scientists' ability to make nature work for them has had clear benefits. Of course some people do question the ethics of certain experiments, and others demand to know just how far we are prepared to go with scientific change. Nevertheless, the benefits to both individuals and the whole of society outweigh these concerns.*

C
> *In conclusion, the problems would seem to be enormous. What right do we have to think that we can tamper with nature in this way? The road the scientists are travelling is a dangerous one, and society should be on its guard.*

> **Exam Strategy**
>
> To write a good essay:
> * plan before you write.
> * don't include too many points, or you may go over the word limit, and you won't be able to develop them.
> * give your main topics, in order, in your introduction.
> * deal with each topic in a separate paragraph.
> * include specific evidence for all your points.
> * use linking devices to signal the relationship of ideas within and between paragraphs.
> * use a fairly formal style, avoiding colloquial language.

8 Write your outline for the task, using the notes you made in Exercise 4.2. Then write your essay.

► Exam Maximiser

1 Think of one word only which can be used appropriately in all three sentences.

1 The accident occurred on the north .... of the mountain.
There seems to be a new .... in today's class.
He was putting on a brave ...., but he wasn't fooling anyone.

2 She .... herself so hard she had a nervous breakdown.
His possessiveness finally .... her away.
The behaviour of their son .... them to despair.

3 Watch out – that wire might be .... – don't touch it.
When we go there, you'll be able to see a real .... elephant.
I would never have believed that was a .... performance.

4 Tragically, the secret papers .... into the hands of the enemy.
In the photograph, her long dark hair .... to her waist.
The moment he entered the country, he .... ill and had to be taken to hospital.

5 The company's prospects look good in the long ....
A contusion is the medical .... for a bruise.
The terrorists each received a 30-year prison ....

6 We've finally .... the date for the wedding – it's September 30th.
The interest rate has been .... at 6.5%.
The shelves were .... to the wall with screws.

2 Complete the second sentence with three to eight words so that it has a similar meaning to the first sentence, using the word given. Do not change the word given.

1 We did not think that cancelling the order was a good idea. **inadvisable**
We thought ....
.... the order.

2 He felt very proud of his mathematical ability. **himself**
He ....
.... his mathematical ability.

3 Whatever you do, don't tell anyone about our discovery. **account**
On ....
.... about our discovery.

4 The gradual introduction of technology would eliminate a lot of opposition. **less**
Were technology ....
.... opposition.

5 The reduction in funding meant that the research was stopped. **cutbacks**
They had to ....
.... in funding.

6 To many people, the development of cloning appears dangerous. **regard**
Many people ....
.... development.

7 I don't really know why, but I don't trust him. **finger**
I can't ....
.... I don't trust him.

8 He will never commit himself to a definite arrangement. **pin**
It's ....
.... to a definite arrangement.

3 Talk about the photo.

1 Describe the photo and the situation.
2 How does it relate to the topic of the unit?
3 This picture was considered to illustrate an article on happy family relationships but was rejected. Discuss why it was unacceptable and suggest an alternative.

The last frontier

Today

Speaking

1

1 Look at the two photographs. Describe and compare the people and the situations. Say:

• what sort of places the people might be travelling to
• how you think they are feeling and why.

Yesterday

The joy of travel: off on holiday from Paddington station in 1923

... and at Gatwick airport.

2 Discuss what the two pictures suggest about the way holiday travel has changed over the last century. Do you think travelling has become:

• safer or more dangerous?
• easier or more difficult?
• more or less comfortable?

2 How far do you agree with this statement?

'Travel abroad is no longer the adventure it used to be. Mass tourism has destroyed the adventure of foreign travel.'

Think about these points.

• increased speed and ease of travel
• popularity of organised adventure holidays
• increasing interest in travel to exotic or remote places

3 Read the extract from the Longman *Dictionary of Contemporary English* below.

tourism *n* [U] the business of providing things for people to do, places for them to stay, etc while they are on holiday.

Now consider the following types of tourism and answer the questions below.

• green, or eco-tourism
• heritage tourism
• space tourism
• virtual tourism

1 What sort of things might people do in the types of tourism listed above, and where might they stay?
2 What sort of people might be interested in each of these types of tourism?
3 What are the advantages and disadvantages of each type for a) the environment b) the inhabitants of the place visited c) the tourist?
4 Which type of holiday would you prefer? Why?

Reading

▶ Paper 1, Part 2

1   You have won a prize of a two-week holiday in Antarctica. How do you feel?

a) disappointed – you'd rather stay in a luxury hotel in your own country
b) horrified – won't it be cold, uncomfortable and dangerous?
c) concerned – is nowhere safe from tourism?
d) thrilled – you'll be able to visit a place few other people have ever set foot in

2   You are going to read four extracts which are all concerned with travel in Antarctica. First, read the extracts quickly to get a general idea of their content and possible sources. Do they make you change your view of Antarctica?

3   Now read the extracts carefully and choose the answer (**A**, **B**, **C** or **D**) which you think fits best according to the text.

Across Antarctica on foot

At nine-thirty Geoff's team rolled out into the lead position, heading south. A misty snow fell and clouds hugged the surface. The dogs were crazy to pull, but their wildness threatened to upset the sleds. The morning's battle was to try to contain them until they burned off their extra energy. For that reason alone, we appreciated the deep snow, because it made the dogs work harder and slowed them down.

By late morning the surfaces levelled out and became harder packed, and the skies cleared. The parting clouds revealed a beautiful scene, resembling a white moonscape. The ice-covered mountains that bordered us on both sides were drifted with deep snow. Delicate ice crystals filled the air, and sunlight refracting off them created a sparkling display of rainbows, pillars and halos. In front of our dog-sleds the snow's surface was covered with gleaming prisms, each reflecting the sunlight in a multi-coloured spectrum. In the distance a low fog hugged the horizon. All day – we travelled nearly nineteen miles – we watched Antarctica's beauty unfold. This was a region few men have seen at this time of year, and we sledded through it reverentially, quiet but for the rasping of the dogs and our own periodic shouting to encourage them.

1 The writer suggests that the explorers
   A found the dogs uncontrollable.
   B had some problems handling the dogs.
   C treated their dogs with little consideration.
   D were threatened by the dogs' lack of discipline.

2 On the afternoon described in this extract, the explorers were
   A deeply affected by what they saw.
   B slowed down by the unusual light conditions.
   C sad to leave the scene they found.
   D hindered by the snow conditions.

Through the ice in a small boat

This was as far south as we'd expected to get, but with the help of long poles, we managed to push the boat through the thick ice clogging the narrow channel into the ice pack. It was heavy going, and, overcome with hunger, we devoured Isso's hot scones and rhubarb jam as fast as she could make them.

'Look out!' screamed Igor, choking on a scone and flinging his arm to starboard. Clinging to the wheel, I glimpsed three black fins, tall as fence posts, slicing though the clear water, hurtling straight towards me. There was a broad blur of mottled black and white patches beneath the surface as the killer whales raced towards us. My nightmare was coming true – they couldn't miss the boat. But suddenly they were gone, slipping beneath the keel and hull and shooting on towards the golden crab-eater seals crouched low on the ice floes. All around, penguins popped out of the water like black corks and flailed in a terrified way up onto the ice, while the floes rocked with the wash of the monsters' charge.

'They must have been stalking us under the ice,' muttered Jon. No-one could argue. We were leading a fragile existence.

3   The people in the boat were
   A   trying to escape from the ice.
   B   becoming short of food.
   C   advancing into the ice.
   D   struggling to survive.

4   What feature of the whales is emphasised most?
   A   size   C   intelligence
   B   power   D   curiosity

Antarctic Adventure Cruise

The Ross Sea region contains some of Antarctica's best mountain scenery and wildlife locations, yet remains far less visited than other parts of Antarctica due to its formidable barriers of pack ice. Only a handful of expedition vessels have ever traversed this superb region, and hundreds of miles of coastline remain little explored.

The *M. S. Bremen* is one of the most modern and environmentally-friendly expedition vessels afloat, unmatched in her combination of First Class luxury plus outstanding ability to reach otherwise inaccessible destinations.

Our journey is at the very peak of summer's wildlife season. Bathed by extraordinary 24-hour daylight, the areas around Antarctica's coastline will be erupting with activity; penguins gather to tend their fast-growing young in rookeries of staggering numbers, whales are seen by the hundreds, seals haul themselves out on ice floes and shorelines, and a myriad of other birds nest in the rocks and circle the air. Everywhere there is the backdrop of the Ross Sea's dramatic glaciers, icebergs and mountains. Our journey will be a time of unparalleled photographic opportunities – a chance to witness the Earth's greatest unspoiled natural wonderland.

5   The Antarctic Cruise advertisement is aimed at people who
   A   want to explore in safety.
   B   are expert photographers.
   C   would like to hunt and shoot.
   D   are young and adventurous.

6   The advertisement emphasises the
   A   approachability of the wildlife.
   B   number of breeding places visited.
   C   beauty of the animals in their habitats.
   D   profusion of animals and birds.

The world's loneliest tourist spot

Guidebooks to Antarctica? The notion that the last wilderness is being colonised by tourists tends to provoke the kind of shock-horror reaction associated with tabloid headlines. Is nothing sacred? Apparently not. Thirty years ago, not a single tourist visited Antarctica. Now, as many as 10,000 tourists visit it each year. What next? Package holidays at the South Pole?

The idea of mass tourism on the ice is shocking, of course, because Antarctica is a powerful symbol of the uncorrupted Earth – the planet before we mucked it up. It is a blank in time, the last wilderness and the only geographical symbol of innocence left unless we set up colonies in space.

The dangerous implications of tourism in Antarctica, however, have been exaggerated. 10,000 people aren't actually all that many on a continent one and a half times the size of Europe. Almost all tourists arrive on cruise ships and spend only a few hours on the continent itself. There is no accommodation available to holidaymakers on the ice, so they are obliged to return to their cruise ships to sleep. Antarctic tourism is now well-policed and all reputable organisations adhere to the environmental regulations of the Antarctic Treaty and the guidelines laid down by the International Association of Antarctic Tour Operators. Whilst it is essential to maintain strict control over all visitors, the reality is that the vast majority of the continent has never seen a Nikon and probably never will.

7   According to the writer, Antarctica is a powerful symbol because it is
   A   untouched.   C   timeless.
   B   unspoiled.   D   empty.

8   The writer says that tourists visiting Antarctica
   A   have an exaggerated idea of the dangers.
   B   may be disappointed by what they actually see.
   C   have little effect on its environment.
   D   travel in comfortable conditions.

4   Discuss the following questions.

1   What sort of controls do you think might be specified by the agreements mentioned in the last text?
2   Which isolated place would you most like to visit? Why?

Listening
▶ Paper 4, Part 3

1 Look at the picture and discuss the questions below.

1 What idea is the picture illustrating and how realistic is it intended to be?
2 What sorts of activity might people really do on a holiday in a place like this?
3 Why might they want to go on such a holiday?

2 You will hear an extract from a radio discussion about the possibility of space tourism. Before you listen, read through the questions below. What can you predict about the content of the discussion?

1 Ben says that commercial interests are
  A hindering serious scientific research projects.
  B trying to take over national space stations.
  C increasingly involved in space travel research.
  D likely to exploit tourists by overcharging.

2 What is likely to be the main attraction of the suborbital trips?
  A the inclusion of specialised training
  B the chance to meet other risk-takers
  C a completely new physical experience
  D a chance to see the Earth from a new viewpoint

3 Which aspect of the suborbital trip concerns Ben most?
  A medical
  B psychological
  C financial
  D professional

4 He says that trips in the second stage might be for
  A wedding venues.
  B older people.
  C children's adventure holidays.
  D company hospitality.

5 The speakers agree that space tourism
  A could have serious consequences for the Earth.
  B should follow environmental guidelines.
  C could destroy signs of life on other planets.
  D needs more research before it should be allowed.

 3 Now listen and choose the answer (**A, B, C** or **D**) which fits best according to what you hear. You will hear the recording twice.

4 Would you like to go on either of these two types of 'holiday'? Why/Why not?

5 Say it again

Re-express these sentences from the Listening text, using the word given.

1 Some tourists are willing to shell out a lot to go somewhere new. **prices**
2 A space station would be more profitable being used as a hotel. **if**
3 They have their eyes on the tourist market. **interested**
4 They look something like big playpens. **bear**

Language Focus: Vocabulary

1 Read the following three texts ignoring the gaps for the moment. Match each text to one of the text types a)–e) below.

a) an advertisement
b) an article from a specialist magazine
c) a guidebook
d) a travel book (giving a personal account of a journey)
e) a review

2 Read the three texts again and decide which answer (**A**, **B**, **C** or **D**) best fits each gap.

TRYING TO LEAVE CORSICA

It was the last train to Ajaccio. I arrived in darkness, passing through the back of the city, and hardly entering it because the station is some distance from the centre.

The next day, I tried to get information about the ferries to Sardinia. The travel agents could give me (1) .... details of the flights to Dallas or Miami, they could (2) .... reservations for me at Disneyland; but they had no (3) .... if, or from where, or when, a ferry travelled the few miles from Corsica to Sardinia. I enquired at eight agencies (4) .... I found one with the right information.

'So a ferry leaves every afternoon at four from Bonifacio,' I said. 'What time does it arrive?'

The clerk did not know.

'Where do I get a ticket?'

The clerk did not know, but guessed that someone in Bonifacio would be selling them.

'Is there a bus or a train that (5) .... the ferry in Sardinia?'

This made her laugh. 'Sardinia is in Italy!' she cried, (6) .... amused, as though I had asked her the question about New Zealand.

1	**A** actual	**B** precise	**C** strict
	D literal		
2	**A** book	**B** do	**C** make
	D order		
3	**A** concept	**B** idea	**C** theory
	D belief		
4	**A** until	**B** when	**C** since
	D before		
5	**A** connects	**B** links	**C** matches
	D meets		
6	**A** highly	**B** eminently	**C** exceptionally
	D seriously		

How Mongkok got its name

Hong Kong is well-known as the most (7) .... populated place on Earth. At the heart of Hong Kong lies the area known as Kowloon, and within Kowloon is a district which is crowded even by Hong Kong standards – Mongkok. Here (8) .... live an estimated 165,000 people per square kilometre. Many stories are told of how Mongkok got its name. In the first (9) ...., the word or name does not exist in any Chinese dialect. The 'kok' part of it means 'corner' in Cantonese, and one popular hypothesis notes that the name of the district was supposed to be Wongkok, meaning 'Wong's Corner' but a (10) .... painter inadvertently stencilled the 'W' upside down, thus making it Mongkok instead. Whatever the truth of the matter, this busy and bustling (11) .... of Nathan Road is a popular tourist area where the shops (12) .... many bargains not found on the lower and pricier end of the 'Golden Mile'.

7	**A** compactly	**B** closely	**C** densely	**D** thickly
8	**A** unequalled	**B** alone	**C** only	**D** uniquely
9	**A** place	**B** instance	**C** case	**D** example
10	**A** notice	**B** sign	**C** board	**D** placard
11	**A** distance	**B** expanse	**C** stretch	**D** extent
12	**A** boast	**B** support	**C** exhibit	**D** vaunt

Tourism and tourists

Whilst it is clearly essential to regulate the tourist industry, the fact (13) .... that this can be very difficult to organise in practice. It is true that tourist organisations themselves have to (14) .... to certain regulations, and when they are operating internationally they have to take care not to (15) .... treaty agreements. Most tourist organisations do follow these codes – their clients, however, may not, and may not even have any (16) .... of what responsible tourism means. The (17) .... majority of holiday-makers never consider the effect of tourism on the other cultures and environments that they visit – they are only interested in their own enjoyment. And the number of travellers is increasing all the time – nowadays there are more opportunities (18) .... to would-be adventurers than ever before, with more and more travel agencies setting up holidays in remote and previously untouched places.

13	**A** remains	**B** stays	**C** exists	**D** applies
14	**A** maintain	**B** follow	**C** adhere	**D** abide
15	**A** contradict	**B** contrive	**C** concede	**D** contravene
16	**A** concept	**B** theory	**C** outline	**D** thesis
17	**A** big	**B** large	**C** immense	**D** vast
18	**A** ready	**B** available	**C** convenient	**D** applicable

Language Focus: Grammar
Indirect speech

1 The writer of the extract below describes a difficult and dangerous journey in which he and two friends crossed the mountains from Afghanistan to Nuristan on foot. They were guided to the border by a young boy, who then left them.

1 Read the text, ignoring the gaps for the moment, to get a general idea of the content. Then choose from the list below the best phrases or sentences to fill the gaps.

In front of us, the desolate beauty of Nuristan stretched out towards the majestic range of the Hindu Kush and freedom. It was late afternoon, the sun had dropped below the mountains and a sharp wind was picking up. (1) ...., but we had been walking for three or four hours already and there was still no sign of it. (2) .... but then (3) ....

An hour later we rounded a bend in the river and saw a thread of smoke drifting from between some large rocks at the bottom of a cliff. The fire belonged to a family from Khunduz (4) ....

We walked on until it grew dark. The moon was high in the sky by the time we came to the glow of a lamp hanging inside a tent. (5) .... (6) .... We had been travelling almost continuously for more than eighteen hours. As we sat drinking tea (7) .... I had already guessed the answer, and I was not disappointed.

"With a good horse – maybe an hour."

A I asked one of them, out of idle interest, how far he thought it might be to the next village.
B We briefly considered spending the night in one of the shelters
C Some men invited us inside to share their meal and stay the night.
D (we) decided to press on.
E The boy had told us of a village an hour's journey over the pass into Nuristan

F who told us that there was, indeed, a village another hour's walk down the river.
G We accepted gratefully.

2 Rewrite the extracts **A–G**, using the words given below. Don't change the original meaning. More than one answer may be possible.

A ' .... ' I asked, out of idle interest.
B We briefly wondered whether we ....
C The men said, '...................... '
D We agreed that ....
E The boy had said that ....
F 'Oh, yes,' they said, ' .... '
G We replied that .... (*Use the previous sentence in the text to help you.*)

2 Now discuss these questions with reference to Exercise 1.

1 What verbs do we use to introduce
   a) indirect statements?
   b) indirect questions?
2 What patterns follow these verbs in indirect speech?
3 What changes do we make to vocabulary and tenses?
4 When we report what someone said, do we always use their exact words?

▶ Grammar reference pp. 224–225

3 Fill each of the gaps with a suitable word or phrase. In which sentences do you have a choice of tense?

1 I told you it didn't matter .... alone or brought someone along with you.
2 Jenny just wanted to check that we .... to the party tomorrow.
3 He claimed that his wallet .... by a pick-pocket, but in fact he'd just left it at home.
4 She told me I .... to go as she could manage on her own.
5 I wasn't able to confirm whether it .... be possible for me to attend the meeting.
6 I wish I .... gone with you, but I had to stay at home with the children.
7 She said she wished they .... insist on bringing their dog with them every time they came to visit her.
8 He said he might possibly come along if he .... time, but we shouldn't wait for him.

4 We can also report statements, orders and questions using a verb + *to*-infinitive or verb + *-ing*, with or without an object.

1 Match sentences 1–7 to the appropriate statements below.

1 'Don't stay any longer – it's dangerous.'
2 'Get out now!'
3 'It would be a good idea if you left now.'
4 'Don't forget to go.'
5 'Please, please, go!'
6 'Would you mind leaving now?'
7 'I've made plans for you to go.'

a) He ordered me to go.
b) He advised me to go.
c) He requested me to go.
d) He reminded me to go.
e) He intended me to go.
f) He pleaded with me to go.
g) He warned me not to stay.

2 In which of the reported statements a)–g) above could the object be omitted? How does this affect the meaning?

3 Read the following anecdote told by a tourist guide. Then fill in the gaps with an appropriate verb in the *-ing* form. Add any other words necessary. In some cases a preposition is needed.

The group of tourists suggested (1) .... for a meal together. I advised (2) .... at a small local restaurant, but they insisted (3) .... to an expensive restaurant in the middle of town. When we got there, they blamed me for (4) .... a parking space immediately outside, and grumbled (5) .... made to walk a few metres from the minibus to the restaurant. They protested (6) .... to wait for a table, and accused the waiter (7) .... them the wrong sort of wine. At the end of the evening, they congratulated (8) .... organised such an enjoyable outing.

5 When we report what people say, we often report the general meaning rather than the exact words. In this case, the reporting verb may carry much of the meaning of the original statement. Read the story again. What do you think the tourists' original words were?

6 Impersonal passive constructions

1 We can use impersonal passive constructions with reporting verbs such as: *allege, believe, know, report, rumour, think*. Read the following examples. What two structures are possible?

1 a) *It is said that* the Department of Tourism *is* very interested in this project.
  b) The Department of Tourism *is said to be* very interested in this project.
2 a) *It is reported that* tenders *have been invited* from several construction companies.
  b) Tenders *are reported to have been invited* from several construction companies.

2 When the action in the subordinate clause relates to the future, pattern b) above is not possible with all verbs. Which of the sentences below are incorrect? Rewrite the incorrect sentences using pattern a).

1 *The authorities are not expected to grant planning permission for the hotel.*
2 *The authorities are feared to refuse permission for the development.*
3 *Fines are hoped to discourage unruly holiday-makers.*

▶ Grammar reference p. 225

7 Read the report below, which was broadcast on the radio. Then complete the second version, which is from a written report, using the passive and including patterns from Exercise 6.

'*To attract more tourists, the authorities are planning to build a new airport on the island. Most islanders expect the plans to go ahead, although there are fears that increased tourist numbers will lead to serious environmental problems. Some residents say that water supplies are insufficient to cope with large numbers of tourists, and no-one knows if there is sufficient electricity generating capacity to supply the new hotels that will be built. Others claim that tourism has already brought valuable revenue and employment to the island, and should be encouraged. There have been reassuring reports that the authorities are drawing up plans for strict control and monitoring of tourist developments.*'

Concern over new airport

A new airport (1) is .... to attract more tourists to the island. The plans are (2) .... go ahead, although it (3) .... could lead to serious environmental problems. Water supplies (4) .... to cope with large numbers of tourists, and it (5) .... there will be sufficient electricity generating capacity to supply the new hotels that are expected (6) .... On the other hand, it (7) .... tourism has already brought valuable revenue and employment to the island, and should be encouraged. Reassuringly, the authorities (8) .... be drawing up plans for strict control and monitoring of tourist developments.

▶ Exam Maximiser

Use of English

▶ Paper 3, Part 5

1

International tourism is on trial, and the charge sheet is as long as it is damning

What arguments can you think of for and against tourism? Think of at least two arguments for and two against.

2 Read the following texts on the effects of tourism. Which text is presenting both positive and negative effects?

3 Answer questions 1–4 with a word or short phrase. You do not need to write complete sentences.

The tourist industry promises some of our happiest times – those two weeks in paradise that we spend the rest of the year longing and saving for. The industry creates over ten per cent of the world's income and provides employment for one in 25 people on Earth. A fast-growing proportion of that trade is going to poorer countries – rather than being a freeloader, the industry is throwing an economic lifeline to emerging nations. It is a quick, lead-free engine of wealth creation, driving fledgling economies and creating much-needed foreign exchange. And even if international tourism is dominated by multinational companies bent on exploiting the new frontiers of the developing world, this hardly distinguishes it from any other form of trade. So if tourism is not so different, why has its development become so controversial?

Tourism is different. It is different because there is an expectation that it should be a force for a fair social change. The industry has billed itself as a place where cultures meet, a catalyst to the transfer of wealth from visitor to visited. Even those most sceptical about the industry's track record in this field are up-beat about the development potential of tourism – if only it were regulated. And yet the development of 'third world' tourism is perhaps the most eloquent metaphor for the unjust world in which we live. Fuelled by the growing gaps in income and ever cheaper travel, tourism has become something the world's rich do to the world's poor. In the words of one Namibian school pupil, 'When I grow up I want to be a tourist'.

It's time we introduced a little bit of honesty into the debate about tourism. We don't go abroad to save the planet. We go to enjoy ourselves. Hardly any of the ethical arguments advanced in support of travelling for fun survive even the briefest examination.

We're told that tourism breaks down barriers between our lives and those of the people we visit. But most tourists remain firmly behind the coach windows, hotel walls and camera lenses that divide them from the countries they travel through. The argument that it brings wealth to local people is equally faulty. Tour companies are adept at ensuring that their customers spend most of their money before they even leave home, or that the money they spend abroad is swiftly repatriated. Local people are frequently dispossessed of their land and resources as fishing villages give way to hotels, and forests are cleared to build airports.

No claim is dafter than that tourism helps protect the environment. It is true that it can finance conservation efforts and encourage countries to preserve the resources they want tourists to see, but few human activities are as destructive as going abroad. Even if we forget the coral reefs smothered in sewage, and the swamps and streams drained so that we can enjoy showers and flushing toilets, our environmental account would still be firmly in deficit, simply because we have to travel to get there. Air transport is now one of the gravest threats to the global environment because of the local pollution and disturbance it generates and the vast amounts of carbon dioxide it releases.

Go, if you have to. But don't pretend you're doing it for anyone other than yourself.

1 What is the writer implying with the phrase 'a quick, lead-free engine'? (lines 17)

2 Explain in your own words why, according to the writer, tourism in the third world is 'the most eloquent metaphor for the unjust world in which we live'. (lines 48–50)

3 According to the writer, how is going abroad 'destructive'? (line 19)

4 Which two phrases in text 1 contradict the idea put forward in the sentence beginning 'Tour companies are ...' (lines 10–13) in text 2?

4 In a paragraph of between 50 and 70 words, summarise in your own words as far as possible the arguments people put forward in favour of tourism.

5 Discuss the following questions.

1 Which of the arguments against tourism put forward in the texts do you find most persuasive? Why?

2 How far do you consider that tourism is or can be 'a place where cultures meet, a catalyst to the transfer of wealth from visitor to visited'? Give examples to support your opinion.

Language Focus: Vocabulary

1 Style

Rewrite the sentences below using idiomatic expressions and metaphors from the box to replace the phrases in italics. You may need to make other changes to the grammar of the sentence.

> thrown an economic lifeline   been fuelled by
> billed itself as   got a good track record
> up-beat   a freeloader

1 The tourist is often seen as *someone who takes without giving in return*.

2 The industry has *provided essential financial support* to poorer countries.

3 The tourist industry has *promoted itself by saying it is* a force for improving international understanding.

4 Some people feel that tourism has not *done very well up to now* in the area of cultural understanding.

5 Many of its supporters are *optimistic* about the future.

6 Tourism has *grown quickly because of* the big difference between rich and poor countries.

2 Sentence adverbials

1 The phrases in italics are all sentence adverbials. Match them to the list of functions a)–d).

1 I would like to extend all our thanks to the person who has done more than anyone else to make this holiday a success – *namely*, Paula, our tour guide.

2 There were some problems but *on the whole* the facilities were satisfactory.

3 *In the first place* I don't like cut glass, *secondly* I don't need another vase, and *last but not least* I can't afford it.

4 *Hopefully*, we'll be able to return later this year – *in fact* we plan to book our next trip soon.

a) signalling organisation of ideas
b) identifying by name what has previously been referred to
c) indicating the attitude of the speaker
d) summarising or generalising

2 Complete the text below by adding a suitable sentence adverbial from the box.

> all things considered   for a start   in addition
> in reality   naturally   not surprisingly
> rather the reverse   that is to say

Tourism may seem to assure those involved of untold riches, but (1) .... it can promise more than it delivers. (2) ...., it depends on a host of factors beyond our control — climate, economics, even politics. (3) ...., the success of a place as a tourist destination may lead to it losing the features that first attracted the tourists there — (4) ...., its unspoiled landscape and welcoming people. But this does not seem to have slowed down the expansion of tourism. (5) .... — more and more countries are opening up their doors to the tourists. (6) ...., no place can remain untouched by time. Tourism may be the way out of a life of grinding poverty for people who can see no other hope and they (7) .... welcome the chance to give their children a better life than they had. So (8) ...., it seems that tourism is here to stay — all over the planet.

3 Look at the question below and decide how you would answer it. List some points to support your answer.

'*Is tourism beneficial or harmful to the world and its people?*'

Then debate the question with the rest of your class.

3   Prepositional phrases

1   The following extract is from an article about a holiday disaster which appeared in the Travel section of a newspaper. Add the correct prepositions to complete each phrase, and underline the whole phrase.

Demand for adventure holidays in exotic places is (1) .... the increase and I was very taken by the idea of going on one. So (2) .... the very last minute, I decided to join a group on a walking holiday in the mountains of northern Spain. From reading the brochure, I was (3) .... the impression that it would be quite easy and not too tiring. It said that for each stage of the trip, your luggage was sent on (4) .... advance, so you weren't expected to carry it. It sounded ideal — but it all went horribly wrong. My backpack, containing everything I needed for the holiday, was put on a flight to Cairo (5) .... mistake. The tour guide wasn't (6) .... fault, and he was (7) .... hand to deal with the situation, but all his efforts to retrieve my luggage were (8) .... no avail. I had to start the trek with only the clothes I stood up (9) ...., and, worst of all, without my walking boots. After the first day's hike, wearing light canvas shoes, I was (10) .... agony. Everyone else in the group seemed much fitter than I was, and I got totally (11) .... (12) .... breath trying to keep up with them. Things went (13) .... bad (14) .... worse ...

2   Add a suitable preposition to each of the phrases below.

1   make up .... lost time
2   walk .... a frantic pace
3   .... my horror
4   .... delay
5   .... the end of the holiday

3   Now use the phrases to make up your own ending to the holiday story.

4   Read the advertisement below. Write your own 150-word account of a good or bad journey or holiday experience for submission to the competition. Try to include some of the prepositional phrases from Exercise 3.

DO YOU HAVE A FUNNY TALE TO TELL ?

Or a horrendous ordeal to get off your chest?

Share your holiday nightmares by sending them to us!

Write an account of your disaster in no more than 150 words. Prizes for the best accounts include return flights to New York, Paris and Amsterdam. A collection of the best submissions will be published in a forthcoming book *Travellers' Tales from Heaven and Hell.*

Exam Focus

▶ Paper 4, Part 1

In Paper 4, Part 1 you will hear four short extracts from monologues or conversations. They will not be connected in topic or theme. You have to answer two multiple-choice questions on each extract; each question will have three options **A–C**. You will hear each extract twice. The questions may test your understanding of:

- the function and purpose of part or all of the extract
- the attitudes and opinions of the speaker (stated or implied)
- main ideas
- details.

You will have fifteen seconds after the instructions are read and between each extract to read the introduction and the two questions. Do not try to read the questions for all four extracts at this time as this will distract you.

Here is a procedure to follow for this task.

- During the first listening eliminate the answers you're sure are wrong.
- During the second listening, choose the correct answer. (If you're not sure, remember to put something.)

 1 You will hear four different extracts. For questions **1–8**, choose the answer (**A**, **B** or **C**) which fits best according to what you hear. There are two questions for each extract.

Extract One

You hear a woman talking about how she became involved in a car rally.

1 The speaker was attracted to the event because it was
  A challenging.
  B unusual.
  C a chance to travel.

2 The problem for the speaker was
  A timing.
  B money.
  C lack of information.

Extract Two

You hear part of an interview with an Olympic gold medal winner.

3 What is suggested as a possible cause of post-Olympic depression?
  A coming to the end of something
  B being let down
  C not winning a medal

4 The second woman did not suffer depression because she was
  A successful.
  B prepared for it.
  C too busy.

Extract Three

You hear a scientist being interviewed about 'designer babies'.

5 The scientist says that the phrase 'designer babies' is sometimes used by people
  A without understanding exactly what they mean.
  B to fit whatever they want to say.
  C in connection with the baby's environment.

6 The woman uses the example of the wheel to suggest that
  A some inventions can have dangerous results.
  B minor developments can have significant results.
  C the possibility of bad results should not prevent progress.

Extract Four

You hear part of a talk about the job of a 'warm-up man'.

7 The speaker talks about the studio environment to emphasise the audience's
  A apprehension.
  B confusion.
  C enjoyment.

8 The job of the warm-up man is to
  A bring the audience together.
  B make the audience laugh.
  C change the mood of the audience.

2 Look back at questions 1, 3, 5 and 7 in Exercise 1. Which question tests your understanding of:

- the function and purpose of part or all of the text?
- the attitudes and opinions of the speaker (stated or implied)?
- main ideas?
- details?

> ### Exam Strategy
> DO
> - remember that each extract will be a different type of text.
> - always put an answer even if you are not sure – you may be lucky!
> DON'T
> - read ahead to the questions on the other extracts. Take each extract in turn.
> - go back once you have gone on to the next extract – your memory may be inaccurate.

Writing

▶ Paper 2, Part 2 (review)

In Paper 2, Part 2 you may be asked to write a **review** of a place, either for a magazine or a newspaper. For this type of task you need to think about:

- the target reader
- the purpose for writing
- an appropriate style.

1

1   What is the writer's purpose in a review? Choose four of the following.

1   to give information about something
2   to persuade the reader to do or buy something
3   to recommend or bring about a change
4   to evaluate something
5   to enable the reader to make a judgement
6   to interest the reader

2   Which three of the following are generally features of the language of a review?

1   use of first and second person
2   use of direct speech
3   use of reported speech
4   fairly formal style

2

1   Read the following writing task and underline the three parts of the task.

TASK

The Visitors' Information Centre in your town has re-opened after re-location and modernisation. A local English language magazine has asked people to write a review of the new Centre for publication in the magazine. Write your review, describing the Centre, giving your personal perspective and evaluating its appeal for both local residents and tourists.

(300–350 words)

2   Read this review which was written in answer to the task. Check your answers to Exercise 1.

The new Visitors' Centre finally opened its refurbished and much grander premises in Market Square this week. Like many residents, I had initially been concerned about the plans to update the Centre, feeling that the proposed hi-tech displays would be out of keeping with the historical surroundings. However, when I visited the Centre on its opening day, I was pleasantly surprised by what I found.

The new Centre has kept the building's original eighteenth-century façade, but inside it opens up into a large, airy reception area leading to a series of rooms, each of which has a special focus. One contains computer programs, allowing visitors to explore historical sites in the area, such as the famous rock paintings. Another has details of accommodation, events and guided tours, with computerised booking facilities. Upstairs there is a gallery with pictures by local artists depicting well-known beauty spots. There is a museum section, with displays of historical artifacts and computer-animated models of street scenes from the past. Headsets are available with recorded commentaries in a number of languages.

The organisation and presentation of the Centre is impressive. Peter Williams, the manager, says that the entire project has been designed to be attractive both to casual visitors and serious historians, and the overseas visitors I spoke to were very taken with the facilities offered and the standard of the displays. Inevitably there is a shop, but again I was pleasantly surprised by the quality of the goods on sale, and its excellent selection of books on local history and the culture of the region.

So how much of an asset is it to the town? In spite of my initial reservations, I now feel that it provides a valuable focus for visitors, who will have a much better idea of what the town and its surroundings can offer them. As for residents, it will provide schools with a much-needed resource for our children to research local history — and maybe provide us all with a greater sense of our own heritage. It can only be a good thing.

(343 words)

3   The review is divided into four paragraphs. Match the following topics to the appropriate paragraph. Some paragraphs have more than one topic.

a) reaction of others
b) factual information
c) writer's overall verdict
d) summary of the Centre's appeal
e) writer's initial attitude
f) establishing topic

Paragraph 1   ....
Paragraph 2   ....
Paragraph 3   ....
Paragraph 4   ....

4   Look at the phrases below, which were used in the review to express the writer's changing opinions.

I had been concerned about the plans ... **However,** *when I visited the Centre on its opening day, I was pleasantly surprised by what I found.*
In spite of *my initial reservations, I now feel that it provides a valuable focus for visitors.*

Complete the sentences below using your own ideas. Think about places you have visited or projects you have been involved in.

1   I had been very dubious about ... but now ...
2   I had my doubts about ... but I have since ...
3   At the outset I was enthusiastic about ... but then I began ...
4   My initial reaction to ... was ... but after a while ...
5   I was sceptical about ... at first, but now ...
6   Although I was unenthusiastic about ... at first, I soon ...

5   The statements below were made about the attraction described in the review in Exercise 2. Match the reporting verbs in the box to the quotes below, to indicate the attitude of the speaker. Then rewrite each sentence as reported speech, to make it appropriate for inclusion in a review.

admire	reject	propose	complain
recommend	praise	urge	

1   'The whole centre was just wonderful!'
    The tourists ....
2   'It's going to ruin the town.'
    She ....
3   'I don't accept any of it!'
    He ....
4   'I think it's ideal for families – everyone should go.'
    They ....
5   'Why don't we discuss the possibility of extending the facilities?'
    The manager ....
6   'I think they've done a terrific job.'
    The mayor ....
7   'You really must go as soon as possible!'
    The manager ....

6

1   Read the following writing task. What information will you include?

> ■ **TASK**
>
> A new exhibition has opened in your town. A local interest magazine has asked people to review it. Write your review, describing the exhibition, giving your personal perspective and evaluating its appeal for local residents.
>
> (300–350 words)

2   Think about what kind of exhibition you will write about – industry, historical artefacts, art, theatre, or a different idea of your own.

3   Plan your answer using the structure given in Exercise 3.

The National Centre for Popular Music, Sheffield.

7   Now write your review. Make sure that you include the features of a review discussed in Exercise 1. When you have finished, check and edit your work carefully.

1 Complete each of the following sentences with one of the words from the box.

> boosted   cramped   culmination   prospect
> provisions   reputable   risky

1 Although the living areas are spacious, the sleeping quarters are .... and uncomfortable.
2 In the early days, we had to carry all the .... we needed in our rucksacks.
3 We had planned to travel by canoe, but accepted that it was too .... under the circumstances.
4 The walkers .... their energy levels by eating chocolate as they went along.
5 There is little .... of persuading him to rest while there's still so much work to finish.
6 The launch of this spacecraft marks the .... of many years' research and experimentation.
7 No .... guide would take newly-arrived tourists to such a dangerous area.

2 Read the text below and decide which answer (**A, B, C** or **D**) best fits each gap.

Taking responsibility for tourism

In too many cases nowadays, travel companies don't (1) .... themselves accountable for what they do. By promoting travel to new destinations they're damaging the environments of developing countries and diluting indigenous cultures wherever they get their (2) .... in the door. But it's not entirely their (3) .... – paying customers should insist on the companies (4) .... up a more responsible attitude. The trouble is that people who travel for pleasure are not prepared to pay over the (5) .... for their holidays – they just want a cheap deal. The only way to get the travel companies to change is for people considering buying such holidays to (6) .... with their feet. If people didn't go on these holidays, then the companies would think again – and that's exactly what I'm trying to make people aware of with this campaign.

1 A put   B hold   C keep   D get
2 A foot   B head   C shoulder   D body
3 A mistake   B blame   C fault   D error
4 A looking   B taking   C getting   D boosting
5 A levels   B margins C odds   D chances
6 A choose   B elect   C decide   D vote

3 Read the text below. Use the word given in capitals at the end of some of the lines to form a word that fits in the space in the same line.

This is the story of an (0) ..*extraordinary*. quest. It begins in a small and (1) .... place on a tributary one thousand miles up the River Amazon and ends in a city of a million people. Between the fears with which my journey started and the new, saddened understanding of my return to (2) .... lies an experience that was for me both exhilarating and (3) ....

I went there because I wanted to examine my (4) .... with, and thoughts about, the natural world, and I chose the Amazon because, in spite of many recent changes, it remains the greatest single expression of (5) .... nature on this planet.

The vast area has inspired dreams and (6) .... ever since reports of the river and forest reached Europe in 1500. Even the name men gave it was (7) ...., based on highly (8) .... accounts from early explorers in the region, of female (9) .... similar to the Amazons of Greek mythology. But soon even this mighty rain forest will be broken up into mere patches of (10) ...., disciplined between roads and fields, towns and plantations, and I wanted to see it while it was still outside man's control.

ORDINARY
SIGNIFY

CIVIL

SETTLE

RELATE

TAME

NIGHT

MYSTERY
SPECULATE

WAR

WILD

13 The price of success

Reading

▶ Paper 1, Part 3

1 Interview a partner using these questions.

1 What ambitions did you have when you were a young child?
2 Are they the same as your ambitions now? If not, what made them change?

2 The following extract is from a novel by Amy Tan, a Chinese-American whose parents emigrated to the USA from China when she was a child. In the novel, she writes about a girl in a similar situation to herself. You will find some examples of non-standard English in some of the direct and reported speech, reflecting the influence of the mother's Chinese background.

Read the main part of the text quickly and answer the following questions. Do not look at the jumbled paragraphs on page 183 yet.

1 What does the woman want for her daughter?
2 How does her daughter feel about this at the beginning of the text?
3 Do the daughter's feelings change?

AMERICA was where all my mother's hopes lay. She had come to San Francisco in 1949 after losing everything in China: her mother and father, her family home, her first husband and two daughters, twin baby girls. But she never looked back with regret. There were so many ways for things to get better.

1 ....

We didn't immediately pick the right kind of prodigy. At first my mother thought I could be a Chinese Shirley Temple*. We'd watch Shirley's old movies on TV as though they were training films. My mother would poke my arm and say 'Ni kan' – you watch. And I would see Shirley tossing her curls and singing a sailor song, or pursing her lips into a very round O while saying 'Oh my goodness.'
'Ni kan,' said my mother as Shirley's eyes flooded with tears. 'You already know how. Don't need talent for crying!'

2 ....

The instructor had to lop off these soggy clumps to make my hair even again. 'Short hair is very popular these days,' she assured my mother. I now had hair the length of a boy's, with straight-across bangs that hung at a slant two inches above my eyebrows. I liked the haircut and it made me actually look forward to my future fame.

3 ....

In all my imaginings I was filled with a sense that I would soon become perfect. My mother and father would adore me. I would be beyond reproach. I would never feel the need to sulk for anything. But sometimes the prodigy in me became impatient. 'If you don't hurry up and get me out of here, I'm disappearing for good,' it warned. 'And then you'll always be nothing.'

4 ....

3 Read the text again carefully. Choose from the paragraphs **A–H** the one which best fits each gap. There is one extra paragraph which you do not need to use. Remember to:

- look backwards and forwards
- check that you have not used the same paragraph twice

4 Read through the whole text again.

1 In what order does the girl experience the following emotions? Find evidence from the text to support your answer.

First she brought out a story about a three-year-old boy who knew the main cities in all the states in America and even most of the European countries. A teacher was quoted as saying the little boy could also pronounce the names of the foreign cities correctly. 'What's the capital of Finland?' my mother asked me, looking at the magazine story. 'Nairobi!' I guessed, saying the most foreign word I could think of. She checked to see if that was possibly one way to pronounce 'Helsinki' before showing me the answer.

5 ....

One night I had to look at a page in the Bible for three minutes and then report everything I could remember. 'Now Jehoshaphat had riches and honor in abundance and ... that's all I remember, Ma,' I said. And seeing my mother's disappointed face once again, something inside of me began to die. I hated the tests, the raised hopes and failed expectations.

6 ....

And then I saw what seemed to be the prodigy side of me – because I had never seen that face before. The girl staring back at me was angry, powerful. This girl and I were the same. I had new thoughts, wilful thoughts, or rather thoughts filled with lots of won'ts. I won't let her change me, I promised myself. I won't be what I'm not.

7 ....

And the next day, I played a game with myself, seeing if my mother would give up on me before it sounded eight times. After a while I usually counted only one, maybe two at most. At last she was beginning to give up hope.

Shirley Temple – a child film star of the 1930s

- [ ] disappointment and frustration
- [ ] rebellion
- [ ] determination to be herself
- [ ] optimism and excitement

2 How do you think the situation described at the end of the extract could have been avoided? Think of some advice you could give to a) the mother b) the daughter.

3 In what ways have your family encouraged you to achieve your potential? In what ways have they left you free to make your own choices?

A So now on nights when my mother presented her tests, I performed listlessly, my head propped on one arm. I pretended to be bored. And I was. I got so bored I started counting the bellows of the foghorn out on the bay while my mother drilled me.

B The tests got harder – multiplying numbers in my head, finding the queen of hearts in a deck of cards, predicting the daily temperatures in Los Angeles, New York and London.

C 'You're just not trying,' said my mother. And she was neither angry nor sad. She said it as if to announce a fact that could never be disproved.

D Soon after my mother got this idea, she took me to a beauty training school and put me in the hands of a student who could barely hold the scissors without shaking. Instead of shiny ringlets, I emerged with an uneven mass of crinkly black fuzz. My mother dragged me off to the bathroom and tried to wet it down to straighten it, complaining loudly as though I'd done it on purpose.

E Every night after dinner my mother and I would sit at the kitchen table. She would present me with tests, taking her examples from stories of amazing children she had read in the magazines she got from people whose houses she cleaned.

F You could open a restaurant. You could work for the government and get good retirement. You could become rich. You could become instantly famous.
   'Of course, you can be prodigy, too,' my mother told me when I was nine. You can be best anything.'

G In fact, in the beginning, I was just as excited as my mother, maybe even more so. I pictured this prodigy part of me as many different images, trying each one on for size. I was a dainty ballerina standing by the curtains, waiting to hear the right music that would send me floating on my tiptoes. I was Cinderella stepping from her pumpkin carriage with sparkly cartoon music filling the air.

H Before going to bed that night, I looked in the mirror above the bathroom sink and when I saw only my face staring back – and that it would always be this ordinary face – I began to cry. Such a sad, ugly girl! I made high-pitched noises like a crazed animal, trying to scratch out the face in the mirror.

Listening

▶ Paper 4, Part 1

1 Work in pairs. What is your definition of success? Write a short definition that you can both agree on.

 2 You will hear four different extracts. For questions 1–8, choose the answer (**A, B** or **C**) which fits best according to what you hear.

Extract One

You hear a woman talking about how she became involved in sport.

1 The speaker says she was successful in the triathlon because she
  A was talented.
  B had little competition.
  C was lucky.

2 She wanted to compete again because she enjoyed the
  A success.
  B acclaim.
  C challenge.

Extract Two

You hear a contestant in a TV quiz show being interviewed after the show.

3 Before Pete went on the show he felt
  A confident.
  B nervous.
  C determined.

4 At the end of the show he
  A was satisfied with his performance.
  B regretted losing the money.
  C wished he had answered a different question.

Extract Three

You hear a man talking about his career.

5 How did the speaker feel about his father when he was younger?
  A grateful for his support
  B afraid of opposing him
  C comfortable talking to him

6 The speaker regrets
  A not having tried acting.
  B becoming a lawyer.
  C taking money from his father.

Extract Four

You hear a motorcycling champion, Darren, talking about his sport.

7 When he doesn't win, Darren
  A makes the best of it.
  B is devastated.
  C hides his feelings.

8 What does Darren suggest about motorcycling?
  A He prefers it to an ordinary job.
  B It's an unpleasant environment to work in.
  C Not all of the skills required can be taught.

3 Look back at the definition of success you came up with in Exercise 1, and discuss it in relation to what you have heard. Which speaker do you consider has actually been the most successful?

Improving your writing

In Units 1, 3 and 9, you identified and corrected errors in the areas of writing listed below. This section gives further practice in these areas.

- accuracy, including grammatical accuracy, spelling, punctuation
- range of grammatical structures used
- range and appropriacy of vocabulary used
- consistency and appropriacy of style and register
- organisation and discourse management

1   The extracts below were written by Proficiency students. Match each extract **A–H** to one of the task types 1–5 below. Think about both content and style. Ignore the underlined mistakes for the moment.

1 argumentative essay
2 magazine article
3 newspaper article
4 review
5 report

A

Those providing financial backing always have to hold competitions in places where they can ¹ make a fortune. Professional sport is only for the rich not for the poor because the tickets ² have been so expensive that the poor can't afford ³ it. ⁴ It's not fair, is it? I recommend that entrance to the football stadium should be cheaper so that all the people who ⁵ fancy the game can come and watch. I recommend to the committee an immediate reduction in ticket prices based on my findings.

B

Modern life ¹ has both good and not good input, especially the young generation. Every day we live with high technology, ² among them are television and cinema. Television and film producers are doing their best to attract people by presenting violence, and this is seen ³ clear in this film.

C

By 14.00 ¹ it was downpouring heavily and four inches of rain had ² increased in the ³ past hour. People were ⁴ informed to stay in their houses because the situation outside was getting worse. People were angry with the authorities. Why ⁵ did the forecasters ⁶ excluded this combination of ⁷ the weather conditions? Many people were trapped in trees and others injured themselves by trying to save their homes.

D

To sum up, it is good to have dreams and to ¹ put goals in your life, and of course to fight to ² fulfil all of them, but even if you succeed, what will ³ be their value if you don't have your health. In short, health is clearly the most important thing in life.

E

So if someone commits a crime, he goes to prison. 'It's fair,' said Judge Taylor, 'provided that the prison has regulations and humane and sanitary conditions.' But I can't ¹ stop thinking that for some crimes another ² way of punishment might be better and more effective. ³ I simply think about a place where they give criminals ⁴ an obligatory work without payment, and provide them only with a place to sleep and something to eat for a period of time.

F

Some people questioned believe that apart from human rights there are also animal rights and consequently we should all be as sensitive to ¹ animals' abuse as to humans' abuse. In my investigation I saw that there is a large number of animals which are used as subjects ² to scientific experiments and unfortunately, nearly ³ most of them die or those which manage to ⁴ go through these experiments are left with some kind of permanent ⁵ disability. So this raises another practical issue to address which has to do with the balance of nature, as ⁶ the numbers of some animals due to these experiments is tending to ⁷ dwindle. These findings lead me to my conclusions and recommendations which I outline below.

G

One of the most famous and ¹ interested museums in the world is the British Museum ² at London. It is a huge building ³ overwhelmed with relics, and works of art that ⁴ can impress every visitor.

H

As we all know, stress has always been a very negative factor in our lives because of ¹ it's bad side effects. Today life is much more stressful. There are thousands of cities overcrowded with people and no jobs. Thus, a lot of people are out of work. Others, in order to ² bring home the bacon and educate their children, ³ work like dogs at any job they can find. So is life actually more stressful than ever before?

2   Work with a partner. Read through the extracts again, looking at the underlined words and phrases. Decide what type of mistake each one is (collocation, grammar, vocabulary or style) and correct each one.

3 The extract below lacks range of vocabulary and structure. Work with a partner. Identify the task type. (Use the list in Exercise 1 to help you.) Then improve the range of vocabulary and structure.

> I live in a small town with about 40,000 habitants. It is situated in the suburbs of Lyon. So it's cleaner and there are more green places. With bus and underground it's really easy to go in Lyon's town centre. So I can have advantages of the town and the country.

4 The extract below is the introduction to an argumentative essay about what makes people happy. The paragraph is badly organised and the ideas are not well linked.

1 Work with a partner. Read the extract and discuss what changes you would like to make.

> Happiness is related to many things such as health, family, career, which we consider to be the ones that give us happiness. Therefore, if money could help us to improve one of the things mentioned above and if we had the money to do so this would mean that money could help us attain happiness. However, how far is this actually true?

2 Read the two rewritten versions **A** and **B** on page 239. Discuss which version is better, and why.

Language Focus: Vocabulary

1 Phrasal verbs with *get* and *go*

1 Read through the text below. Then choose a phrasal verb from the box to replace each of the words or expressions in italics.

After (1) *passing* his final law exams with flying colours, Oscar (2) *applied for* a variety of highly-paid jobs, and soon found one he liked. It was hard work at first, but he soon found his feet and (3) *concentrated on* making as much money as possible. However, his money-making schemes were so complex that he did not (4) *have enough time for* making friends or building up a social life.

Feeling stressed, he went to his doctor who warned him that his lifestyle was leading him to a nervous breakdown. She said he'd (5) *escaped* it up to now, but needed to change his lifestyle. She advised him to (6) *take part in* some type of sport and recommended climbing, saying it would suit his drive to reach the top. She was right. He became so successful as a climber that he gave up his job and (7) *managed to make a living* with the money he earned writing about his exploits. When his third book was published he was asked whether he was happier now than when he was making a lot of money. 'Of course,' he replied. 'There's more to life than just (8) *being successful* financially.'

get on	go ahead with
get through	go in for
get away with something	
get by	go for
get down to	go into
get round to	

2 Read the story again. Do you agree with Oscar's changed attitude to success?

3 Look at the phrasal verbs you didn't use. Write a sentence about your own ambitions using each one.

2 Idioms with *get* and *go*

1 Read the following text. Then replace the words in italics with an idiom from the box. You may need to make other changes.

> I've always believed there's only one way to achieve success: you've just got to (1) *put all your effort into* it. Even if you seem to be (2) *making no progress whatsoever*, you have to (3) *strive to get what you want.* You may find you've got no-one to lend a helping hand, you may have to (4) *struggle without help*, but if you can (5) *achieve more than* the rest, then you'll make it to the top.

get up and go
get your act together
get nowhere/somewhere
go one better than ...
go for it
go all out for something/to do something
go it alone
have a go at something

2 What difference have these changes made to the style of the text?

3 Look at the expressions you didn't use. What do they mean? Write a sentence including each of them.

4 Do you agree that it is always possible to achieve success by individual effort?

3   Compound nouns formed from verbs

✗ *it was downpouring heavily* (text, p. 185)
✓ *the rain was pouring down*
✓ *there was a heavy downpour*

Complete the sentences below with a compound noun including the word given. You may need to change the form of the word.

1   The students hardly cooked at all, but lived on .... TAKE

2   Finally, we'll give you some .... on the course and a few suggestions for how it could be improved. FEED

3   We are anxiously waiting for the .... of the negotiations. COME

4   We've got far too much rubbish in this house – it's time we had a .... CLEAR

5   In 1999 there were two major .... in research into spinal injury. BREAK

6   None of the .... took any notice, in spite of his shouts. PASS

7   The .... among the peasants was cruelly put down by the king's army. RISE

8   The cat had numerous ...., all of whom inherited her timid nature. SPRING

9   There were a few ...., but in general the project went well. SET

10 The .... of the disease was gradual, and at first they hardly noticed its effects. SET

4   Use of English: Paper 3, Part 3

Think of one word only which can be used appropriately in all three sentences.

1   Insects such as mosquitoes and lice .... many serious diseases.
    He was required to .... all the details in his head, as it was too dangerous to commit them to paper.
    All our products are fully refundable in case of dissatisfaction and .... a full twelve month guarantee.

2   Pam's husband has supported her every .... of the way, in spite of the problems.
    As part of her job, Alison tries to keep in .... with all new developments in fashion.
    He needed to be one .... ahead of his opponent in order to win.

3   He has an interesting .... of videos and CDs, including several not usually available in this country.
    They knew they were in great danger as the ship was within .... of the enemy guns.
    We finally reached the top of the pass, only to find another mountain .... facing us.

4   He spent about an hour trying to explain it all to me but I still felt totally .... – it just seemed impossible.
    His kind words were completely .... on her – she was too immersed in her own thoughts.
    Celia didn't notice how long the flight took; she spent the whole time .... in her book.

5   Add the flour and sugar to the eggs and .... them together until the mixture becomes light and fluffy.
    The bird .... its wings in a desperate effort to escape from the trap.
    The administration claim that they are about to .... inflation.

6   She asked if I wanted a hand with the bags but I told her I could .... them on my own.
    I honestly don't know how we're going to .... now Keith's lost his job.
    I've really had enough, but think I could .... another of those delicious cakes if you insist.

Listening
▶ Paper 4, Part 2

1

1 Look at the situations below. In which situation do you think mental attitude might play the greatest part in succeeding or failing?

2 Discuss the following questions.

1 Have you ever been afraid of failing?
2 What caused this fear?
3 How did it affect you?
4 Did you overcome it? How?

2 You will hear a talk being given to a group of students by a businessman. Before you listen, look through the gapped sentences below. What can you predict about his talk?

1 The speaker says that everyone feels [1   ] when they are successful.

2 The fear of [2   ] can be encouraging.

3 Time pressure may be given as a reason for not using the [3   ] of life.

4 The speaker suggests that people should first [4   ] their main fear.

5 He says that even if you fail, this can make you [5   ] than you were.

6 You can't anticipate the [6   ] of others.

7 You can control your fears better if you visualise the [7   ] of success.

8 The speaker denies that success is based on [8   ].

9 For him, the [9   ] he got from success was its main reward.

3 Now listen and complete the sentences with a word or short phrase. When you have finished, check that the words you have written are spelled correctly and that they make sense in the sentence as a whole.

4

1 Match the verbs and nouns to form phrases connected with achieving success.

1	play	a)	a chance
2	take	b)	in glory
3	set	c)	your mark
4	seize	d)	results
5	handle	e)	an aim
6	bask	f)	it safe
7	make	g)	something well
8	accomplish	h)	yourself a target
9	get	i)	an opportunity

2 Can you think of a time when you or someone you know did any of the things in the list above? Tell your partner what happened.

Use of English
▶ Paper 3, Part 1

1 Look at the picture and discuss these questions.

1 How is the man feeling?
2 What kind of sacrifices do you
   think he might have had to make to achieve his success?

2 The following text is by Roger Black, a British athlete who won both team and individual Olympic medals. First, read the text through to get a general idea of its content, then fill each of the gaps with one suitable word. Finally, read the text again to make sure your answers make sense.

The meaning of success

Success is simple. It comes when you focus solely (0) ....*on*.... what you can control and don't put (1) .... under the pressure of worrying (2) .... what everybody (3) .... does. Even though someone (4) .... beat you in a race, they cannot (5) .... away your own sense of achievement. Many people feel, 'I've (6) .... to win or it's not (7) .... doing.' Only one person is going to win, so if winning is everything, you will be disappointed. But you can be a winner (8) .... saying, 'I ran my perfect race', because then your success is not (9) .... on a gold medal.

In 1996 I was looking (10) .... an art gallery. It had been at the (11) .... of my mind to see if I could (12) .... upon any inspiration in what was an Olympic year, (13) .... I was drawn to a magnificent sculpture of a gymnast inspired by an Olympic motto I had never heard of until then: *The essence lies not in the victory but in the struggle.*

The (14) .... I thought about it the better it got. To me the message is that there is no (15) .... in achieving any goal if you have not learned from or enjoyed the journey. I bought the sculpture.

3 Discuss these questions.

1 Compare the writer's attitude towards success with others you have discussed in this unit.
2 The writer found inspiration in a sculpture. Discuss any objects, ideas, or people that have inspired you personally, and explain why they were important to you.

Language Focus: Grammar
Clauses of concession

1 How else could the idea below be expressed? Look back at the cloze exercise opposite to help you.

'Another man may beat you in a race, but he cannot take your sense of achievement from you.'

2 Use of English: Paper 3, Part 4

Complete the second sentence with three to eight words so that it has a similar meaning to the first sentence, using the word given. Do not change the word given. These transformations all involve different ways of expressing concessions. If necessary, refer to the Grammar reference on page 225 to help you.

1 That leather jacket is too expensive for me, even though I really like it.   **as**
  I can't afford ....
  .... I like it.

2 He could never win the game, although he did his best.   **hard**
  However ....
  .... lost the game.

3 Although they were incredibly nervous, their performance was brilliant.   **yet**
  They were incredibly nervous, ...
  .... performance.

4 In spite of all her efforts, she failed the tests.   **even**
  She didn't manage ....
  .... very hard.

5 'She can dance, but, her singing leaves a lot to be desired,' said the casting director.   **while**
  The casting director pointed out that ....
  .... good enough.

6 Whatever you do, you'll always be successful in my eyes.   **no**
  To me you'll always be a ....
  .... do.

7 She got the job even though she had no qualifications.   **being**
  She was appointed ....
  .... the job.

8 Although I understand his position, he must still make a written apology.   **same**
  I understand his position, ...
  .... writing.

▶ Grammar reference p. 225

Exam Focus

▶ Paper 5 (complete interview)

The complete interview lasts nineteen minutes, and you have to take it with a partner. There will be an examiner who will just listen and an interlocutor who will ask you questions and give you tasks to complete.

You are assessed on:

- the accuracy and range of grammar you use
- the range and appropriacy of your vocabulary
- discourse management, e.g. the way you organise your ideas and how relevant they are
- pronunciation
- the skills you display when you interact with your partner and the interlocutor.

There is also a general mark given for your overall performance throughout the test.

Although it is very important that you interact with your partner, you will always be assessed on your own individual performance, and you will not be compared with your partner.

The interview has three parts, which are not connected in theme or topic.

In **Part 1** the examiner will ask you about yourself and your opinions.
In **Part 2** you have to work with your partner to complete a task based on pictures.
In **Part 3** you each have a 'long turn' where you are given a prompt card and have to talk on your own for two minutes. This is followed by general discussion between you, your partner and the interlocutor, based on the topic of the two long turns.

Part One

In the first part of the interview the interlocutor will ask each of you some general questions to make you feel at ease and to give you the chance to show how you can talk socially. You may be asked to give opinions as well as facts about yourself.
You will do this with the interlocutor in the exam, but to practise this you will work with your partner.

1 Work with a partner. Look at the following areas of conversation. Ask your partner questions that will give them a chance to talk naturally and fluently.

- home and family
- interests and hobbies
- experience at work or school
- achievements

Can you tell me about your home and family?

2 Now answer your partner's questions. Try to give interesting answers which express your personality and background, and which demonstrate how much vocabulary you know.

Part Two

In the second part of the interview you have to work with your partner. You will be given a task to complete based on pictures. It is important that you listen carefully to the interlocutor's instructions so that you can complete the task correctly. The task will have two sections: the first section is one minute and the second is three minutes.

In the exam you will be given a number of pictures, from one up to a maximum of seven, to look at together. In the first section of the task, you may have to talk about only one or two of the pictures, but in the second section you will have to talk about them all. Don't simply describe the pictures. You have to talk about the issues or points that the pictures raise, **not** about the pictures themselves.

1 Work with a partner. Read the task below.

1 Here are some pictures of people in the public eye. Look at pictures 3 and 5 and say how you think the people might be feeling.

2 Now look at all the pictures.
   An enquiry is being held into the behaviour of the
   press, and all the pictures will be used as evidence.
   Talk together about the different aspects of press
   behaviour suggested by the pictures, and decide
   which aspects you find most unacceptable.
   (HINT: *There are two points to cover here: the different
   aspects of press behaviour – including both positive and
   negative effects of such photos – and the discussion of
   which one is most unacceptable. Remember to discuss
   both.*)

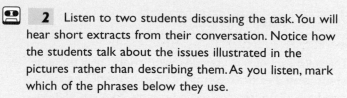

2 Listen to two students discussing the task. You will
hear short extracts from their conversation. Notice how
the students talk about the issues illustrated in the
pictures rather than describing them. As you listen, mark
which of the phrases below they use.

> It seems to me that one of the important points
>   to bear in mind is ...
> Well, that might be true, but what about ...?
> That's a good point ...
> What I think is ...
> Don't you think that ...?
> What I mean is ...

Exam Strategy

Listen carefully to the interlocutor's instructions and
remember to talk about the issues illustrated in the
pictures. Remember that this is a shared task and
that you should try to reach an agreement.

Part Three

The third part of the interview takes twelve minutes, and is not related to the topic of Part Two. You will be given a card with a question and some prompts. You have to talk about the topic for two minutes. You do not need to use the prompts on the card if you already have lots of ideas about the topic, but they will help if you can't think of anything to say. If you run out of ideas, try to relate the topic to your own experience. After you have spoken for two minutes, your partner will be asked a follow-up question based on what you have said. Then you will both be asked another general follow-up question by the interlocutor.

Your partner will then be given a prompt card on a related topic and asked to talk for two minutes. After the follow-up questions, the interlocutor will start a general discussion by asking further questions related to the theme of the two prompt cards.

Look back at Unit 1, page 18 for a procedure for dealing with the prompt card.

1   Read the prompt card below. Make notes on the ideas you would include.

> How would you define success in the modern world?
> - relationships
> - opportunities
> - finances

2   Listen to a student discussing the question on the prompt card and compare his answer with your notes. Did he include the same ideas? Was the talk logical and clear?

3   Work with a partner. You should each talk for two minutes about the topic on the prompt card. Then give each other feedback on the ideas and organisation of your talks.

(HINT: *Look back over the topics you have studied in this coursebook to practise this part of the interview. Set yourself questions to talk about for two minutes. You could record your talk and listen for accuracy and general interest.*)

4   To finish the interview, the interlocutor will ask some further questions, which you will not see. The interlocutor will only ask as many questions as are necessary to keep the conversation going. This part of the interview lasts about four minutes, so you will need to talk about the topic in detail. To practise this, discuss the following questions, which develop the theme of success.

1   Do you think that financial success is more important than fame?
2   What kinds of success do you think go unnoticed?
3   Whose success do you particularly admire, and why?
4   What part does luck play in success?
5   How would you like to be successful and why?
6   Do you think that the right kinds of people become role models in society today?
7   Do you think that modern society is too hard on people who fail?

Exam Strategy

- Although you will not have any time to prepare your talk, try to think in a logical way and organise your ideas into an introduction, a main part and a conclusion. Remember that the prompts are there to give you ideas on the topic but you do not need to use them.

- Always listen carefully to your partner's talk as you will be asked a question by the examiner on what they have said.

- In the final part of the interview you have the opportunity to interact with your partner without having a task to complete. You need to have plenty to say about the topic and to use strategies to maintain a good flow of conversation.

- Don't try to dominate the conversation when you are interacting with your partner. You will get marks for asking questions and using conversation strategies.

Writing

▶ Paper 2, Part 1 (article)

In Unit 9 you wrote an article for Paper 2, Part 2. This had a descriptive focus.
For Part 1, you may also be asked to write an **article**. In this case you will have to discuss the topic rather than describe a situation or event, and you will be given some input to use as the basis for your writing.

1   Read the following writing task.

TASK

You have seen the extract below in an article in a local newspaper and have read the letter sent in to the newspaper in response to the article. Readers have been asked to send in their opinions. You decide to write an article discussing the points raised by both the original article and the letter.

(300–350 words)

Rare award for Scouting

A PRESTIGIOUS scouting award was handed out to Joseph Reynolds on Saturday night in front of an audience of over 300 local people. Mr Reynolds received the Silver Acorn in recognition of his 34 years of service to scouting. He said, 'Not many people get this award – I was overjoyed.'

To the Editor:
Do we really need to gather 300 people together to see someone being given a 'Silver Acorn'? Ceremonies such as this are a waste of time and money – and what good is a silver acorn to anyone? Surely such awards are meaningless in today's world.

---

2   In groups, discuss the following questions.

- What do you know about scouting? How do you think it benefits children?
- What other organisations do you know of that work with children?
- What is your opinion of people who give up their free time to work with children? What kind of reward do you think they should have (if any)?

3   Read the article below, which was written in answer to the task. What is the writer's opinion about the value of awards for outstanding achievements? (There are some problems of language and organisation; ignore these for now.)

There are many awards given out these days in many different walks of life – pop music, film, social service, scouting – but what is the value of these awards in real terms? I saw a pop group get an award on television last week and there was a big dinner for them afterwards. Some people, like the writer of the letter, believe that they are worthless. When I first read the letter, I agreed with this point of view but then, thinking of what such awards may mean to those who actually receive them, I started to revise my opinion. The modern world is very cynical and materialistic; the majority of people seem to be out for what they can get, seeing reward solely in terms of material gain. But when a person achieves something special in their particular field, or spends years working for others, as Mr Reynolds has done, why should they not receive some symbol of recognition from the society they live in? After all, it was a really nice award, silver with writing around the base. Mr Reynolds' hard work has clearly been of benefit to the young people he worked with. Although he may feel that their appreciation is reward enough, it must be gratifying for his efforts to be publicly recognised. Is acknowledging the achievements of others old-fashioned? I don't think so. In fact, I think it's great if they can really enjoy it, and I bet Mr Reynolds is dead pleased, and so are all the other people who get awards. If society ignores the efforts made by individuals, there is a danger that they may feel their work is not worthwhile. And anyway, I think people get a kick out of being told they've done well. All in all I feel such awards are valuable – they do not cost the tax payer anything and they make those who receive them feel appreciated. If we lose such symbols, we lose more than a 'Silver Acorn'.

(333 words)

4 Look back at both the newspaper extract and the letter. Which points has the writer used from each?

5

1 This article should be divided into three paragraphs. Look back at the article and mark where you think each new paragraph should start.

2 What is the focus of each paragraph?

6

1 Two sentences in the article give information which is irrelevant to the topic. Find these sentences and cross them out.

2 Two further sentences contain language which is too informal, or ideas which are expressed too personally. Find these sentences, underline them, and rewrite them in a more appropriate way.

7

1 Read the following writing task.

> **TASK**
>
> You have seen the following extract in a newspaper article. Readers have been asked to send in their opinions. You decide to write an article for publication in the newspaper addressing the points raised and expressing your own views.
>
> Write your article.
>
> (300–350 words)

Government withdraws funding for gifted children

THE MINISTER of Education today announced that funding would no longer be available for schools for children of exceptional intellectual ability. 'We feel that priority should be given to disadvantaged children, rather than to those who are likely to succeed in any case,' he said.

Jane Harries, Head Teacher of one of the affected schools, said, 'It is a tragic decision. Gifted children cannot realise their full potential without the challenge and support we provide; they are our country's future and we can't afford to let them down.'

2 Decide what your opinion is. (Do you agree with the point of view of the Minister of Education, or the Head Teacher?)

3 Make notes on ideas to support your point of view.

4 Plan your article using the organisational structure you identified in Exercise 5.

8 Write your article. When you have finished, check and edit your work carefully. Pay special attention to the organisation of ideas, and the use of an appropriate style.

1 Think of one word only which can be used appropriately in all three sentences.

1 I found that the sports car .... particularly badly on wet roads.
The advice service .... a useful function until it was closed last year.
He .... in front of a live audience last week for the first time.

2 We need a new captain who can .... the team to regain their past form.
The new manager doesn't exactly .... confidence in his workers.
His meeting with this unknown woman was to .... his greatest poem.

3 He was so shocked after the accident that the police couldn't get any .... out of him at all.
They were certainly under a lot of pressure, although this in no .... excuses their actions.
The whole sorry affair left me with a .... of complete helplessness.

4 The existing range will soon be .... by an entirely new generation of multifunctional products.
If he had .... in this round, he could have gone on to the finals.
Once Flavia had .... Simon as chief executive, she revealed her plans for the company.

5 The police have several theories about the case, but no .... evidence as yet.
She found all this sudden concern for her welfare rather .... to take.
He found that running 50 miles a week was very .... on his knee joints, and finally gave it up.

6 Winning the championship was a personal .... for Boardman, as well as for everyone in his team.
There were yells of .... from the campaigners when the result of the election was announced.
The revolutionary new museum building has been acclaimed as a .... of modern design.

2 Use the word given in capitals at the end of some of the lines to form a word that fits in the space in the same line.

When we think of the future we think of
a (0) _digital_ world opening out in front of us, where   DIGIT
vast amounts of data are transmitted at the speed of
light for the general good (or bad) of (1) ....   HUMAN
We try to (2) .... a new type of existence, where   VISUAL
limits are broken and things happen that we can't
even dream about. Not (3) .... so, cry many   NEED
social (4) .... who say that our society is in fact   COMMENT
becoming more medieval.

Their argument goes like this: the greatest gulf
between medieval and 21st-century thought is the
(5) .... today that no matter what things may   ASSUME
look like on the surface, the world is fundamentally
(6) .... and there is no order. In the Middle Ages   COHERE
the exact opposite was the case – but there is now a
hankering to return to this happier order. People
nowadays think that progress only causes anxiety
and (7) .... They see it as creating   STABLE
divisions between its (8) .... and those who are   BENEFIT
left behind, remaining as confused (9) .... living   STAND
on the (10) .... of society.   SKIRT

3 Why would this photo be suitable for inclusion in a magazine article about pension schemes and their benefits?

Speaking

1 Read the following statement and discuss the question below.

'Books, art and music all contribute to the development of individual members of society.'

What do you think individuals can gain from:

- reading books?
- looking at art?
- listening to music/playing music?

Think of three benefits of each.

2

1 How important are the following in your own life? Discuss the questions below.

- music
- dancing
- film
- theatre
- poetry

Why are they important to you?
How are you involved in them?
Do you take an active part in any of them?

2 Choose two of the areas listed. Work out three arguments to persuade others to become involved in them.

Use of English

▶ **Paper 3, Part 5**

1 Do you think that people will still be reading books in fifty years' time? Why/Why not?

2 Read the following texts on the place of the book in modern society and decide what answer each of the writers would give to the question in Exercise 1.

Text 1

Frantic efforts are now being made to render the traditional book as 'obsolete' as the stage
5 play or the symphony orchestra. Small fortunes have been spent putting books on the Internet. The plug-in book is now being
10 produced by Research and Development bureaucrats in media conglomerates. Books could be stored in the electronic spines of
15 hand-held light-boxes. They could be loaded into photosensitive pages for carrying on trains and planes. But all those
20 developments have encountered consumer resistance. People appear to find flickering screens tiring. They make eyes
25 ache since the scanning pulses are in constant movement. The flicker is said to limit lateral vision and make speed-reading
30 (and mistake spotting) difficult. The eye is also strained since the screen is brighter than ambient light. And all screens need electronic power.
35
What these souls are struggling to do is merely to reinvent what Caxton discovered half a millennium ago. It is called
40 a book. Technologists dislike books because they are 'low tech', yet the market loves them. The book needs no power
45 supply and creates no radio interference. It is cheap, small and portable, usable on the beach, while walking or curled up in bed. It is
50 virtually indestructible. A book can be read fast or slow at the flick of a finger. It can be dog-eared, ripped up, passed around and
55 shelved for instant and easy retrieval. A row of books is a joy to behold. This object is, in short, a technical and aesthetic masterpiece. Had
60 the Internet been around for years and had I invented printing on paper, I would be hailed as a genius.

Text 2

The book seems as obvious a candidate for redundancy now as it has since the middle of the 20th century. But we should be aware of pessimism's poor record.
5 People previously assumed that the cinema and television would finish off reading, yet the book, to an extraordinary degree, has learned to coexist with its rivals.

Most Hollywood projects derive from
10 novels: often trashy ones, it is true, but also the classics. And not only do movies and television series descend from books but, almost routinely, they return to them as nearly every screen product has its tie-in book. It all
15 suggests that the desire of the viewer to follow the visual experience with a print experience is even more tenacious than ever.

The threat to the conventional book in the 21st century is, though, subtly different. Where
20 the first challengers were alternatives to reading, the current ones are alternative ways of reading: CD Rom, computer disk, the Internet, recorded books. The smart money would bet that the standard home or library
25 reference book is going the way of the dodo simply because the new technology can make information more visually appealing. But, with regard to fiction, it seems a reasonable assumption that the portability of the standard
30 book, and the aesthetic affection that established readers still have for it as a product, will confound pessimism in the future.

3 Read the texts again and answer questions 1–4 with a word or short phrase. You do not need to write complete sentences.

1 What is the writer actually suggesting about the stage play and symphony orchestra in the first sentence?
2 Who is the writer referring to when he says 'these souls'? (line 36)

3 Explain briefly in your own words the way in which the threat to traditional books has now changed.
4 What phrase in paragraph 3 echoes the idea that 'a row of books is a joy to behold'? (text 1, lines 57–58)

4 In a paragraph of between 50 and 70 words, summarise in your own words as far as possible, the reasons given in the texts for why books have remained popular up to the present and are likely to survive into the future.

5 The writer of text 1 says that the main advantage of the new technology is that it makes information 'more visually appealing'.

1 How far do you agree with this?
2 What other advantages can you think of for having fiction and non-fiction on electronic books?
3 Would you prefer to read on screen or on paper? Why?

Language Focus: Vocabulary
▶ **Paper 1, Part 1**

1 Read the text and decide which answer (**A**, **B**, **C** or **D**) best fits each gap

Youth's guilty secret – they love books

In today's youth culture, books are seen as boring and old-fashioned (1) .... to a recent study which claims that children only spend fifteen minutes a day reading, and are (2) .... to the television or computer screen for the rest of their leisure time.

However, this is totally at (3) .... with other research, which suggests that children are reading more books than ever before. Although technology has been accused of destroying their desire to read, it appears that using the Internet actually stimulates children to look for more information about the things they come (4) .... there, and the easiest way for them to do this is by reading books.

It is true that children often try to (5) .... their enjoyment of books in case they are seen as 'soft'. But it does in fact seem possible that (6) .... lowering standards of literacy, computers and television have actually contributed to raising them.

1	**A** due	**B** according	**C** referring	**D** owing
2	**A** glued	**B** fixed	**C** attached	**D** stuck
3	**A** differences	**B** opposition	**C** variation	**D** odds
4	**A** over	**B** across	**C** to	**D** through
5	**A** bottle up	**B** cover up	**C** blot out	**D** put away
6	**A** rather than	**B** as well as	**C** in spite of	**D** more than

2 In the light of what you have read and talked about in this unit so far, discuss the two statements below and decide which you agree with.

'The development of technology and mass media has given young people today a far greater awareness and understanding of culture than their parents.'

'People spend so much more time nowadays involved in passive leisure pursuits such as watching television and playing computer games that they have far less interest in cultural activities than their parents and grandparents.'

3 Do you prefer reading short stories or full-length novels? Why?
What different challenges do you think the two types of writing offer authors?

4 Read the following statement. How far do you agree with it?

'The ability to see our life as a narrative with a beginning, middle and end is one of the things that distinguishes humans from other living creatures.'

Exam Focus
▶ Paper 4, Part 4

In Paper 4, Part 4 you have to listen to a conversation with two main speakers and match statements to one or both of the two speakers. (You will **not** be given any statements which do not match either speaker.) You need to identify the speakers' opinions and whether they agree or disagree.

Here is a procedure to follow for this task.

- Read through the statements before listening, to get an idea of the subject and the opinions given.
- As you listen, try to identify key expressions from both speakers relating to the written statements.
- As you listen for one statement, try to look ahead at the next statement as well, to avoid missing important information.

1   You will hear two writers of fiction, Philip and Angela, discussing their work. For questions **1–6**, decide whether the opinions are expressed by only one of the speakers, or whether the speakers agree.

Write   **P**   for Philip,
       A   for Angela,
or   **B**   for Both, where they agree.

1   As a writer, I feel most at ease with the full-length novel.   ☐ 1

2   Most writers begin by writing short stories.   ☐ 2

3   I did not return to short stories once I'd written a full-length novel.   ☐ 3

4   People build up awareness of stories from their own lives.   ☐ 4

5   Only humans have the ability to tell themselves stories.   ☐ 5

6   To be successful, a short story needs a definite ending.   ☐ 6

2   To analyse your answers, refer to the extracts from the tapescript on page 239.

3   **Say it again**

Re-express the following sentences using the word given, without changing the meaning.

1   They're a good tool, whether or not people do a writing programme.
  even
2   They seldom or never go back to the short story.
  ever
3   I'm not talking about thinking about it consciously.
  conscious
4   It's extremely short on plot.
  doesn't

> **Exam Strategy**
> - Remember that the second speaker may use pronouns, e.g. *this/it* to refer back to what the first speaker has said.
> - The key expressions from each speaker may come quite closely together. These may be actual opinions or expressions of agreement or disagreement, which will probably be implied rather than direct, e.g. *Are you sure?* often suggests disagreement.

Language Focus: Grammar

Comparisons

1 The following sentences show different ways of making comparisons. Complete the sentences using **one** word in each gap.

1 Books seem to be just .... popular now .... they were in the past.

2 The book seems .... obvious .... candidate for redundancy now as it has been since the middle of the 20th century.

3 The rise of cinema and TV has not had .... a negative effect on the book .... some people predicted.

4 A high proportion of TV series are based on novels, ... are many films.

5 I much prefer reading .... watching TV.

6 I'd much .... see a film at the cinema .... on TV.

7 .... than watching sport on TV, I much prefer going to a real game.

> ► Grammar reference p. 226

2 Use of English: Paper 3, Part 4

Complete the second sentence with three to eight words so that it has a similar meaning to the first sentence, using the word given. Do not change the word given.
(These transformations all involve different ways of expressing comparison. If necessary, refer to the Grammar reference on page 226 to help you.)

1 The original version of the film was superior in every way to the new version.   **nothing**
The new version of the film ....
.... the original version.

2 The first time I went I enjoyed myself more than I did on the second visit.   **good**
I didn't ....
.... on the second visit as I had done on the first.

3 The critics predicted the musical would be very successful, but in fact it didn't do very well.   **hit**
The musical wasn't as ....
.... the critics had predicted it would be.

4 Like many other people, she was impressed by the sculpture.   **did**
She thought the sculpture impressive, ...
.... other people.

5 She greeted him less enthusiastically than he had expected.   **warm**
She ....
.... a greeting as he had expected.

6 The President had thought the public would be more affected by the news.   **of**
The news ....
impression on the public than the President had expected.

7 Books are still more portable than the majority of computers.   **around**
At present, few ....
.... easily as books.

8 It was fortunate that more workers kept their jobs than had been expected.   **laid**
Fortunately, not so many workers ....
.... had been feared.

Reading

For Paper 2 of the Proficiency exam, you may choose to study a set text.

In this section you will study a short story in detail. The same principles of analysis can be applied to the longer set text that you choose to study.

1 You are going to read a short story called *Machete* by the Australian writer, Robert Drewe. The story is set in a newly built suburb on the outskirts of an Australian town. It tells how a man finds a machete on his front lawn one morning when he goes to collect his newspaper from the mail box at the end of his driveway. Before you read the story, look at the illustration and read the definition of a machete below. Then discuss these questions.

> **machete** *n* [C] large knife with a broad heavy blade, used as a weapon or a tool

1 What do you associate a machete with? What can it be used to do?
2 If you found a machete on your front doorstep,
• how might you feel?
• what questions would you ask yourself about it?
• what would you do?

2 Read the story to find out what happened.

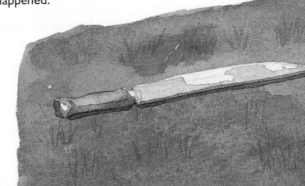

MACHETE

At eight this morning there was a machete lying on the lawn, flat in the middle of my front yard. It gave me a jolt. It's hard to describe the feeling of seeing a machete lying on your lawn when you're picking up the morning paper. I don't own a machete. It's not a common garden tool around here. In my mind a machete is a weapon of foreign guerrillas. Rural terrorists. I associate machetes with the random slaughter of innocent villagers, the massacre of peasant farmers who backed the wrong party.

Well, I picked it up – my heart beating faster – and hefted it in my hand. The blade was heavy and sharp; it was in good order. All the while I couldn't believe it was there in my yard, in my hand. I was peering around to see if the machete's owner was about to appear but there were only the usual sleepy-looking suburban houses coming to life. People were backing cars out of their driveways and leaving for work; children were setting off for school; a woman down the street watered her garden. In a moment I began to feel self-conscious standing there in my suit and tie all set for work, with the rolled newspaper in one hand and a machete in the other.

Belleview is a new suburb. Gillian and I moved here six months ago but we don't know anyone yet. These sandy, gravelly plains on the outskirts of the city were never thickly vegetated, and the developers bulldozed those trees and bushes, mainly spindly acacias, which had persevered. The residents are just starting to establish their lawns and gardens, but it's a battle in the sand. Everything blows away, and when it rains your topsoil washes half a kilometre down the road. What I'm saying is that it's not tropical rainforest or anything. A rake, a spade and a pair of secateurs will see you through. There is no need for slashing and hacking.

So I was standing in the front yard holding the machete and thinking all sorts of imaginative things. How a machete came to get here in the middle of the night, and so forth. It's a long drive to work, to the bank, and I knew the highway would be jammed already, but now I'd found the machete I couldn't just leave.

My mind was whirling. Gillian left work three weeks ago, in her seventh month of pregnancy, and she would be at home, alone, all day. It was our first baby and she was in a state just being pregnant, without me mentioning the machete.

So whose machete was it? I didn't know the neighbours, only that the other young couple on the right worked long hours and that the fellow on the left kept Rottweilers. His wife was Filipino and stayed indoors all the time. Her face peeping through the curtains looked wistful. We'd heard him shouting at night. My guess was that a Rottweiler owner was more likely to own a machete, and to care for it so well.

From where I was standing with the machete I lined up with the front door of the Rottweiler residence. There was only the low paling fence separating us. Someone could have thrown the machete from the front door to where I stood if they were impelled to do that. But it was hard to think of a reason why.

I couldn't see myself going next door past all the Rottweilers and asking "Excuse me, did you leave your machete in my yard? When you were trespassing last night?" By then, it was well after eight and my one clear thought was not to frighten Gillian with any quirkiness. Things were making her weepy and anxious lately: all those children on TV with rare diseases, the hole in the ozone layer, fluoride in the water. I wanted to keep her serene. I took the machete around to the back of the house. I pushed it hard into the sandy flowerbed until only the handle stuck up, and that was hidden by shadow. Then I got into the car, drove to work and forgot about it.

But tonight, as I was driving home past the Hardware Barn I remembered it. The strange feeling came back and I speeded up. These nights the sun sets well before five and our end of the street was in darkness when I pulled up. I left the headlights on and ran to the back of the garage.

There is something more alarming than the presence of a machete. The absence of a machete.

3

1 Answer the following comprehension questions about the story on page 201.

1 Why is the narrator shocked when he finds the machctc? (para. 1)

2 Why does he feel self-conscious when he is holding it? (para. 2)

3 What does he suggest a machete could be used for in some areas and why would it not be needed here? (para. 3)

4 Why does he not want to upset his wife? (para. 5)

5 What makes him think that his neighbour might be the owner of the machete? (para. 6)

6 Why does he hide the machete? (para. 8)

7 What does he do when he returns home from work? (para. 9)

2 How do the last two lines make you feel? What do you think may have happened to the machete?

4 The writer uses the following techniques to build up suspense, and a sense of unease and foreboding in the story.

- revealing important information bit by bit so that it has maximum impact
- implying that something is strange when it could be quite normal

The following exercises focus on those techniques.

1 Number the events below in the order that they are described in the story (**not** the order in which they actually happened). How does the sequence in which the information is revealed help to build up suspense?

☐1 The narrator finds the machete lying on the lawn.
☐ He can't find the machete.
☐ His wife leaves her job because she is going to have a baby.
☐ He goes to work.
☐ He hides the machete.
☐ He and his wife move to the suburb.
☐ People go to work as usual.

2 What is the effect of the first sentence? How does it contribute to the suspense in the story?

3 Look at the following sentences and find how the same information is expressed in the text. What associations does the writer set up through his inclusion of these details? What are the possible implications?

1 A machete is used by people who fight.

2 This machete had been looked after well.

3 The neighbour owned dogs.

4 The neighbour's wife often looked out of the window.

5 The narrator felt worried driving home.

5 In the exam you may need to refer to the writer's use of language to explain how he creates an effect.

1 Answer the following questions, which focus on how the choice of language and use of stylistic devices contribute to creating a sense of unease.

1 Which two words in the first paragraph connect the machete with the idea of killing? What kind of killing is it? Who are the victims?

2 What is the effect of the word 'sleepy-looking' in the description of the suburb?

3 Paragraph 3 gives more details of the new suburb. How do you know
a) that there are no trees?
b) that the soil is dry and dusty?
What is the relevance of this information to the story?

4 Which two words in paragraph 3 emphasise the violent way a machete cuts?

5 What is the effect of the direct speech in paragraph 8?

6 Underline the verbs used in paragraph 9 to describe the man's actions. What idea do they share? What effect do they have?

2 Find examples in the story to support the following statement.

'The story is written in an informal and personal style, with colloquial expressions, and direct appeal to the reader.'

3 How does the style emphasise the strangeness of the discovery of the machete?

6 In the exam you may need to describe how the writer conveys a character's personality, feelings and emotions.

1 Answer the following questions with reference to the writer's choice of language.

1 What does the phrase 'my heart beating faster' tell you about the narrator's state of mind when he finds the machete? (para. 2)

2 How do you know that the man is confused and uncertain? (paras. 4 and 5)

3 How do you know his wife is feeling emotional and upset? (para. 8)

2   Which of the words in the box below would you use to describe:

a) the narrator?
b) the neighbour with the dog?
c) Gillian?

Find evidence in the text to support your ideas.

> nervous   anxious   weird
> thoughtful   secretive   strange
> sensitive   emotional
> quick-tempered

7   People react to this story in different ways. Do you think it is:

a) ironic – a parody of a horror story?
b) funny – a comedy not to be taken seriously?
c) menacing – a real horror story in which the writer is trying to scare you?

Find evidence in the text to support your answer.

8   What do you think happened when the man entered his house after the end of the story? Discuss different ways in which the story might continue.

Writing
▶ Paper 2, Part 2 (set text)

In Paper 2, Part 2 you can choose to answer a question on a **set text**. You may be asked to write:

- an article
- an essay
- a letter
- a review
- a report.

For part or all of your answer you may have to write about:

- different aspects of the structure and plot of the book
- the main characters
- the importance of a character or an incident in the story.

Remember that you should always support your ideas with evidence from the text.

Discussing structure and plot

1   **An article**

1   Read the following writing task, which is based on the short story *Machete* on page 201.

> **TASK**
> A literary magazine has invited readers to contribute articles to a series called *I'll Never Forget It* about stories that have remained fresh in their memory. Write an article on *Machete*, explaining how interest is built up and why you found it memorable.
>
> (300–350 words)

2   Look back at the work you did in the Reading section and at the story itself. What ideas would you include in this article?

2   Read the following article which was written in answer to the task and answer the questions below.

1   Look at the introduction to the article. Why does the writer find *Machete* so memorable?
2   Find the main point of each paragraph. How do these points build up to the final conclusion?
3   What examples from the text are used to support the points in paragraphs 2–5? Underline them in the article.

1   'Machete', by Robert Drewe, stays in the memory long after you have read it, because of the careful way in which suspense is built up throughout the story. Even at the end you are left hanging, uncertain of the final outcome.

2   The writer builds up suspense through suggestion rather than through events. One way he does this is by his choice of words. At the outset, he links the machete to the idea of terrorists. Words like 'random slaughter' and 'massacre' of innocent people arouse suspicions that something similar will happen in the story, even though there is no immediate evidence for this. He also contrasts the negative associations of the machete itself with the 'sleepy-looking', very normal suburb where the narrator lives. This mixture of normal and abnormal creates a sense of real unease.

3   Suspense is also created through the details he gives about the neighbours. The man's choice of pet (dogs with a reputation for viciousness) and the fact that his wife is seen 'peeping through the curtains' with a 'wistful' expression imply that he is dangerous, though we don't know how or why.

4   A third device used by the writer is to hold back information so that when it is revealed it has a greater effect. Not until halfway through the story does the unnamed narrator introduce the fact that his wife is pregnant, so possibly weak and vulnerable. This creates an image of a potential victim.

5   Towards the end, the pace of the story changes. Returning home, the narrator remembers the machete and words like 'speeded up' and 'ran' suggest urgency and possible danger. Such associations, on top of the suggested vulnerability of the wife, build up the tension even further. The last line leaves the reader in total suspense – everything is left to the imagination. And when you look back at the actual story there is nothing concrete to be afraid of. It is all in the mind. And that is where it stays!

(330 words)

3   Look back at the story *Machete*. How far do you agree with the ideas in the article? What further details could you add to support the ideas? Do you agree with the article's conclusion or not?

4   The essay

1   Read the following writing task.

TASK

'There is little suspense in the story because hardly anything actually happens.' Write an essay for your tutor discussing this statement and using examples from the story to support your ideas.

(300–350 words)

This question is on the same topic as Exercise 1, but here you are asked to discuss a statement. This means that you must decide whether you agree with the statement or not before you write, and then present an argument supporting your point of view.
The article in Exercise 2 describes ways in which the story provides suspense, but its introduction and conclusion are inappropriate for a discussion.

2   Read the paragraph below and compare it with the introduction in the article in Exercise 2. What differences do you notice?

'Machete', by Robert Drewe, stays in the memory long after you have read it, although in fact very little happens in the story. A man finds a knife in his garden, hides it, goes to work, and comes home. So why is the story so memorable? To me, the lack of events does not mean that there is 'little suspense'.

3   For the middle part of the essay you need to provide similar information to that given in the article. However, your final paragraph should relate to the introduction and include a summary of your opinion about the statement.
Write a final paragraph for the essay begun in the introduction above.

Discussing character

1

1   Read the following description of the narrator of *Machete*. Notice how every aspect of character mentioned is supported by reference to the text.

> The narrator is a fairly young man, with a regular job. He is obviously not a violent man, because his reaction to the machete suggests he does not like the idea of terrorists – he uses the words 'random slaughter of innocent villagers' and 'massacre', which are very strong. He was also a little frightened by the machete – his heart 'beat faster' when he picked it up. He seems to be a sensitive person. For example, he feels sorry for the woman next door, and describes her as 'wistful'. He is also reluctant to worry his wife by telling her about the machete.

2   The following description of the neighbour was written by a student. It does not give any evidence from the text to justify the opinions expressed, and there are also two factual mistakes. Rewrite the description, adding evidence where indicated.

> The strange neighbour is a man who lives on the right of the narrator. He is clearly <u>interested in dogs</u> although the type of dog he sells might indicate that he is worried about security or <u>has something to hide</u>. This <u>adds to the interest of the story.</u>
>
> *How do you know?*
>
> *Why? How?*
>
> We can also guess that he <u>does not take good care of his wife</u> and he may be quick-tempered.
>
> *What evidence is there?*

2   The letter

1   Read the following writing task.

> **TASK**
>
> You have read a magazine review of *Machete* criticising the writer's portrayal of Gillian on the grounds that her character is poorly described and that she contributes little to the plot. Write a letter to the editor of the magazine defending the writer's portrayal of Gillian and explaining her importance in the story.
>
> (300–350 words)

Look back at the story on page 201. Use your answers to Exercise 6 on page 202 to help you.

1   Decide what kind of person you think Gillian is.
2   Decide what her importance is to the story.
3   Choose evidence from the text to support your ideas.

2   Using the introduction on page 206, write your letter. Use Exercise 1 to help you with the description of Gillian if necessary.

In a letter you need to use the same techniques as in a discussion but the style will be more direct. You will need to use both description and argument, and support your points with evidence from the text. There will be a clear purpose for writing which you should mention in your opening paragraph.

Dear Sir,

I am writing to complain about the review of 'Machete' published in last month's magazine, which I think was extremely unfair. In particular, the criticism of the way the writer has portrayed the character of the narrator's wife was unjust.

Although Gillian does not actually do anything in the story, we know a lot about her and what kind of person she is. In fact, she also plays a central role in the development of the plot because of the type of person she is.

She is ...

3 The essay

Read the following writing tasks. Both involve discussion as well as description.

> **TASK**
>
> 'Without the character of the neighbour there would be no story.' Write an essay for your tutor discussing the statement, and illustrating your points with evidence from the text.
>
> (300–350 words)

> **TASK**
>
> 'Gillian is the most important character in the story.' Write an essay for your tutor comparing the role of Gillian with other characters in the story. Illustrate your arguments with evidence from the text.
>
> (300–350 words)

4 Choose one of the tasks in Exercise 3.

1 Using your ideas from Exercises 1 and 2, plan the first part of the essay. Then look back at the story and plan the second part of the argument.

2 Now write your essay.

5 The review

In the exam you may also be asked to write a review or a report on the set text that you chose to study. In this section you can base your answers on the set text you are studying, another book you have read recently, or on *Machete*.

1 Which of the statements below refers to a book review and which to a report on a book?

A The main aim is to assess the suitability of the book for a particular purpose and to make suggestions about how and why it could achieve that purpose. It is written for a particular person or group of people.

B The main aim is to give the reader an overall idea of the content, characters and setting of the book and to evaluate its effectiveness or literary value. It is usually written for the general public.

2 Decide which of the following are features of a review and which are features of a report.

- objective analysis
- personal opinion
- colourful language
- formal style
- rhetorical questions
- headings

3 Read the following writing task.

> **TASK**
>
> An EFL magazine has asked for a review of a book written in English which is appropriate for advanced learners of English and which broadens the reader's knowledge of the culture of England or an English-speaking country.
>
> Write your review.
>
> (300–350 words)

You may use your set text as the basis for the review, or any other suitable book (alternatively, you could refer to *Machete*).
Look back at Units 3 and 12 for help in writing a review.

Your review should be divided into four parts:

- introduction of topic
- description of book
- evaluation of how it can help to improve understanding of English language and culture
- conclusion.

(Remember **not** to use sub-headings in a review.)

4   Decide which ideas you will include from the text you have chosen to write about, and plan your review. Make sure that your points are all supported with evidence from the text.

5   Exchange your plan with a partner, and comment on the organisation and ideas. Then write your review.

6   The report

1   Read the following writing task.

> ### TASK
>
> A film company is interested in making a film of a book that you have read. Write a report on the book for the company, summarising the plot and evaluating how suitable the book is for a film.
>
> (300–350 words)

2   Make notes under the headings below.

Introduction
Background information

Main part
a) Brief summary of plot
b) How suitable is the book for a film?
  genre and audience
  * what type of film would the book make, e.g. thriller, romance?
  * who would it appeal to?

  plot: is it
  * dramatic?
  * interesting/original?
  * full of twists?
  * fast-moving?
  * well-constructed?
  * true to life?

  characters: are they
  * interesting and well-developed?
  * likeable?

  other selling points
  * suitable parts for any famous actors?
  * interesting locations
  * possibility of special effects
  * international appeal

Find examples from the text to support your ideas and note them down.

Conclusion and recommendations
Close your report appropriately, with your recommendation.

3   Now write your report, using the headings to help you. Remember to use evidence from the text to support your points.

> ### Exam Strategy
> In the exam you won't have your book with you.
> To prepare, make notes in advance on character, plot and other aspects you have worked on in this unit. Include in your notes any key evidence for your ideas, including quotations. (You aren't expected to quote exact words from the text in the exam, though using an appropriate short phrase can give a good impression and make your point quickly and effectively.) Use these notes to help you with revision. You will not be allowed to take them into the exam with you.
> In the exam, remember to:
> * read the question carefully. If it is an essay, decide whether it is a discussion or a description.
> * think carefully about the style of the letter, article, review or report.
> * plan your writing carefully.
> * always give evidence from the text to support your ideas.

1 Multiple-choice lexical cloze

For questions 1–6, read the text below and decide which answer (**A**, **B**, **C** or **D**) best fits each gap.

Experiments with gravity

The gold and lead balls that Galileo (1) .... dropped off the leaning Tower of Pisa have entered into scientific legend, although the story may have no (2) .... in fact. What is certain is that three years later, in 1586, a Flemish mathematician named Simon Stevin published an account of a strikingly similar experiment.

Like Galileo, Stevin was keen to (3) .... Aristotle's claim that heavy bodies fall faster than light ones, and reported that two lead spheres both fell a distance of 30 feet in exactly the same time (4) .... one being ten times heavier than the other.

It seems that Galileo may have been (5) .... for an experiment he never actually performed, though he undoubtedly confirmed its conclusion many times.

In 1971 the airless moon was the scene of a similar experiment when astronaut Dave Scott let a hammer and a falcon's feather fall onto the surface and they (6) .... hit the ground simultaneously.

1 **A** hypothetically **B** supposedly
  C notionally **D** presumably
2 **A** support **B** footing
  C basis **D** rationale
3 **A** debunk **B** puncture
  C explode **D** expose
4 **A** in the face of **B** regardless of
  C against **D** despite
5 **A** approved **B** credited
  C attributed **D** charged
6 **A** correctly **B** deservedly
  C duly **D** fittingly

2 Open cloze

Read the text below and fill each space with one suitable word.

Motivation in the novel

What kind of knowledge (0) ..*can*.. we derive (1) .... reading novels, which (2) .... us stories we know are not 'true'? One traditional answer is: knowledge of the human mind. (3) .... the biologist nor even the psychologist has such intimate access to the secret thoughts of his subjects (4) .... does the novelist. Novels thus provide us with models of how and why people act as they (5) .... , based on the idea of the individual's responsibility (6) .... his or her own acts. We value them, (7) .... , for the light they (8) .... on human motivation.

A novel generally aims to convince us that the characters act in a particular (9) .... not simply because (10) .... actions further the interests of the plot (11) .... because a complex combination of factors leads them to do (12) .... In traditional folk-tales a single cause suffices to explain behaviour – the hero is courageous because he is the hero, the witch is malevolent because she is a witch, and so (13) .... In the realistic novel, (14) .... , things are not so black and white. Any action tends to be the product of several levels of the personality, as it is in real life, and (15) .... is maybe what provides us with the knowledge we seek.

3 Word formation

Use the word given in capitals at the end of some of the lines to form a word that fits in the space in the same line.

Woman alive three days after jungle fall

A 72-year-old London woman has survived three days in the Sri Lankan jungle after falling down a cliff while chasing exotic butterflies.

Delphine Czartoryska – a Polish princess through marriage – is now making a good (0) ..*recovery*.. in hospital in Colombo. Mrs Czartoryska was only a day into her holiday when she went on a walk alone to admire the plants and (1) .... She was just half a mile from the hotel when she fell and hit her head, losing (2) .... as a result of her injuries.

In the (3) .... , her friends were becoming increasingly worried, and eventually alerted the holiday company, who instigated a full-scale search involving police, hotel staff and guests. After more than 72 hours, Mrs Czartoryska was found almost within (4) .... of the hotel, lying in dense (5) .... at the foot of a cliff. She was suffering from (6) .... and concussion, but otherwise unharmed.

Grace Hall, a (7) .... for the holiday company, said, 'Mrs Czartoryska's (8) .... of what happened is hazy. The area where she was found is almost (9) .... jungle, and she is very lucky to have survived. The (10) .... says she is in remarkably good condition considering what she has been through, and should soon be able to leave hospital.'

COVER

WILD

CONSCIOUS
MEAN

EAR
UNDER
HYDRATE

SPEAK
COLLECT

PENETRATE
CONSULT

4 Gapped sentences

For questions 1–6, think of one word only which can be used appropriately in all three sentences.

1 I've decided to paint the bedroom a .... peach colour.
Don't be too .... with that class or you'll have trouble with them later on.
He had no chance of winning the fight – he'd got .... with years of easy living.

2 She couldn't .... the pressures of her new job and eventually resigned.
He was unwilling to .... the goods the two men offered him, as he suspected they were stolen.
It wasn't very polite of you just to .... off without saying goodbye to anyone.

3 He thought that a few illustrations or anecdotes would add .... to his report.
The fascinating old market is full of .... and activity and is well worth a visit.
You're looking better today – you've got a bit more .... than you had yesterday.

4 Just look at Richard – he's .... proof that you don't need a degree to be successful.
It was the worst storm in .... memory, but thankfully the sailors all returned safely.
People say that he is the .... image of his father, but I can't see it myself.

5 When the police interviewed him, he .... he'd been miles away at the time of the crime.
The avalanche is believed to have .... almost a hundred lives, although exact figures are not yet available.
When he was made redundant, he swallowed his pride and .... unemployment benefit.

6 A mobile phone is an absolute .... for this job, as you will need to be available at all times.
The summary of his findings is, of .... , very brief, but it gives as much information as is relevant.
There was no .... for her to give up her job – it was entirely her own choice.

5 Key word transformations

Complete the second sentence with three to eight words so that it has a similar meaning to the first sentence, using the word given. Do not change the word given.

1 The job will probably be much simpler than they say.
anything
The job should ....
.... complicated as they say.

2 She didn't seem at all surprised to hear the news.
hair
She ....
.... she heard the news.

3 The original version of the song was not much like this new recording.
resemblance
The new recording of the song ....
.... the original version.

4 When she heard the story of his final journey, she found herself crying.
tears
She found ....
.... by the story of his final journey.

5 Nowadays, most people automatically lock their doors at night.
nature
It's ....
.... their doors at night nowadays.

6 We always had to tell her exactly when we would arrive and when we would leave.
times
She always insisted on us ....
.... and departure.

7 Even though all their money had been returned they continued to complain.
spite
They kept on ....
.... a full refund.

8 She was exhausted from trying to satisfy the demands of her large family.
cope
She was wearing ....
.... the demands of her large family.

---

6 This picture was suggested for the cover of a travel brochure. Discuss what it suggests about travel today and then decide if a different cover might be more effective.

Grammar reference

UNIT 1

Talking about the past (p. 12)

The main uses of the tense forms relating to the past are as follows.

1 Past simple

We use this tense when we describe a state, an event or an action (single, repeated or habitual) at a point in the past or within a completed past time period.

> My parents **met** in Canada in 1975.
> When I was a child, we **lived** in Vancouver.

Note: The past simple is often used to tell a story or describe a sequence of events. Initially, a time referent or other specific detail is often given to anchor the events to a specific time or situation.

> When Chris Marris came to Queensmill **in 1982**, he was astonished by Stephen's drawings.
> Something really amazing happened to us **in the USA**. (= when we were in the USA)

2 Past continuous

1 One use of this tense is to describe something which was already in progress at a point in the past, and which continued after that point.
> I **was still working** at eight o'clock.
> The plane **was just taking off** when I found I didn't have my bag with me.
> When I first saw him, Stephen **was sitting** on his own, drawing.

2 We also use this tense to describe something which was interrupted by another event.
> We **were just setting off** to the airport when we heard that all flights were cancelled due to the snow.

3 We can also use it to describe two events occurring simultaneously over a period of time.
> Stephen **was producing** these amazing drawings when other children his age **were drawing** stick figures.

Note: In narratives, the past continuous is often used to set the background to the story before the actual events are related.

> I **was sitting** on my balcony, enjoying the spring sunshine, when the telephone rang.

3 Past perfect simple

1 We use this tense to make it clear that something happened *before* another event in the past. We usually need to use it if the events are not described in chronological order.
> Chris was amazed. Nothing **he had ever seen had prepared** him for this.

Note: Once the time reference is clear, it is not always necessary to use the past perfect for all verbs.

> By the time I was 21, I **had lived** in four different countries. I **lived** in England until I was five. Then my parents **emigrated** to New Zealand, where I **went** to school, and then I **went** to university in Australia. Finally I **ended up** doing my PhD in California.

2 We may also use the past perfect to make the order of events clear when conjunctions such as *when* and *because* are used.
> She **switched off** the TV when he walked in. (= he walked in first)
> She **had switched off** the TV when he walked in. (= she switched it off first)

Note: With conjunctions such as *before*, *after* and *as soon as*, the past perfect is optional as the order of events is shown by the conjunction.

> The bell rang before they **(had) finished**.

4 Past perfect continuous

This tense describes a continuing or repeated activity or event leading up to a particular time or event in the past. The event or activity may stop just before or at this point, or it may continue.

> By 1982, Marris **had been teaching** disabled children for nine years.
> She'**d just been swimming**, and her hair was still wet.

5 used to/would

Both of these can describe past habits (often long ago rather than the recent past).

1 **used to** can describe habitual actions, repeated actions and states.
> When I was six or seven, I **used to enjoy** spending holidays with my grandparents.

2 **would** is used for habitual or repeated actions (but not for states) when a specific time period is being referred to.
*Sunday mornings at the cottage were always the same. My grandfather **would get up** early and milk the cows while my grandmother got* breakfast ready.*

Note: *As with the past perfect, once the time referred to has been established, it is not necessary to continue using *would* or *used to* with every verb.

Linking the past to the present (p. 13)

1 Present perfect simple
1 We use the present perfect simple with *since, for* or *How long ...?* to describe a state beginning in the past and continuing up to the present.
*Ever since he was very young, Lee **has enjoyed** reading.*
*How long **have you had** this car?*
2 We also use it for an event or events in a period leading up to the present. The time period may or may not be specified.
*He **has made** a fortune through his writing.*
*He **has just published** his 45th book.*
*I **have lost** my keys three times **this week.***
*Since last year, he **has attended** five training courses.*
*I've **never been** skiing **before** – in fact, this is **the first time I've ever seen** snow!*

Note: We may introduce a topic with the present perfect, and then switch to the past simple as we add more details of the time and situation.
*I've **taken** my driving test six times. The first time I took it **was** in London.*

2 Present perfect continuous
This may be used in the same situations, but may also:
1 convey the idea of continuation or non-completion.
*Susie **has been writing** an essay.*
2 emphasise the duration of the event.
*She's **been working** all morning.*

Note: In some cases, both simple and continuous forms may be possible, without much change in meaning.
*Stephen King **has lived** / **has been living** in the same small town for many years.*

State and event (p. 13)
Simple tenses are normally used for single events, states and habits. Continuous tenses describe activities in progress. They suggest that the activity is temporary, and may not be complete.

1 States
Verbs which describe states are sometimes called *stative* verbs. They describe activities and situations that may not have a definite beginning or end. They are not generally used in the continuous form (but see below). They include verbs of:
perception: *hear, see, feel, smell, taste, notice*
mental states and feelings: *love, hate, hope, imagine, remember, forget, understand, want, wish, prefer, seem, appear*
relationships and states of being: *have, own, possess, belong to, consist of, cost, depend on, require*

2 Events
Verbs which describe events are sometimes called *dynamic* verbs. They describe activities with a definite beginning and end. They may be used in the simple or continuous form. They include verbs describing:
momentary acts: *kick, jump, knock*
activities: *walk, study, work, eat, drive*
processes: *grow, change, develop, enlarge*

Many state verbs can in fact be used in the continuous form in the following situations:
1 to focus on the temporary nature of the action or event. Compare:
You're very warm-hearted.
*You're **being** silly.*
2 with a change of meaning.
*He **appears** to be quite a cold person. (= seems)*
*He's **appearing** in a play. (= performing)*
*He **doesn't have** a car. (= possess)*
*We're **having** a party! (= holding)*
*I **can see** the car headlights. (= they are in sight)*
*Tamara **is seeing** Steve quite regularly. (= meeting)*
*I **think** it's a good idea. (= in my opinion)*
*I'm **thinking** about it, but I'm not sure.*
(= considering)

UNIT 2

Conditionals (1) + wishes and preferences (p. 28)

Four types of conditionals are practised in this unit. Other possibilities for conditional sentences are described in Unit 7.

1 *Children **learn** if they are **exposed** to new ideas.*
*You **have to be prepared** to commit yourself if you **want** a good job.*
These sentences are about things which the speaker believes to be generally true. They don't refer to any particular time. They have:

main clause with a present tense + subordinate (*if-*) clause with a present tense

Note: It is also possible to have a modal verb in the main clause.

> He **can/might** do it if he's given the chance.

2 *He'll get* the contract if the price **is** OK.
Here, the speaker thinks the situation in the main clause (*he'll get the contract*) is definitely possible. The sentence has:
main clause with a future tense + subordinate (*if-*) clause with a present tense

Other modal verbs or future forms can also be used in the main clause.

> He **can/might** do it if he gets permission.
> She's **driving/going to drive** there tomorrow if she has time.

Note: In spoken English, the part of the sentence stressed would give further information about the speaker's view of how likely the event is.

> He'll (quite probably) get the contract if the **price is** OK.
> He'll (almost certainly) **get** the contract if the price is OK.

3 *I would buy* a new car if I **got** that job.
I would go with you if I **were** younger.
Depending on the context, the speaker in the first example might regard getting the job as very unlikely, or as impossible. In the second example, the situation in the *if-*clause is absolutely impossible. To describe hypothetical situations like this in the present or future we use:
main clause with *would* plus infinitive + subordinate (*if-*) clause with a past tense

Notes:
1 You will see other examples of this use of the past tense below.
2 Other modal verbs can also be used in the main clause.
> If she entered, she **might** get the prize.
> She **could** win if she was very lucky.
3 If the verb *be* is used in the *if-*clause, it is usually written in the form *were* for all persons, especially in more formal and/or written contexts (*If I were you* ...). This is an example of the subjunctive form in English. (See also Unit 6.)

4 *I would have been* very upset if I **hadn't got** on the course.
This speaker is describing a hypothetical situation in the past. Neither the situation nor the result actually happened – the speaker did get on the course, and so wasn't upset. Sentences about hypothetical situations in the past have:
main clause with *would have* + past participle + *if-*clause with past perfect

Note: Other modal verbs can be used instead of *would*.
> He **might/could** have gone to the USA if he hadn't got that job.

wish/if only (p. 28)

1 We use the verb *wish* to express regret that something is not the case.
> I wish (that) I **knew** his name. (referring to the present)
> I wish we **weren't doing** the exam tomorrow! (referring to the future)
> I wish (that) I'**d learned** to drive earlier. (referring to the past)
2 Sentences with *wish* (*that*) refer to unlikely or hypothetical situations. Tenses used are similar to those in hypothetical conditions.
3 *If only* can replace *I wish*, giving the sentence the force of an exclamation.
If the wish is in the past, the tense of the following verb stays the same.
> I **wished** I **knew** him.
> I **wished** we **weren't doing** the exam the next day.
> I wish **he would do** the shopping.
> I wish **I could do** the shopping.
> NOT I wish **I would** do the shopping. ✗
It is not correct to say *I wish I would* ... *Wish* can only be followed by *would* if the subjects of the two verbs are different. If the subjects are the same, use *could* instead of *would*.

Note: *Wish + would* can only be used to describe an event, not a state.
> His parents wish he **liked** sport. (state)
> NOT ... wish he would like sport. ✗
> I wish he **would go** home. (event)

4 *wish* and *hope*
We use *wish* when we would like things to be different from the way they are in reality. We use *hope* to refer to things we would like to happen.

5 *Wish* can also be used:
- when giving good wishes for particular events.
  *I **wished** him a happy birthday.*
- as a formal way of saying *want to*.
  *Do you **wish** to make a complaint?*

It's time, I'd rather, I'd prefer (p. 29)

These phrases can be followed by a past tense or an infinitive.

1 It's time

It's (high) time + clause with verb in past tense (referring to present or future time)
> *It's high time that child **was** in bed – it's nearly midnight!*

It's time + infinitive
> *It's time **to go** – it's almost eight o'clock.*

Notes:

1 ***High** time* is more emphatic, suggesting that the event is overdue. It is not generally followed by the infinitive.

2 When the infinitive is used to refer to a specific person who is not the speaker or the person being spoken to, then the expression *It's time **for x** to …* must be used.
> ***It's time for him to decide** what he wants to do with his life.*
> NOT *It's time to decide what he wants …* ✗

2 I'd rather

I'd rather + clause
> *I'd rather you **didn't tell** him – he'd be upset.* (referring to future time)
> *I'd rather you **hadn't told** him – he was upset.* (referring to past time)

I'd rather + infinitive (without *to*)
> *I'd rather **tell** him myself.* (referring to future time)
> *I'd rather **be** anywhere than here!* (referring to present time)
> *I didn't enjoy the holiday at all – I'd rather **have stayed** at home.* (referring to past time)

Note: The infinitive is only possible if both parts of the sentence are about the same person.

3 I'd prefer

I'd prefer it + *if*-clause
> *I'd **prefer it** if they **were** left on their own.* (future time)
> *I'd **have preferred it** if I **could have studied** maths.* (past time)

I'd prefer + infinitive (present or perfect)
> *I'd prefer **to be** left on my own.*

UNIT 3

Participle clauses (p. 46)

Participle clauses contain a participle instead of a full verb. Participles may have the following forms:
present: *showing*
past: *shown*
perfect: *having shown*
passive: *being shown, having been shown*

Present participle clauses are much more common than past participle clauses. They are used to avoid repetition and make a point more economically in written texts, and are particularly common in fiction. However, they are not used much in spoken English.

Participle clauses can describe:

1 events happening at the same time (present participle).
> ***Drinking his coffee slowly**, he thought about the problem.* (= He drank his coffee slowly and …)

2 events happening in rapid sequence (present participle).
> ***Tearing the envelope open**, he took out the letter.* (= He tore the envelope open, and took out …)

3 events happening with a longer time gap between them (perfect participle).
> ***Having retired**, he found himself with time on his hands.* (= When he had retired, he found …)

4 other time relations when used with an appropriate conjunction.
> ***Before being shown** round, we were welcomed by the Principal.*
> ***After finishing** his speech, he took a sip of water.*
> *Wear protective gloves **when** using this equipment.*
> ***On arriving**, you will find someone waiting for you.*
> ***While travelling** to work, she usually reads a novel.*
> *She has been much happier **since changing** schools.*

5 concession when used with an appropriate conjunction
> *She intends to go, **despite it being** so far.*

6 cause or reason (perfect participle).
> ***Not having had** any breakfast, I was hungry.* (= Because I had not had …)
> *(As a result of) **having appeared** once on television, she became a local celebrity.*

Note: The present participle of state verbs such as *be*, *have*, *know* and *live* can also be used in participle clauses expressing reason.
> ***Being** a kind man, he agreed to help.*

7 condition (past participle).
> ***Left to follow** his own inclinations, he would do no work at all.* (= If he were left to follow …)

Note: If the subject of a participle clause is not stated, we assume it is the same as the subject of the main clause.

> *Feeling tired, he stopped for a cup of tea.*

If the subject of the participle is different from that of the main clause, it must be stated.

> *The weather being perfect, we decided to go swimming.*

If this is not done, the sentence may be confusing.

> *Kicking with all his strength, the ball went straight into the goal.*

(The ball was not 'kicking', but we don't know who was. This is known as a 'dangling' participle.)

There is more information on participle clauses in Unit 6 Language Focus: Grammar (Relative clauses).

Inversion after negative adverbials (p. 48)

Starting a sentence with a negative adverbial (e.g. *at no time*) or an adverbial with a negative implication (e.g. *hardly, seldom*), and reversing the order of the subject and verb is a way of adding emphasis or creating a dramatic effect in English.

> *He was never in the slightest danger.*
> ***At no time was he*** *ever in the slightest danger.*

This structure is a feature of more formal writing, but can also be used in speech.

Expressions that can be used in this way include:

on no account	*in no circumstances*
at no time	*nowhere*
not once	*not one … /not a single …*
not until …	*not only … but also …*
never (before)	*rarely*
seldom	*only now*
only by chance	*only recently*
hardly/scarcely …	*no sooner …. than*
when …	

Notes:

1 If there is no auxiliary verb, *do/does/did* are added (as with a question).

> *He never once came to see her in hospital.*
> *Never once **did** he come to see her in hospital.*

2 *Hardly/scarcely … when*

In this expression, *when* introduces a time clause.

> ***Scarcely*** *had we sat down **when** the alarm went off.*
> *No sooner … than* has a similar meaning.
> ***No sooner*** *had we sat down **than** the alarm went off.*

UNIT 4

Emphasis: preparatory *it* (p. 60)

By using structures with the pronoun *it*, we can change the order of words or phrases in a sentence to highlight specific information.

1 *it* as a 'preparatory' subject

It can be used as the subject of a sentence referring *forwards* to a noun or phrase occurring later. This may be done:

- if the subject is a long phrase. Usually in English longer or more complicated phrases are placed towards the end of the sentence. A common pattern here is *It + be* + adjective + *that*-clause.
  > *It was clear **that everything he'd ever done had been for his own benefit**.*

- to place the main topic at the end of the sentence. This is where new information is usually found, and this information can therefore be emphasised.
  > *It is vital **for Alicia to go to London**.*

2 *it* as a 'preparatory' object

It may also act as the object of a sentence, referring forwards to a noun or phrase. Again, this puts the noun or phrase in a more emphatic position, and allows a longer phrase to be used.

> *She finds **it** difficult **to walk to the shops on her own**.*
> *They thought **it** strange **that he had not told anyone**.*

Note: *It* also has the following non-emphatic uses.

- to refer back to something that has already been mentioned. This may be a singular noun, or a general idea.
  > *Many products sink without trace soon after they've been launched. Why? Well, a lot of **it** is to do with marketing.*

- as an empty or 'dummy' subject when talking about dates, times and the weather.
  > *It's six o'clock.*
  > *It's cold.*

UNIT 5

Modals and related expressions (1) (p. 70)

Modal and semi-modal verbs give us information about the speaker's attitude towards or judgement of an event, e.g. Is it desirable? Is it necessary? Is it probable?

The type of information provided by modals can also be given through structures with adjectives (*it is advisable to ...*), adverbs (*probably*) and lexical verbs (*I forbid you to ...*). It is useful to learn these expressions together with the related modal verbs.

Note: Modal verbs are verbs such as *can, must, will, should,* etc. They always come first in the verb phrase, and do not have a 3rd person 's' ending. They are followed by the 'bare' infinitive (infinitive without *to*).

> He **could** have told her earlier.

Semi-modals have some, but not all, of these features.

> He **ought to** tell someone.
> He **has to** see her now.

1 Obligation/necessity
Present/future

> I **must**/**have to** finish now. I/I'll **have to** go soon.

Past

> We **had to** get the report finished that day.

Other expressions

> She **needs** to get more information.
> She's **got to** go now.
> He **was obliged** to give up his job.
> Strong shoes **will be necessary**.
> You **are to** wait here until I give you permission to leave.

Note: In conversational English, *have to* is much more common than *must*. (We generally use *have to* when the obligation is imposed on us from outside, rather than from our own feelings or beliefs.)

2 Prohibition
Present/future

> You **mustn't** touch that, it's dangerous.
> You **can't** go in there – it's not allowed.

Other expressions

> **It is forbidden** to walk on the grass.
> You **are not allowed** to go there.
> Smoking **is prohibited**. (formal)
> You **are not to** run in the corridors.
> Mobile phones **are banned** in my school.

3 Lack of obligation/necessity
Present/future

> You **needn't** come if you don't want to.
> You **don't have to** do it now.

Past

> They said it was quite near, so he **didn't need** to take the car. (= it wasn't necessary to take the car, and he didn't)
> When he got there he found it was quite near, so in fact he **needn't have taken** the car. (= he took the car unnecessarily)

Note: With *didn't have to* either meaning can be conveyed, depending on the stress and intonation used.

> He didn't **have** to go to London (but he did).
> He didn't have to go to **London** (so he didn't).

Other expressions

> She's **not obliged** to go.
> It's **not obligatory/compulsory**.
> It's **not (absolutely) necessary** for you to go.
> These classes **are voluntary**.

4 Advice
Present/future

> You **should/ought to** ask for more money.

Past

> You **should/shouldn't** have gone there on your own.

Note: The perfect form expresses disapproval of something that was done.

Other expressions

> I **wouldn't recommend** you to go there.
> It **would be a good idea** to tell him.
> Customers **are advised** to retain their receipts.
> It **is advisable** to book first.
> **If I were you**, I'd do it.
> It was **wrong of** him to borrow the money.

5 Opportunity/free choice
Present/future

> You **can** take whatever you want.
> You **could** always go tomorrow (if you wanted to).

Past

> You **could** go anywhere without problems.
> He **could have been** a doctor if he'd wanted.

Other expressions

> **It's up to you** whether you go or not.
> **It's your decision/choice** whether you stay or go.
> He's **free** to do whatever he wants.
> You will **have the opportunity** to travel wherever you want.

215

6 Permission

Present/future

'**Could** I borrow this book?' 'Of course you **can**!'

Past

They said I **could** go wherever I wanted.

Note: It is also possible to say *May*/*Might I borrow this book?* but this is rather formal and old-fashioned and is not frequently used.

When talking about a particular occasion in the past, *could* is not possible.

I ~~could~~/**was allowed** to drive my father's car whenever I wanted.

On her tenth birthday, Lisa ~~could~~/**was allowed** to ride her bicycle to school.

Other expressions:

He **lets me go** wherever I want.

The librarian **gave me permission** to take the book.

7 Ability

Present/future

Can you manage on your own?

Past

I **could** speak English when I was six.

Note: When talking about a particular occasion in the past, *could* is not possible.

I **could**/**was able** to swim when I was very young. (general ability)

Although I was very frightened, I **could**/**was able** to tell the police officer what had happened. (particular event)

Other expressions:

After a lot of effort, I **managed** to do it.

I **know how** to swim.

She **has the ability** to sense the feelings of others. (formal)

She **is capable of** doing very well if she wants to.

Notes:

1 *need*/*need to*

When *need* is used as a modal verb, it is followed by the bare infinitive. (This is most common in the negative form.) It removes obligation imposed by the speaker.

He **needn't come** if he doesn't want to.

When it is used as a main verb, it is followed by the full infinitive, and can refer to obligation from an external force.

He really **needs to be** careful.

It is often used in the question form.

Do we need to bring our own sheets and towels?

2 *be supposed to*/*suppose*

Compare:

You're **supposed to** be working. (suggests criticism = You're meant to be working – and you're not.)

I **suppose** I'll have to go. (expresses reluctance = I'm afraid I'll have to go, even though I don't want to.)

Modals and related expressions (2) (p. 74)

1 Logical deduction/assumption

Present

It **must be** true.

'There's someone at the door.' 'It'll be Carla.'

We **should be able** to get there on time.

Past

It **must have been** an accident.

Other expressions

I **expect** that's Mrs Stevens on the phone.

I'm **convinced** that he's right.

I'm **sure**/**certain** that he did it.

He's **bound**/**sure**/**certain** to tell everyone.

We **can conclude** that he was the murderer. (formal)

It follows from this that she was not guilty. (formal)

We **can assume** that the house was empty.

The child **was presumably** away at the time.

The answer **is thus**/**therefore**/**hence** x minus 2y. (formal, academic)

2 Possibility

It might	conceivably	be happening. (present)
It may	well	happen. (future)
It could	possibly	have happened. (past)

Note: The adverb *well* makes the possibility stronger.

It could well be true – there's plenty of evidence.

The other adverbs stress that the situation is not certain, but do not tell us any more about the speaker's own viewpoint.

Other expressions:

It's **possible**/**conceivable** that she was murdered.

There's **a strong possibility** that it was **Ira**.

Possibly/**Perhaps**/**Maybe** she got lost.

It's **quite likely** that he'll tell us.

The likelihood is that they'll arrive late.

The chances are that she'll pass the exam.

I **bet** she'll be pleased! (informal)

3 Uncertain possibility

Present It **might**/**may** not be true.

Future Cheer up – it **might**/**may** never happen.

Past It **might**/**may** **not have** happened.

Other expressions
> There's **very little/not much chance/possibility** that we'll find it.
> They're **not likely** to see him.
> It's **(highly) unlikely** that she'll come.
> **I don't think** he'll come.
> **I doubt** that you'll see them.
> **I can't see** them finishing today.

4 Impossibility
Present It **can't** be true.
Future It **couldn't/can't** ever happen.
Past It **couldn't/can't** possibly **have** happened.

Note: When used as an exclamation, *could* and *might* often express annoyance or criticism.
> You **could/might** have told me!

UNIT 6

Passives: Special points (pp. 85–87)

1 *make, see, hear, help*
These verbs are all followed by the infinitive without *to* when they are active, and the infinitive with *to* when they are passive.
> They **made** him **stand** at the front.
> He **was made to stand** at the front.

2 *let*
This is never used in the passive.
> They usually **let** him **stand** at the front.
> He **is** usually **allowed to stand** at the front.

3 Future with *is to*
This is often used in the passive for reporting news items. It is a fairly formal structure.
> New measures to support the homeless **are to be introduced** (by the government).

It is common in newspaper headlines, where it is usually shortened.
> New measures to support homeless **to be introduced**

4 *need doing*
This structure has a passive meaning.
> The house **needs painting**. (= The house needs to be painted.)

5 *by, with* and *in*
The agent of a passive verb is introduced by *by*. *With* or *in* may be used to introduce the means by which something is done.
> The drain was cleared **by** the workmen.
> The drain was blocked **with** rubbish.

> The roads were crowded **with** people.
> Service is included **in** the price.

Subjunctives (p. 86)

Subjunctive verb forms are not used very often in English. There are two basic forms.

1 The subjunctive of most verbs is the same as the bare infinitive with no 3rd person 's' or past form. In formal contexts, this form of the subjunctive is used in *that*-clauses after verbs and adjectives such as the following:
   advise   demand   insist   propose   recommend   require   vital   urge   preferable   desirable   essential   obligatory   suggest

   > It is vital (that) every employee **attend** the meeting.
   > I suggest (that) large fines **be introduced**.

   The same structure can also be used after related nouns.
   > Their **suggestion** is that the system **be** reviewed carefully after trialling.

   In rather less formal contexts, the subjunctive is avoided and clauses such as the following are used instead.
   > It is vital (that) every employee **should attend** the meeting. (should + bare infinitive)
   > It is vital (that) every employee **attends** the meeting. (present simple)

   This form of the subjunctive is also used in some fixed phrases.
   > **Come what may**, we shall achieve our goal.
   > **Suffice it to say** that I was disappointed.
   > **Be that as it may**, your behaviour was unacceptable.

2 *Be* has a past subjunctive form *were*. In conditional clauses and after *wish*, the past subjunctive form *were* is often used instead of *was*.
   > If I **were** you, I'd go.
   > If I **were** in charge, I would make great changes.
   > I wish I **were** rich.
   > He shouted at her as if she **were** deaf.

Note: Speakers in informal contexts may use *was* in these situations.
> If I **was** going, I'd take her.

However, it is best to use the subjunctive form *were* in Papers 1–4 of the Proficiency exam.
In conditional sentences using inversion, *were* must always be used – *was* is not possible.
> **Were** he to refuse permission, we would be in trouble.

Relative clauses (pp. 91–92)

Relative clauses are usually introduced by a relative pronoun, e.g. *who, whom, whose, which, that, where, when*. These clauses function as adjectives, and modify a noun which has been given (or sometimes only implied) earlier.

Defining relative clauses

1 We use defining relative clauses to distinguish one thing or person from similar things or people. If the information in the relative clause is omitted, the sentence will not make sense. The clause is therefore not separated off by commas.
*Curitiba is an example of a city **which has been successful in avoiding transport problems.***

2 They can be introduced by the relative pronouns *who* (subject), *whom* (object), *whose* (possessive), *which/that* (for things), *where* (place), *when* (time).

3 If the relative pronoun is the *object* of the clause, it can be omitted.
The man (whom) I met yesterday phoned me up.
(See also below – participle clauses/verbless clauses.)

Note: In informal English *who* may be used as an object as well as a subject and *that* may be used to replace *who/whom*.
*The girls **who** I saw last night …*
*It was the same man **that** had spoken to me earlier.*

Non-defining relative clauses

1 Non-defining relative clauses give additional information about the preceding noun. If they are omitted, the sentence will still make sense. They are separated off by commas, which have a similar function in this case to brackets.
*The city, **which I had visited once before,** was huge.*

2 They can be introduced by the same relative pronouns as defining relative clauses, except for *that*, which is not normally used.
*My grandparents' house, **which was very old,** was surrounded by fruit trees.*

3 The relative pronoun cannot be omitted.

Relative clauses with prepositions

If a preposition is required, this may be placed before the relative pronoun in formal English, or at the end of the clause in less formal English.
*He's the man **to whom** the prize was awarded.*
(formal)
*He's the man **(who)** the prize was given **to**. (informal)*

Notes:
1 *Whom*, not *who*, must be used after a preposition.
2 When we are referring to a place, if the relative clause includes a preposition, *which* must be used instead of *where*. (This is because the relative pronoun is the object of the preposition.)
*The area **where** I lived was very prosperous.*
*The area **(which)** I lived **in** was very prosperous.*

Sentence relatives

A non-defining relative clause can refer back to the whole of the previous clause.
*I had left my money at home, **which** meant I had to borrow from my friend.*
The following phrases are also used to refer back to a whole clause.
in which case   as a result of which   by which time
at which time/point   since when   since which time

Relatives with quantifiers

Quantifiers (e.g. *some, a few*) can also be used in non-defining relative clauses, with *of whom/of which/of whose*. Examples of quantifiers which can be used in this way are:
all   both   some   many   a few   several
enough   hardly any   neither   none
one/two/three   half/one third   the majority
a (large/small) proportion   a number
This structure can also be used with comparatives and superlatives.
*He had two sisters, **the younger of whom** still lived at home.*

Participle and verbless clauses (p. 92)

Participle clauses

These can be used to replace relative clauses (both defining and non-defining). They are sometimes known as 'reduced relatives'.

1 With an *-ing* form
-ing participle clauses can replace a relative pronoun followed by an active verb.
*A new road has been built, **which bypasses** the town.*
*A new road has been built, **bypassing** the town.*

2 With an *-ed* form
If the verb in the relative clause is passive, both the relative pronoun and the auxiliary verb can be omitted.
*The area **(which was) designated** for development was near the river.*

Verbless clauses

If a relative clause contains a relative pronoun and the verb *be* as a main verb, both the relative pronoun and the verb can be omitted.

> The people, **(who were)** *tired of traffic pollution, decided to take action.*
> His daughter, **(who is)** *now a famous actress, visits him regularly.*

UNIT 7

Conditionals (2) (pp. 211–213)

As well as the four types of conditionals described in Unit 2 pages 211–212, many other variations are possible, depending on the time period being referred to. The following examples show some of the possibilities, but other combinations of tenses can be used.

Hypothetical conditionals referring to different time periods

1 *If you* **hadn't worked** *so hard then, you* **wouldn't be** *so well-off now.*

This speaker is connecting a hypothetical situation in the past to a present consequence (also hypothetical – the person *is* well-off). Sentences like this have:

If-clause with past perfect + main clause with *would/could/might* + infinitive

2 *If I* **weren't** *so busy all the time, I* **would have been able** *to help.*

Here the speaker is thinking of a hypothetical state (not being busy) and explaining its consequences in the past. The result is also hypothetical – the speaker wasn't actually able to help.

Sentences relating hypothetical states or habits to a particular event (also hypothetical) in the past have:

If-clause with subjunctive or past simple + main clause with *would have* + infinitive

Note: Again, alternative modals can be used.

> *If he didn't speak French, he* **might** *not have got the job.*

Open conditionals referring to different time periods

Again, the two clauses may refer to different times, and many different combinations are possible, but in all cases the tenses used depend on the time being referred to. The following are some examples of possible combinations.

1 *If I* **was** *sad, my grandmother* **comforted** *me.*

Here the speaker is describing a repeated event in the past, and implying that the situation in the *if*-clause did in fact happen. In fact, *if* could be replaced by *when* or *every time* with very little change in meaning. Sentences like this have:

If-clause with past simple/past continuous + main clause with past simple

Note: Modals can also be used in both clauses.

> *If she* **could find** *a spare moment, she* **would** *often* **tell** *me a story.*

2 *If he* **cheated** *then, he's probably* **cheating** *now and he'll probably* **cheat** *again.*

Here the speaker is basing a prediction about a present and future event on a past situation.

3 *If we've* **finished** *the bread we* **can get** *some more at the shop.*

The speaker is describing a possible situation around the present time.

4 *If there's no hot water, someone* **must have** *just* **had** *a shower.*

We are inferring what happened in the past from a present situation.

5 *If it* **needs** *mending, they'll usually* **do** *it for nothing.*

This suggests one event typically follows another.

6 *If we* **are to** *get there by evening, we* **ought to** *set off now.*

The speaker is making a recommendation.

7 *I'll buy the drinks if you'll bring the food.*

In both clauses, *will* expresses willingness to do something.

Note: A future form is not normally used in the *if*-clause. However, modals such as *will/would* and *could* may be used in the following cases:

- to say someone is willing or unwilling to do something.
  If you won't help me, I'll do it on my own.
- in polite requests (*would/wouldn't/could/couldn't*).
  If you wouldn't mind sitting here for a minute, I'll see if anyone is free.
- to suggest that someone is insisting on doing something.
  If you <u>will</u> *tease him, of course he'll cry.*

Inversion in conditional sentences

Conditions may be expressed without using *if* by inverting the first auxiliary verb. This is a fairly formal structure.

> **Had** *I seen him, I would have told you.* (= *If I had …*)
> **Were you** *to go there, you would find it disappointing.* (= *If you were to …*)

If the first auxiliary verb in the conditional is a form of *be*, the form *Should ... be* must be used instead of simple inversion.

> **Should** this **be** true, there will be serious consequences.
> ~~Be this true~~, there will be ...
> (= *If this is true …/If this should be true …*)

Other structures expressing condition (without *if*)

1 imperative + *and* (a fairly emphatic structure, often used in advertising)
   Buy *our new washing powder,* **and** *you'll be amazed at the results!* (= *If you buy …*)
2 negative imperative + *or* (emphatic)
   Don't *touch it* **or** *it will explode!* (= *If you touch it …*)
3 past participle or preposition + noun
   Deprived *of light and water, the plant will soon die.*
   (= *If (it is) deprived of …*)
   Without *your help, he won't be able to manage.* (= *If he doesn't have …*)

Other words expressing condition

- *unless*
  Don't come **unless** *I ask you to.*
- *provided/providing that*
  I'll do the work **provided that** *I can finish by lunchtime.*
- *as long as*
  I'll do the work **as long as** *I can finish by lunchtime.*
- *suppose/supposing*
  Suppose *it were to break! What would we do?*
- *imagine*
  Imagine *we lived on Mars. What sort of life would it be?*
- *assuming (that)*
  We're planning to fly, **assuming** *it's not too expensive.*
- *but for (the fact that)*
  But for your help, *we'd never have managed.*
  We'd have got there on time, **but for the fact that** *we got a flat tyre.*
- *otherwise*
  We need to set out soon, **otherwise** *we'll miss the train.*

in case

In case is used to talk about things we do to prepare for a possible later situation. Notice that *will* is not used in the clause with *in case*.

> *I've brought a towel* **in case** *we* **decide** *to go swimming.*

It often refers to things we do to prevent or prepare for something bad.

> *Make a note of your passport number* **in case it gets stolen.**

Sentences with *in case* cannot be rewritten with *if* without changing the meaning.

> *Take an umbrella* **if it rains**. (= *if it is raining when you leave*)
> *Take an umbrella* **in case it rains**. (= *to be prepared for the possibility of rain*)

However, the structure *in case of* + noun can be rewritten with an *if*-clause.

> **In case of** *any problems, phone 0014–829020.*
> **If you have** *any problems …*

even though/even if

Even though refers to something that is actually the case.

> *I went alone,* **even though** *I knew it was dangerous.*

Even if refers to a possible condition.

> *I want to go,* **even if** *it might be dangerous.*

UNIT 8

So and such (p. 115)

The intensifier *so* is used with adjectives, and *such* with nouns. They may be used in the following ways.

1 **For emphasis**
   It's **so** *hot! I can't stand it!*
   It's **such** *a big effort to get up in the morning!*
   Be careful. This is a fairly colloquial and emphatic use. In most situations it is more appropriate to use *very* instead.
   It is **very** *difficult to give a clear answer to this question.*

2 **To describe cause**
   A *that*-clause must follow, giving the result.
   It's **so** *hot* **that** *I can't do anything.*
   It was **such** *a hot day/***such** *hot weather* **that** *we decided to stay indoors.*

Note: In formal contexts it is also possible to use *so* + adjective (e.g. *so hot*) with the indefinite article and a noun (e.g. *a day*). In this case the article must go immediately in front of the noun.

> *It was a difficult journey.*
> *It was* **so difficult a journey** *that they feared they would never achieve their goal.*

Inversion can be used for dramatic effect in clauses describing causes or reasons. Again, this is more common in formal contexts.

*The weather **was so hot** that no-one could work.*
→ ***So hot was** the weather that ...*
→ ***Such was the heat** that ...*
*It was **such a difficult journey** that ...*
→ ***So difficult a journey was it** that ...*

When the main verb is not *be*, and there is no auxiliary verb, *do* is added.

*He **travelled so far** that ...*
→ ***So far did he travel** that ...*

UNIT 9

Verb patterns (p. 126)

When one verb follows another, various patterns are possible.

Some verbs do not take an object but are immediately followed by the second verb.

*I **hoped to go**, but I couldn't.*

Other verbs may, or must, have an object. In this case the second verb refers to the object. (See note below.)

*I **wanted her to go**, but she couldn't.*

In addition, depending on the first verb chosen, the second verb may be:
- an infinitive with *to*
- an infinitive without *to* (a 'bare' infinitive)
- an *-ing* form.

Most verbs take only one of these patterns, but some may take more than one pattern, with or without a change of meaning.

Finally, instead of being an infinitive or an *-ing* form, it may be possible or obligatory for the second verb to be in a *that*-clause.

*I **told him to go**.*
*I **told him that** he should go.*

Verbs which can also take a *that*-clause are marked * in the lists below.

Note: If the second verb does not refer to the preceding object, then a *that*-clause must be used.

*I **told him that** Maria should go.*

1 verb + verb (no object)

1 verb + *to*-infinitive
*I have **applied to go** to university.*
*He **promised to help** us. (= He promised that he would help us.)*
agree* arrange* apply appear* decide*
fail hope* intend long plan* pretend*
promise*

2 verb + *-ing*
*We **postponed making** any decision.*
*The doctor **suggested taking** a holiday. (... that we should take a holiday)*
admit* advise consider* deny* finish
postpone suggest* recommend*

3 verb + *to*-infinitive or *-ing*
a) with little change in meaning.
*I **prefer working/to work** alone.*
begin continue hate like love prefer
start

b) with a change in meaning
- *dread*
*I **dread to think** what he will do. (Only used with I ... think ...)*
*I **dread seeing** him again.*
- *forget*/remember*/stop*
***Remember to phone** him.*
*I can't **remember** ever **having seen** him before.*
- *go on*
*After school he **went on to study** at university.*
*He **went on studying** until six o'clock in the morning.*
- *mean**
*I didn't **mean to insult** him.*
*The new job **meant leaving** everything she knew.*
- *regret**
*I **regret to tell** you that your application has been unsuccessful.*
*I **regret not having been** to university.*
- *try*
*Please **try to remember**.*
*I've **tried being** strict with him, but it's no good.*

Notes:
1 In phrases such as *I would like/love to ...*, which refer to specific hypothetical situations, the infinitive is always used.
*I **love going** to New York. (= I often go.)*
*I would **love to go** to New York. (= I've never been.)*

2 For several of the verbs in point b), the use of the infinitive suggests a 'forward-looking' meaning, while the *-ing* form is used when something happened before or at the same time as the action.

2 verb (+ optional object) + verb

1 verb (+ object) + *to*-infinitive
*He **chose (her) to be** the leader.*
ask choose expect* intend need want
wish*

2 verb (+ object or possessive) + *-ing*
*We **insisted on them/their being** present.*
*I **recall him/his having won** first prize at school.*
*I **appreciate you/your doing** that for me.*
anticipate*   appreciate*   describe   dislike
enjoy   insist on   recall*   risk

Notes:

1 The use of the possessive rather than the object is more formal. It is more common when the second verb applies to a person rather than an object.

2 If *appreciate* is followed by a *that*-clause, the pronoun *it* must be used.
*I do **appreciate it** that you did all that work.*

3 verb + *for* + object + *to*-infinitive
*I **have arranged for the neighbour to feed** the cat.*
apply   arrange*   long   wait

Note: These verbs cannot be followed by an object alone.

3 verb + compulsory object + verb

1 verb + object + *to*-infinitive
Verbs in this pattern generally have the meaning of imposing one's will on someone else, either asking or forcing them to do something.
*I **forced him to take** the job.*
allow   compel   force   invite   order   tell
want

Other verbs include verbs of opinion. They are often used passively and are often followed by *be* + adjective.
*We **knew him to be** trustworthy.*
*He **is known to be** trustworthy.*
assume*   believe*   consider*   imagine*
know*

2 verb + object + bare infinitive
*She **made him go** to school on his bike.*
make   let   help

Note: *Help* can also be followed by a *to*-infinitive.
*She **helped him (to) cross** the road.*
Can't/couldn't help can also be followed by the *-ing* form when it means that someone couldn't prevent themselves from doing something.
*I **couldn't help laughing**.*

3 verb + object + bare infinitive or *-ing*
*They **saw her walking** in the park.* (action in progress)
*They **saw her walk** across the field.* (the whole action)

hear*   listen to   notice*   see*   observe*
watch

Note: These are all verbs of perception.

Emphasis: Cleft sentences (p. 129)

In cleft (divided) sentences, two clauses are used instead of one in order to highlight specific information. They always have a form of the verb *be* in one clause. There are two types of cleft sentences.

1   *It + be*
This type of cleft structure emphasises the word or phrase that immediately follows *be*. This may be a subject or object of a sentence, or an adverbial. It cannot be used to emphasise the verb.
Jane saw Peter here.
→ *It was **Jane** who saw Peter here.* (subject)
→ *It was **Peter** (whom/who) Jane saw here.* (object)
→ *It was **here** that Jane saw Peter.* (adverbial)

If there is a modal verb in the sentence, it goes before the verb *be*.
*Jane **must have seen** Peter.*
*It **must have been** Jane who saw him.*
It was Jane who must have seen him. ✗

2   *What .../All ... + be*
1 In this type of cleft structure a noun clause beginning with *what* or *all* is used. It can emphasise any part of the sentence, including the verb.
*I particularly enjoyed **going to the theatre**.*
→ ***What I particularly enjoyed** WAS going to the theatre.*
→ *Going to the theatre WAS **what I particularly enjoyed**.*

2 The verb can be emphasised by using *do* in the *wh*-clause.
We're searching for the best solution.
*What we're **doing** IS searching ...*

3 To emphasise the whole sentence, we can use *happen*.
The population has increased.
→ ***What has happened** IS that the population has increased.*

4 *All* can be used to replace *what* if it refers to the object of the clause.
I just wanted my own car.
→ ***All** I wanted WAS **my own car**.*

3   Cleft sentences with relative clauses
It is also possible to emphasise part of a sentence by using a general word such as *person/time/place*, followed by a relative clause.

Simon is doing the best job.
→ The **person who** *is doing the best job* **is** *Simon.*
She went there to make some contacts.
→ The **reason why** *she went there* **was** *to make some contacts.*
This can also be used to focus on an adverbial or a prepositional phrase.
They decided on January.
→ The **month** *they decided on* **was** *January.*

UNIT 10

Adverb + adjective collocation (p. 143)

Some adjectives can have comparative and superlative forms, and can be modified with words like *very* or *absolutely*. These are called gradable adjectives. Examples of 'ordinary' gradable adjectives are *small*, *young* and *sad*. They are modified with adverbs such as *fairly*, *very*, *moderately* and *exceedingly* (Group 1 on page 143).

Examples of 'strong' gradable adjectives are *astonished*, *wonderful* and *terrifying*. They are modified with adverbs such as *absolutely*, *completely* and *totally* (Group 2 on page 143).

Other adjectives do not normally have comparative and superlative forms as they refer to classes or groups. These are called ungradable or classifying adjectives. Examples of ungradable adjectives are *French*, *perfect* and *boiling*. They are not normally modified.
The temperature of boiling water is 100°C.
However, in some cases we may want to make these adjectives gradable. In this case, we treat them as strong gradable adjectives and use Group 2 adverbs.
The weather today is **absolutely** *boiling!*

Future forms (p. 148)

A large number of different verb forms can be used to refer to the future. The future form chosen may depend on:
• the speaker's view of the likelihood of the future event
• the relation of the event to another point in time
• the duration in time of the future event
• the context – formal or informal, spoken or written.

Here are some of the most important future forms and their uses:

1 *going to*
This may express certainty, based on present evidence.
You're **going to** *miss the train – it's six o'clock.*
Look at those clouds – it's **going to** *rain.*
It may express intention.
I'm **going to** *look for a new job.*

Note: The time need not be stated.

2 Present continuous
This suggests that something is planned; the time is either stated or can be understood from the immediate context.
What are you doing tonight? I'm **staying** *at home.*

3 *will*
This is used for general predictions, which are not necessarily based on present evidence and not pre-planned. The speaker is often an authority on the subject.
House prices **will** *rise.*
(It is often accompanied by an adverbial: *probably*, *almost certainly*, etc.)
It is also used in speech for a spontaneous decision made at the moment of speaking, and in spoken and written language for a promise.
I'll make you a cup of tea.
I'll work as hard as I can.

4 Future continuous
This is a common way of referring to something which has already been decided or planned.
I'll be driving to London tomorrow anyway, so if you want I can give you a lift.

Note: It is often used when offering to do something for someone.

It can also be used for an ongoing or repeated action which will be in progress at a specified time in the future. It is used with time expressions such as: *quite soon*, *in ten years' time*, *for a few more years*, *when I'm 40*.
At six o'clock tomorrow I'll be sitting on the plane.

5 Future perfect, future perfect continuous
The future perfect is used for an action which will have finished before a point in the future. It is used with time expressions with *by* such as:
by 2050, by the time ..., by this time (next week/year).
By the time she's thirty, she'll have started her own business.
The continuous form describes something continuing up to a point in the future, and emphasises the duration of the activity. It is often used with time expressions *for* and *since*.

*By this time next month, I'll **have been working** here for a year.*

6 *could, may, might*

These suggest that the future event is seen as uncertain.

*I **might** be late, I'm not sure.*

7 Present simple

This is used for events that are felt to be fixed and certain, like timetables. It is generally used with a time adverbial.

*The exams **begin** next Tuesday.*

8 *be to*

This also suggests that something is fixed and inevitable. It is more common in written language than in spoken.

*The office **is to be** closed for a week.*
*The Prime Minister **is to visit** Poland.*

9 Other expressions

Events in the near future

*He's **on the point of** leaving.*
*She's just **about to** make a decision.*

Expected or predicted time of event

*The train's **due to** arrive in ten minutes.*

Probability

*He's **quite likely** to accept the job.*
*It's **not very likely** that they'll win.*

Note: In many situations when referring to the future, it is possible to use several different forms without changing the meaning very much.

I'm going to see him tomorrow so ...
I'm seeing him tomorrow so ...
I'll be seeing him tomorrow so ...
I'll probably see him tomorrow so ...
} *I can discuss it with him then.*

In written English, writers may use different forms just to add variety.

Tenses in time clauses (p. 149)

Future verb forms are not used in time clauses introduced by *when, after, as soon as, by the time, while, once,* etc. Instead a present tense must be used.

*He'**ll phone** as soon as he **arrives** at the airport.*
*She'**ll be** happy once she'**s lying** on the beach.*

Note: This is similar to the use of the present tense to refer to future time in *if*-clauses.

The present perfect is used to show that the action in the subordinate clause is completed before the action in the main clause.

*They'll buy the house when they've **saved** enough money.*

UNIT 11

Reflexive pronouns (p. 159)

Reflexive pronouns such as *myself, yourself, ourselves,* etc. are used to refer back to the subject, in cases where the subject and object are the same. They always agree with the subject of the verb.

*He prides **himself** on his good taste.*

The following verbs are always reflexive:

busy   content   pride

Most transitive verbs can be used reflexively as long as it is possible for the subject and object to be the same.

*He introduced **himself** to the hostess.*
*I adapted **myself** to the climate.*
*Enjoy **yourselves** at the party!*

However, some verbs which are reflexive in other languages are generally used without a reflexive pronoun in English. They include:

wash   dress   shave   shower   adapt   readjust
move   hide   concentrate

*She **washed** and **dressed** hurriedly, hoping not to be late for work.*

Future forms with modal verbs

For future forms with modals, see Unit 10 above.

UNIT 12

Indirect speech (p. 173)

1 Indirect statements

Verbs that can be used to introduce indirect statements include:

acknowledge   agree   answer   argue   describe
explain   order   recommend   refuse   reply
say   tell

The following patterns are used with these verbs.

a) reporting verb (+ object) (+ *that*) + reported clause
   *They said **that it was an hour's journey**.*
   *They suggested **that we should rest for a while**.*

b) reporting verb + object + infinitive
   *They told **us to carry on**.*

c) reporting verb + *-ing*
   *They recommended **going on**.*

d) reporting verb + object + prepositional phrase
   *They told **us of a nearby village**.*

See also Unit 9 Verb patterns; Unit 6 Subjunctives.

2 Indirect questions

Verbs which may be used to introduce indirect questions include:

ask   enquire   wonder

The following patterns follow these verbs.

a) reporting verb + object
   *They asked **our names**.*
b) reporting verb + preposition + object
   *They enquired **about our families**.*
c) reporting verb + *wh-/if*-clause
   *I asked **where he was going**.*
   *He asked **if I would go with him**.*

Note: Remember that in indirect questions there is no inversion in the question form.

3 Sequence of tenses

When the situation being reported is no longer the case, tenses, pronouns and other expressions may all change to make this clear. This is usually necessary in a written narrative where there is a big time gap between the events and the time of reporting.

- **Tenses** shift backwards.
- **Pronouns** change from first and second person to third person.
- **Time expressions** change so that they are no longer based on the time of speaking.
- **Expressions of place** change so that they no longer refer to the immediate setting.
   *'I'm hoping to stay **here** until **tomorrow**,' she said.*
→ *She said **she was** hoping to stay **there** until **the following day**.*

These changes may not be necessary or appropriate if the situation has not changed.

   *She says she's **hoping** to stay **here** until **tomorrow**.*
   *He told me he **isn't** very happy at school.*

4 Paraphrasing

When we report what someone said, we often report the general meaning rather than the exact words.

   'You must be tired. Come inside and sit down with us,' they said.
→ *They invited us to come in.*

Impersonal passive constructions (p. 174)

After the following reporting or thinking verbs, a passive construction may be used.

allege   believe   expect   fear   hope   know
report   rumour   say   think

The following patterns are possible.

1   It + passive verb + *that* + subject
   ***It is rumoured that he** plans to resign.*
2   subject + passive verb + present/perfect infinitive
   ***He is rumoured to be planning** to resign.*

These structures are often used in newspapers to avoid naming the source of the information.

Note: When the action in the subordinate clause refers to the future, the second pattern is only possible if the active sentence has an object and an infinitive. Compare:

Active: *Everyone expects **Bradley to get** the contract.*
Passive: ***Bradley is expected** to get the contract.*

Active: *People hope **that fines will discourage littering**.*
Passive: ***It is hoped** that fines will discourage littering.*
   NOT *Fines are hoped to discourage littering.* ✗

UNIT 13

Clauses of concession (p. 189)

Clauses of concession can be introduced in the following ways:

1   *although, even though, while, whilst* (formal), *whereas* + clause
   *She carried on training, **even though** she had little hope of winning the race.*

Note: *May* is often used in clauses of concession to express possibility.
   *While some people **may** disagree, I feel the plan is basically sound.*

2   *whatever, whoever, however, whichever, wherever* (+ noun/adjective/adverb) + clause
   ***However** hard I try, I just can't find the answer.*
   ***Whatever** you say, they won't agree.*
3   *no matter what/who/how/which/where* + clause
   ***No matter what** you do, you'll never manage on your own.*
4   *much as* (= *although*) + clause
   ***Much as** I like him, I don't feel he's the right person for this job.*
5   adverb/adjective + *as/though* + clause
   ***Strange as** it may seem, I found I was beginning to like him.*
   ***Hard though** it was, I struggled on.*
   ***Talented though** he may be, he does not have the determination to win.*
6   *and yet/but still* + clause
   *It was a warm day, **and yet** she was shivering.*
   *He'd been warned many times, **but still** he continued to misbehave.*

7 *even so/all the same* + clause
   *It was almost impossible, but **even so**, she decided to try.*

8 *despite/in spite of* + noun or *-ing* form
   ***In spite** of the fact that she knew the answer, she refused to reply.*
   ***Despite** having lost the last match, he did not give up.*

Note: These must be immediately followed by a noun or an *-ing* form, not a clause.

UNIT 14

Comparison (p. 200)

1 We can use the following structures to say that things are similar to or different from one another.
   a) *as* + adjective or adverb + *as* ...
      not so/as + adjective or adverb + *as* ...
   *Books seem to be just **as popular** now **as** they were in the past.*
   *The effect of TV has not been anything like **as detrimental** to reading habits **as** people feared it would be.*
   b) *as* + adjective + *a/an* + noun + *as* ...
   *The book seems **as obvious a candidate** for redundancy now **as** it did in the 20th century.*
   c) (*not*) *such a/an* + noun + *as* ...
   *The rise of cinema and TV has **not** had **such a** negative **effect** on book sales **as** some people predicted.*

Note: This structure is mainly used in negative sentences. Compare the position of the article *a/an* with the example in point b) above.

   d) *as* + clause
   In comparisons, *as* is a conjunction introducing a clause.
   *I believe that the book will continue to survive, **as it has done in the past.***
   Inversion can also be used.
   *A large proportion of TV dramas are based on novels, **as are many films.***

2 We can use the following structures to express preferences.
   ***I much prefer** playing music **to doing** sport.*
   ***I'd far sooner** stay at home **than** go out tonight.*
   *TV producers should concentrate on quality **rather than** quantity.*
   ***Rather than** watching sport on TV, **I'd prefer to** go to a live game.*

Speaking prompt cards

Unit 1

What effect does growing older have on relationships?

- in the family
- friends
- at school and work

1 What kind of relationships do you think last the longest? Why?
2 Do you think that the skill of making relationships should be taught at school?
3 How important do you think it is to like the people you work with?

Unit 2

What do you think is the best way to prepare children for life?

- in the home
- at school
- leisure activities

1 Do you agree that schooldays are wasted on the young?
2 What do you regret about your own schooldays?
3 What skill would you most like to learn in the future? Why?

Unit 3

How important do you think film will be as the entertainment of the future?

- technological developments
- costs
- changing lifestyles

1 What kind of films do you like to see and what do you dislike?
2 How influential do you think films are on young people's behaviour?
3 Do you think that films should be censored more? Why/Why not?

Unit 4

What do you think makes some types of advertising potentially dangerous?

- content
- medium
- target market

1 How much are you influenced by advertising?
2 Do you think that society has become too materialistic?
3 Why do you think that shopping has become a leisure activity?

Unit 5

Is crime a bigger social problem now than it was in the past?

- types of crime
- detection of crime
- control of crime

1 Do you agree with some people who say that the police should never carry guns?
2 How do you feel about the way crimes are reported in the media nowadays?
3 What effect do you think the Internet could have on crime?

Unit 6

How do you imagine life in cities in the future?

- work
- leisure
- travel

1 Some people feel that modern buildings are ugly. What do you think?
2 Which city would you most like to visit? Why?
3 How far do you agree that there are more disadvantages than advantages in living in a city?

Unit 7

What responsibilities do you think individuals have towards the environment?

- lifestyle
- shopping
- financial

1 What is being done in your area to improve or protect the environment?
2 How would you like to see people made more aware of environmental problems?
3 What do you think is the biggest environmental problem in your area?

Unit 8

How important is it for young people to have good role models?

- at school
- in leisure time
- at work

1 Who do you think is a good role model for young people in your country? Why?
2 What would you most like to be admired for?
3 How much is success due to individual effort and how much to luck?

Unit 9

Do you think that having a good imagination is important in life?

- personal happiness
- personal well-being
- personal achievement

1 Do you think that people can learn to be creative? How?
2 Do you think that technology limits imagination?
3 Some people say that reading fiction is a waste of time. How far do you agree?

Unit 10

What kind of work do you think should be rewarded most highly?

- risk and training
- difficulty
- responsibility

1 How far do you agree that job satisfaction is more important than financial reward?
2 Do you think the age of retirement should be changed? Why/Why not?
3 How far do you agree that computer skills are essential for every worker in today's world?

Unit 11

What aspects of technological development do you find most exciting?

- medical
- communications
- agricultural

1 What aspect of technological development do you find most worrying?
2 What aspects of life do you think have been made easier by the development of technology?
3 If you could have invented one thing, what would it be? Why?

Unit 12

What do you think people gain from foreign travel?

- personal
- cultural
- financial

1 What dangers do you see in foreign travel?
2 How important do you think it is that there should be a common world language?
3 Which country would you most like to visit and why?

Unit 13

How do you think success should be measured?

- at home
- at school
- at work

1 How would you most like to be successful? Why?
2 Do you think that there is too much emphasis on formal qualifications nowadays?
3 What kind of people are usually successful in life?

Unit 14

Why do you think books continue to be popular in this technological age?

- for children
- for workers
- for travellers

1 Do you think that people should be encouraged to read more books? Why?
2 What is the best book you have ever read?
3 Do you think that writers should be well-paid? Why/Why not?

Writing reference

The writing reference section contains:
- a variety of key expressions and linking words and phrases
- an editing checklist of key points you should be thinking about when you complete a task for Paper 2
- a checklist for different task types.

Useful linking expressions

The lists below provide a selection of linking expressions that you will find useful in your writing.

1 Time sequence
- *When/As soon as/The moment* they arrived, the meeting began.
- *On hearing* the news, we immediately phoned to congratulate them.
- *From early childhood/an early age*, she showed great aptitude for music.
- *Throughout his adult life*, he has dedicated himself to helping others.
- *Up to that time*, she had never even been abroad.

2 Listing
- *First of all*, it must be stated that ...
- *Secondly*, it could be argued that ...
- *Last but not least*, it must be remembered that ...
- *Finally*, it is important to ...

3 Adding information/emphasising a point
- He left early – and *on top of that/to cap it all*, he didn't pay for his share of the meal. (*informal*)
- She didn't really want to see the film, and *besides/anyway/anyhow* she was too tired to go to the cinema now. (*informal*)
- The rent is reasonable and *moreover/furthermore/in addition* the location is perfect.
- *Not only* has he achieved a great deal, *but* he has *also* set an example for a generation.
- They want new regulations in the hostel; *above all*, they want to restrict the noise level in the evenings.

- These new medicines are perfectly safe. *Indeed*, they can be given to young children.

4 Giving examples
- Many things contributed to her success, *for instance/for example/such as* hard work, good fortune and the support of her friends.
- *To illustrate this point*, ...
- *Let's take the example of* ...

5 Explaining/reformulating
- Some cars are more environmentally friendly than others. *That is to say/In other words*, they cause less pollution.
- He read the newspaper to confirm what he knew already, *that is/namely* that his team had lost.
- You should treat your colleagues as friends, or, *better still/rather*, as close friends if you want to create a good working atmosphere.

6 Contrast
- She was very kind. *By/In contrast*, he seemed very callous.
- Some people learn languages easily. *Conversely*, others find it very difficult.
- It wasn't a good thing; *on the contrary*, it was a huge mistake.
- They decided not to take the car. *Instead*, they caught the next train.
- *On the one hand* I enjoyed their company, but *on the other hand* their strange lifestyle disturbed me.

7 Concession
- *Although/Even though* he was feeling unwell, he attended the meeting.
- *Despite* feeling unwell, he attended the meeting.
- He felt unwell; *however/nevertheless/nonetheless*, he attended the meeting.
- He was feeling unwell *but* he attended the meeting *all the same/even so*. (*informal*)
- My friends left the cinema before the end of the film *whilst/whereas/while* I stayed until it had finished.
- *No matter how many/However many* times I listen to that music, it still moves me to tears.
- *Whoever* comes, it will be a valuable opportunity to discuss the problem.

8 Giving opinions

- *In my opinion/view*, he is one of the most impressive writers of our generation.
- *It seems to me that* one of the biggest problems facing us today is ...
- *(Personally,) I feel that* more needs to be done to encourage young people to take responsibility for the environment.
- *I can honestly say* that ...

9 Commenting/expressing own attitude (sentence adverbials)

- *Surely* it must be obvious to anyone that this plan is doomed to failure.
- *Clearly*, more needs to be done to persuade people to use public transport.
- *Not surprisingly*, there has been considerable opposition to this plan.
- *Irritatingly/Annoyingly*, the authorities have decided to cut the funds available for the project.

10 Giving reasons

- *Seeing that/As* it was getting late, they decided to return home.
- Trains are being delayed *owing to/due to/because of* the inclement weather.
- They liked his idea, *in so far as/to the extent that* it made money for the company.

11 Purpose

- *In order for* her *to* live a comfortable life, she had to find a well-paid job.
- She spoke quietly *in order not to/so as not to* wake the sleeping child.

12 Results/consequences

- A lot of people voted for his entry and *thus/consequently/therefore/as a result/accordingly* he was awarded the prize.
- He became a citizen in 1999, *thereby* gaining the right to vote.
- Many areas have been modernised *in such a way as to* make the city more attractive to tourists.

13 Comparisons

- It's *a good deal/a great deal/very much* easier to watch sport than to take part.
- She looked *as if/as though* she'd seen a ghost.
- He was *nowhere near/nothing like as* good at tennis *as* (he was at) basketball.
- *The more* cities expand, *the less* access we have to the countryside.

14 Summing up

- Although the day was not a complete success, *all in all* it went as well as could be expected.

- *To sum up/In short*, it was a highly successful visit.
- *Overall*, what I most admire is their determination to succeed.
- *In conclusion/Finally/To conclude*, it seems clear that tourism is having an adverse effect on the area.
- The team played well, but *at the end of the day* they just weren't good enough to win. (*informal*)

Checklist of key points for editing

1 Understanding the question

*Your writing will be assessed on relevance to the task set; you must identify and answer the **exact** question set.*

- Have you identified the key words in the question and answered **all** parts?
  You must make sure that you have answered the questions fully and clearly.

- Have you taken any given input into account?
  If you are completing a Part 1 task, make sure that you read the given input carefully so that you can use it to structure your answer. Remember that a Part 1 task is usually discursive so you will need to put forward a point of view and support it with ideas or evidence.

- Have you identified the appropriate style required by the task?
  You must think about the appropriate style to use – e.g. a report is more formal than an article.

2 Planning and organisation of material

Your writing will be assessed on both the organisation of the whole answer and on the organisation of individual paragraphs. Careful planning is very important.

- Have you decided on the main points you want to make before you start to write?
  If you have not made a plan, then your writing will not be well organised. In a Part 1 answer you must plan in order to make sure that you include all the relevant information from the input text.

- Does your introduction make it clear what ideas your writing will develop?
  In a **discursive (Part 1) task** you should give a clear indication in your introduction of the main areas you are planning to cover and follow this structure throughout the task. The input may give you ideas for these areas.

In a **formal letter** you should state your reasons for writing in the first paragraph.

In an **essay**, **report** or **proposal** your introduction should state the main topic areas you will be covering – this is the 'plan of development'.

In an **article** your introduction should set the scene and capture the reader's interest, e.g. by referring to a specific incident.

- Have you started a new paragraph for each new topic (but not each new point)?
  Each paragraph should have one main topic only (though in a discursive answer there may be more than one piece of evidence provided to support the idea).

- Do the topics in your supporting paragraphs match the opening statement or plan of development stated in your introduction?
  Make sure that you haven't strayed from your main theme and included any unrelated points.

- Does each paragraph include plenty of supporting evidence for the main idea?
  You should provide enough details or examples to support your main point so that your writing will be convincing.

- Have you linked your paragraphs so that they follow on from each other clearly?
  Your supporting paragraphs should follow a sensible, logical sequence and should be linked clearly either by linking words or phrases or by the underlying meaning.

- Have you used a clear method of development to organise the supporting details within each paragraph?

Common methods of development are:
Chronological time order
Emphatic order – listing points from the least important to the most important or 'saving the best until last'
Contrast/concession – making a point followed by an opposite point

- Have you used appropriate linking words to help link the sentences within each paragraph?
  Linking words signal the method of organisation you have chosen, and help the reader to follow the direction of your thoughts – but don't overuse them as this is unnatural.

- Is your conclusion prepared for?

In a **discursive answer** (Part 1), your conclusion should summarise your answer to the question and state your own opinion or conclusion.

In a **report** or **proposal**, your conclusion should summarise the points made or make final recommendations.

In an **article**, your writing should round off with a quotation from a person interviewed in the article or a rhetorical question to the reader that echoes the introduction.

3 **Range and appropriacy of language**
You will be assessed on the range of vocabulary and structures you use and the appropriacy of your language for the type of writing.

- Have you used a style and register appropriate to the task?
  Check that you haven't used language that is too formal or informal for the task and that you have been consistent. For example, you shouldn't use features of informal language in a formal letter, report or proposal (see Register table Unit 4 p 62, correction of register mistakes Unit 3 page 47).

- Have you used a variety of structures and vocabulary?
  Try to vary the way you start your sentences, by using participle clauses, inversions, etc. where appropriate.

4 **Accuracy**
You will be assessed on the range of grammatical structures you use and how accurate your writing is.

- Have you made any basic mistakes in grammar, spelling and punctuation?
  Make sure that you check tenses and verb agreements – basic mistakes such as 'he don't' and misuse of capital letters create a very bad impression. (See correction of mistakes Unit 1, page 19.)

5 **Overall impression**
- Is your writing interesting and enjoyable to read?
  You will have a better chance if the examiner enjoys reading your work!

Be careful that you don't:
- forget to answer the compulsory question in Part 1
- forget to use the input given in Part 1 as the basis of your answer
- include information that is not relevant to the

question you are answering

- use too many connecting words and phrases – they should be used when necessary, not in every sentence
- write more than the number of words required
- take longer than one hour for each composition. Your timing should be:

    10 minutes thinking and planning
    40–45 minutes writing
    5–10 minutes checking

There is no advantage in taking one and a half hours over one answer and then only having 30 minutes for the second. You should spend an equal time on each answer.

A checklist for different task types

Part 1

All task types must use the given input as the basis of the answer, and the focus will be discursive.

An **article** is written for unknown readers often to raise issues or provoke thought. It should:

- involve presentation and/or discussion of a point of view supported by evidence
- have an introduction which states the overall topic
- be divided into clear paragraphs according to the topic of each
- return to the question or round off the argument in the conclusion
- use a variety of structures and vocabulary to retain the reader's interest
- use a style appropriate to the specified audience.

An **essay** is written for a tutor or a specific reader and is usually academic. It should:

- involve presentation and/or discussion of a point of view supported by evidence
- state the general position in the introduction and outline the frame of the essay
- be divided into clear paragraphs according to the topic of each
- return to the question and state the writer's own opinion in conclusion
- use a formal style.

A **proposal** is written for a specific reader or readers, for a specific purpose and focuses on the future. It should:

- involve discussion of a situation and recommendations for future action, supported by evidence
- have an introduction giving background information to the current situation
- be divided into clear sections (possibly with headings) and topic paragraphs
- summarise the proposal in the final paragraph with recommendations
- use a formal style.

A **letter** may be personal (either formal or informal) or it may be written for publication in a magazine or newspaper. It should:

- involve presentation and/or discussion of a point of view with supporting evidence
- use appropriate phrases for the register and focus of the task (formal or informal)
- be divided into clear topic paragraphs
- make recommendations or call for action in the final paragraph
- begin and end appropriately.

Part 2

Answers will be more descriptive than discursive. The article, proposal and letter should follow the same guidelines as given for Part 1, but the answers will be more descriptive than discursive.

A **report** is written for a specific group of readers for a specific purpose and focuses on a past or present situation. It should:

- involve description of a past or present situation or event in an official context
- have an introduction giving background information
- be divided into clear sections (possibly with headings) and topic paragraphs
- make recommendations or suggestions in the final paragraph
- use a formal style.

A **review** is written for unknown readers to give information about a place, film, book, etc. with evaluation and advice. It should:

- involve presentation of a point of view supported by evidence
- have an introduction which states the overall topic
- be divided into clear paragraphs according to the topic of each
- return to the question or give a final opinion or verdict in the conclusion
- use a variety of structures and vocabulary to retain the reader's interest
- use a style appropriate to the specified audience.

Communication activities

Unit 1, Grammar Ex. 3 (p. 12)

Student A: Annette's story.

My husband and I were working as cook and waiter at a hotel in the south of England, and living with our six-month-old baby in a cottage nearby. For once we (1) .... (*manage*) to get an evening off together, and one of the hotel staff had volunteered to babysit for us so that we could go out to the cinema together.

We caught the bus to the nearest town, about ten kilometres away, but we (2) .... (*not watch*) the film for more than a few minutes before I (3) .... (*start*) to feel terribly uneasy. I could distinctly smell burning. I told my husband, but he couldn't smell anything and told me I (4) .... (*imagine*) things. But the smell persisted, and eventually I told him I was leaving. He (5) .... (*follow*) me reluctantly, muttering something under his breath.

As we made the journey home on the bus I prayed for it to go faster. At each stop I almost died. At last we (6) .... (*rush*) down the lane leading to the cottage. The smell of burning was now very definite to me, though my husband still couldn't smell anything. We reached the door and burst in. As we did, dense smoke (7) .... (*pour*) out and a chair by the fire burst into flames. I rushed through to the bedroom and got the baby, while my husband dragged out the unconscious babysitter. She (8) .... (*smoke*) and had fallen asleep and (9) .... (*drop*) her lighted cigarette onto the chair. We later worked out that it must have happened just as I first (10) .... (*smell*) smoke in the cinema.

Unit 4, Writing Ex. 3 (p. 64)

Student A

Unit 6, Exam Focus Ex. 2 (p. 83)

Extract 1

In the following extract from the tapescript, single underlining relates to the wrong answers (distractors) and double underlining indicates the section which gives the correct answer. Read Question 1 below and circle the words which have been changed.

Woman: Yeah ... there were big changes going on, it was all developing very fast and ... well, when I first went, I lived quite near to the city centre, and in the centre there, in the old town, it was all ... mostly old, narrow streets, with lots of sharp corners, and it was too narrow for cars at all really, but they managed to edge their way through anyway (**B**) and there were these high old buildings on either side (**D**) – with windows with lovely carved wooden shutters, all rather falling to bits, and children playing and things like cats and goats along the streets as well, even whole herds of cattle occasionally.
Interviewer: Was it like that where *you* lived?
Woman: More or less ... though I lived in a new block of flats, (**C**) but there weren't any big office blocks around (**A**) then, or things like international hotels. And another thing ... although it was a port and it was built by the sea, you weren't actually all that conscious of it, of the sea.

1 When the speaker first went to Jeddah, there were no
   A large commercial buildings.
   B cars in the city centre.
   C modern buildings.
   D tall buildings.

Extract 2

Use underlining in the same way to highlight the distractors and the correct answer in the following extract from the tapescript. Match the options A–D to each section you have underlined and decide exactly why each of the distractors is wrong.

Interviewer: So when did it start to change?
Woman: Oh it was already changing fast, before long there were office blocks and multi-storey hotels shooting up all over the place ... a lot of the old town was pulled down, and for a time it seemed as if all the history was going to be lost, but then just at the last moment they started doing up some of the old houses and some of the streets were pedestrianised so you could walk around there without being mown down by traffic. But they kept the old souq, the big covered market, where you could buy things like spices and gold ... and cassettes and electrical equipment too, of course.
Interviewer: So it became more of a tourist centre then?
Woman: No, tourism doesn't exist at all – it was done for the people who lived there.

2 The speaker was relieved that
   A more goods were available in the market.
   B unsafe buildings were pulled down.
   C some buildings were restored.
   D there were no tourists.

Woman: But it wasn't just a matter of preservation – I mean the whole infrastructure was developed: roads, services like telephones and public transport, shopping malls, a huge new airport ... and the whole city just expanded outwards at an amazing rate. You'd go out one morning and there'd be a whole new road where there hadn't been one before ... at least that's what it felt like ... and a lot of the roads didn't have names yet ... so if you were looking for a friend's apartment or something, out in the new suburbs, tempers could get quite frayed.
Interviewer: What about social life – did you go out much?
Woman: Yes ... although it is a very family-orientated society ... life is quite private. And then it's so hot for a lot of the year that people tend to stay inside where it's air-conditioned.

3 One problem she had was that
   A her friends lived far out of town.
   B most social life was family-based.
   C it was difficult to find her way around.
   D there was no telephone or public transport service.

Unit 5, Language Focus: Grammar Ex. 3.3 (p. 74)

Agatha Christie was found nine days after her disappearance. She had been staying in a hotel in the town of Harrogate, in the North of England. She claimed to have lost her memory: 'For 24 hours I wandered in a dream and then found myself in Harrogate as a well-contented and perfectly happy woman who believed she had just come from South Africa.' The truth was only discovered half a century later, when secret documents were at last made available. Agatha Christie in fact staged her own disappearance, not as a publicity stunt, as many believed, but because she wanted to ruin a weekend that her husband was planning to spend with his mistress. To avoid public disgrace, she and her husband stuck to the story that a blow to her head had resulted in amnesia, but it was the end of their marriage. However, the affair did make Christie the most famous crime writer in Britain.

Unit 4, Writing Ex.3 (p. 64)

Student B

Unit 8, Exam Focus Ex. 1 (p. 114)

wear² n **1** [U] damage caused by continuous use over a long period: *The carpet is showing signs of wear.* **2** [U] the amount of use an object, piece of clothing etc has had, or the use you can expect to get from it: *Considering the wear it's had, your coat's in good condition.* | **have/get a lot of wear out of sth** *You'll get a lot of wear out of a canvas tent.* | **a lot of wear is left in sth** (=it is still useful or can still be worn) **3 sportswear/evening wear/childrens' wear etc** the clothes worn for a particular occasion or activity, or by a particular group of people: *a new range of casual wear* | *the menswear department* | *footwear* (=shoes) **4 wear and tear** the amount of damage you expect to be caused to furniture, cars, equipment etc when they are used for a long period of time: **normal/everyday wear and tear** *The washer should last for ten years allowing for normal wear and tear.* —see also **the worse for wear** (WORSE¹ (8))

Unit 8, Exam Focus Ex. 4 (p. 114)

Student A

You are going to make up three gapped sentences for your partner. The word gapped in each case is the adjective *heavy*. Look at the dictionary extract below and choose three different uses of the word. Remember that the word should be in exactly the same form each time but should have a different meaning. Then make up three sentences but leave a gap for the word *heavy* each time. You can use or adapt the examples given or make up ones of your own, but remember that you need to write **complete sentences**. (**Note:** The uses listed are in order of frequency – so you may find that the first ones are too easy and the last ones may be too difficult.) The dictionary extract gives you information about collocations and idioms – try to include some of these.

heav-y[1] /ˈhevi/ *adj* **heavier, heaviest**
1 ►**WEIGHT**◄ weighing a lot: *I can't lift this case – it's too heavy.* | *The baby seemed to be getting heavier and heavier in her arms.* | **how heavy?** (= how much does it weigh) *How heavy is the parcel?* – opposite LIGHT[3] (4)
2 ►**A LOT**◄ **a)** a lot or in very large amounts: *The traffic was heavier than normal, and I was late for work.* | **heavy rain/snow** *flooding caused by heavy rain over the weekend* | **heavy use/consumption** *the film's heavy use of special effects*
3 heavy smoker/drinker someone who smokes a lot or drinks a lot of alcohol
4 ►**SERIOUS/SEVERE**◄ serious or severe: *heavy winter storms* | *a heavy burden of responsibility* | **heavy fine/penalty** *heavy fines for possession of hard drugs* | **a heavy cold** (= a very bad cold) *She's in bed with a heavy cold.* | **heavy losses** *Most insurance companies suffered heavy losses last year.*
5 ►**NEEDING PHYSICAL EFFORT**◄ needing a lot of physical strength and effort: *heavy manual work*
6 ►**NEEDING MENTAL EFFORT**◄ not easy or entertaining and needing a lot of mental effort: *I want something to read on holiday – nothing too heavy.*
7 heavy going difficult to understand or deal with: **find sth heavy going** *I found Balzac's books pretty heavy going.*
8 be heavy on *informal* to use a lot or too much of something: *The car's rather heavy on oil.*
9 heavy schedule/timetable/day etc one in which you have a lot to do in a short time: *I'd had a heavy day at the office.*
10 heavy sleeper someone who does not wake easily

Unit 9, Exam Focus Ex. 3 (p. 128)

Look at the extracts from the tapescript and at questions 1–5 on page 128. For which question do you have to:

a) choose the correct adjective from two with similar meanings?
b) understand who is referred to by a pronoun in the tapescript?
c) match a general verb in the tapescript to an earlier more specific verb?
d) match a noun in the tapescript to an earlier more specific noun?
e) give someone's opinion?

A few months after my accident I had an idea for a short film about a quadriplegic. During the day, lying in his hospital bed, he can't move. But at night he dreams that he's whole again. This is someone who had been a lifelong sailor, and he had a beautiful sailing yacht. In his dream he sails down the path of a full moon – the kind of romantic night-sailing anyone can imagine. But in the morning, he's back in his bed and everything is frozen again. The dream is very vivid. At first it's just a dream, and he recognises it as such. But one night he finds himself getting out of bed and walking down the corridor and out the door and then into the boat, which, magically, is anchored not far away. Soon these voyages become so real to him that when he wakes up in his bed, his hair is wet. And the nurse comes in and says, 'Oh, I'm sorry. 1 didn't dry your hair enough last night when I gave you a shampoo. You slept with wet hair.' He says nothing, but he's thinking that his hair is wet from the spray when he was out on the water. ...

Up to this time his wife and children have been very distressed because, since he became paralysed, he has not been able to pull out of a very serious depression. His children are afraid of him because he is not himself and they don't know how to be with him. But as he continues to go sailing in his dreams, this begins to improve. His wife notices the change ...
Well, there comes a time when our protagonist realises that these voyages offer a way of escaping from his paralysed condition, that he could just sail on happily – it's what he loves most in the world – until one night he would go out into the middle of the ocean and he wouldn't take supplies. He would just sail. And he would die happy that way, just sailing down the path of the moon. And one night he starts to do that ...

Unit 1, Grammar Ex. 3 (p. 12)

Student B: Judi's story

It was in May 1989, about two weeks before the end of the school year. My son Corey, along with many of his classmates, had decided to skip school that day to have a party at the country home of a friend who (1) .... (*graduate*) the previous year. Corey had borrowed a motorbike from his older brother for the day. I (2) .... (*know*) nothing about any of this and just assumed that he was at school as usual.

Around noon as I (3) .... (*stand*) in my kitchen looking out of the window, I (4) .... (*was*) suddenly (5) .... (*fill*) with intense fear and immediately thought of Corey. I (6) .... (*tell*) myself that this was ridiculous because I knew Corey was in school and was just fine. But the feeling grew stronger and I (7) .... (*start*) shaking and crying uncontrollably – all I could do was to think of Corey and to pray that he was alright. When I was able to calm myself I went and sat on the sofa, trying to understand what (8) .... (*happen*) to me.

Ten minutes later the telephone rang. It was Corey's best friend.

'Mrs Gradey, it's about Corey. He's been involved in an accident. You mustn't worry, he's OK. But he's been taken to hospital.'

I rushed to the hospital and found Corey had miraculously escaped with only a few scratches. Later I found that as he (9) .... (*go*) round a curve in the highway, he (10) .... (*lose*) control of the motorbike and been thrown off into a small ditch at the side of the road. He had skidded along the ditch on his stomach, passing directly between a cement post and a pile of rocks. If he had gone a couple of inches in either direction, he would have been killed.

As far as I can work out, I (11) .... (*have*) my experience just as Corey was involved in the accident.

Unit 4, Writing Ex. 2 (p. 63)

British Nuclear Fuels plc
Adjudication:

1. Complaint not upheld.
The advertisers said they had decommissioned the sites of old nuclear reactors and made this land available for general commercial use. [...] The Nuclear Installations Inspectorate had declared there was no longer any danger from ionising radiation on a site they had decommissioned. They also said they had the expertise to transform former commercial sites into reusable land, and cited an example of an old nuclear site that would be re-used in Colorado, USA. The ASA considered that, because of the context of the advertisement – it was addressed to the nuclear industry in the trade press – it was unlikely to mislead.

2. Complaint upheld.
The advertisers believed the claim was justified because they were the most experienced company in the industry. They said they had perfected their knowledge and expertise to solve customers' waste problems in ways that complied with international regulations and were unsurpassed in the industry. They believed that in the context of a trade magazine most readers would understand what they meant by the claim. The ASA was satisfied that the advertisers dealt with waste to within UK standards but was concerned that the readers would interpret the claim to mean the advertisers had advanced their methods significantly beyond those standards. The Authority asked the advertisers not to repeat the claim.

Unit 13, Improving your writing Ex. 4 (p. 186)

Look at the two rewritten versions of the extract. Which version do you think is better? Why?

A

> Happiness is related to many things which we consider to be the ones that give us happiness. Therefore, if money could help us to improve health, family and career and if we had the money to do so, this would mean that money could help us attain happiness. However, how far is this actually true?

B

> Happiness is related to many things such as health, family and career. If money could help us in any of these areas, then this would mean that money too could bring us happiness. However, how far is this actually true?

Unit 14, Exam Focus Ex. 2 (p. 199)

1 Look at the tapescript extract below and discuss the meaning of the underlined words and phrases.

Philip: But by temperament <u>I'm usually in for the long haul</u>, even though it's a considerable investment in all sorts of ways ...

Interviewer: Angela?

Angela: Well, in this context people often talk about sprinters and marathoners, and I think by nature and metabolism <u>I'm a marathoner</u>. We mostly – those of us who end up being professional writers – cut our teeth on the short forms. They're a good teaching tool, whether or not people do their apprenticeship in an actual writing programme ...

Philip: ... and then <u>they</u> get the hang of it and begin to write novels and I suppose the typical pattern is that <u>they</u> never go back to the short story ...

Angela: <u>That's</u> been true for me, certainly ... but I suppose sometimes the form chooses the writer, rather than the other way round.

Philip: Absolutely ... <u>it's</u> happened to me twice, twice in my four decades or so of writing fiction I've been seized, *possessed* by the muse of short-windedness ...

2 Now look back at Exercise 1 questions 1–3 on page 199. For which question do you have to understand that:

a) one speaker implies agreement with the other speaker by continuing that speaker's sentence?

b) both speakers agree about one point, but this is not the subject of the statement?

c) both speakers make the same point by using different metaphors?

Unit 8, Exam Focus Ex. 4 (p. 114)

Student B

You are going to make up three gapped sentences for your partner. The word gapped in each case is the noun *patch*. Look at the dictionary extract below and choose three different uses of the word. Remember that the word should be in exactly the same form each time but should have a different meaning. Then make up three sentences but leave a gap for the word *patch* each time. You can use or adapt the examples given or make up ones of your own, but remember that you need to write **complete sentences**. (**Note:** The uses listed are in order of frequency – so you may find that the first ones are too easy and the last ones may be too difficult.) The dictionary extract gives you information about collocations and idioms – try to include some of these.

> **patch**[1] /pætʃ/ *n* [C]
> **1 ▶PART OF AN AREA◀** a part of an area that is different or looks different from the parts that surround it: *Lost: a small dog, white with brown patches.* | **patch of dirt/grease/damp etc** *Watch out for icy patches on the roads.* | **patch of light/sky etc** *Patches of blue sky peeked through the clouds.*
> **2 ▶OVER A HOLE◀** a small piece of material used to cover a hole in something: *a jacket with leather patches at the elbows*
> **3 ▶FOR GROWING STH◀** a small area of ground for growing fruit or vegetables: *a strawberry patch*
> **4 ▶ON YOUR EYE◀** a piece of material that you wear over your eye to protect it when it has been hurt
> **5 ▶DECORATION◀** a small piece of cloth with words or pictures on it that you can stitch onto clothes
> **6 a bad/difficult/sticky patch** *informal especially BrE* a period of time when you are having a lot of difficulty: *Gemma's going through a bad patch right now.*
> **7 sb's patch** *BrE informal* an area that someone knows very well because they work or live there; TURF[1] (4) *AmE: The boss knows everything that's going on in our patch.*
> **8 not be a patch on** *BrE informal* to be much less attractive, good etc than something or someone else: *She's no great beauty – not a patch on Maria.*
> **9 good/interesting/boring etc in patches** *especially BrE* good etc in some parts, but not all the time

Pearson Education Limited
Edinburgh Gate
Harlow
Essex CM20 2JE
England
and Associated Companies throughout the world.

www.longman.com

© Pearson Education Limited 2001

First published 2001

ISBN-13: 978-0-582-50727-2
ISBN-10: 0-582-50727-8

Set in Admark10/13pt

Printed by Graficas Estella.

Eighth impression 2006

The authors would like to thank the following people: Nigel, Neil, Ralph, Ken and Marjorie for their patience and support; the staff and students of the Bell Language School, Saffron Walden; all the Longman team, in particular Jenny Colley (Publisher) and our editors Helena Gomm and Frances Cook.

The authors and publisher wish to express thanks and appreciation to Mike Gutteridge, Hilary Maxwell-Hyslop and Martin Parrott for reporting on this new edition. They would also like to thank the following for their help in developing the original course, in particular Christine Barton, Frederika Beer, Raphaelle Collins, Patrick Dare, Bob Davis, Elizabeth Heliotis, Sarah Hellawell, Philip Kerr, Richard Mann, Nick Shaw, Elsa Silivestra, Mark Skipper, Tasia Vasilatou, Georgia Zographou and Heather Jones (Senior Exams Publisher, Longman).

We are grateful to the following for permission to reproduce copyright material:

The authors' agent for an extract from *The Anatomy of Relationships* by Michael Argyle and Monica Henderson published by Penguin Books Ltd; BT plc for an extract adapted from their advertisement on fingerprinting; Carlton Books for an extract from *How Long's the Course* by Roger Black published by André Deutsch Limited; Constable & Robinson Limited for extracts from *Mother Love* by Cassandra Eason; Friends of the Earth for an extract from "Take action" by Tony Juniper published in *Earthmatters* Winter 1998; Peter Gillman for an extract from his article "Mount Everest" published in the *Daily Telegraph*; Gruner & Jahr Ltd for an extract from "Windsurfing the edge" by Roger Turner published in *Focus Magazine* September 1995; Guardian Newspapers Limited for extracts from "Big sell ring targets" by Sarah Boseley published in *The Guardian*, "Help, mom, I'm stuck under a train" by Michael Ellison published in *The Guardian* 5th April 1999, "Big bird is back" by Martin Kettle published in *The Guardian* 7th May 1998, "Cod is dead" by Bill McKibben published in *The Guardian* 14th June 1998, and "Biodiversity: tearing up the map" by Tim Radford published in *The Guardian* 11th August 1998; HarperCollins Publishers Ltd for extracts from *Hare Brain, Tortoise Mind* by Guy Claxton, and *The God of Small Things* by Arundhati Roy; HHL Publishing for an extract from "Future shock" by Simon Reeve published in *Hotline Magazine* Autumn / Winter 1998; Hutchinson & Co for an extract from *The Hungry Spirit* by Charles Handy; Independent Newspapers (UK) Limited for extracts from "A winning formula" by Nick Harris published in *The Independent on Sunday* 10th October 1998, "Will our children read books?" by Mark Lawson published in *The Independent on Sunday* 9th April 1995, and "Why can't we say no to brands?" by Deborah Orr published in *The Independent* 17th October 2000; Jossey-Bass Inc., a subsidiary of John Wiley & Sons, Inc. for an extract from *Tuning in Trouble* by Geanne Albronda Neaton and Noona Leigh Wilson; Sir Alexander Macara, chairman of the BMA 1993-1998, for an extract from his article "Spare-part surgery success" published in *Tomorrow's World Magazine* April 1998; the McGraw-Hill Group of Companies for an extract from *Social Psychology* 5/e by J Wiggens and Vander Zanden; Macmillan Publishers Ltd (London) for extracts from *The Greenway* by Jane Adams, *Machete (Bay of Contented Men)* by Robert Drewe, and *An Anthropologist on Mars* by Oliver Sachs; New Horizons for Learning for an extract from "Thoughts about education" by Mihaly Czikszentmihalyi

published in *Creating the Future* edited by Du Dickinson, on-line at www.newhorizons.org; News International Newspapers Ltd for extracts from "Robonurse takes care of the elderly" by Sean Hargrave published in *The Times* 4th January 1998, "Trip of a life (the salaryman)" by Joanna Pitman published in *The Times Magazine* 22nd August 1998, and "Maybe I'm amazed / A hard day's nightie" by Lesley White published in *The Sunday Times Magazine* 8th March 1998; Orbit Magazine for an extract from "Issues for the 90s volume 3" by Craig Donellen published in *Orbit* March / April 1996; Orion Publishing Group Ltd for an extract from *The Death of Distance* by Frances Cairncross; the Ottawa Citizen for an extract from "Robber stitched up by jeans" by Trent Edwards published in *The Ottawa Citizen* May 1998; Random House Group Ltd for extracts from *Goodness* by Tim Parks published by William Heinemann, *Still Me* by Christopher Reeve published by Century, *This Game of Ghosts* by Joe Simpson published by Jonathan Cape, and *In the Mind of the Machine* by Kevin Warwick published by Arrow; Reed Business Information Ltd for an extract from "All God's children" by Margaret Wertheim published in *New Scientist* 20th December 1997; Solo Syndication for extracts from "Back for the future" by Danusia Hutson published in *Evening Standard* 5th October 1998, and "Taking a liberty with our cities" by Rowan Moore published in *Evening Standard* 23rd February 1999; Taylor & Francis Books Ltd for an extract from *The Brain Book* by Peter Russell published by Routledge 1979; Understanding Global Issues Ltd for an extract from "The Curitiba experience / healthy cities" published in *Understanding Global Issues* April 1996; Virgin Publishing Ltd for extracts from *Film Review 1992/3, 1993/4* and *1995/6* by F Maurice Speed and James Cameron-Wilson; and Sara Wheeler for an extract from her article "Welcome to the world's loneliest tourist spot" published in *Waterstone's Quarterly Guide* Summer / Autumn 1997.

In some instances we have been unable to trace the owners of copyright material and we would appreciate any information that would enable us to do so.

The Publishers are grateful to the following for their permission to reproduce copyright photographs:

The Advertising Archives for 57 (inset) and 64 (all); All Sport for 110 left, 110 middle, 110 right, 115 and 119; BBC for 184 bottom; Barnardo's for 236; Bubbles Photo Library for 138; Corbis Images for 53 top right, 57 (main) and 67 middle bottom; Corbis Stock Market for 67 bottom right, 182 bottom left and 182 top right; Greg Evans International for 87; Mary Evans Picture Library for 88/89; Gamma Presse, Paris for 45 and 82 bottom right; Getty One Stone for 23, 26 top right, 36 (all), 37 left, 37 right, 54 middle, 54 right, 63 (main) and (inset), 76, 82 middle, 82 left, 96 bottom left, 105, 107, 111, 122, 142 left, 154 left, 154 middle bottom, 154 middle right, 154 top right, 154 right, 182 top left, 195 and 196 middle right; Ronald Grant Archive for 38, 39 top left, 39 bottom left, 39 top right, 39 bottom right, 42, 46 top, 46 bottom, 50 top left, 50 top right and 50 bottom left, 128 middle left, 156 left, 156 middle right, 156 right, 156/157 middle and 157 middle; Elizabeth Handy for 25; Robert Harding Picture Library for 53 bottom right and 169; Hulton Getty for 168 left; Image Bank for 51 middle right, 51 bottom right, 67 middle right, 73, 82 middle right, 121, 137, 139 bottom left, 182 bottom right, 184 top and 198; Image Select International for 30, 94 left and 182 top; Image State for 194 right; The Independent on Sunday for 171; The Kobal Collection for 50 bottom right and 156 middle left; London Features International for 8 (all); Mothercare for 54 left; Panos Pictures for 116, 182 middle bottom and 194 left; Pearson Education/Gareth Boden for 167 and 179; Photofusion for 51 bottom left and 72 bottom; Pictor International for 28 bottom and 82 top right; Popperfoto for 51 top left, 191 top right, 191 bottom left and 191 top left; Rex Features for 21, 67 bottom left, 72 top, 118, 128 top right, 128 middle right, 130, 139 top right, 140, 142 right, 191 bottom right, 196 middle left, 197 and 199; Redferns for 196 top right; Ann Ronan Collection for 148; Sainsbury's for 53 bottom left; Science Photo Library for 96 bottom right, 154 middle left and 154 middle top; Spectrum Colour Library for 52, 82 middle left, 101 bottom right and 139 bottom middle; Frank Spooner Pictures for 190; Still Pictures for 26 middle left, 63 top, 94 right, 96 left, 96 middle top, 96 middle bottom, 96 top right, 101 top, 109, 139 middle right, 139 top left; The Sunday Times for 158; Telegraph Colour Library for 51 top right, 53 top left and 67 top; John Walmsley for 26 bottom, 28 top, 28 middle and 151.

Illustrated by Alan Rowe, Brian Sweet, Mark Oldroyd, Aldo Balding, Kate Charlesworth, Oxford Designers and Illustrators

Designed by Oxford Designers and Illustrators
Project managed by Helena Gomm